THE SCHOOLS HISTORY PROJECT

S·H·P

OFFICIAL TEXT

COMMUNIST RUSSIA

UNDER LENIN AND STALIN

Terry Fiehn and Chris Corin

Series Editor: Ian Dawson

Hodder Murray

A MEMBER OF THE HODDER HEADLINE GROUP

In the same series

Britain 1790–1851	Charlotte Evers and Dave Welbourne	ISBN 0 7195 7482 X
The Early Tudors: England 1485–1558	David Rogerson, Samantha Ellsmore and David Hudson	ISBN 0 7195 7484 6
Fascist Italy	John Hite and Chris Hinton	ISBN 0 7195 7341 6
The Reign of Elizabeth: England 1558–1603	Barbara Mervyn	ISBN 0 7195 7486 2
Weimar and Nazi Germany	John Hite with Chris Hinton	ISBN 0 7195 7343 2

The Schools History Project

This project was set up in 1972, with the aim of improving the study of history for students aged 13–16. This involved a reconsideration of the ways in which history contributes to the educational needs of young people. The project devised new objectives, new criteria for planning and developing courses, and the materials to support them. New examinations, requiring new methods of assessment, also had to be developed. These have continued to be popular. The advent of GCSE in 1987 led to the expansion of SHP approaches into other syllabuses.

The Schools History Project has been based at Trinity and All Saints' College, Leeds, since 1978, from where it supports teachers through a biennial bulletin, regular INSET, an annual conference and a website (www.tasc.ac.uk/shp).

Since the National Curriculum was drawn up in 1991, the project has continued to expand its publications, bringing its ideas to courses for Key Stage 3 as well as a range of GCSE and A level specifications.

Acknowledgement

The authors would like to thank Beryl Williams, Reader in History, Sussex University, for her enormous contribution to this book. Not only have her advice and guidance been invaluable, but much of the material in this book has been drawn from her published work and her own papers and notes, freely and generously made available to us.

Hodder Headline's policy is to use papers that are natural, renewable and recyclable products and made from wood grown in sustainable forests. The logging and manufacturing processes are expected to conform to environmental regulations of the country of origin.

© Terry Fiehn, Chris Corin 2002

First published in 2002
by John Murray (Publishers) Ltd, a member of the Hodder Headline Group
338 Euston Road
London NW1 3BH

Reprinted 2002, 2003, 2004, 2005, 2006

Layouts by Janet McCallum
Artwork by Oxford Designers & Illustrators
Typeset in 10/12pt Walbaum by Wearset Ltd, Boldon, Tyne & Wear
Printed and bound in Great Britain by Martins the Printers, Berwick upon Tweed

A catalogue entry for this book is available from the British Library

ISBN-10: 0 7195 7488 9
ISBN-13: 978 0 7195 7488 7

Contents

Using this book

This is an in-depth study of Communist Russia under Lenin and Stalin. It contains everything you need for examination success and more. It provides all the content you would expect, as well as many features to help both independent and class-based learners. So, before you wade in, make sure you understand the purpose of each of the features.

Focus routes

On every topic throughout the book, this feature guides you to produce the written material essential for understanding what you read and, later, for revising the topic (e.g. pages 24, 49). These focus routes are particularly useful for you if you are an independent learner working through this material on your own, but they can also be used for class-based learning.

Activities

The activities offer a range of exercises to enhance your understanding of what you read and to prepare you for examinations. They vary in style and purpose. There are:

- a variety of essays, both AS exam-style structured essays (e.g. pages 122, 315) and more discursive A2 level essays (e.g. pages 134, 315)
- source investigations (e.g. pages 106, 217)
- examination of historical interpretations, which is now central to A level history (e.g. pages 267, 310)
- decision-making exercises which help you to see events from the viewpoint of people at the time (e.g. pages 155, 186)
- exercises to develop Key Skills such as communication (e.g. page 315), ICT (e.g. page 199), and numeracy (e.g. pages 43, 180) and much more.

These activities help you to analyse and understand what you are reading. They address the content through the key questions that the examiner will be expecting you to have investigated.

Overviews, summaries and key points

In such a large book on such a massive topic, you need to keep referring to the big picture. Each chapter begins with an overview and each chapter ends with a key-points summary of the most important content of the chapter.

Learning trouble spots

Experience shows that time and again some topics cause confusion for students. This feature identifies such topics and helps students to avoid common misunderstandings (e.g. page 28). In particular, this feature addresses some of the general problems encountered when studying history, such as assessing sources (e.g. page 105); analysing the provenance, tone and value of sources (e.g. page 28); handling statistics (e.g. page 196); and assessing historians' views (e.g. page 59).

Charts

The charts are our attempts to summarise important information in note or diagrammatic form (e.g. page 113). There are also several grid charts that present a lot of information in a structured way (e.g. pages 316–317). However, everyone learns differently and the best charts are the ones you draw yourself! Drawing your own charts in your own way to summarise important content can really help understanding (e.g. page 26) as can completing assessment grids (e.g. page 171).

Glossary

We have tried to write in an accessible way but occasionally we have used advanced vocabulary. These words are often explained in brackets in the text but sometimes you may need to use a dictionary. We have also used many general historical terms as well as some that are specific to the study of Communist Russia. You won't find all of these in a dictionary, but they are defined in glossary boxes close to the text in which they appear. The first time a glossary word appears in the text it is in SMALL CAPITALS like this.

Talking points

These are asides from the normal pattern of written exercises. They are discussion questions that invite you to be more reflective and to consider the relevance of this history to your own life. They might ask you to voice your personal judgement (e.g. pages 42, 74); to make links between the past and present (e.g. pages 42, 112, 315); or to highlight aspects of the process of studying history (e.g. pages 59, 95, 197).

Communist Russia is one of the most popular A level history topics. The content is deeply relevant to the modern world. But the actual process of studying history is equally relevant to the modern world. Throughout this book you will be problem solving, working with others, and trying to improve your own performance as you engage with deep and complex historical issues. Our hope is that by using this book you will become actively involved in your study of history and that you will see history as a challenging set of skills and ideas to be mastered rather than as an inert body of factual material to be learned.

COMMUNISM

Last stage in Marx's notion of the evolution of history where there would be no state; everybody would be equal and share in an abundance of goods produced by machinery rather than by workers' labour; more leisure and people would take what they needed from central pool of goods. Never clearly defined.

SOCIALISM

Workers' control of state. At first exercised through the dictatorship of the proletariat, a period of strict control necessary to deal with counter revolution and to root out non-socialist attitudes. Factories, machines owned collectively and run by state; everybody equal, class system brought to an end; wealth and goods shared out fairly; equal entitlement to good housing and standard of living.

AUTOCRAT

All-powerful ruler.

Introduction

The Russian Revolution of October 1917 is arguably the most important event in the twentieth century, since it led to the creation of the world's first Communist state which lasted for over 70 years and had a huge impact on world affairs for the greater part of the twentieth century. From its very beginning, Communist Russia represented a philosophy and worldview that terrified countries in the West. The governments of Western Europe and the USA regarded COMMUNISM as a kind of virus that could, if unchecked, infect their countries. Fear of Communism affected the internal politics and foreign policies of numerous countries. For example, in Germany, it helped Adolf Hitler come to power. It also made some governments unwilling to stop the aggressive Nazi rearmament programme because they saw a strong Germany in Central Europe as the best bulwark against the expansion of Communism from the East.

After the Second World War, the Soviet Union emerged as a superpower vying with the USA for influence in the post-1945 world. The Cold War between these two great powers – the propaganda, spying, intrigue and interference in the affairs of other countries which this entailed – dominated international relations over five decades and nearly brought the world to the point of self-destruction. The Communist model was exported to Eastern Europe, China, South-Eastern Asia and parts of Africa and the Caribbean. So there is little doubt that the Bolshevik, or Communist, Revolution of 1917 had a major impact on the course of the twentieth century.

The aim of this book is to tell the story of how this Communist state came into being and how it developed under the leadership of two major historical figures – Vladimir Ilyich Ulyanov, better known as Lenin, and Joseph Dzhugashvili, better known as Stalin. Lenin and Stalin are among a very small group of individuals who have had real influence over events that have changed and shaped the world.

Lenin was a follower of the teachings of Karl Marx who believed that human history passed through a series of evolutionary stages leading to SOCIALISM and then on to Communism, the highest form of society. Marx thought that this would be achieved by a revolution of the working classes in highly industrialised countries. Lenin brought to Marxism a specifically Russian tradition in revolutionary thought. He developed the notion of a disciplined revolutionary party run by professional, hard-working revolutionaries who would seize power in Russia and set in motion a world revolution. In 1917, Lenin and his party, the Bolsheviks, hijacked a revolution that had been generated by the Russian people desperate to rid themselves of an AUTOCRATIC regime run by Tsar Nicholas II. Lenin used the momentum of this 'revolution from below' to set up a Communist state which he was sure would be the precursor to Communist revolution throughout the world.

The world revolution never materialised, and Lenin only lived long enough to see his new regime secure in power. The Soviet Union remained isolated from other countries as the only Communist state in the world. After Lenin's death, the mantle of power was taken up by Stalin who was determined to build socialism in one country – Russia. He equated the building of the socialist state with national pride and achievement.

Stalin envisaged nothing less than the complete economic and social transformation of Soviet Russia that would help it catch up with and overtake the industrialised capitalist countries of the West. With the ruling elite of the Communist Party, Stalin planned a 'revolution from above' which would not only change the way people lived but also their fundamental attitudes and

TOTALITARIANISM
A state in which power is concentrated in the hands of one man or small group, exercising excessive control of individuals and denying them fundamental civil and political liberties; monitoring and control of aspects of individuals' lives carried out by secret police who are accountable only to the political élite.

CAPITALISM
Economic system based on private enterprise and the profit motive in which the market determines the price of goods and regulates the supply and distribution of raw materials and products.

values. There was a high price to be paid for this revolution – millions of deaths, including leading figures in the Bolshevik Party, and immense suffering which resulted from Stalin's policies and the operation of the new command economy. In the process of carrying his policies out, Stalin created a TOTALITARIAN state that provided the models for George Orwell's *1984* and Aldous Huxley's *Brave New World*.

By the end of the 1930s, Stalin had changed a backward agricultural country into an industrialised country, one that was able to take on the might of the Nazi war machine and defeat it in the Second World War. He had also given shape and form to the institutions of the Soviet state and economy which remained largely unchanged until the 1980s. It was Lenin who made the October Revolution happen and it was Lenin who laid the foundations of the Communist state. But it was Stalin who shaped it into the Soviet totalitarian system that competed with the democratic countries of the CAPITALIST world until the collapse of Russian Communism in 1991. Whether Lenin would have approved of the Soviet state that emerged under Stalin, and how far he was responsible for the shape it took, is an issue that is dealt with at the end of this book.

SOURCE 3   D. Volkogonov, *The Rise and Fall of the Soviet Empire*, 1998, p. 81

Trotsky wrote: 'Marx was all in the Communist Manifesto, *in the preface to his* Critique *and in* Capital. *Lenin, on the contrary, was all in revolutionary action. If he had never published a single book, he would still have gone down in history as he does now, as the leader of the proletarian revolution and founder of the Third International'. Trotsky was right. It was not his writings, but his ability to convert Marx's concept of the class struggle into a tool for the achievement of his main goal, the seizure of power, that made Lenin a giant in history. The world changed in the twentieth century in a large measure because of Lenin's intervention. While one part of mankind began to live 'according to Lenin', the other recoiled in horror and fear of repeating the experiment themselves. To avoid it, many countries sought acceptable reform and social change, and concentrated their efforts on economic growth and the rights of their citizens. It was not armed force and barbed wire that saved the people of the capitalist countries from the temptations of the revolution. It was their incomparably higher standard of living and the guarantee of their civil rights.*

SOURCE 4   D. Volkogonov, *The Rise and Fall of the Soviet Empire*, 1998, p. 139

The marks left by Stalin on the face of the earth cannot easily be wiped away. Whether the thousands of buildings in the 'Stalinist' style of architecture, the canals, highways, blast furnaces, mines and factories – built to a large extent by the slave labour of millions of anonymous inmates of his Gulag – or nuclear weapons, his traces are steeped in blood. Between 1929 and 1953 the state created by Lenin and set in motion by Stalin deprived 21.5 million Soviet citizens of their lives. No one in history has ever waged such a war on his own people.

ACTIVITY

1 What image of Lenin and Stalin is conveyed by Sources 1 and 2?
2 Consider Sources 3 and 4. What is Volkogonov's view of the contributions that Lenin and Stalin made to the development of Communism in Russia and to world history?
3 What reasons can you suggest for the differences between the visual sources and Volkogonov's views?

TALKING POINT

1 Do you agree with Volkogonov that the high standard of living and guarantee of civil rights in capitalist countries are the main factors that have prevented revolutions in them?
2 Do you think attitudes towards capitalism are changing in western societies, particularly in view of developments connected with globalisation?

SOURCE 2   Stalin appeared on many posters and paintings leading the workers who were engaged in the transformation of the USSR

Why were the Bolsheviks successful in October 1917?

In January 1917, the leader of the revolutionary Bolshevik Party, Vladimir Ilyich Ulyanov, also known as Lenin, said that he did not expect to see a revolution in his lifetime. Yet in 1917 two revolutions took place in Russia. In the first, the old regime of the tsars was swept away; in the second, the Bolsheviks, soon to be called Communists, seized power. In this section we look at why the Bolsheviks were successful and how Lenin became leader of the USSR.

February 1917

SOURCE 1   The head from a vandalised statue of Tsar Alex III lying on the ground

SOURCE 2   A demonstration in Petrograd on International Women's Day, 23 February 1917

POPULAR REVOLUTION
By this we mean a revolution that is accepted and welcomed by the majority of the people in a country. Many of the people may have been involved in carrying out the revolution.

ACTIVITY

What is a revolution?

Are revolutions always carried out by masses of people? Do they always have to have leaders and revolutionary parties that organise and direct the people? Historians have debated the popular nature of the two revolutions in Russia in 1917 and the extent to which revolutionary parties were important in carrying them out. Sources 1–4 on pages 1–2 will help you to form some first impressions. At the end of Section 1 you will be able to reach your own conclusion about whether there were two POPULAR REVOLUTIONS in 1917.

1 What do you think a revolution is?
2 What ideas about revolution in Russia are suggested by Sources 1–4?
3 Does there seem to be any difference between the February 1917 pictures and those of October 1917?
4 Do you think you can have a revolution without leaders?
5 What do you think are the main causes of revolutions? Look at the possible causes suggested below and rank them in order of importance. Add any others you can think of.
   a) wanting more democracy
   b) economic distress
   c) wanting political change
   d) wanting a new leader
   e) losing a war
   f) a crisis or lack of confidence within the existing government
   g) mismanagement of the economy by the government
   h) leaders who put forward a different way of running society.
6 What aspects of a society need to change in order to justify the term 'revolution'?

October 1917

SOURCE 4 A painting made in Russia in the 1930s by Sokolov-Skalya, showing the storming of the Winter Palace

SOURCE 3 A street theatre event staged in the years after the Revolution, celebrating the storming of the Winter Palace

What led to the downfall of the Tsar?

CHAPTER OVERVIEW This chapter provides a brief background history for those readers who may not have studied Russian history before or need to refresh their knowledge. Its aim is to provide a basic understanding of Russian society and government before the revolutions of 1917, and more particularly to introduce the key players who become important after the fall of tsarist Russia.

A Russia under the tsars before 1914 (p. 4)

B The social structure of tsarist Russia (pp. 5–6)

C How was Russia governed under the tsars? (pp. 7–8)

D Background history to the downfall of the last tsar (pp. 8–15)

E Who were the key players? (pp. 16–23)

■ IA Russia and its people before 1914

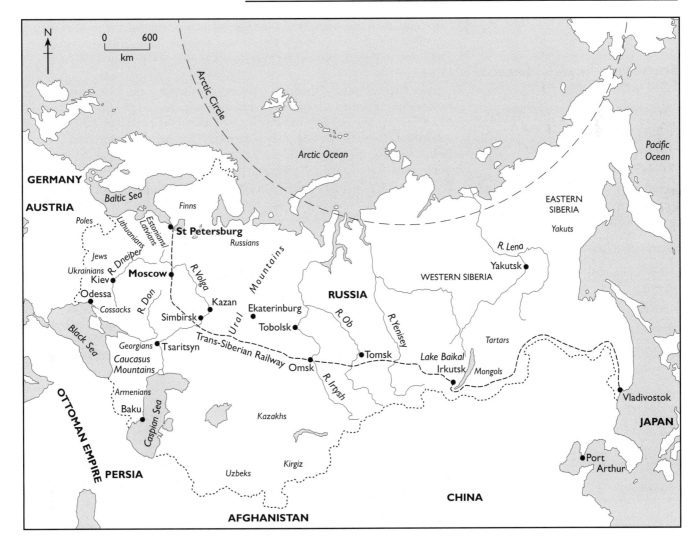

WHAT LED TO THE DOWNFALL OF THE TSAR?

A Russia under the tsars before 1914

FOCUS ROUTE

Make notes under the following headings: Size; Communications; National groups; Policy of Russification. Explain why Russia was a difficult country to govern before 1914.

One of the most startling features of tsarist Russia in 1900 was its size. It was a vast empire crossing two continents – Europe and Asia. From west to east it measured over 6400 km and from north to south over 3000 km. It covered about one-sixth of the world's total land mass. The USA could fit into it two and a half times and Britain nearly a hundred times. Large parts were (and still are) either uninhabited or sparsely populated. The northern part of Russia is frozen for most of the year.

Communications across this huge area were poor. There were few paved roads outside the big cities. Most of the roads were hard-packed earth which turned to mud in heavy rain and became impassable in winter. For longer journeys, rivers were used. Most of Russia's major cities had grown up along important river routes. The other main form of travel was the railway. Although there had been a great expansion of the railways at the turn of the century, Russia in the early twentieth century had only as much track as Britain. The most important route was the Trans-Siberian railway which crossed Russia from Moscow in the west to Vladivostok in the east. This journey took more than a week of continuous travel.

The Russian people

The Russian empire had been built up over centuries. The Russians who lived in the area around Moscow gradually extended their state (Muscovy) from the fifteenth century onwards by conquering the peoples around them. But large parts of the empire were added only in the nineteenth century. The Caucasus region was secured as late as 1864, bringing into the empire the Georgians and fierce mountain tribespeople like the Chechens. Vladivostok, the most eastern part of the empire on the Pacific Ocean, was added in 1859 and the central Asian area of Russia, including Turkestan, was conquered in the 1860s and 1870s.

So by the beginning of the twentieth century, Russia was a vast sprawling empire that contained a large number of different national groups (see Source 1.1). The Russians themselves formed about half of the population, the vast majority of whom lived in the European part of Russia west of the Ural Mountains. The diversity of culture, religion and language throughout the empire was astonishing, ranging from sophisticated European Russians living in St Petersburg, to nomadic Muslim peoples in the desert areas of the south, to the peoples who wandered the vast spaces of Siberia, living and dressing very much like native Americans.

Russification

The size and diversity of the empire made it extremely difficult to govern. Many of the national minorities resented Russian control, particularly the policy of russification that was imposed more rigorously in the second part of the nineteenth century. This policy involved making non-Russians use the Russian language instead of their own, wear Russian-style clothes and adopt Russian customs. Russian officials were put in to run regional government in non-Russian parts of the empire like Poland, Latvia and Finland. It meant that the Russian language was used in schools, law courts and regional governments; for instance, in Poland it was forbidden to teach children in the Polish language. Usually it was Russians who got the important jobs in government and state-sponsored industry. The national minorities saw russification as a fundamental attack on their way of life and a monstrously unfair policy that discriminated against them. During the nineteenth century there were a number of uprisings and protests from national groups seeking more autonomy (self-government) in their parts of the empire.

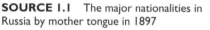

SOURCE 1.1 The major nationalities in Russia by mother tongue in 1897

Nationality	Millions
Russian	55.6
Ukrainian	22.4
White Russian	5.8
Polish	7.9
Jewish	5.0
Kirgiz	4.0
Tartar	3.4
Finnish	3.1
German	1.8
Latvian	1.4
Bashkir	1.3
Lithuanian	1.2
Armenian	1.2
Romanian/Moldavian	1.1
Estonian	1.0
Murdrinian	1.0
Georgian	0.8
Turkmenian	0.3
Tadzhik	0.3

B The social structure of tsarist Russia

■ **Learning trouble spot**

It is difficult to determine the size of
social classes in Russia at the end of
the nineteenth century. The 1897
Census looks at 'social estates', not
classes. There is no category for
middle classes. The nearest to the
Marxist definition of bourgeoisie is
the merchants and honoured
citizens, only 0.5 per cent of the
population. The 'urbanites' category
comprised small tradesmen,
shopkeepers, white collar workers
and artisans. Similarly, there is no
category for industrial workers.
About 7 per cent of peasants lived in
towns but were not all factory
workers. The 'others' category,
referred to as 'settlers', covers much
of the population of Russian Central
Asia. The Cossacks were categorised
as a separate ethnic group.

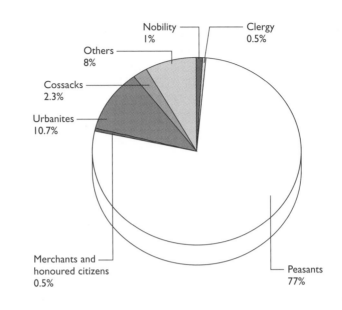

SOURCE 1.2 A breakdown of Russia by class in 1900, based on the census of 1897

The most noticeable features of Russian society around 1900 were the high
proportion of the population, almost 80 per cent, who were peasants and the
small proportion in the professional and merchant classes. The absence of a
significant middle class played an important part in the development of Russia
during the early twentieth century. Chart 1B gives some idea of the character of
these different groups.

■ **1B The social structure of tsarist Russia**

NOBILITY
• Made up just over one per cent of the
population but owned 25 per cent of all
the land. Some were extremely rich, with
enormous country estates.
• Few spent much time on their estates.
They lived for most of the year in St
Petersburg or Moscow, doing the round
of social events that constituted 'society'.
• Some had important jobs in government
or in the army but were often there
more because of their position in society
than on merit.

MIDDLE CLASSES
• Although small in number, there was a
growing class of merchants, bankers and
industrialists as industry and commerce
developed.
• The lifestyle of the middle class was very
good. They had large houses, and enjoyed
a wide variety of food, as well as the
cultural life (theatres, ballets and operas)
of major cities.
• The professional class (doctors, lawyers,
teachers) was growing and beginning to
play a significant role in local government.
Lawyers, in particular, were becoming
active in politics.

SOURCE 1.3 The ball of the coloured wigs at Countess Shavalova's palace, 1914

PEASANTS

- Life for most peasants was hard and unremitting, slogging out their lives on small patches of land they owned and working on the estates of the nobility.
- Most were poor, illiterate and uneducated. Some peasants, however, were quite well off and some areas were more prosperous than others.
- Most peasants got by in good years, but in years of bad harvests there was widespread starvation, e.g. 400,000 died in 1891.
- Disease was widespread, with regular epidemics of typhus and diphtheria.
- Many lived in debt and squalor, prone to drunkenness and sexually transmitted diseases, especially syphilis.

Land and agriculture

- Agricultural methods were inefficient and backward: most peasants practised subsistence farming, using the outdated strip system and few animals or tools, e.g. they still used wooden ploughs.
- There was not enough land to go around. The vast expansion of the peasant population in the second half of the nineteenth century led to overcrowding and competition for land.
- Before 1905, most peasants had serious debt problems because of land repayments to the government. Before 1861, the Russian peasants had been serfs, virtually owned by their masters, the nobility. In 1861, they had been emancipated (freed) and given plots of land from the estates of the nobility. But they had been forced to pay for their land by making yearly redemption payments to the government. Most could not afford the payments and went further and further into debt. The peasants felt betrayed by this. They believed that the land really belonged to the people who worked it – them! They wanted the rest of the big estates to be given to them. The government cancelled the land repayments in 1905.

SOURCE 1.4   Peasants in a village near Nizhny-Novgorod, *c.* 1891

URBAN WORKERS

- Most workers were young and male. Although many were ex-peasants, by 1900 over a third were young men whose fathers had worked in factories, mines and railways.
- The 1897 Census showed that literacy among them (57.8%) was twice the national average. They could articulate their grievances and were receptive to revolutionary ideas.
- There were large numbers of women in textile factories in St Petersburg and Moscow.
- Wages were generally very low and working conditions very poor. There were a high number of deaths from accidents and work-related health problems.
- Living conditions were generally appalling: shared rooms in tenement blocks or in barrack-style buildings next to factories or mines. People had no privacy or private space: men, women and children often lived together in rooms divided only by curtains.

Industry

- There was a low level of industry at the beginning of the century but it was growing fast. By 1914, Russia was the world's fourth-largest producer of coal, pig-iron and steel.
- Because of Russia's late industrial development, many of its factories used up-to-date methods of mass production, although there were also many small workshops with low levels of technology.
- By 1914, two-fifths of factory workers were in factories of over 1000 workers. This made it much easier to organise strike action.

SOURCE 1.5   Inside a workers' lodging house *c.* 1900

C How was Russia governed under the tsars?

FOCUS ROUTE

1 How did the tsars run Russia?
2 What was the role of the Orthodox Church in tsarist Russia?
3 In the late ninteeenth and early twentieth centuries, what sort of opposition to the tsars had developed and how did the tsars deal with it?

WHO WERE THE COSSACKS?

The Cossacks were a fiercely independent people who came from the Don area of Russia. Once they had been conquered by the Russians they became loyal supporters of the tsar and could be trusted to act against other peoples in the empire, including the Russians. The Cossacks were famed for their horsemanship and formed the best cavalry units in the Russian army. They were feared because they could be brutal and ruthless. According to the 1897 Census, Cossacks made up 2.3% of the population.

Tsarist Russia was an autocracy. The tsar was an autocrat, an absolute ruler, who had supreme power over his subjects. As far as the tsar was concerned, he had been appointed by God to lead and guide his people. Article 1 of the Fundamental Laws, 1832, makes it clear: 'The Emperor of all the Russias is an autocratic and unlimited monarch; God himself ordains that all must bow before his supreme power, not only out of fear but also out of conscience.'

The tsar had an imperial council to advise him and a cabinet of ministers who ran the various government departments. But they were responsible to him alone, not to a parliament or to a prime minister. They reported directly to the tsar and took instructions from him. This meant that the tsar was the pivot on which the system rested.

To run this enormous empire, there was a huge bureaucracy of civil servants and officials. It was a rigid hierarchy (orders were passed down from superiors to the lower ranks) marked by its inefficiency: it took ages to get things done. The lower ranks who had contact with the people were generally badly paid and there was a culture of corruption in which bribery was common. The bureaucracy was virtually impenetrable for ordinary citizens, who rarely found that their interests were served properly. The different regions of the empire were under the control of governors who had their own local bureaucracies.

Opposition was not tolerated. Political parties were illegal before 1905 and newspapers and books were censored. The government made use of an extensive secret police network, the Okhrana, to root out dissidents and people likely to cause trouble. Political critics who organised strikes and protests were often put in prison or sent to exile in Siberia. The large-scale protests, demonstrations and riots that often broke out in times of famine were suppressed by force. The much-feared Cossacks were used to deal with any trouble. Tsarist Russia was an oppressive and intolerant regime.

■ 1C The structure of the tsarist state

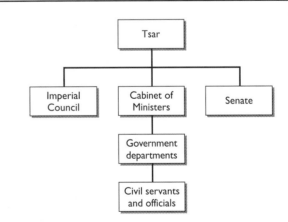

The Russian Orthodox Church

This regime was underpinned by the Russian Orthodox Church. It had, for various historical reasons, become independent of the Pope and Rome. It had developed its own traditions and customs, which included a heavy dose of mysticism and superstition. Holy men, or starets, were held in special regard. One who played an important role in the story of the Russian Revolution was Grigory Rasputin (see page 13). The Orthodox Church was closely aligned with the tsarist system. It supported the divine right of the tsar to rule and exhorted believers to obey the tsar as the agent of God. It was a deeply conservative organisation.

CONSTITUTIONAL MONARCHY
One where the monarch's political powers are limited as agreed in a constitution (the body or principles or precedents by which the State is acknowledged to be governed); most usually, power is held by an elected parliament of one or two houses.

Opposition to the tsars

There was considerable opposition to the tsars in the late nineteenth and early twentieth centuries. This opposition included revolutionary populist movements like the People's Will, which planned to bring down the government through terrorist acts: in 1881, members of this movement managed to assassinate Tsar Alexander II. Towards the end of the nineteenth century a new revolutionary party, the Social Democrats, grew up, centred around the ideas of Karl Marx. His 'scientific' theories of history and revolution were attractive to many Russians who were disillusioned with the populist movement.

The other main strand of opposition to the tsars were the liberals, who came mainly from the middle classes. They wanted political reform rather than revolution, and were looking for a parliamentary-style system that would reduce the tsar's power, and turn him into a CONSTITUTIONAL MONARCH like those in Britain. (You can read more about these movements on pages 16–18.)

WHAT IS POPULISM?

Populists put their trust in, and seek support from, ordinary people. From the 1860s to the 1880s the populists, or narodniks, largely well-to-do intellectuals, believed that the peasants in Russia could develop their own form of socialism. Life would be based around co-operation and sharing in peasant communes on a fairly small scale. This would mean that capitalism and its evils could be avoided altogether. They believed in 'going to the people' and spreading their socialist ideas to the peasantry by peaceful propaganda. Many populists, particularly students and young people, did 'go to the people' in the 1870s, only to be rejected. The peasants had nothing in common with middle-class youngsters and their strange ideas. When this move failed, some populists formed the People's Will, turning to terrorism to bring down the tsarist regime.

FOCUS ROUTE

Make notes using the following questions as guidelines:

1 Why was modernisation needed?
2 Why was modernisation dangerous to the Tsar?
3 How did Witte try to build up industry?
4 How successful was Witte's economic policy?

D Background history to the downfall of the last tsar

The last tsar of Russia was Nicholas II. Any ruler would have found the challenges facing tsarist Russia formidable, but Nicholas was ill-equipped to fulfil the role of an autocratic leader.

Modernisation

At the beginning of the twentieth century Russia was a very backward, agricultural country compared to highly industrialised countries like the USA, Germany, Britain and France. There was an urgent need to modernise and industrialise for two basic reasons:

1 To be a great power in the twentieth century – and the Tsar and ruling élite wanted their country to play a major role on the world stage – Russia had to industrialise. You could not be an important military power without a strong industrial base to provide weapons, ships, munitions and the other military equipment required for modern warfare.
2 Russia was poor. Agriculture was hopelessly inefficient, still using outdated traditional methods, such as strip farming, and making minimal use of machinery and modern farming methods. Partly as a result of this and partly because of the ballooning population (a 50 per cent increase between 1860 and 1899), hundreds of thousands of peasants starved in years when

the harvest was poor. With little to lose, there would often be peasant uprisings and revolts which made the tsarist regime unstable. It was essential to modernise agriculture and industrialise to increase the general wealth of the country and take the surplus labour off the overcrowded land and into the towns.

The contradictions of modernisation

The dilemma for Nicholas II was that while modernisation was desirable in many respects, it also posed a serious threat to the tsarist regime.

- It would be difficult to maintain the institutions of tsarist autocracy in a modernised Russia. Most modern industrial countries had democracies and parliaments in which the middle class featured strongly and the power of monarchs was limited.
- Industrialisation created social tensions when millions moved from the countryside to the cities. A discontented working class living and working in poor conditions became volatile and led to instability. Packed together in the cities they would find it easier than the peasants to undertake concerted action.
- The need for a more educated workforce would make people more able to challenge the government.
- The growth of the middle classes would create pressure for political change and for more accountable and representative government.

So somehow the government had to steer a path between modernisation on the one hand and revolution on the other. It was very difficult to modernise within the framework of an autocracy.

Tsar Nicholas II
Nicholas came to the throne in 1894 after his father, Alexander III, died unexpectedly. Nicholas was not prepared for this role and admitted that he did not want to become tsar. He was simply not up to the job. His many inadequacies have been well documented – his inability to make decisions; his unwillingness to engage in politics (even to read government reports); his lack of organisational skills ('Unfit to run a village post office', was the comment of an unknown cabinet minister); his weakness; his obstinacy. Yet this was the man who faced the enormous problems of modernising Russia and bringing it into the twentieth century. Moreover, he made clear throughout his reign that he had the God-given duty to uphold the autocracy and proved unwilling to make any moves towards constitutional government, which may have aided his survival and helped Russia solve its political problems. He believed that democracy, with its elections and parliaments, would bring about the collapse of the Russian empire. Above all, he was a family man, devoted to his wife and children. He had photographs of them everywhere, including in the lavatory. Although charming and kind to those around him, commanding respect and loyalty, he could be vicious and merciless. He was a Jew-hater and encouraged pogroms (attacks) on Jewish settlements by the Black Hundreds (right-wing paramilitary gangs). He praised regiments that put down disorders, and he oversaw the vicious repression that took place after the 1905 Revolution.

CAPITAL EQUIPMENT
Machinery used to manufacture goods.

Witte's economic policy

The problem for Russia, then, was how to build up its industries and generate more wealth. Sergei Witte, the Finance Minister from 1892 to 1903, thought he had the answer. Witte's plan was to make a huge investment in industry to create a spiral of upward industrial growth: the more industry grew, the more demand there would be for other industrial products, which would lead to further growth, and so on. He placed much of his faith in the development of the railways. Whilst these would improve communications between cities, they would also create demand for iron, steel, coal and other industries associated with railway building. During his time in office, the high level of state investment in the railways nearly doubled the kilometres of railway in operation.

However, developing the railways was not enough. The government needed to invest in industry on a huge scale to really get it going. This meant buying expensive machinery – CAPITAL EQUIPMENT – from countries like Germany to equip factories until Russia could manufacture its own. The big question was: where was the money for this going to come from? Witte had two sources available:

1 Foreign investment – he negotiated huge foreign loans, particularly from the French. The problem with foreign loans was that interest payments had to be made at regular intervals.
2 The peasants – he increased both the state taxes they paid and the taxes on everyday items that they used, such as salt, kerosene and alcohol. He used the surplus grain from harvests to sell abroad, to pay off the interest on foreign loans and to buy more capital equipment.

Witte's policy (see Chart 1D) was to squeeze resources out of the peasants to pay for industrialisation. He also kept urban workers' wages low so that all the money available went into industrial development. He hoped that industrial growth would lead to more wealth for everyone before the squeeze hurt too much. At first things went well. There was great expansion in the late 1890s and early 1900s. But in 1902 it all went wrong. There was an international slump and Russia could not sell the products of its industry. The home market was not strong enough because the peasants had been squeezed so hard they did not have money to spend on manufactured goods. Thousands of the new industrial workers lost their jobs. Strikes and protests broke out in most cities.

There were also problems in the countryside. Bad harvests in 1900 and 1902 pushed the peasants into starvation. They had already been squeezed by Witte's policies and now they were at breaking point. From 1902 to 1904, peasant uprisings erupted sporadically and there was widespread violence in which the homes of landowners were looted and burnt. The government's only response to this was to use force to suppress the disturbances.

The 1905 Revolution

In 1904, in the midst of the economic depression, the Tsar decided to divert attention by starting a war with the Japanese. But the war exacerbated the economic and social plight of industrial workers and peasantry by creating shortages of goods and raising prices. Military catastrophe in the war, especially defeat by a small country regarded as inferior by the Russians, led to growing dissatisfaction with the government and pressure for reform. Tension built up towards the end of 1904. Then, at the beginning of 1905, revolution broke out in St Petersburg following the events of Bloody Sunday (22 January) when the Tsar's troops fired on a peaceful demonstration. By the end of January, 400,000 workers were out on strike. The strikes spread to other cities and into the countryside.

FOCUS ROUTE

1 What were the main long-term and short-term causes of the 1905 Revolution?
2 What acted as a catalyst for the Revolution? Why?
3 Why was the Tsar forced to make concessions during 1905?
4 What were the concessions?

LONG-TERM DISCONTENT

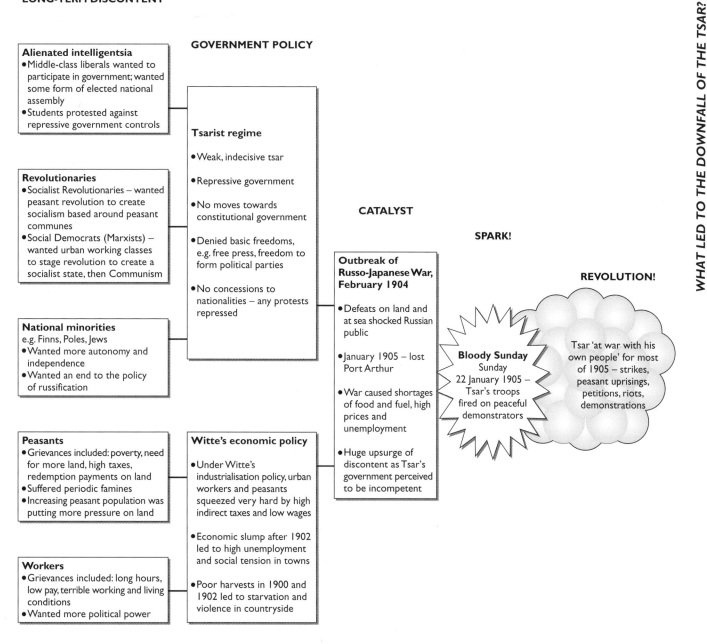

For most of 1905, the Tsar was 'at war with his own people' – an endless series of strikes, demonstrations, barricades, petitions and political meetings. All groups joined in the protests: workers, students, civil servants, teachers, doctors and even imperial ballet dancers went on strike. The liberals, who were the most powerful political opposition force at this time, demanded reforms in the light of the shameful way the Tsar and his government had handled the war and the economy. They demanded representative government and elections. In addition, the national minorities, such as the Finns and the Poles, demanded independence, while the Jews demanded equal civil rights.

In many towns and cities, the workers started to form new organisations, called soviets, to co-ordinate strikes. They were loose organisations – workers' councils – to which workers were sent to represent their factories. The most important was the St Petersburg Soviet, which soon became an influential and powerful body which threatened the government. A popular and important figure in the Soviet (see page 17) was Leon Trotsky (see page 23). In October, matters reached a head as a general strike spread throughout major cities in Russia, bringing the country to a standstill.

Faced with this opposition and a lack of control in town and countryside, the Tsar had a choice: to put down the uprisings and strike movement with bloodshed or to make concessions. He made concessions in the form of the October Manifesto which he issued on 30 October 1905. This promised:

- a duma or parliament that would be elected by the people and represent their views and interests
- civil rights – freedom of speech and conscience
- the right to form political parties
- an end to press censorship.

After this, the middle classes, worried by the growing unrest and violence, swung back to the side of the Tsar. The October Manifesto had given them what they wanted and they now wanted to see the restoration of law and order. By this time the Tsar also had at his disposal the soldiers returning from the Russo-Japanese War which had ended in September. He made sure that they received all their back pay and improved their conditions of service so that they stayed loyal. Nicholas now felt he was in a position to reassert control. He used force to crush the St Petersburg Soviet and the soviet movement in other cities; there was a particularly nasty struggle in Moscow where the soviet was suppressed violently. Then he turned his forces on the peasants and brought the countryside under control, although it took most of 1906 to do this.

1906–14
For almost a whole year in 1905, the Tsar had lost control of the country. Nicholas II now had the opportunity to make some fundamental changes to the way Russia was run, to try to improve the conditions of the people and make the political system more representative. How well did he do?

FOCUS ROUTE

What developments between 1906 and 1914 were:

a) likely to reduce the chance of revolution in the future?
b) likely to increase the chances of further revolution?

Note down your answers to these questions.

1 Political change
The Tsar did set up the Duma (parliament) as he had promised in the manifesto, but he curtailed its power drastically. It could not pass laws or control finance, and ministers were still responsible to the Tsar and not to the Duma. The electoral system was weighted in favour of the well-off and against the working classes and peasants. The revolutionary parties decided to boycott the Duma when they could not get any changes made. After a rocky beginning, the Duma did do some useful work, but it was clear that the Tsar was not prepared to make the jump to constitutional government.

2 Economic and social change
a) The peasants
In the countryside, Stolypin, the chief minister, brought in land reforms to encourage higher production. He aimed to encourage the KULAKS to become efficient producers for the market. He allowed them to consolidate their land into one holding (previously the old strip system had been used) and to buy up the land of poorer, less efficient peasants. To some extent this worked and production did increase, leading to record harvests by 1913, although some historians maintain this was more to do with favourable weather conditions. Recent research suggests that peasants in some areas were more prosperous than previously thought. But the reforms had not gone far enough by 1914 to judge whether they were a permanent solution to Russia's agricultural problems, which were very complex. The reforms certainly had a serious

KULAK
Rich peasant who owned animals and hired labour.

downside: they produced a growing class of alienated poor peasants. Many drifted into the cities to work in the factories while others became disgruntled farm labourers.

b) The workers

Between 1906 and 1914 there was an industrial boom, with tremendous rates of growth in industries like coal, iron and oil. Huge modern factories grew up in the cities, employing large numbers of workers. Entrepreneurs and business people were very prosperous. However workers did not, on the whole, benefit from the increasing prosperity (although in some areas they did quite well). Average wages did not rise much above their pitiful 1903 levels. Conditions at home and in the workplace were just as dreadful as they had always been. As a result, there was a growing number of strikes before the First World War. Workers remained disillusioned with their economic and political progress.

The downfall of the Tsar

The causes of the revolution in February 1917 are complex. We can identify two broad lines of thought amongst historians. The first suggests that Russia was beginning to make the changes required, that agriculture and industry were making real progress, and that there was some political progress which suggested the Tsar would make some concessions to parliamentary government in the not-so-distant future. Historians who take this line see the First World War as the main reason for the downfall of Tsar Nicholas II.

Other historians accept that progress had been made on the industrial front, but stress that the benefits had not filtered down to the working class who remained discontented and strike-prone in 1914. They maintain that the case for the success of the agricultural reforms has not been proven and point to the continued alienation and antagonism of the peasantry, who wanted more land. They claim that little real progress had been made in the political sphere and that the Tsar remained an entrenched autocrat, reluctant to give up any of his powers. The historians who take this line believe that the regime was unable to adapt to changing conditions and would have fallen even without the impact of the First World War. However, they agree that the war acted as a catalyst for the revolution and accelerated events.

Grigory Rasputin

Grigory Yefimovich, born into a Siberian peasant family, gained a reputation as a holy man, or 'starets', and the name Rasputin. It was rumoured that he belonged to the Kylysty, a sect that found religious fulfilment and ecstasy through the senses and, in particular, sexual acts. Men and women flogged themselves and, it is said, engaged in sexual orgies as a way of achieving a religious experience. In 1905, Rasputin was introduced into polite society in St Petersburg and became known to the royal family as a holy man. He seemed to have an ability to control the haemophilia which afflicted the Tsar's son, Alexis. Rasputin appeared to be able to stop the bleeding associated with this disease. It is not known how, though he may have had some skill with herbal remedies. However, this convinced the Tsarina that he had been sent by God to save her son and this brought him an elevated position at the Russian court. Women from higher social circles flocked to him to ask for advice and healing or to carry petitions to the Tsar to advance their husbands' careers. There were rumours that Rasputin solicited sexual favours for this help and stories of orgies emerged. However, secret police reports and subsequent investigations seemed to show that his sexual activity – and he was very active – was restricted mainly to actresses and prostitutes rather than society women. His influence at court and his growing reputation for degeneracy caused Nicholas political problems. The Tsar censored newspaper reports about Rasputin heavily, which meant some papers appeared with huge white spaces where they had been removed. He fell out with the Duma over this and Rasputin's influential position at court. But the Tsar, largely because of the urgings of the Tsarina, continued to support Rasputin despite the political damage he was doing the royal family.

The impact of the First World War

The vast majority of historians acknowledge that the First World War played a major role in bringing down the regime in February 1917. The key ways in which it did this are outlined in Chart 1E.

■ 1E How the First World War contributed to the Tsar's downfall

Military failures

- Heavy defeats and the huge numbers of Russians killed in 1914 and 1915 led to disillusionment and anger about the way the Tsar and the government were conducting the war. Losing a war is always bad for a government.

- In September 1915, the Tsar went to the Front to take personal charge; from then on he was held personally responsible for defeats.

Difficult living conditions

The war caused acute distress in large cities, especially Petrograd and Moscow. Disruption of supplies meant that food, goods and raw materials were in short supply; hundreds of factories closed and thousands were put out of work; prices rocketed and inflation was rampant; lack of fuel meant that people were cold as well as hungry. Urban workers became very hostile towards the tsarist government. In the countryside, the peasants became increasingly angry about the conscription of all the young men, who seldom returned from the Front.

Role of the Tsarina and Rasputin

- The Tsar made the mistake of leaving his wife, the Tsarina Alexandra, and the monk Rasputin in charge of the government while he was at the Front. They made a terrible mess of running the country, dismissing able ministers in favour of friends or toadies who performed poorly. Ministers were changed frequently. As a result, the situation in the cities deteriorated rapidly with food and fuel in very short supply.

- The Tsarina and Rasputin became totally discredited. The odium and ridicule they generated (cartoons were circulated showing them in bed together) also tainted the Tsar, who was blamed for putting them in charge. The higher echelons of society and army generals became disenchanted with the Tsar's leadership and support for him haemorrhaged away. By the beginning of 1917, few were prepared to defend him.

Failure to make political reforms

During the war the Tsar had the chance to make some concessions to political reform that might have saved him. Russia could have slipped into a constitutional monarchy and the pressure would have been taken off him personally. The Duma was fully behind the Tsar in fighting the war. A group called the 'Progressive Bloc' emerged who suggested that the Tsar establish a 'government of public confidence', which really meant letting them run the country. However, the Tsar rejected their approach. He had opted to retain autocracy and was to pay the price for it.

The winter of 1916 was particularly harsh. Rasputin was murdered by Prince Yusupov who hoped to save the Tsar by getting rid of the monk and the damage he was doing to the royal family. A secret police report at the end of 1916 said that the workers in Petrograd were on the verge of despair, with the cost of living having risen by 300 per cent, food virtually unobtainable and long queues outside most shops. The secret police reported a rising death rate due to inadequate diet, insanitary and cold lodgings and 'a mass of industrial workers quite ready to let themselves go to the wildest excesses of a hunger strike'.

As the new year, 1917, began, things seemed to be getting worse and a serious mood of discontent was taking hold of the population in the cities. The story of the February Revolution and the final fall of the Tsar is taken up in Chapter 2.

TALKING POINT

1 Do you think it is likely that a revolution would have taken place in 1917 if there had not been a war?
2 Why are wars accelerators of change?

FOCUS ROUTE

Make a list of the ways in which the First World War weakened the Tsar's position.

■ 1F The causes and build-up to the February Revolution

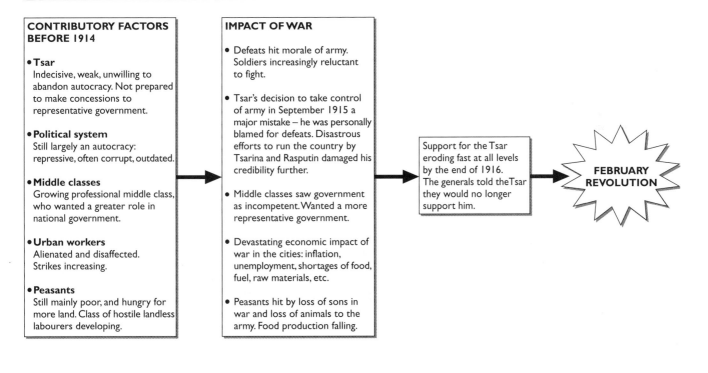

CONTRIBUTORY FACTORS BEFORE 1914

• **Tsar**
Indecisive, weak, unwilling to abandon autocracy. Not prepared to make concessions to representative government.

• **Political system**
Still largely an autocracy: repressive, often corrupt, outdated.

• **Middle classes**
Growing professional middle class, who wanted a greater role in national government.

• **Urban workers**
Alienated and disaffected. Strikes increasing.

• **Peasants**
Still mainly poor, and hungry for more land. Class of hostile landless labourers developing.

IMPACT OF WAR

• Defeats hit morale of army. Soldiers increasingly reluctant to fight.

• Tsar's decision to take control of army in September 1915 a major mistake – he was personally blamed for defeats. Disastrous efforts to run the country by Tsarina and Rasputin damaged his credibility further.

• Middle classes saw government as incompetent. Wanted a more representative government.

• Devastating economic impact of war in the cities: inflation, unemployment, shortages of food, fuel, raw materials, etc.

• Peasants hit by loss of sons in war and loss of animals to the army. Food production falling.

Support for the Tsar eroding fast at all levels by the end of 1916. The generals told the Tsar they would no longer support him.

FEBRUARY REVOLUTION

E Who were the key players?

Before we go on with the story of 1917, we need to be clear on who the main players were after February 1917.

■ 1G Key players after February 1917

THE LIBERALS
Liberal parties: Kadets, Octobrists and Progressive Bloc

The liberals had been the major political opposition up to, during and after the 1905 Revolution (political parties were not legal in Russia until 1906). They had been active in the zemstva – town and district councils that had been established in the 1860s and 1870s – where the professional middle classes had developed skills of local government. Zemstva, described as 'the seedbeds of liberalism', gave them the taste for more participation in government.

Before 1905 they had called for a national zemstvo elected by universal suffrage. In the 1905 Revolution, the Tsar had been forced to make concessions in the form of the Duma (parliament) and civil rights.

The main liberal party was the Kadets (Constitutional Democrats), established in 1905. Along with the Octobrists (more conservative liberals who wanted to stick to the agreement in the October Manifesto), they had played an important part in the Duma before the First World War.

More progressive liberals had formed the 'Progressive Bloc' in the Duma in the war years, pushing the Tsar towards constitutional monarchy, but he had rejected their advances.

The idea of 'liberalism' was not very Russian and it was regarded as an alien Western creed by most Russians. The Kadets did not identify themselves as a liberal party with its middle-class connotations. In Russian they called themselves the 'Party of Popular Freedom' and saw themselves as a national, not a class, party.

Main beliefs: Parliamentary democracy, civil rights, free elections in which all men could vote.

Methods: Non-violent political channels: the zemstva, the Duma, articles in the press, meetings, etc.

Support: They did not have a large popular base, with few active supporters outside Moscow, Petrograd and a few other large cities, although the Kadets did try to establish local provincial party bases. The Kadets were mainly supported by the middle-class intelligentsia, such as academics, lawyers, doctors and progressive landlords. Octobrists tended to find support amongst industrialists, businessmen and larger landowners.

THE SOCIALIST REVOLUTIONARIES

The Socialist Revolutionary (SR) Party had been formed in 1901, emerging from the ruins of the populist movement of the 1870s, most particularly the People's Will (a populist movement hit hard by the backlash following the assassination of Alexander II in 1881).

The Socialist Revolutionary Party was a loose organisation accommodating groups with a wide variety of views and did not hold its first congress until 1906. It was never well co-ordinated or centrally controlled. It had initially taken part in the Duma but later boycotted it. Peasants were represented in the Duma by the Trudoviki labour group, of which Alexander Kerensky was a member. This was a loosely knit group whose main policy line involved redistributing land to the peasants.

Main beliefs: SRs placed their main hope for revolution in the peasants, who would provide the main support for a popular rising in which the tsarist government would be overthrown and replaced by a democratic republic. Land would be taken from landlords and divided up amongst the peasants.

Unlike the old populists, the SRs accepted the development of capitalism as a fact. The leading exponent of their views was Victor Chernov.

He accepted that the growth of capitalism would promote the growth of a proletariat (working class) who would rise against their masters. But he saw no need for the peasants to pass through capitalism; he believed they could move straight to a form of rural socialism based on the peasant commune (the *mir*) which already existed. He saw SRs as representing 'all labouring people'.

Methods: Agitation and terrorism, including assassination of government officials.

Support: Peasants provided the party with a large popular base but industrial workers formed perhaps 50 per cent of the membership by 1905. This is probably because many urban workers were ex-peasants recently arrived in the cities, who recognised the party and supported its aims of land and liberty. Most had regular contact with their villages.

The SRs also attracted intellectuals who wanted to make contact with the mass of the population. SRs often bemoaned their lack of strength in villages because most SR committees were run by students and intellectuals in towns and communication was difficult. Most peasants could not read the leaflets they published. Nevertheless, they were the party the peasants recognised as representing them.

FOCUS ROUTE

Draw up your own chart to show the following information about the key players:

- who they were
- their main aims
- their main beliefs
- their main areas of support.

THE SOCIAL DEMOCRATS

In the 1880s, it seemed to some Russian intellectuals that there was no hope of a revolutionary movement developing amongst the peasantry. Instead they turned to the latest theories of a German philosopher, Karl Marx (see page 19). The 'scientific' nature of Marxism appealed to them; it was an optimistic theory in which there was progress through the development of industry and the working class to the ultimate triumph of socialism.

Marxist reading circles developed and societies and groups were formed. They believed in action and soon became involved in organising strikes in factories. The working class, not the peasants, were the key to the revolution.

In 1898, Marxists formed the Russian Social Democratic Labour Party but it split into two factions at the Second Party Congress in 1903 – the Bolsheviks (Majoritarians) and the Mensheviks (Minoritarians).

This split was largely caused by the abrasive personality of Vladimir Ulyanov, or Lenin, who was determined to see his notion of the revolutionary party triumph. During the congress the votes taken on various issues showed the two groups were roughly equal. But in a particular series of votes, Lenin's faction came out on top (mainly because some delegates had walked out of the conference) and he jumped on the idea of calling his group the majority party (Bolsheviki), which gave them a stronger image. In fact, until 1917 they always had fewer members than the Mensheviks, for reasons that will become clear below.

It is worth noting that the Bolsheviks played a relatively unimportant role in the 1905 Revolution and events leading up to February 1917.

Main beliefs: Both factions accepted the main tenets of Marxism (see page 19), but they split over the role of the party.

Bolsheviks

Lenin believed that a revolutionary party should:
- be made up of a small number of highly disciplined professional revolutionaries
- operate under centralised leadership
- have a system of small cells (three people) to make it less easy for the police to infiltrate them.

It was the job of the party to bring socialist consciousness to the workers and lead them through the revolution. Critics warned that a centralised party like this would lead to dictatorship.

Mensheviks

They believed that the party should:
- be broadly based and take in all those who wished to join
- be more democratic, allowing its members to have a say in policy-making
- encourage trade unions to help the working class improve their conditions.

It took the Marxist line that there would be a long period of bourgeois democratic government during which the workers would develop a class and revolutionary consciousness until they were ready to take over in a socialist revolution.

Support: Their support came mainly from the working class. The Bolsheviks tended to attract younger, more militant peasant workers who liked the discipline, firm leadership and simple slogans. The Mensheviks tended to attract different types of workers and members of the intelligentsia, also a broader range of people – more non-Russians, especially Jews and Georgians.

ACTIVITY

1 Sources 1.6–1.9 contain the views and ideas associated with the various parties.
  a) Identify the party.
  b) Explain what points about the party the writer of each source is making.
2 Source 1.10 has a very different message. What warning does it contain for which party?

SOURCE 1.6

And thus I confirm that:

1 no revolutionary movement can be firm without a solid and authoritative organisation of leaders;

2 that the wider the masses spontaneously drawn into the struggle, acting as a basis of the movement and participating in it, all the more urgent is the necessity of such an organisation . . .

3 that such an organisation should consist primarily of people who are professional revolutionaries

4 that in an autocracy, the more we restrict the membership of such an organisation to those who are professional revolutionaries and who received professional training in the art of struggle against the political parties, the harder it will be to 'draw out' such an organisation.

SOURCE 1.7

Fundamental civil rights

1 All Russian citizens, irrespective of sex, religion or nationality, are equal before the law . . .

2 Each citizen shall have freedom of conscience and religious belief . . .

3 Each individual is free to express himself orally, in writing and in published works . . . censorship will be abolished . . .

The state structure

14 Popular representatives shall be elected by universal, direct, equal and secret ballot . . . No resolution, regulation, edict or similar act can become law without the approval of the representatives . . . Ministers are responsible to the assembly of popular representatives.

SOURCE 1.8

A great peasant upheaval must come, such as would enable the peasantry to confiscate all land not already held by the communes. The land would be socialised and made available to the peasant toiler in accordance with his needs. The peasants might either become members of a co-operative or till the soil as small 'proprietors' . . .

The combat organisation ought first to disorganise the enemy; second, terrorism would serve as a means of propaganda and agitation, a form of open struggle taking place before the eyes of the whole people, undermining the prestige of government authority.

SOURCE 1.9

A man can be sincerely devoted to a cause but quite unsuited for a strongly centralised militant organisation consisting of professional revolutionaries. For this reason the party of the proletariat must not limit itself to the narrow framework of a conspiratorial organisation because then hundreds, and even thousands, of proletarians would be left outside the party. We can only be glad if every striker, every demonstrator . . . can describe himself as a party member.

SOURCE 1.10 L. Trotsky, *Our Political Tasks*, 1904

In the internal politics of the party these methods lead, as we shall yet see, to this: the party organisation is substituted for the party, the central committee is substituted for the party organisation, and finally a 'dictator' is substituted for the central committee.

FOCUS ROUTE

Start to compile a separate file on Lenin. Here you can note down details of his career before 1917.

■ **Learning trouble spot**

Photographs

Throughout this book you will examine many photographs which will yield a great deal of valuable information. Photographs can capture some people or moments in history in a way that words cannot. They also give a lot of supplementary information about the way people lived, dressed etc. However, photographs have to be treated with care when using them as historical evidence; they can be unreliable and misleading. Many of the Soviet photographs you meet in this book are propaganda photographs, designed for consumption in the USSR or abroad. Here are some points you need to look for:

- when the photograph was taken – a photograph captures a moment in time but things may have looked very different just before or just after
- who took it – often difficult to establish
- the reason why it was taken
- the purpose for which it is being used
- whether the photograph was posed or staged – many personal or family photographs are posed to make the people look as they wish others to see them; in Soviet Russia many photographs were elaborately staged so that they could be used for propaganda purposes
- whether it is likely to have been faked or altered in some way.

Quite often you do not have all this information available but, you have to make a judgement based on awareness of the problems photographs present.

Karl Marx (1818–83)
Marx was a German philosopher who spent the last years of his life in London. He wrote the *Communist Manifesto* which encouraged workers to unite to seize power by revolution. He also wrote *Das Kapital* which explained his view of history. His views became known as 'Marxism' and

influenced the thinking of socialists throughout Europe in the late nineteenth and twentieth centuries.

Marxism

Marxism was attractive because it seemed to offer a 'scientific' view of history, similar to the evolutionary theories of Charles Darwin. According to Marx, history was evolving in a series of stages towards a perfect state – Communism. Each stage was characterised by the struggle between different classes. This was a struggle over who owned the 'means of production' (resources used to produce food, goods, and so on) and so controlled society. In each stage, Marx identified a ruling class of 'haves' who owned the

means of production and exploited an oppressed class of 'have-nots' who sweated for them for little reward. He saw change as being brought about by a revolutionary class who would develop and contest power with the existing ruling class. Economic change and development (economic forces) would bring this new class to the fore and eventually allow it to overthrow the ruling class in a revolution (see Chart 1H on pages 20–21).

Marx was a determinist: he thought that there were certain forces (economic forces, e.g. changes in technology) driving history which would lead to the changes he predicted. However, he did give individuals a role in history. He believed that they could affect the course of events, though not the general pattern: 'Men make their own history but do not make it just as they please; they do not make it under circumstances chosen by themselves but under circumstances directly encountered, given or transmitted from the past.'

He gave middle-class revolutionaries an important role in that they saw what the true nature of history was and could help to bring it about.

Marx did not think his theories were the final word and he did not think all countries would go through the pattern described; he thought it applied particularly to countries in Western Europe. He expected that experience would lead to changes in his theories; he even had a name for this – *praxis*.

■ 1H The route to Communism

FEUDALISM
Government: Absolute monarchy
Means of production: Land; land ownership gives power.
Social organisation: Aristocracy is the dominant group controlling the mass of the population – peasants – who work on their estates. Peasants are virtually owned by their lords and masters.
Revolutionary change: The revolutionary class is the middle class (merchants, traders, manufacturers). As this group gets wealthier, it begins to break down the rules of feudal society which hinder its development, e.g. wants an economy based on money and labourers free to work in towns.

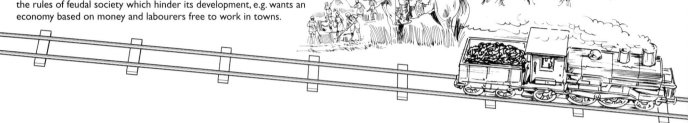

COMMUNISM
Government: There is no state, just people who are interested in managing the day-to-day business of keeping society going.
Social organisation: Everybody is equal. There is an abundance of goods produced by machinery rather than by workers' labour, so everyone has much more leisure time. People work on the principle, 'From each, according to their ability, to each according to their needs' – they take out what they need from a central pool and contribute to society in whatever way they can. (Marx's view of Communist society is not very clear.)

THE TRANSITION TO COMMUNISM
The need for government declines because there are no competing classes.

SOCIALISM
Government: Workers control the state. At first, government is exercised through the **dictatorship of the proletariat**, a period of strict control necessary to deal with counter-revolution (old capitalist enemies trying to recover power) and to root out non-socialist attitudes.
Means of production: Factories, machines, etc., as in the capitalist period but not owned by individuals. They are owned collectively by everybody.
Social organisation: Everybody is equal, the class system is brought to an end. Wealth and goods produced by industry are shared out fairly. Everybody has an equal entitlement to good housing and decent standards of living.

BOURGEOIS (MIDDLE-CLASS) REVOLUTION

The growth of trade and industry sees the middle classes becoming larger and more powerful. Eventually, they want to reshape society and government to suit their interests, e.g. they want to have a say in how the country is run and do not want landed aristocrats determining national policy. The middle classes take power from the monarch and aristocracy. The bourgeois revolution can be violent, as in France in 1789, or more peaceful and gradual, as in Britain during the eighteenth and nineteenth centuries.

CAPITALISM

Government: Parliamentary democracy with civil rights, elections, freedom of the press, etc., but largely run by the middle classes.

Means of production: Industrial premises, factories, capital goods like machinery, banks owned by **capitalists**. Land becomes less important as industry and trade create greater share of national wealth.

Social organisation: Middle classes or **bourgeoisie** are the dominant or ruling class although the aristocracy may still hold on to some positions of power and prestige. The mass of the population move from being peasants to being industrial workers – the **proletariat**, who are forced to work long hours in poor conditions for little reward.

Revolutionary change: As capitalism grows so does the proletariat, since more workers are needed to work in factories and commercial premises. Great wealth and material goods are produced, but these are not shared out fairly. A small bourgeoisie gets increasingly wealthy while the proletariat remains poor. Gradually, the proletariat develops a class consciousness and realises that it is being oppressed as a class.

LENIN'S CHANGES TO MARXIST THEORY (MARXISM-LENINISM)

1 Revolution would be accomplished by a small group of highly professional, dedicated revolutionaries. They were needed to develop the revolutionary consciousness of workers and focus their actions.

2 Lenin believed that the revolution would occur during a period of conflict between capitalist powers. He accepted Trotsky's 'weakest link' theory – revolution would start in an underdeveloped country (just like Russia) where the struggle and conflict between proletariat and bourgeoisie was very great, then spread to more advanced industrial countries.

3 He did not think that the middle classes in Russia were strong enough to carry through a bourgeois-democratic revolution. He believed that the working class could develop a revolutionary government of its own in alliance with poor peasants who had a history of mass action in Russia – the bourgeois and socialist revolution could be rolled into one.

SOCIALIST REVOLUTION

The proletariat moves from class consciousness to a revolutionary consciousness aided by revolutionary leaders (often from the middle classes). They now form the great bulk of the population whilst the bourgeoisie are a tiny minority. They rise up and seize power, ousting their class enemies – the bourgeoisie. The socialist revolution starts in a highly industrialised country.

Lenin

Vladimir Ilyich Ulyanov, later known as Lenin, was born in Simbirsk in 1870 into a privileged professional family. His father was a Chief Inspector of Schools, his mother the daughter of a doctor and a landowner. They were a family of mixed ethnic origin (Jewish, Swedish, German and Tartar) and Lenin may not have had much Russian blood in his ancestry. According to Robert Service in *Lenin, A Biography* (2000), new archival evidence about Lenin's early life suggests he was a raucous, self-centred little boy who gave his brothers and sisters a hard time. He had tantrums and would beat his head on the floor. However, he was a gifted school pupil, doing exceptionally well in exams.

Service suggests that the Ulyanovs were a self-made, upwardly mobile family, anxious to succeed. However, the involvement of Lenin's elder brother in a plot to assassinate Tsar Alexander III saw the family ostracised: people refused to speak to them. Service thinks that Lenin may have learned to hate at this time. Certainly he was deeply affected by his brother's execution and seemed, by some accounts, to have become harder and more disciplined.

Lenin went on to university at Kazan where he studied law and soon became involved in student revolt. This led to his expulsion but he was eventually allowed to sit his exams and, for a short time, practised as a lawyer. He was becoming more interested in revolutionary ideas and, after flirting with populism, was drawn to the scientific logic of Marxism.

In 1893, he moved to St Petersburg and joined Marxist discussion groups where he met his future wife, Nadezhda Krupskaya. He became involved in propaganda for a strike movement in 1895 and was arrested. He spent the next four years first in prison and then in exile in Siberia, where he married Krupskaya, a kind of revolutionary working relationship, and enjoyed with her possibly the happiest years of his life, writing, walking and hunting.

After his release from exile in 1900, Lenin moved to London with Krupskaya. He founded a newspaper, *Iskra* ['The Spark'], with his friend Martov (Julius Tsederbaum). He wanted to establish it as the leading underground revolutionary paper which would drive forward the revolutionary movement. In 1902, he published his pamphlet *What Is To Be Done?* which contained his radical ideas about the nature of a revolutionary party (see below). He wanted to put forward his ideas at the Second Congress of the Social Democratic Party which met in 1903 (first in Brussels and then in London). His abrasive personality helped to cause the split in the party into Bolsheviks and Mensheviks. He lost control of *Iskra* to the Mensheviks.

The Bolsheviks played a relatively minor role in the 1905 Revolution and Lenin returned to St Petersburg only in October. But when the revolution failed, he left for exile abroad once more. The years from 1906 to 1917 were frustrating. There were arguments and splits in the Bolshevik Party and membership collapsed. Lenin seemed destined to remain a bit player in history.

SOURCE 1.11   Lenin with his wife Krupskaya

Political theorist

Lenin is regarded as an important political theorist. The body of his work, including adaptations of Marxist theory, has been called Marxism–Leninism. But he really saw his writings as plans for action. His principal writings include:

- *What Is To Be Done?* (1902) – here he argued for his idea of a revolutionary party:
  - it was to be highly centralised; a clear line of policy would be laid down by the central committee of the party
  - there would be a network of agents who would be 'regular permanent troops'
  - it would be a small, conspiratorial party made up of professional, dedicated revolutionaries
  - it would act as the vanguard of the working class who would not attain a revolutionary consciousness without clear guidance from the revolutionary élite.

  Lenin encouraged the individual revolutionary to be hard with himself and others to achieve his aims; there was no room for sentiment.

- *Imperialism: the Highest Stage of Capitalism* (1916) – here he claimed that capitalism was a bankrupt system and would collapse in a series of wars between capitalist countries over resources and territory. This would lead to civil war and class conflict within countries, which would facilitate the socialist revolution. This could start in a relatively undeveloped country – the weakest link in the capitalist chain – and then spread to other industrialised countries. Russia seemed to be this weakest link.

- *The State and Revolution* (1917) – this book discussed what the state would be like after revolution and dismissed the need for constitutional government. Existing state structures should be taken over and smashed by revolutionaries. The transformation of the economy and society would be relatively easy – the spontaneous will of the people would support revolution and they would play a large part in managing their own affairs in industry and agriculture.

REVOLUTIONARY NAMES

Many of the revolutionaries adopted pseudonyms or aliases to protect their families and confuse the tsar's secret police so that they would have trouble tracking down their associates. Vladimir Ulyanov's pseudonym 'Lenin' was probably derived from the River Lena in Siberia and was first used in 1901. The name Trotsky was taken from a prison guard during Trotsky's escape from Siberia in 1902. Other well-known pseudonyms are Stalin meaning 'Man of Steel' which Joseph Dzhugashvili was supposed to have acquired whilst in prison camps; Martov (Julius Tsederbaum) leader of the Mensheviks; and Parvus (Alexander Helphand).

Trotsky

Lev Bronstein was born in 1879 in the Ukraine, the son of a well-to-do Jewish farmer. He had a flair for writing and for foreign languages. He, too, was dissatisfied with the society he lived in, particularly its treatment of Jews. He was drawn to Marxism in his teens and had joined a Marxist discussion group by the age of sixteen. He fell in love with the leader of the group, Alexandra Sokolovska, and they were soon involved in inciting strikes. They were both arrested in 1900, got married in prison and were exiled together to Siberia. Aided by his wife, he escaped dramatically in 1902 by using a false passport signed with the name of a prison warder – Leon Trotsky.

Arriving in Paris he met a young Russian art student, Natalia Sedova. He was to live with her for the rest of his life and have two sons by her. He soon made the journey to London, where he got on well with Lenin and his wife Krupskaya, who were busy writing and editing the Social Democratic journal, *Iskra*. They admired his writing skills, giving Trotsky the nickname 'The Pen'. But at the 1903 Social Democratic conference he would not side with Lenin. He prophesied that Lenin's concept of a revolutionary party would lead inevitably to dictatorship. He remained in the Social Democratic Party somewhere between the Bolsheviks and Mensheviks but not in either camp.

He first made his mark in the 1905 Revolution, where his oratorial talents led to his becoming deputy chairman of the St Petersburg Soviet. His subsequent arrest and escape established his credibility in revolutionary circles. His analysis of the situation in Russia moved closer to Lenin's when, with 'Parvus' (Alexander Helphand), he developed the theory of the weakest link (see page 20) concerning the weakness of the Russian bourgeoisie and how revolution might begin. He was in the USA when the revolution broke and arrived back to find the Mensheviks collaborating with the Provisional Government. This horrified him as much as it did Lenin and it was not long before he threw in his lot with the Bolshevik Party. Like Lenin, he was anxious for a workers' government to be put in place at the earliest possible opportunity.

KEY POINTS FROM CHAPTER 1

What led up to the downfall of the Tsar?

1 Tsarist Russia was a huge country with a diverse population, making it a very difficult country to govern.
2 In 1900, an overwhelming majority of the population were peasants.
3 Russia was an autocracy, ruled by a tsar who was at the head of a vast, unresponsive and inefficient bureaucracy.
4 The tsars used repressive measures to keep control but despite this a number of opposition parties developed.
5 The last tsar, Nicholas II, was an ineffective and weak leader, unable to cope with the pressures of modernising Russia whilst trying to retain autocratic institutions.
6 The task of modernising Russia was one that even the most able leader would have found difficult.
7 Nicholas received a warning in 1905 when revolution broke out all over Russia. He survived the 1905 Revolution by making concessions but was unwilling to make the move to a more democratic, representative form of government.
8 The First World War put the Tsar and his regime under tremendous pressure and in February 1917 it collapsed.

2

Who took control of Russia after the February Revolution?

CHAPTER OVERVIEW   In February 1917, revolution exploded on the streets of Petrograd (from 1914 the new name for St Petersburg), the capital of Russia. Tsar Nicholas II was forced to abdicate and a Provisional Government took over the running of Russia. But the Provisional Government had little real power. A mixture of committees and soviets appeared all over Russia to run the affairs of cities, towns and rural areas. Chief amongst these was the Petrograd Soviet (a council representing workers and soldiers) which held the real power in the capital. Initially, it decided to co-operate with the Provisional Government, but a huge wave of expectations was building up in the Russian people that was going to strain this relationship.

A   How popular was the February Revolution? (pp. 25–28)

B   Which was more powerful: the Provisional Government or the Soviet? (pp. 28–32)

C   The honeymoon of the revolution (p. 32)

D   What was happening in the rest of Russia? (p. 33)

FOCUS ROUTE

Draw an annotated timeline as you read through this chapter. Mark on key dates and use brief notes to show how the revolution developed. Identify key turning points.

THE CHANGING NAME OF ST PETERSBURG

The German-sounding St Petersburg (Peter's town) was changed to the more Slavonic Russian-sounding Petrograd in 1914 as a wave of anti-German feeling swept Russia on the outbreak of war. After the death of Lenin in 1924, it was renamed Leningrad (Lenin's town). After the break-up of the Soviet Union in 1991, it reverted to its original name.

■ Learning trouble spot

The Russian calendar

The tsarist Russian calendar was based on the Julian calendar (introduced by Julius Caesar in 46BC). Although a new calendar had been introduced by Pope Gregory in 1582 and gradually adopted throughout Europe – Britain had changed to the Gregorian calendar in 1752 – Russia had kept the old Julian calendar. By 1918, there was a difference between the two calendars of thirteen days. The Bolshevik government adopted the Gregorian calendar on 31 January 1918; the next day was declared to be 14 February.

Some books (including this one) use the old-style calendar, which was in use in Russia at the time, to date the events of 1917. Others use the Gregorian calendar, which was used in the rest of Europe.

Event	Date under old-style calendar	Date under Gregorian calendar
First revolution of 1917	23 February	8 March
Second revolution of 1917	25 October	7 November

A How popular was the February Revolution?

In February 1917, a wave of popular unrest swept Tsar Nicholas II from office and the Romanov dynasty to oblivion. By the time Nicholas abdicated, it was clear that support for him had almost universally collapsed and there were few people left who wanted to see him or his family continuing to run the country.

The main push came from the workers in the cities whose pent-up frustration exploded after the hard, cold winter of 1916. Shortages of food, fuel and other materials – caused by the war – had driven up prices. Strikes and lock-outs had created high levels of tension in the capital, Petrograd.

■ 2A Map of Petrograd, 1917

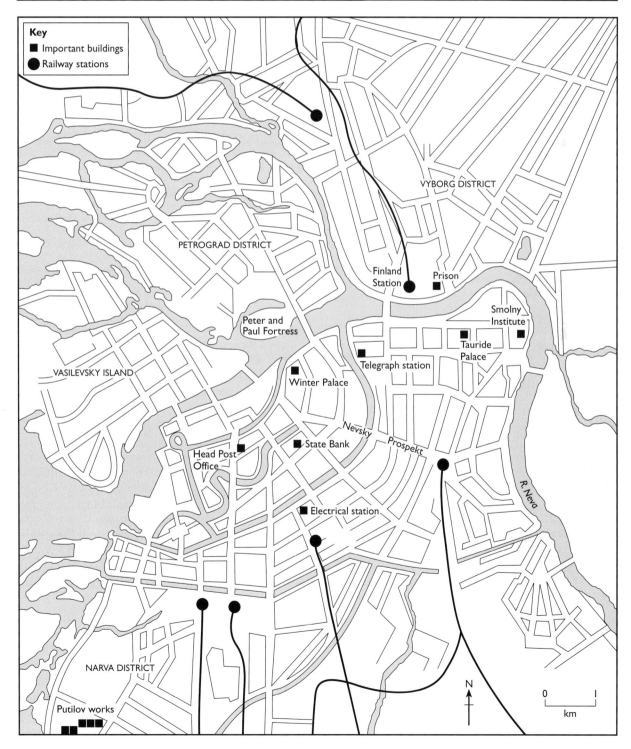

Key
■ Important buildings
● Railway stations

VYBORG DISTRICT

PETROGRAD DISTRICT

Finland Station

Prison

Smolny Institute

Peter and Paul Fortress

Tauride Palace

Telegraph station

VASILEVSKY ISLAND

Winter Palace

Nevsky Prospekt

R. Neva

Head Post Office

State Bank

Electrical station

NARVA DISTRICT

Putilov works

N

0   1
km

CENTRES OF RADICALISM: VYBORG AND THE PUTILOV ENGINEERING WORKS

The Vyborg district of Petrograd was a working-class area that had a history of radical action. The Putilov engineering works in the Narva district had as many as 40,000 men working in several huge factories. If the Putilov workers went on strike then the authorities had a sizeable demonstration on their hands. A strike by the Putilov workers had contributed to the beginning of the 1905 Revolution.

SOURCE 2.1 O. Figes, *A People's Tragedy: The Russian Revolution 1891–1924*, 1997, p. 310

The first symbolic battle of this war of nerves was fought out on the Nevsky Prospekt – and won decisively by the people – on the afternoon of the 25th. Part of the crowd was brought to a halt by a squadron of Cossacks ... not far from the spot where, twelve years before, on Bloody Sunday 1905, the Horseguards had shot down a similar crowd. A young girl appeared from the ranks of the demonstrators and walked slowly towards the Cossacks. Everyone watched her in nervous silence: surely the Cossacks would not fire at her? From under her cloak the girl brought out a bouquet of red roses and held it towards the officer. There was a pause. The bouquet was a symbol of peace and revolution. And then, leaning down from his horse, the officer smiled and took the flowers. With as much relief as jubilation, the crowd burst into a thunderous 'Oorah!' From this moment the people began to speak of the 'comrade Cossacks', a term which at first sounded rather odd.

Workers who had been laid off wandered the streets. Some women spent almost 24 hours in queues for food and other goods. When the news of the introduction of bread rationing hit the streets towards the end of February 1917, the flood gates opened. Queues and scuffles over remaining bread stocks turned into riots. Anti-government feelings in Petrograd were running high.

On Thursday 23 February, International Women's Day, the discontent became more focused. What started off as a good-humoured march in the morning – 'ladies from society; lots more peasant women; student girls' – took on a different mood in the afternoon. Women, many of them textile workers on strike, took the lead in politicising the march. They went to the factories in the Vyborg district of Petrograd and taunted the men, calling them cowards if they would not support them. Women tram drivers went on strike and overturned trams, blocking streets. Women took the initiative while men were more cautious. Local Bolshevik leaders actually told the women to go home because they were planning a big demonstration for May Day, but the women took no notice.

By the afternoon, the women had persuaded men from the highly politicised Putilov engineering works and other factories to join them. A huge crowd began to make its way towards the centre of the city. They crossed the ice of the frozen River Neva and burst on to Nevsky Prospekt, the main street in Petrograd. The protest started to gather momentum.

FOCUS ROUTE

1 As you read pages 26–28, note down evidence using this grid:

	Evidence for	Evidence against
The revolution was spontaneous		
The revolution was popular		

2 Why was the role of the army so important in the February Revolution? Make a note of your answer to this question.

The protest grows

Over the next three days, the demonstrations grew and took on a more political nature. Demands for bread were accompanied by demands for an end to the war and an end to the Tsar. Observers reported that there was almost a holiday atmosphere in the city as all classes of people – students, teachers, shopkeepers, even well-dressed ladies – joined the ranks of the workers marching towards the centre of the city. There seemed to be no general organisation of events. Certainly no political party was in charge: all the main leaders of the revolutionary parties were abroad or in exile. But socialist cells, particularly from the Bolshevik revolutionary party, were active in spreading protest and getting the workers out on the streets with their red flags and banners. By Saturday, there was virtually a general strike as most of the major factories shut down and many shops and restaurants closed their doors.

The weekend of 25 and 26 February was the testing time. There had been demonstrations in the past and these had been dealt with effectively by the Cossacks (see page 7) and other troops. The difference this time was that the soldiers joined the demonstrators. The NCOs in the army, like the sergeant in Source 2.2 on page 27, played a key role in this. These men had a more direct relationship with the soldiers than their senior officers did and it seems that the NCOs had decided that the time had come when they would no longer fire on the crowds. Also, many of the soldiers in the Petrograd garrison were young reservists, some fresh from the villages, who identified more easily with the people on the streets. They were desperate not to be sent to the front line where the Russian army was suffering huge losses, and they shared the dissatisfaction with the way the war was being conducted and the impact it was having on the living conditions of ordinary Russians in the cities.

Revolution!

It was, paradoxically, Tsar Nicholas himself who initiated the mutiny of his own soldiers. Hearing about the trouble in Petrograd, he ordered that troops put down the disorders. On Sunday 26 February, some regiments opened fire on the crowds, killing a number of demonstrators. This tipped the scales. The crowds became hostile and the soldiers now had to decide which side they were on: were they going to join the people or fire on them? One by one, regiments moved over to the side of the people. There was some fighting between the soldiers in different regiments and a number of officers were killed, but this was largely over by 27 February. As Orlando Figes puts it, 'The mutiny of the Petrograd garrison turned the disorders of the last four days into a full-scale revolution.'

The main struggle now took place between the soldiers and the police. The police had taken the main role in attacking demonstrators and had a habit of putting snipers on rooftops to fire down on the crowds. Soldiers rooted them out, throwing them off the roofs on to the streets to the cheers of the crowds below. Police stations were attacked and police records destroyed. The prisons were thrown open and the prisoners released.

The revolution of February 1917 was not a bloodless revolution. Some estimates put the death toll at around 1500 with several thousands wounded. Also, by 28 February the situation in the capital was starting to get out of control. Although in many ways the people showed remarkable self-restraint, crime was beginning to grow (partly because of all the criminals released) and there was increasing violence. Armed gangs looted shops, and private houses of the well-to-do were broken into (see Source 2.4). Somebody had to take control of the situation. Most people looked to the Duma, the Russian parliament, although the socialists were already forming their own organisation to represent the interests of the workers – the Soviet.

SOURCE 2.2   O. Figes, *A People's Tragedy: The Russian Revolution 1891–1924*, 1997, pp. 313–14, quoting a young peasant sergeant, Kirpichnikov

I told them that it would be better to die with honour than to obey any further orders to shoot the crowds: 'Our fathers, mothers, sisters, brothers, and brides are begging for food,' I said. 'Are we going to kill them? Did you see the blood on the streets today? I say we don't take up positions tomorrow. I myself refuse to go.' And as one, the soldiers cried out: 'We shall stay with you!'

SOURCE 2.3   B. Williams, *The Russian Revolution 1917–21*, 1987, pp. 8–9

The fall of the Russian monarchy was accomplished over a ten-day period from 23 February to 4 March 1917. Ten days of popular demonstrations, political manoeuvring and army mutiny developed imperceptibly into a revolution which no one expected, planned or controlled ... Moreover, there was no doubt that the initiators of the revolution were the workers and the reserve troops in the capital ... All the major leaders of the revolutionary movement were in Siberia or abroad when the movement started, and certainly no political party organized the revolution.

SOURCE 2.4   B. Moynahan, *The Russian Century*, 1994, p. 81

Countess Kleinmikhel was dining with the Prince and Princess Kurakin. They had started the first course when servants burst into the dining room. 'Run! Run!' they cried. Bandits had broken into the building, wounding two doormen, and were making their way through the rooms. The countess led her guests out into the night to refuge in the house opposite. From there they watched fascinated as a group of soldiers and sailors were served their meal on silver plate and ordered up dozens of bottles of wine from the countess's cellar.

SOURCE 2.5 A quotation attributed to Trotsky

To the question 'Who led the February uprising?' we can answer definitely enough: conscious and tempered workers educated in the main by the party of Lenin.

SOURCE 2.6 W. H. Chamberlain, *The Russian Revolution, 1917–1921*, 1935

The collapse of the Russian autocracy ... was one of the most leaderless, spontaneous, anonymous revolutions of all time.

ACTIVITY

1 To what extent do you think the February Revolution was both a spontaneous and a popular revolution? Use the evidence you collected in the Focus Route on page 26 to answer this question.
2 How do Trotsky (Source 2.5) and Chamberlain (Source 2.6) disagree about the question of who led the revolution? Is one right and the other wrong? Or could both be true in certain ways?
3 What do you think were the main reasons why the revolution was successful?

The end of the Romanovs

When Tsar Nicholas had finally realised that the situation in Petrograd was spiralling out of control, he had ordered loyal troops to march on the capital to restore order. He had also suspended the Duma when its chairman had suggested that he give more power to the people's representatives (i.e. make the first moves towards a constitutional monarchy). But Duma members remained in the Tauride Palace, where they normally met, and held informal meetings. Meanwhile crowds of people milled around outside demanding that the Duma take control of the situation.

On Monday 27 February, the Duma formed a special committee made up of representatives of the main political parties. It soon became clear to the committee that the revolution in Petrograd had gone too far for the Tsar to be involved in any form of government. Luckily for them, the Russian Army High Command had come to the same conclusion; they now placed their hopes in the Duma committee and ordered the troops advancing on Petrograd to halt. When the generals told the Tsar that they would not support him, he knew the time had come to go. On 2 March he abdicated for himself and his sick son in favour of his brother Michael; but Michael, realising the extent of antimonarchical feeling, refused and the Romanov dynasty came to a swift end. The Duma committee set about forming a new government.

■ **Learning trouble spot**

Duma and soviets

The Duma had been established after the 1905 Revolution in Russia. It was an elected parliament but had little real power and was not truly representative of the mass of the people – the workers and peasants. The voting arrangements were weighted heavily in favour of the upper and middle classes. However, it did represent the first move towards some form of constitutional monarchy and had played a more important role during the First World War.

The word *soviet* in Russian simply means 'council'. Factories sent representatives along to the council (soviet) to look after their interests and to put their point of view to the wider community. The soviets had appeared as a form of working-class organisation during the 1905 Revolution, when over 80 had been set up in towns across Russia. They were not controlled by one party and were often led by non-party men of local repute. The word *soviet* did not have the political connotation that it later assumed under the Bolshevik regime. It was not surprising that workers and soldiers looked towards this form of organisation when the old regime collapsed in 1917, particularly in Petrograd. The Petrograd (or St Petersburg as it was then) Soviet had played a very significant role in 1905 under the chairmanship of Leon Trotsky.

SOURCE 2.7 The Tauride Palace, where both the Provisional Government and the Petrograd Soviet met in 1917

B Which was more powerful: the Provisional Government or the Soviet?

CONSTITUENT ASSEMBLY

When an old system of government collapses (in this case, the tsarist autocracy), a new system of government has to be set up. But somebody has to work out what the new system will consist of: will there be a president? will there be one house of representatives or two? how will these be elected? and so on. The constituent assembly, a parliament elected by everyone, would have the authority to do this. For instance, it writes the new constitution.

On 2 March a Provisional Government was declared, made up largely of leading figures of the various liberal parties. It was dominated by the Kadets and their leader, Milyukov, who became Foreign Minister. There was one socialist minister, Alexander Kerensky, who became Minister of Justice; he was soon to become a major player in the events that unfolded during 1917. The new Prime Minister, Prince G. E. Lvov, was a strange choice but a popular one. He had headed the union of zemstva (town and district councils), and had been widely praised for his efforts in providing support and medical help for soldiers at the Front. The avowed job of the Provisional Government, and hence its title 'provisional', was to run Russia until elections to a Constituent Assembly could take place.

Another important body was taking shape at the same time in the same building – the Tauride Palace – where the Duma members were meeting. The Petrograd Soviet was formed on Monday 27 February. The idea for this seems to have come from Menshevik intellectuals. It quickly became the focus of working-class aspirations. Factories were asked to elect delegates to attend a full meeting of the Soviet. When it met, an Executive Committee was chosen. This was dominated by Mensheviks and non-party socialist intellectuals. Its first chairman was a leading Menshevik, Chkheidze.

Soldiers were also anxious to protect their own interests. On Wednesday 1 March, they went to the Soviet and demanded representation. They gained the famous Order No. 1 (see Source 2.10). Each regiment was to elect committees that would send representatives to the Soviet. It was now called the 'Soviet of Workers' and Soldiers' Deputies'.

SOURCE 2.8 Members of the first Provisional Government

■ 2B The membership and role of the Petrograd Soviet and the Provisional Government

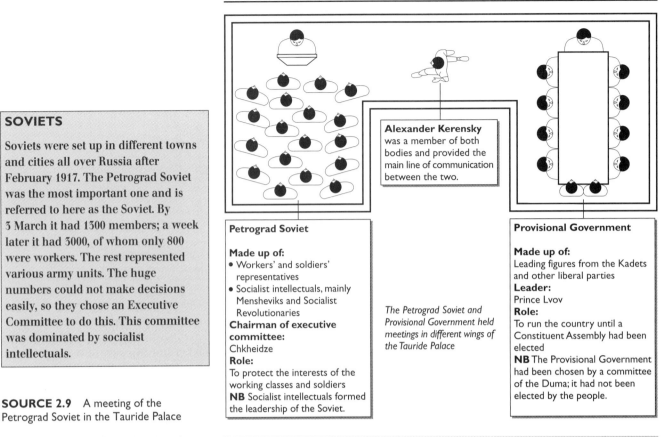

SOVIETS

Soviets were set up in different towns and cities all over Russia after February 1917. The Petrograd Soviet was the most important one and is referred to here as the Soviet. By 3 March it had 1300 members; a week later it had 3000, of whom only 800 were workers. The rest represented various army units. The huge numbers could not make decisions easily, so they chose an Executive Committee to do this. This committee was dominated by socialist intellectuals.

SOURCE 2.9 A meeting of the Petrograd Soviet in the Tauride Palace

Alexander Kerensky was a member of both bodies and provided the main line of communication between the two.

The Petrograd Soviet and Provisional Government held meetings in different wings of the Tauride Palace

Petrograd Soviet

Made up of:
• Workers' and soldiers' representatives
• Socialist intellectuals, mainly Mensheviks and Socialist Revolutionaries
Chairman of executive committee:
Chkheidze
Role:
To protect the interests of the working classes and soldiers
NB Socialist intellectuals formed the leadership of the Soviet.

Provisional Government

Made up of:
Leading figures from the Kadets and other liberal parties
Leader:
Prince Lvov
Role:
To run the country until a Constituent Assembly had been elected
NB The Provisional Government had been chosen by a committee of the Duma; it had not been elected by the people.

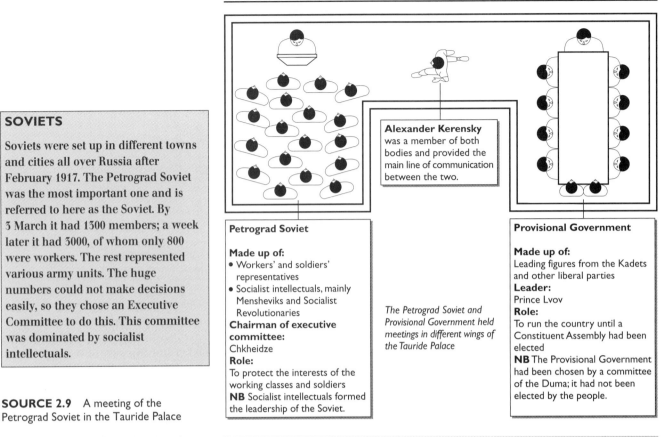

2C The power of the Petrograd Soviet

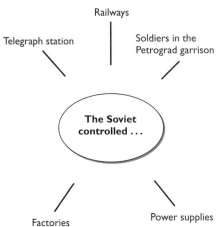

Railways

Telegraph station

Soldiers in the Petrograd garrison

The Soviet controlled ...

Factories

Power supplies

SOURCE 2.10 Extracts from Order No. 1, adapted from *A Source Book of Russian History*, Vol. 3, by G. Vernadsky, 1972, p. 882

The Soviet of Workers' and Soldiers' Deputies has decided:

- *In all companies, battalions, squadrons and separate branches of military service of all kinds and on warships, committees should be chosen immediately.*
- *The orders of . . . the State Duma [Provisional Government] shall be carried out only . . . [when] they do not contradict the orders and decisions of the Soviet of Workers' and Soldiers' Deputies.*
- *All kinds of arms, such as rifles and machine guns, must be under the control of the company and battalion committees and must in no case be handed over to officers even at their demand.*
- *The addressing of officers with titles such as 'Your Excellency', 'Your Honour', etc., is abolished and these are replaced by 'Mr General', 'Mr Colonel' and so on.*

Order No. 1 was extremely significant. It not only gave the soldiers representation but also gave their committees control of all weapons. It stated that soldiers would only obey the orders of the Provisional Government if the Soviet agreed. Thus a situation known as 'dual power' was created. The Provisional Government was the popularly accepted, although unelected government but the real power lay quite clearly with the Soviet. Chart 2C shows the areas the Soviet controlled through its soldier and worker representatives. The Provisional Government could not move around or send a message without the Soviet's knowing. The Soviet could determine which factories stayed open and which services, such as electricity, would be provided.

The policy of the Soviet was to keep its distance from the middle-class Provisional Government, to act as a sort of watchdog to make sure that it did nothing to damage the interests of the working class. It decided not to participate directly in the government. There was one exception – Alexander Kerensky. He was vice-chairman of the Soviet and Minister of Justice in the Provisional Government (see pages 44–47). He served a useful role, running, sometimes literally, between the two to make sure there were no misunderstandings.

Why did the Soviet not take power?

The obvious question here is: why didn't the Soviet simply take over and form its own government? There are a number of answers to this:

1. The leaders of the Soviet did not think the time was right for the workers to form the government. The Mensheviks and the Socialist Revolutionaries believed that Russia had to go through a 'bourgeois revolution' before the workers could assume power. They were following the classical Marxist line (see page 19) and believed that there had to be a long period in which capitalism developed more fully, society became more industrialised and the proletariat became much larger. During this time, Russia would be run by a democratically elected government. They believed the workers needed a period of education before they could play a role in running a country, though they did see a powerful role for the soviets in local government.

2. There was a practical reason behind this theoretical position: they wanted to avoid a civil war and COUNTER-REVOLUTION. They needed to keep the middle classes and the army commanders on their side. The Russian High Command had kept their troops outside the city because they were reassured that the Duma politicians (solid middle-class citizens) were in control of the situation. If they thought that a socialist government hostile to them and to military discipline was going to assume power, then they might well send in their troops.

3. The leaders of the Soviet, mainly intellectual socialists, were scared; they were not sure they could control the masses. They thought all the anger in the streets might be turned against them if they became the government (see Source 2.11).

COUNTER-REVOLUTION

A counter-revolution is when the supporters of the old system of government try to take back power and re-establish the old system, if not the old ruler.

SOURCE 2.11 Mstislavsky, a Socialist Revolutionary leader

Oh, how they feared the masses! As I watched our 'socialists' speaking to the crowds . . . I could feel their nauseating fear . . . As recently as yesterday it had been relatively easy to be 'representatives and leaders' of these working masses; peaceable parliamentary socialists could still utter the most bloodcurdling words 'in the name of the proletariat' without blinking. It became a different story, however, when this theoretical proletariat suddenly appeared here, in the full power of exhausted flesh and mutinous blood.

Therefore, the leaders of the Soviet, most of whom had little experience of government, decided to step back and let others steer the ship in the dangerous waters of February–April 1917, while they kept a close eye on events.

■ **Learning trouble spot**

Dangerous times and difficult decisions

When looking back at events like the February Revolution, students can make the error of thinking that it was bound to be successful and that it all happened relatively smoothly. But it was a period of great turmoil, when people could not see the future and so were fearful. The members of the Duma were acting illegally and would have been arrested if the Tsar had returned with loyal troops. Trapped between a vengeful tsar and the noisy crowds outside who might turn violent, they argued about what they should do. Some slipped out of the back door and went home. It was only when the Soviet formed itself that they thought they had better do something.

Similarly, the meetings in the Soviet were chaotic with people running in and out while, outside, groups of soldiers and workers, many of whom were drunk, roamed the streets. The situation in Petrograd was very worrying for the middle classes and for socialist intellectuals. The socialist writer Maxim Gorky, for instance, was very depressed by the looting and violence (see page 301). He said that it was 'chaos', not revolution at all. So, people were trying to make decisions that held the situation together and the best policy to them seemed to be one of co-operation between the Provisional Government and the Soviet.

TALKING POINT

Why do the middle classes and intellectuals get frightened in times of unrest and fear the growth of working-class action? Is this still an issue in our society today and in other societies?

THE FREEST COUNTRY IN THE WORLD

When we look at the Provisional Government, we often think of it as a group of rather staid middle-class liberals compared with the radical left-wing revolutionaries. But if all of their ideas had been put into practice Russia would have been the most radical liberal democracy in Europe in 1917. At the same time, in Britain, women did not have the vote at all and trade unionists would have looked in envy at the rights that their Russian counterparts had won.

C The honeymoon of the revolution

For the first two months of the revolution, there was little to bring the Provisional Government and the Soviet into conflict. The first measures taken by the Provisional Government met with Soviet and public approval:

- Tsarist ministers and officials were arrested and imprisoned. The police, on the whole, put themselves under arrest; this was a desperate move to stop the workers and soldiers from literally pulling them to pieces.
- The secret police were disbanded.
- The first decree of the Provisional Government (worked out with the Soviet) granted an amnesty for political and religious prisoners and established freedom of the press and freedom of speech. The death penalty was abolished. Discrimination on social, religious or national grounds was made illegal.
- The Provisional Government promised it would arrange for elections for a Constituent Assembly that would determine the future government of Russia. These elections were to be by secret ballot and universal suffrage.

Support for the new government flooded in from outside the capital and harmony was maintained between the Provisional Government and the Soviet. The soldier representatives on the Soviet were happy since it was agreed that soldiers in the Petrograd garrison would not be sent to the Front. The workers were happy because they had secured the right to strike and to organise trade unions, an eight-hour working day and the recognition of the factory committees. It was an optimistic time, when it seemed that the worst aspects of tsarism had been ditched and a bright future beckoned. Lenin remarked in the summer of 1917 that Russia was the freest country in the world.

D What was happening in the rest of Russia?

There is a tendency to focus on Petrograd in 1917 and ignore what was happening in the rest of Russia. The tsarist administrative order was being dismantled: what would take its place? The Provisional Government dismissed the old tsarist governors and replaced them with commissars. These were usually the old zemstvo (town council) chairmen, some of whom were landowners. But they were largely ignored and were given little respect.

In many areas 'Committees of Public Organisations' were set up. At first, these tended to be multi- or non-party bodies run by middle-class zemstvo members, but their membership rapidly expanded to take in representatives of various workers', soldiers', trade union and other popular committees that mushroomed at the time. However, these bodies were being outstripped by the growth in towns and districts of soviets that were set up to represent workers' interests. As news of the revolution spread into the countryside, peasants also started to set up committees and give voice to their opinions and demands. The Prime Minister, Lvov, who was more radical and populist than other liberals in the Provisional Government, encouraged localities to run their own affairs.

Things were moving fast and a great wave of expectation was building up. The honeymoon of the revolution was coming to an end and some hard decisions had to be taken. The main issue that was causing problems was the war. The war was still being fought and soldiers were dying in large numbers; there were still shortages of food and fuel, too. And, soon, the capital was to be shaken up by the arrival at the beginning of April of a new personality – Lenin!

KEY POINTS FROM CHAPTER 2

Who took control of Russia after the February Revolution?

1 The downfall of the Tsar had been swift because there was very little support left for him in any section of society.
2 The February Revolution seems to have been a spontaneous and popular revolution with little involvement from revolutionary leaders.
3 A Provisional Government was formed by liberal politicians to rule Russia during a transition period until a Constituent Assembly could set up a new system of government.
4 The Provisional Government had little power in Petrograd.
5 The power lay with a rival body – the Soviet – which had been formed at the same time.
6 The Soviet, led by socialist intellectuals, represented workers and soldiers. It controlled the armed forces, industries and services in the capital.
7 The Soviet could have taken control but had several reasons for not doing so and for co-operating with the Provisional Government. In particular, the Soviet leaders did not want a civil war to break out.
8 Things seemed to start well, as the Provisional Government announced elections and civil rights for the Russian people.
9 In the rest of Russia, all sorts of bodies were set up to run local government. The soviets were the most important of these bodies. They were simply councils or committees run by local people, non-party socialists, Mensheviks and Socialist Revolutionaries, pretty much outside of anybody else's control.
10 Things did not immediately get better after the revolution. The war was still going on and food and fuel were still in short supply.

Was the Provisional Government doomed from the beginning?

CHAPTER OVERVIEW   The Provisional Government was hit by a wave of rising expectations that it could
not satisfy in 1917. On major issues – the war, land, social reform, food supplies,
the status of national minorities – it could not supply the policies the populace
craved. By the end of August, the problems it faced had deepened and were
driving it on to the rocks. The situation was made much worse by the return of
Lenin, who offered radical alternatives which were more to the people's liking.

A What were the policies of the key players in March 1917? (pp. 34–35)

B What difference did the return of Lenin make? (pp. 36–38)

C What problems faced the Provisional Government? How well did it deal with them from April to August? (pp. 39–43)

D What was the position at the end of August 1917? (pp. 44–47)

E Review: Was the Provisional Government doomed from the beginning? (p. 48)

A What were the policies of the key players in March 1917?

The honeymoon of the revolution did not last long. Different groups in society
started to make conflicting demands, which the Provisional Government found
hard to meet. The situation was becoming highly charged as groups began to
argue about the policies the new government should adopt. You can see a
summary of the key issues in Chart 3A and the policies of the main groups in
Chart 3B.

■ 3A Key issues in March 1917

War
Should Russia sue for an immediate peace, with all
the national shame, humiliation and loss of territory
that this implied? If not, should Russia fight a defensive
war (i.e. seek only to defend its own existing
territory), or should it continue to fight alongside
the Allies in the hope of winning more territory?

Land
Should land be taken from the nobility and big
landowners and handed over immediately to
the peasants for them to divide amongst
themselves? Or should the issue of land
redistribution be left to an elected government
of Russia to organise in a more controlled way?

Social reform
How quickly could a programme of social reform
for the workers (e.g. greater power in the
workplace, improvements in working and living
conditions) be put into action and how far
should it go?

KEY ISSUES IN MARCH 1917

National minorities
Many national groups, such as the Finns, the
Poles and the Ukrainians, were clamouring for
independence or more self-government now
that the tsarist regime had collapsed. Should
the old Russian empire be allowed to break up?

Economy
How could the economic
situation be improved, particularly
the supply of food and fuel?

THE LIBERALS

The Kadets (Constitutional Democratic Party) were the dominant liberal force in the Provisional Government but there were liberal groups that were more right wing, such as the Octobrists (see Chart 1G, pages 16–17).

The Kadets were not united:

- Some of the Kadets – including their leader, Milyukov – had moved further to the right. They believed that the revolution was over in March and should go no further. They wanted to set up a sound constitutional framework, with a democratically elected government, but in a centrally controlled state.

- Left-leaning Kadets wanted much greater social reform, with a larger role for people in government, and more power to regional and local centres.

Main policies
- **War**   They were committed to continuing the war on the side of Britain and France. After the war they wanted Western help for their fledgling democracy and to remain an important power internationally. Milyukov (who was the War Minister as well as the leader of the Kadets) wanted to make territorial gains if the Allies won.

- **Land issue**   They wanted the problem of land redistribution to be sorted out by the elected Constituent Assembly.
- **National minorities**   They did not want the old empire broken up; they wanted to maintain the integrity of the state.

- **Elections to Constituent Assembly**   They realised that the majority of the population were not going to vote for them, and therefore sought to delay the elections until the war was over, when a more settled atmosphere might improve their chances.

SOCIALISTS

The socialists were a very mixed grouping. The main socialist groups in Petrograd were the Socialist Revolutionaries, the Mensheviks and the Bolsheviks. The first leading Bolsheviks to arrive, in mid-March, were Stalin and Kamenev. Like the Mensheviks, they assumed that this was the 'bourgeois' stage of the revolution. There was even talk that the Bolsheviks and Mensheviks would reunite. There were also many socialists who did not belong to any party but could be powerful on local soviets.

Main policies
The main socialist parties shared broadly the same policies in March 1917:

- **Co-operation**   They were prepared to co-operate with the Provisional Government while acting as a watchdog to ensure that the people's interests were not jeopardised.

- **War**   They wanted to fight a defensive war only, to prevent defeat by the Germans; they did not want to fight to gain territory.

- **Land issue**   They wanted to leave this to the Constituent Assembly. The Socialist Revolutionaries were anxious to redistribute land as soon as possible but were prepared to wait until the Assembly met.

- **National minorities**   They wanted to accede to the national aspirations of non-Russian people, offering more self-government and local control; in particular, they wanted to grant self-government to the Ukraine.

Both the Mensheviks and the Socialist Revolutionaries (SRs) were split over the war:

- **Socialist Revolutionaries**   Chernov and moderate SRs favoured continuation of a defensive war while left-wing SRs opposed war.

- **Mensheviks**   Tsereteli and moderate Mensheviks supported continuation of the war but Menshevik-INTERNATIONALISTS led by Martov opposed it.

The liberals were dominant in the Provisional Government.

The moderate wings of both the Socialist Revolutionaries and the Mensheviks were dominant in the Petrograd Soviet.

INTERNATIONALISTS
Socialists opposed to the First World War who campaigned for an immediate peace through international socialist collaboration.

■ Learning trouble spot

Making policy in the political parties
It is easy to fall into the trap of thinking that the political parties in Russia had fixed policy lines and stuck with these all the time. But if you think of parties today, you know that there are various groups inside a party that disagree with each other. This was particularly the case in Russia in 1917. Many of the parties were loose-knit organisations, particularly the Socialist Revolutionaries, and there were many internal disagreements. They had not expected to be in the position they were in in 1917 and were working things out as they went along.

B What difference did the return of Lenin make?

It was into this highly charged situation that Lenin arrived at the beginning of April. Lenin had been in Switzerland and the events of February 1917 had taken him completely by surprise. As soon as he realised what was happening, he hurriedly made preparations to get to Petrograd. However, the journey involved crossing German territory and Lenin had no desire (as a Russian and a revolutionary) to end up in a German prison. In the event, it was the Germans who helped him. They provided him with a railway carriage which was sealed when the train entered German territory and unlocked on the other side. The German authorities hoped that he would cause some mischief in Russia and hinder the Russian war effort.

Lenin's train pulled in at Finland Station in Petrograd, where an excited crowd was waiting for him. He was greeted by the Menshevik chairman of the Soviet, Chkheidze, who told Lenin politely, but firmly, that the revolution was going very well and that they did not need him, Lenin, to rock the boat. But that was exactly what Lenin intended to do. He brushed Chkheidze aside and immediately made a speech welcoming the revolution, but saying that it was far from complete. He called for:

• a worldwide socialist revolution
• an immediate end to the war
• an end to co-operation with the Provisional Government
• the Soviet to take power
• land to be given to the peasants.

ACTIVITY

What questions do you need to ask about the painting in Source 3.1 before you can decide whether it is useful evidence for historians?

SOURCE 3.1   After Lenin had brushed aside the welcoming committee, he jumped onto an armoured car and made a speech calling for a worldwide socialist revolution. This painting of the occasion was made in the 1930s

N. N. Sukhanov

In this section of the book, we use the eyewitness accounts of Sukhanov several times. Sukhanov was the diarist of the revolution. He was in a unique position. He knew the Bolshevik leaders well and his wife was a Bolshevik. Indeed, the very meeting at which Lenin and the Bolsheviks decided to seize power was held in his flat (he was out and his wife had not told him about the meeting). He was a Menshevik-Internationalist, one of a small group headed by Martov, Lenin's old friend and eventual antagonist. So his observations about the Bolsheviks and what was going on amongst the masses are often acute and extremely useful. He published his eyewitness testimony of the five years of the revolution in seven volumes in 1922.

TALKING POINT

What are the likely strengths and weaknesses of Sukhanov's diary as a source?

These demands were set out in the so-called 'April Theses', which he had jotted down on the journey from Switzerland. The day after his arrival he delivered his Theses at a meeting of the Social Democrats. They were received with boos and whistles from the Mensheviks, who claimed he was ignoring the lessons of Marx. One called the Theses 'the ravings of a madman'; another said, 'Lenin is a has-been'. The Bolsheviks, too, reacted with astonishment. The Theses went beyond anything that even the most radical had imagined. Some believed that Lenin had lived abroad for too long and was out of touch. His ideas were opposed by some members of the Bolshevik Central Committee. But, by the end of the month, Lenin's personality and power of argument ensured that the April Theses were party policy.

The Bolsheviks now provided a radically different alternative to the Provisional Government and the moderate socialists in the Soviet. The main points of the Theses were turned into slogans: 'Bread, Peace and Land!', and 'All Power to the Soviets!' These appealed to the soldiers and workers whose expectations and demands were becoming more radical and were moving ahead of the ability of the Provisional Government and the Soviet to satisfy them.

SOURCE 3.2   J. Carmichael, *A Short History of the Revolution*, 1967, pp. 80–81. Here, Carmichael is quoting extracts from N. N. Sukhanov's diary in which Sukhanov describes the impact of Lenin's speech at the Finland Station

'Dear Comrades, soldiers and sailors and workers! I am happy to greet in your persons the victorious Russian Revolution, and greet you as the vanguard of the worldwide proletarian army ... long live the worldwide Socialist Revolution!'

... Suddenly, before the eyes of all of us, completely swallowed up by the routine drudgery of the Revolution, there was presented a bright, blinding beacon ... Lenin's voice, heard straight from the train, was a 'voice from outside' ...

I shall never forget that thunderlike speech, which startled and amazed not only me, a heretic who accidentally dropped in, but all the true believers. I am certain that nobody expected anything of the sort.

How did Lenin justify the April Theses?

Lenin believed that the bourgeoisie (middle classes) were too weak in Russia to carry through the democratic revolution. He said that the proletariat had already assumed power in the soviets – they were driving the Russian Revolution in the form of the Petrograd Soviet. It was therefore a backward step to move to a middle-class-dominated parliamentary democracy. He claimed that in Russia the poorer peasants could be treated as proletarians because they had a consciousness of their class position and were active players in the revolution.

But Lenin saw this as part of a wider picture. Along with Trotsky, he believed that a worldwide socialist revolution would start, not in a highly industrialised society as Marx had suggested, but in a backward country where capitalism was just developing and the conflict between the industrialists and the employees was more acute (as a result of low wages, bad conditions, etc.). Trotsky and Lenin thought that 'the weakest link' in the capitalist chain would break first and that once the revolution had begun it would spread to the proletariat in other countries. They considered that Russia was the weakest link and that the war had acted as a catalyst to bring Europe to the brink of a socialist revolution. Lenin was sure that Germany, at least, was about to explode into revolution. Both thought that once the revolution started, the proletariat of the advanced capitalist countries would come to the aid of the Russian proletariat and help them to develop the conditions in which socialism could be built.

■ 3C How Lenin's radical policies distinguished the Bolsheviks from other socialist parties

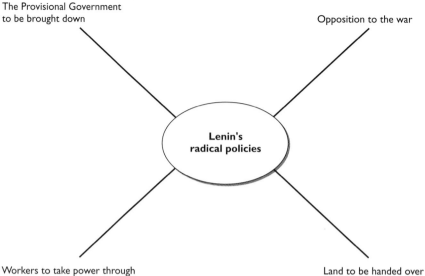

The Provisional Government to be brought down

Opposition to the war

Lenin's radical policies

Workers to take power through the Soviet

Land to be handed over to the peasants immediately

FOCUS ROUTE

1 Use the table below to summarise the positions of the key players at the end of April 1917 and the alternatives they presented to the populace. You will need to refer to sections A and B.

	Provisional Government	Petrograd Soviet	Bolsheviks
Who were they?			
What general policy statements did they make?			
What were their attitudes to each other?			
What were their attitudes to the war?			
What were their attitudes to the land question?			

2 a) Why did Lenin's arrival in Petrograd have such an impact?
   b) Draw an annotated diagram showing and explaining the main ways in which he distinguished the Bolsheviks from the other socialist parties.
   c) How did Lenin justify his April Theses?

■ Learning trouble spot

Political parties

It is easy to get confused about the various parties. Here's a brief summary:

- Liberals, mainly from the Kadets, dominated the Provisional Government.
- Moderate socialists from the Menshevik and Socialist Revolutionary parties were running the Petrograd Soviet.
- Both of these parties had radical wings – Menshevik-Internationalists and left-wing SRs.
- The Bolshevik party, led by Lenin, was more disciplined and centrally controlled, but at this time did not have a strong presence in the Soviet.

C What problems faced the Provisional Government? How well did it deal with them from April to August?

FOCUS ROUTE

1 As you work through this section, fill out a table like the one below to evaluate the policies and actions of the Provisional Government.

Issue	How the Provisional Government dealt with it	How successful its response was

2 Look closely at the moderate socialists. Make notes on how:
   a) the socialist groups (apart from the Bolsheviks) became associated with the policy of continuing the war
   b) the moderate socialist leaders of the Soviet were losing the support of the workers
   c) the Socialist Revolutionary leaders were losing touch with the mood of the peasants.

Four key issues faced the Provisional Government. These were:

- the war
- the land
- national minority demands
- the deteriorating economic situation.

1 The war

It was clear from early on that the conduct of the war would be a crucial factor and would determine the way in which the revolution developed. It is central to understanding why the Provisional Government failed.

Matters came to a head at the end of April when it was apparent that Milyukov, Minister of War, not only wanted to defend Russia but also hoped to make territorial gains if the Allies won; in particular, he was after Constantinople and control of the straits into the Black Sea, which the Russians had wanted for centuries. This outraged the socialists in the Soviet who were committed to a defensive war only. Milyukov was forced to resign and the Provisional Government was in crisis.

The crisis ended when the Provisional Government was reformed on 5 May. Five socialist leaders joined the new COALITION government. The most important of these were the Menshevik leader Tsereteli and the leader of the Socialist Revolutionaries, Chernov. The significance of this cannot be underestimated. From now on, the Menshevik and Socialist Revolutionary leaders would be associated with the conduct of the war and therefore would be criticised and risk losing support if the war went badly.

COALITION
Combination government formed by people drawn from different political parties.

The summer offensive, 1917

At the beginning of the summer of 1917, the Provisional Government decided to launch a major offensive against the Germans. The reasons are not altogether clear, but it seems to have resulted from the following factors:

- Britain and France had requested strongly (even desperately) that Russia attack on the Eastern Front to take the pressure off their forces in the West. The Provisional Government was responding to its treaty obligations to the Allies.

A SEPARATE PEACE

Some commentators believe that if the Russians had negotiated a separate peace treaty with the Germans in May or June 1917, the Bolshevik Revolution of October would probably not have taken place. Such a treaty would have offended Britain and France but Russia would have been able to focus on its internal problems. The socialists in the new coalition did try to set up an international peace conference, but they failed to get anywhere. However, peace would have meant the loss of territory and, even in March 1918, would have been very unpopular.

- There was still a strong nationalist and patriotic element in Russian society, across classes, that did not like to surrender to the Germans. For them, defeat, which would probably mean giving up Russian land in any negotiation, would be a national humiliation.
- The Kadets and other conservative forces in Russia thought that a successful offensive might put the generals and officers back in control of the armed forces and that they might then be able to bring the revolution under control. Joined by the liberal press, they called for the masses to unite under the banner of Russia.
- Some socialists felt that a successful offensive would put them in a better bargaining position with the Germans in peace negotiations.

In the event, the socialists allowed themselves to be persuaded by their liberal coalition partners that a summer offensive should be undertaken. The new Minister for War, Alexander Kerensky, threw himself into a propaganda campaign to mobilise the armed forces and the people for a massive attack. Kerensky, who was still immensely popular, made patriotic speeches and toured the Fronts. To some extent it worked. Middle-class civilians volunteered to fight in shock battalions designed to raise the army's morale. However, Kerensky was not so successful with the soldiers, who were increasingly unwilling to fight. Soldiers' committees argued that they could see little point in fighting for territory when everybody wanted peace. There was considerable fraternisation between German and Russian troops and thousands ran away before the offensive began.

SOURCE 3.3 O. Figes, *A People's Tragedy: The Russian Revolution 1891–1924*, 1997, p. 419

The crucial advance towards Lvov [a town] soon collapsed when the troops discovered a large store of alcohol in the abandoned town of Koniukhy and stopped there to get drunk. By the time they were fit to resume fighting three days and a hangover later, enemy reinforcements had arrived and the Russians, suffering heavy casualties, were forced to retreat . . .

. . . Bochareva's Battalion of Death did much better than most. The women volunteers broke through the first two German lines, followed by some sheepish male conscripts. But then they came under heavy German fire. The women dispersed in confusion, while most of the men stayed in the German trenches, where they had found a large supply of liquor and proceeded to get drunk. Despite the shambles around her, Bochareva battled on. At one point she came across one of her women having sexual intercourse with a soldier in a shell-hole. She ran her through with a bayonet; but the soldier escaped. Eventually, with most of her volunteers killed or wounded, even Bochareva was forced to retreat. The offensive was over. It was Russia's last.

The offensive began on 16 June and lasted for about three days. Then it began to fall apart. The rate of desertion was extremely high. Soldiers killed their officers rather than fight. The result was that hundreds of thousands of soldiers were killed and even more territory was lost. The failure of the offensive produced an immediate effect in Petrograd – an armed uprising in early July, known as the July Days (see page 50). Although the Provisional Government survived this, in the longer term the effect of their war policy was that the moderate socialist leaders in the government lost their credibility with the soldiers and workers.

TALKING POINT

Russians wanted the war to end but many did not want to see it end in a humiliating defeat. What if your country were in a situation where your enemies were about to be your conquerors and take much of your best territory? Would you carry on fighting even though you knew defeat was certain?

THE WOMEN'S DEATH BATTALION

Maria Bochareva, who had fought in the war and been twice wounded, was given permission to form a women's volunteer unit. Shocked by the breakdown of military discipline, she hoped that a women's unit would shame male soldiers into fighting. The women shaved their heads and put on standard army uniform. It did not have the intended effect. Some soldiers refused to fight alongside the women and others saw it as an indication of how desperate the army had become.

SOURCE 3.4 Members of the Women's Death Battalion, formed in July 1917 by Maria Bochareva. The top photo shows the battalion being blessed by Patriarch Nikon, a Russian Orthodox Church leader

2 The land

By May 1917, there was significant unrest in the countryside. The peasants were hungry for land and the collapse of central authority meant there was no one to stop them taking it. They had always believed that the land belonged to them and had felt betrayed by the emancipation of 1861 (see page 6). Now they saw a chance to complete the process that had been started then. However, they wanted government approval to give legitimacy to their actions.

But the liberals in the Provisional Government were not willing simply to hand over the land to the peasants. They were not against land redistribution, but they wanted it to be done within the framework of law set down by the Constituent Assembly and they wanted landowners (often their supporters) to be compensated. They were also concerned that a land free-for-all would lead to the disintegration of the army as peasant soldiers rushed back to claim their share. This seemed a reasonable position, but not to the peasants. As the summer wore on they began taking more and more land, as well as livestock, tools, timber and anything they could grab from private estates.

When the Socialist Revolutionaries joined the Provisional Government in May, it seemed that a better relationship might develop between government and peasants. Chernov, their popular leader, was Minister of Agriculture and the Socialist Revolutionaries had played a leading part in helping to organise peasant soviets. But, broadly, the Socialist Revolutionaries, too, urged that the land problem be resolved by the Constituent Assembly. Chernov did want to try

D What was the position at the end of August 1917?

Disagreements grew within the Provisional Government as it became harder to find solutions to the problems facing Russia. On 2 July, three Kadet (liberal) ministers resigned from the Provisional Government over the concessions given by socialist ministers to Ukrainian demands for self-government and land reform. The liberals also blamed socialist leaders for the militant strikes in the cities. A day later, Lvov resigned as Prime Minister, equally fed up with both liberals and socialists.

Alexander Kerensky became Prime Minister. He was seen as the only man who could unite the country – since he was acceptable to workers, the middle classes and the military – and stop the drift into civil war. He was therefore keen to keep a coalition government which included Kadets, although the balance had shifted in favour of the socialists. However, the people in the streets saw the Kadets and other liberals as reactionaries working in the interests of landowners and industrialists. Urban workers, peasants and soldiers were demanding more radical action from the government over land reform, the economy and the war, and were becoming increasingly impatient.

■ **Learning trouble spot**

The changing Provisional Government

The changes in the Provisional Government coalition can be confusing. There are three key ones:

1 In March 1917, it was dominated by the liberals (Kadets). The only socialist was Kerensky.
2 In May, five socialists joined but the liberals still dominated.
3 In July, Kerensky became Prime Minister and the balance shifted in favour of the socialists, although there was still a strong liberal presence.

Who was Alexander Kerensky?

Alexander Kerensky was a lawyer. Like Lenin, he was born in Simbirsk. Both had fathers who became Chief Inspectors of Schools (strangely enough, Kerensky's father was Lenin's headmaster) and both trained in the law. Kerensky became involved in radical politics in his teens but did not favour Marxism or terrorism. He set up an office in St Petersburg to advise workers on their rights and represent them free of charge. In the 1905 Revolution he published a socialist newspaper and was arrested. The four months he served in prison cemented his position in radical socialist circles and in 1912 he was elected to the Duma. He joined the Trudoviki group, left-wing socialists on the edge of the Socialist Revolutionary party.

Kerensky was a master of the art of twentieth-century political communication. In his biography of Lenin, Robert Service refers to Kerensky as 'the real master of the modern technology of politics in 1917' (R. Service, *Lenin*, 2000, page 277). In comparison, the propaganda techniques of the Bolsheviks were not very imaginative and posters of Lenin were not made until after the October Revolution. Kerensky had great skills as an orator and was famous for his passionate speeches which left his 'whole body trembling with sweat pouring down the pale cheeks'. At the end of his dramatic speeches, he would collapse in a faint through nervous exhaustion. An English nurse marvelled as people 'kissed him, his uniform, his car and the ground on which he walked. Many of them were on their knees' (F. Farmborough, *Nurse at the Russian Front*, 1977, pages 269–70). He was very popular with women.

He was the ideal man for February 1917, the link man between the Provisional Government and the Soviet because he was generally liked in all

circles and the workers trusted him. In the early months after February, he was referred to as 'the first love of the revolution', the 'poet of freedom' and the 'saviour of the fatherland'. He was a popular choice for Prime Minster in July 1917. He was seen as the 'human bridge' between socialists and liberals, acceptable to the workers and soldiers as well as to the military leaders and the bourgeoisie.

Kerensky was energetic and tenacious, but he was also temperamental and vain. He had a picture of himself at his huge desk printed on tens of thousands of postcards (see Source 3.8) and newsreels made of his public appearances. He deliberately struck a Napoleonic pose, making tours of the Front in a smart military uniform with his arm in a sling. When he became Prime Minster he seemed to see himself as the man destined to save Russia and adopted a self-important air. He moved into Tsar Alexander III's rooms in the Winter Palace. He kept on the old palace servants and had the new red flag on the palace raised and lowered as he came and left, just as the old flag had been for the tsars.

SOURCE 3.8 A photograph of Kerensky at his desk

SOURCE 3.9 Kerensky (right) addresses the troops at the Front in mid-May 1917

SOURCE 3.10 O. Figes, *A People's Tragedy: The Russian Revolution 1891–1924*, 1997, p. 337, describing Kerensky's speech to the Soviet on 2 March 1917, in which he asked for approval of his decision to join the Provisional Government as Minister of Justice

'Comrades! Do you trust me?' he asked in a voice charged with theatrical pathos. 'We do, we do!' the delegates shouted. 'I speak, comrades, with all my soul, from the bottom of my heart, and if it is needed to prove this, if you do not trust me, then I am ready to die.' . . . He told them that 'his first act' as the Minister of Justice had been to order the immediate release of all political prisoners and the arrangement of a hero's welcome for their return to the capital. The delegates were overcome with emotion and greeted this news with thunderous cheers. Now Kerensky turned to ask them whether they approved of his decision to join the government, offering to resign from the Soviet if the answer should be no. But there were wild cries of 'We do! We do!' and, without a formal vote, his actions were endorsed. It was a brilliant coup de théâtre. *What might have been the moment of his downfall had in fact become the moment of his triumph. Kerensky was now the only politician with a position in both the government and the Soviet. He was the undisputed leader of the people.*

SOURCE 3.11 A hostile cartoon mocking Kerensky's 'Napoleon Bonaparte' image

SOURCE 3.12 Sir Robert Bruce Lockhart, British Consul in Moscow 1911–17, quoted in R. Abraham, *Alexander Kerensky, The First Love of the Revolution*, 1987, p. 207. Lockhart describes an address given to a packed meeting in the Bolshoi Theatre in Moscow on 11 June 1917

The whole theme of his speech was built around the idea that without suffering nothing that was worth having could be won. He himself looked the embodiment of suffering. The deathly pallor of his face, the restless movements of his body as he swayed backwards and forwards, the raw, almost whispering tones of his voice . . . all helped to make his appeal more terrible and more realistic. . . . And, when the end came, the huge crowd rose to greet him like one man. Men and women embraced each other in a hysteria of enthusiasm. Old generals and young praporshicks *wept together over the man who all Russia feels can save the country from ruin. Women gave presents of jewellery, officers sacrificed their orders. An autographed photogravure of [M.] Kerensky was sold for 16,000 roubles and the whole theatre rained roses.*

ACTIVITY

1 **a)** What impression of Kerensky do you get from Sources 3.8 and 3.9?
   b) He had many copies of Source 3.8 made and sent out to people. Why?
2 What do Sources 3.10 and 3.12 reveal about Kerensky's abilities and why he was a popular leader?
3 What aspects of Kerensky's character and history made him the ideal man for February 1917 and the popular choice for Prime Minister in July 1917?

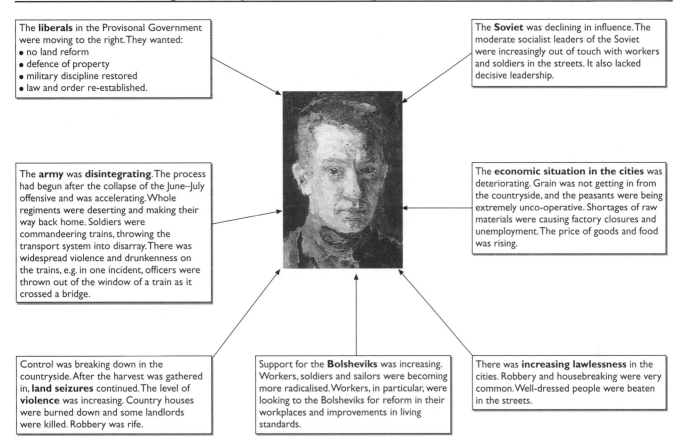

The **liberals** in the Provisional Government were moving to the right. They wanted:
- no land reform
- defence of property
- military discipline restored
- law and order re-established.

The **Soviet** was declining in influence. The moderate socialist leaders of the Soviet were increasingly out of touch with workers and soldiers in the streets. It also lacked decisive leadership.

The **army** was **disintegrating**. The process had begun after the collapse of the June–July offensive and was accelerating. Whole regiments were deserting and making their way back home. Soldiers were commandeering trains, throwing the transport system into disarray. There was widespread violence and drunkenness on the trains, e.g. in one incident, officers were thrown out of the window of a train as it crossed a bridge.

The **economic situation in the cities** was deteriorating. Grain was not getting in from the countryside, and the peasants were being extremely unco-operative. Shortages of raw materials were causing factory closures and unemployment. The price of goods and food was rising.

Control was breaking down in the countryside. After the harvest was gathered in, **land seizures** continued. The level of **violence** was increasing. Country houses were burned down and some landlords were killed. Robbery was rife.

Support for the **Bolsheviks** was increasing. Workers, soldiers and sailors were becoming more radicalised. Workers, in particular, were looking to the Bolsheviks for reform in their workplaces and improvements in living standards.

There was **increasing lawlessness** in the cities. Robbery and housebreaking were very common. Well-dressed people were beaten in the streets.

ACTIVITY

Alexander Kerensky, the Prime Minister, has a few headaches at the end of August. Can he and the Provisional Government survive?

a) Using Chart 3E and other information in this chapter, list the main problems and challenges to his government's authority.

b) Four courses of action are identified below; these were all realistic choices for Kerensky.
  i) Negotiate an immediate peace treaty with the Germans.
  ii) Find a loyal general to help you to restore discipline, law and order.
  iii) Suppress the Bolsheviks who present a continuing threat by demanding the overthrow of the government and attracting growing support in the cities.
  iv) Hold immediate elections for the Constituent Assembly.

Draw a table like the one shown below. Give each course of action a mark out of ten showing whether you think it is a good idea or not and note down how it might help. Then work out the risks or problems involved. Discuss your decisions with the rest of the class.

Course of action	Mark out of ten	How this might help	Risks or problems involved
Negotiate immediate peace treaty with Germany			
Find a general to restore law and order			
Suppress the Bolsheviks			
Hold elections to the Constituent Assembly			

E Review: Was the Provisional Government doomed from the beginning?

Any government faced with the sort of demands confronting the Provisional Government – complete redistribution of land, radical social reform, autonomy and independence for national minorities, conflicting views about the conduct of the war – would have been in trouble. In addition to this, the Provisional Government was a temporary body and it did not have the power to enforce its decisions. So we might say that it was in an impossible position and that too much was being expected of it in too short a time.

On the other hand, the Kadets in the government had effectively blocked the government from taking measures that would have gained it popular support. They had:

- blocked the land deal and Chernov's suggestions for a compromise, thereby siding with the landowners and antagonising the peasants
- supported the war and wanted to continue it aggressively, to the dismay of the soldiers and many other citizens
- sided with the employers against the workers over workers' power and working conditions. They had refused to intervene in the running of the economy, for example by preventing further price rises, to the increasing frustration of the workers.

By the summer of 1917, it was clear that the liberals did not want the revolution to go any further. They wanted it reined in and would prefer military control to soviet control.

ACTIVITY

Do you think the Provisional Government was doomed from the beginning? Given its status and the situation in Russia, could it have met the expectations of the mass of the people?

a) Note down reasons for and against the idea that it was doomed from the start.

b) What would you identify as the most significant or important factors in deciding whether it was doomed or not?

KEY POINTS FROM CHAPTER 3

Was the Provisional Government doomed from the beginning?

1 Lenin offered a radically different programme from that of the Provisional Government and the moderate socialist leaders of the other parties.

2 The Mensheviks and Socialist Revolutionaries were drawn into the Provisional Government and thereafter became associated with its weakness and failures.

3 War was the source of many of its problems but the Provisional Government, for a number of reasons, was unwilling to make a separate peace with Germany.

4 The peasants were increasingly taking matters into their own hands after the Provisional Government refused to legitimise their right to redistribute land amongst themselves.

5 There were splits in the Provisional Government between the liberals and the socialists over how to treat the national minorities.

6 The workers became more radicalised as the summer turned into autumn, and class antagonisms with employers became more acute.

7 Soldiers, increasingly war weary, did not want to fight.

8 The Provisional Government could not meet the expectations of the people in such a short space of time.

9 By the end of August the new socialist Prime Minister, Alexander Kerensky, faced a formidable range of problems.

4

Was the Bolshevik seizure of power in October 1917 inevitable?

CHAPTER OVERVIEW

The popularity of the Bolshevik Party grew in the summer of 1917 as the workers became more disillusioned with the policies of the Provisional Government and the moderate socialist leaders in the Soviet. At the beginning of July there was an explosive rising – the July Days – in Petrograd which reflected the frustration of workers, soldiers and sailors. The Bolsheviks were drawn into this but the rising collapsed and leading Bolsheviks were arrested. Kerensky tried to assert his authority by taking military control of the capital, with the help of General Kornilov, but the plan backfired on him and he was discredited. The Bolsheviks exploited this situation to seize power in October 1917.

A Why did the Bolsheviks become so popular and how did they almost ruin their chances of taking power? (pp. 50–52)

B The Kornilov affair and its consequences (pp. 53–54)

C The October Revolution – did Kerensky hand power to the Bolsheviks? (pp. 55–57)

D Popular revolution or *coup d'état*? (pp. 58–63)

E Review: Was the Bolshevik seizure of power inevitable? (p. 64)

Note: Section A of this chapter looks at the fortunes and misfortunes of the Bolsheviks from April to August 1917. This covers the same time period described in sections C and D in Chapter 3. The story of the Revolution from September to October starts in section B (page 53).

FOCUS ROUTE

1 As you work through this chapter, follow the ups and downs of the Bolshevik Party from April to October. The timeline in Chart 4A will help. Annotate your copy of the graph to explain key points in their progress, showing why their popularity increased from May to November.

2 Throughout this chapter you are going to think about the question of whether the Bolshevik seizure of power was always the most likely outcome. At various points, you will be asked to note down your opinions. Then at the end you will be asked to reach a final judgement.

Support for the Bolshevik Party

April May June July August September October

■ 4A Timeline of the revolutions in 1917

FEBRUARY
23 Women's Day parade
25 General strike
27 Duma committee and Petrograd Soviet formed

MARCH
1 Order No. 1 issued
2 Provisional Government formed (Tsar abdicates)

APRIL
3 Lenin returns to Petrograd

MAY
2 Milyukov resigns as Minister for War; Provisional Government in crisis
5 Coalition government of socialists and Kadets formed

JUNE
3 First All-Russian Congress of Soviets begins
16 Launch of military offensive

JULY
3–4 'July Days'
5–6 Bolsheviks arrested in Petrograd; Lenin flees to Finland
8 Kerensky becomes Prime Minister, at head of new coalition government

AUGUST
26–30 Kornilov affair

SEPTEMBER
9 Bolshevik majority in Petrograd Soviet
15 Bolshevik Central Committee rejects Lenin's first call for insurrection

OCTOBER
7 Lenin returns to Petrograd
10 Bolshevik Central Committee confirms decision to seize power
25–26 Bolsheviks seize power

 Why did the Bolsheviks become so popular and how did they almost ruin their chances of taking power?

The Bolshevik Party became the main focus for the masses dissatisfied with the government's performance. Their programme of ending the war, controlling employers, social reform for workers and prioritising food supplies was appealing. During May and June the workers and soldiers in Petrograd and Moscow began to differentiate between the Bolsheviks and the other socialist groups. Left-wing members of the Socialist Revolutionary and Menshevik parties were increasingly drawn towards the Bolshevik camp. Support for the party grew and membership increased enormously (see Source 4.11, page 61). Probably the most famous recruit to the Bolshevik Party in the summer of 1917 was Leon Trotsky.

■ Learning trouble spot

The workers and political parties

It is easy to think that workers supported one or other of the socialist parties in the same way as people support political parties today. But in *The Russian Revolution 1917–21* (1987), Beryl Williams has pointed out that workers in the first months after the February Revolution in 1917 did not tend to think in party terms. Most would not have known the difference between a Menshevik and a Bolshevik. Workers tended to identify more with their own craft or industry and placed most of their trust in their workplace committees and local soviets, most of which were multi-party or non-party organisations. However, it seems that by June many workers were becoming aware of the Bolsheviks as a separate party with a different programme – one which tied in with their own demands and aspirations.

The July Days

The mounting frustration of workers and soldiers erupted at the beginning of July in what became known as the July Days, several days of uncontrolled rioting on the streets. This was sparked by the failure of the summer offensive against Germany, workers' anger at their economic plight and the Petrograd garrison's fear that its regiments were to be sent to the Front.

For two days the capital was defenceless. On 3 July, Sukhanov, the diarist of the revolution, reported lorries and cars rushing about the city full of 'fierce-faced' civilians and soldiers, and armed groups marching in the streets. On 4 July, events took a more violent turn when 20,000 armed sailors from the Kronstadt naval base arrived in Petrograd. Red Kronstadt, as it was known, was a hotbed of revolutionary activity. The sailors marched to the Tauride Palace where they demanded that the Soviet take power. Chernov, the Socialist Revolutionary leader, was sent out to calm them down but was seized and bundled into a car. He was rescued by Trotsky who barely escaped with his own life (see Source 4.2).

KRONSTADT

Krondstadt was a naval base on an island just off the coast near Petrograd. The sailors who lived in the base were, in 1917, extremely radical and supported revolutionary change. However, there is a common misconception that they were, to a man, Bolsheviks. Many were Bolsheviks, but anarchists and Socialist Revolutionaries were also very influential. The sailors had their own fiercely independent soviet which was multi-party and chaired by a Socialist Revolutionary.

51

WAS THE BOLSHEVIK SEIZURE OF POWER IN OCTOBER 1917 INEVITABLE?

SOURCE 4.1 Troops fire on demonstrators in Petrograd during the July Days

SOURCE 4.2 J. Carmichael, *A Short History of the Revolution*, 1967, p. 116, quoting from Sukhanov's diary

A group of workers rushed [into the room where the Soviet leaders were meeting] . . . shouting out: 'Comrade Chernov has been arrested by the mob! They're tearing him to pieces right now! To the rescue! Everyone out into the street!'

Chkheidze, restoring order with difficulty, proposed that Kamenev, Martov and Trotsky should hasten to rescue Chernov. [Trotsky and several others went out to help] . . . The mob was in turmoil as far as the eye could reach. A number of sailors with rather savage faces around the motor car were particularly violent. Chernov, who had plainly lost all presence of mind, was in the back seat.

[Trotsky climbed on to the bonnet of the car.]

All Kronstadt knew Trotsky and, one would have thought, trusted him. But he began to speak and the crowd did not subside. If a shot had been fired nearby at that moment by way of provocation, a tremendous slaughter might have occurred, and all of us, including Trotsky, might have been torn to shreds.

[Trotsky said:]

'You hurried over here, Red Kronstadters, as soon as you heard the revolution was in danger . . . Long live Red Kronstadt, the glory and pride of the revolution . . . You've come to declare your will and show the Soviet that the working class no longer wants to see the bourgeoisie in power. But why hurt your own cause by petty acts of violence against casual individuals? . . . Every one of you is prepared to lay down his life for the revolution. I know that. Give me your hand, comrade! Your hand, brother!'

Trotsky stretched his hand down to a sailor who was protesting with especial violence. The latter moved his hand out of reach. . . . But I think they were Kronstadt naval ratings who had, in their own judgement, accepted Bolshevik ideas. It seemed to me that the sailor, who must have heard Trotsky in Kronstadt more than once . . . was confused. Not knowing what to do, the Kronstadters released Chernov. Trotsky took him by the arm and hurried him into the Palace. Chernov sank nervelessly into his chair.

[Later a worker jumped on to the platform of a Soviet executive committee meeting and shouted:]

'Comrades! How long must we workers put up with treachery? You're all here debating and making deals with the bourgeoisie and the landlords . . . You are busy betraying the working class. Well, just understand that the working class won't put up with it! There are 30,000 of us all told here from Putilov. We're going to have our way. All power to the soviets! We have a firm grip on our rifles! Your Kerenskys and Tseretelis are not going to fool us!'

FOCUS ROUTE

Make a note of your answers to the following questions:

1 How did the Bolsheviks differentiate themselves from other socialist parties?

2 a) What was the significance of the July Days?

   b) How involved were the Bolsheviks in the uprising?

   c) Why did they look weaker after the July Days?

3 Were the Bolsheviks really a highly disciplined and organised party?

ACTIVITY

1 What do Sources 4.1 and 4.2 and the incidents described above show about:

   a) the feelings of the workers and soldiers

   b) their attitudes towards the Provisional Government

   c) the position of revolutionary leaders in July 1917

   d) the situation in Petrograd regarding control and order?

WAS THE BOLSHEVIK SEIZURE OF POWER IN OCTOBER 1917 INEVITABLE?

52

What was the position of the Soviet at this time?

In the summer of 1917, the Petrograd Soviet was controlled by the moderate leaders of the Mensheviks and the Socialist Revolutionaries. However, it was becoming increasingly weak and identified with the Provisional

FOCUS ROUTE

Did it look at this point as if the Bolshevik seizure of power was inevitable?

Some historians have seen the July Days as an early attempt by the Bolsheviks to take power. There is little doubt that the rising was encouraged by middle-ranking Bolshevik officials, and Sukhanov talks of armed groups led by 'Bolshevik lieutenants', but it seems that the Bolshevik leadership were far from committed. In fact, when the rioting began and the Kronstadt sailors marched into Petrograd, Lenin was on a short holiday. When he returned on 4 July he appealed for restraint and the Bolshevik Central Committee called off the demonstration it had planned for early the next day. Lenin adopted a 'wait and see' policy. He did not dissociate himself from the demonstrations but he did not provide coherent leadership or make a concerted attempt to seize power.

This lack of leadership proved the undoing of the July rising. Without a clear purpose, the rising lost momentum. Troops loyal to the Soviet arrived and the crowds were dispersed. The steam was also taken out of the demonstrations by the leaking of a letter by the Provisional Government which appeared to show that Lenin was in the pay of the Germans and had come back to Russia to undermine the Russian war effort. Several leading Bolsheviks and Trotsky were arrested; Lenin was forced into hiding in Finland. The Soviet newspaper, *Izvestia*, denounced the role of the Bolsheviks in the July Days and it seemed that the Bolshevik cause had been dealt a blow from which it might not recover.

LENIN'S ESCAPE

Lenin, dressed as a working man, had to shave off his beard to escape. You can tell if a Soviet film of the events of October 1917 is genuine by looking to see if Lenin has a beard, as it had not grown back by the time the Bolshevik seizure of power took place. Lenin's hiding place was just on the other side of the Finnish border.

■ Learning trouble spot

Lenin and the Bolshevik Party

One important historical question during this period concerns the relationship between Lenin and the Bolshevik Party:

- Was it Lenin's conviction and force of personality alone that was driving them forward?
- Was Lenin in control of a highly disciplined party that obeyed orders?

Lenin had certainly changed party policy in April from co-operation with the Provisional Government to outright opposition and had called for the Soviet to take power. But revisionist historians like Edward Acton (*Rethinking the Russian Revolution*, 1990, page 196) point out that Bolshevik Party activists had been calling for these changes before Lenin's return. Lenin was more in tune with grassroots Bolsheviks than other Bolshevik leaders were. Lenin himself remarked that the body of the party was more radical than the leadership.

Acton goes on to say that Lenin was not in a position to impose control over the party. Membership soared, cells sprang up, elections and meetings took place, committees operated at different levels and communications were poor – all of which made close supervision difficult, especially outside Petrograd. The party's policy was fiercely debated at every level and there were often divisions even at the top. According to Acton, 'Formal policy directives from the centre were followed only in so far as they corresponded to local Bolshevik opinion.' The July Days appear to be an example of lower-ranking party members running ahead of their leaders.

B The Kornilov affair and its consequences

FOCUS ROUTE

Make notes to explain how the Kornilov affair helped the Bolsheviks.

The arrests of leading Bolsheviks and the closure of Bolshevik newspapers after the July Days gave the moderate socialists and the liberals in the Provisional Government a boost, but not for long. You know from Chapter 3 that their problems – war, pressure for land reform, pressures from the national minorities, and a deteriorating economic situation – got worse as August progressed. (See Chart 3E and the Activity on page 47.)

■ 4B How did Kerensky respond to his problems?

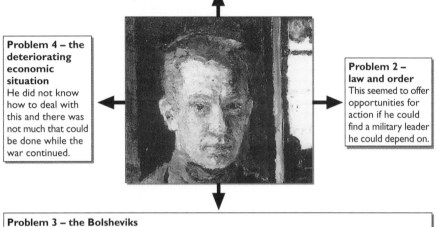

Problem 1 – the war
He was still unwilling to make a separate peace with Germany. The moderate socialists and liberals in the Provisional Government agreed with him because they knew it would cost Russia dearly in territory and they did not want to be defeated by Germany.

Problem 4 – the deteriorating economic situation
He did not know how to deal with this and there was not much that could be done while the war continued.

Problem 2 – law and order
This seemed to offer opportunities for action if he could find a military leader he could depend on.

Problem 3 – the Bolsheviks
Along with other moderate socialists, he did not want to go for full-scale suppression of the Bolsheviks. He thought such a move might lead to rioting and violence.

By the end of August, Kerensky had come to the conclusion that the only course open to him was to restore law and order in the cities and discipline in the army. He desperately needed troops he could count on to carry out his orders and deal with any threat presented by the Bolsheviks. Kerensky appointed a new Supreme Commander of the Russian forces, General Kornilov, and entered into an agreement with him, as he saw it, to bring trustworthy troops to Petrograd. But Kornilov, who was fast becoming the middle-class hope for salvation, saw it as an opportunity to crush the radical socialists, prevent the worst excesses of the revolution, and restore order and authority in Petrograd. He sent his troops marching towards the city in what was the beginning of an attempt to seize control of the government and establish military control.

Kerensky panicked when he realised what was happening. He denounced Kornilov and called on the Soviet to help to defend Petrograd from counter-revolution. Whilst some of the middle classes would undoubtedly have welcomed Kornilov and the restoration of order that would protect their property and interests, the mass of the people were terrified by the prospect. To them it meant the return of the old order, the loss of the gains of the Revolution, and bloodshed in the fighting that would inevitably result. The soldiers in Petrograd were also alarmed: they might lose the power they had gained over their officers, old-style discipline would be restored and they might be forced to go to the Front to fight. In their alarm and panic, the people desperately wanted help – and it was the Bolsheviks that provided it. Soldiers, workers and sailors prepared to defend the city, but much of this defence was organised by the Bolsheviks. The Bolshevik Red Guard (militia trained secretly by the Bolsheviks) appeared on the streets and Kerensky was good enough to supply

54

WAS THE BOLSHEVIK SEIZURE OF POWER IN OCTOBER 1917 INEVITABLE?

them with weapons. In the event, Kornilov's troops did not arrive. Railway workers halted the trains carrying them to Petrograd and Bolshevik agents persuaded them to desert their officers. Kornilov was arrested.

The consequences of Kornilov's ill-judged intervention were very significant:

1 Kerensky's reputation was irretrievably damaged. Kerensky's wife wrote: 'The prestige of Kerensky and the Provisional Government was completely destroyed by the Kornilov affair; and he was left almost without supporters.'
2 The Menshevik and Socialist Revolutionary leaders were discredited by their association with Kerensky. Their inability to change their policies also condemned them in the eyes of the people. All that the moderate socialist leaders could do was to place their hopes on the forthcoming Constituent Assembly.
3 The mass of the people completely distrusted the Kadets and other liberals as the agents of the industrialists and large landowners.
4 Soldiers, infuriated by what they thought was an officers' plot, murdered hundreds of officers. It became clear that generals could not rely on 'loyal' troops to carry out their orders. Officers, for their part, felt that Kerensky had betrayed Kornilov and were not prepared to fight for him in the coming confrontation with the Bolsheviks.
5 The Bolsheviks rode back on a wave of popular support as the saviours of the city, the true defenders of the Revolution. They were elected in huge numbers on to soviets. On 9 September, the Bolsheviks gained overall control of the Petrograd Soviet and on 25 September Trotsky was elected its President. They also took control of the Moscow Soviet and dominated the executive committees of soviets throughout urban Russia.

Kornilov
Kornilov, the son of a Siberian Cossack, had shown some sympathy towards revolutionary change, even approving soldiers' committees in the army. He was liked and supported by his own soldiers, and did not seem to have political ambitions. He seemed a good choice as Supreme Commander for Kerensky, who desperately needed stability in the army and loyal troops. But Kornilov quickly became the darling of right-wing conservative forces (industrialists, army officers and landowners) who saw in him their main hope for turning the tables on the revolutionaries. This may have swayed him to make his move on Petrograd. It is not clear whether he wanted to set up a military dictatorship or not. He said he would not move against the Provisional Government but he did want it 'cleansed and strengthened'. What Kornilov was clear about was that his main aim was to 'Hang the German spies, headed by Lenin … and disperse the Soviet'.

FOCUS ROUTE

Did it look as if the Bolshevik seizure of power was inevitable at this point? Note your opinion, explaining any pointers that suggest it was increasingly inevitable and any reasons why it was still not inevitable.

■ **Learning trouble spot**

Was the rise in support for the Bolsheviks in September due only to the Kornilov affair?
In *From Tsar to Soviets: The Russian People and their Revolution 1917–21* (1996, page 147), the historian Chris Read makes the point that support for the Bolsheviks was rising again even before Kornilov's attempted coup. In August in the elections to the Petrograd City Duma, the Bolsheviks polled 33 per cent of the votes, coming a close second to the Socialist Revolutionaries. Menshevik supporters, in particular, were moving to the Bolsheviks because of, as one Menshevik paper put it, a 'lack of concrete results' for the masses. The Kornilov affair hastened this process.

55

WAS THE BOLSHEVIK SEIZURE OF POWER IN OCTOBER 1917 INEVITABLE?

C The October Revolution – did Kerensky hand power to the Bolsheviks?

WHO WERE ZINOVIEV AND KAMENEV?

Zinoviev (top) and Kamenev were important Bolshevik leaders who had been close to Lenin while he was in exile abroad before 1917. Zinoviev had been in hiding with Lenin in Switzerland. He had returned with Lenin on the train from Switzerland in April 1917. Both men had consistently opposed the idea of the Bolsheviks seizing power on their own, and wanted to work with other socialist groups.

Lenin had been in hiding in Finland watching events unfold. He judged that the time was now right for the Bolsheviks to seize power. He thought that a number of factors were working in their favour:

- the Bolsheviks had control of the Soviet
- their popularity was at an all-time high and they had done very well in elections to soviets across Russia
- the liberals and other conservative forces were demoralised after the Kornilov affair
- the Provisional Government was helpless.

A power vacuum had been created after the Kornilov débâcle and Lenin was determined to fill it. He was worried that events might turn against the Bolsheviks, particularly if the Germans made a sudden move and a separate peace was negotiated.

On 12 September, he wrote to the Bolshevik Central Committee urging action. He wrote: 'History will not forgive us if we do not assume power now.' But the other leading Bolsheviks in the Party Central Committee thought his plans were premature and remained unconvinced. They rejected his initial demands and it was only after he had come secretly to Petrograd and talked to them all night on 10 October that they finally agreed. Even then Zinoviev and Kamenev thought that it was too risky and opposed the seizure of power. To Lenin's intense displeasure, they publicised their views in a letter published in Gorky's newspaper, *Novaia zhizn*.

SOURCE 4.3 A letter from Zinoviev and Kamenev, published in *Novaia zhizn* on 18 October 1917

To call at present for an armed uprising means to stake on one card not only the fate of our Party, but also the fate of the Russian and international revolution ... A majority of workers and a significant part of the army is for us. But the rest are in question. We are convinced, for example, that if it now comes to elections for the Constituent Assembly, then the majority of peasants will vote for the Socialist Revolutionaries ... If we take power now and are forced into a revolutionary war, the mass of the soldiers will not support us.

Zinoviev and Kamenev feared civil war and believed the Bolsheviks would end up isolated and defeated by other forces combining against them. There was a real danger for the Bolsheviks that they did not have enough support in the army or amongst the workers to make a success of their rising. Trotsky urged Lenin to wait until the meeting of the Second Congress of All-Russian Soviets on 26 October. He thought that the Bolsheviks could use this as an opportunity to take control since it would appear that the seizure of power was done with the support of the soviets rather than by the Bolsheviks on their own.

Kerensky's response to the growing crisis

Once again Kerensky played into the Bolsheviks' hands. He tried to send the most radical army units out of the capital and there were rumours that he planned to abandon Petrograd to the Germans. This allowed the Soviet (now under Bolshevik control) to set up a Military Revolutionary Committee (MRC) in case there was another attempted right-wing coup. The MRC, dominated by the Bolsheviks and controlled by Trotsky, now had more direct control over soldiers in the capital and seized great quantities of arms and ammunition.

It was now an open secret that the Bolsheviks intended to seize power. Kerensky, in a last-ditch attempt to recover the situation, tried to close down two Bolshevik newspapers, restrict the power of the MRC and raise the bridges

56

WAS THE BOLSHEVIK SEIZURE OF POWER IN OCTOBER 1917 INEVITABLE?

FOCUS ROUTE

Did the Bolshevik seizure of power seem inevitable at this point?

SEIZING POWER

From our viewpoint the Bolshevik seizure of power looks very easy, with little risk involved. But it would not have appeared so to the Bolsheviks. Lenin and Trotsky were quite gloomy on the night of the take-over. They were concerned that Kerensky might turn up with troops loyal to the Provisional Government and they had no idea how the mass of the working class and other socialists would receive the news of their actions. Just a few days earlier, Bolshevik activists had reported that workers would not come out *en masse* in support of the Bolsheviks alone.

■ **Learning trouble spot**

Why did the Bolsheviks want to use the All-Russian Congress of Soviets in their bid for power?

The first congress, held at the beginning of June 1917, was dominated by the Mensheviks and Socialist Revolutionaries. Delegates were sent from soviets across Russia.

The congress was an important forum and, as such, it was potentially very powerful. The Second All-Russian Congress was called for 25 October. It was not entirely representative but reflected the Bolshevik success in elections to the soviets. The Bolsheviks had the most delegates but not a majority until the other parties walked out. Trotsky used the congress to claim that they were taking power in the name of the soviets.

linking the working-class districts to the centre of Petrograd. This was a blunder – it gave the Bolsheviks an excuse for action. They could now say that Kerensky was attacking the Soviet and the Revolution. Kerensky, dosing himself on brandy and morphine, sought loyal troops to help him deal with the Bolshevik threat but, finding none in the city, he left for the Front. He even had to borrow a car from the American embassy to get him there.

The Bolsheviks seize control

At the Smolny Institute, the Bolsheviks' headquarters, Trotsky and Sverdlov (see page 71) organised the final stages of the revolution. On the night of 24–25 October, units of the Red Guard, sailors and garrison soldiers were sent out to seize key points in the city – the bridges, telephone exchange, the main railway stations and the power stations. There was a bit of trouble at the main telegraph office but on the whole any troops on duty just faded away as the Red Guards appeared.

The next day in Petrograd began as normal and indeed, to a casual observer, it might have appeared that nothing special was happening. The shops opened as normal, the trams were running and people went about their everyday business. There was no furore in the streets. Many of the foreign observers in the embassies expected the Bolshevik move to crumble when people realised what was happening. Meanwhile, the Bolsheviks had decided to move in on the Provisional Government in the Winter Palace. On the night of 25–26 October, Bolshevik soldiers entered the Palace and at 2am arrested what remained of the government. The storming of the Winter Palace was to become a great Bolshevik myth defining the heroism of the revolutionaries and the popular nature of the revolution (see pages 58–63).

The same evening the All-Russian Congress of Soviets met. Socialists from other parties denounced the actions of the Bolsheviks. They argued first, that the Bolsheviks did not represent the ordinary Russian people – only a broadly based coalition of socialist parties could do that – and, second, that the Bolshevik action would set in motion a backlash which would set back the cause of socialism for decades. Trotsky replied:

'A rising of the masses of the people needs no justification . . . The masses of the people followed our banner and our insurrection was victorious. And now we are told: renounce your victory, make concessions, make compromise. With whom? . . . to those who tell us to do this we must say: you are miserable bankrupts, your role is played out; go where you ought to be – into the dustbin of history!'

The main socialist parties stormed from the hall. Only the left-wing Socialist Revolutionaries remained. This was fortunate for the Bolsheviks as it gave them a majority in the congress. Later, Lenin arrived and announced the formation of a Bolshevik government, immediate moves to end the war and a decree transferring land to the peasants.

Whilst the insurrection in Petrograd was relatively bloodless, this was not the case in Moscow and in some other towns. There were ten days of bloody fighting in Moscow between the Bolsheviks and forces loyal to the Provisional Government before a truce was agreed. There was an immediate threat to Petrograd by forces under General Krasnov, organised by Kerensky. But they got no nearer than the edges of the city where a mixed force of workers, sailors and soldiers repulsed them. However fragile their hold was for the moment, the Bolsheviks were in power in Russia.

57

WAS THE BOLSHEVIK SEIZURE OF POWER IN OCTOBER 1917 INEVITABLE?

THE ROLE OF TROTSKY

Trotsky had finally joined the Bolsheviks in August, although in spirit he had been with them for longer and was anxious for the Soviet to seize power. He had been a valuable addition to the party. He was by far the best orator and could really sway crowds. He was probably better known than Lenin because of his role in the 1905 Revolution when he had been chairman of the St Petersburg Soviet. Trotsky's role in the preparations for the October Revolution – persuading Lenin to wait until October; setting up and controlling the Military Revolutionary Committee; reacting to Kerensky's blunders; planning the details of the take-over – has led some to suggest that he was more important than Lenin in the actual seizure of power.

SOURCE 4.4   Bolsheviks outside the Smolny Institute

TALKING POINT

Does anything you have read in this chapter change your ideas about whether the Provisional Government was doomed from the beginning?

ACTIVITY

Assessing the role of Kerensky

After August, the pressure of leadership seems to have affected Kerensky. One commentator said, 'He is like a railroad car that has left the rails. He sways and vacillates, painfully and without any glamour.' Rumours spread of his love affair with his wife's cousin and of his drunkenness and addiction to morphine and cocaine.

Kerensky has been criticised for poor political judgement in 1917 which made it easier for the Bolsheviks in October and hastened the revolution. The best examples of this are:

- his involvement with Kornilov (Kerensky did appoint Kornilov) and the subsequent débâcle, leading to his loss of credibility, and the creation of a power vacuum which Lenin was only too willing to fill (see pages 53–54)
- his disastrous underestimate of the support for Lenin in October. He believed that any Bolshevik rising would be a repeat of the July Days and easily crushed
- his actions on 24 October, closing two Bolshevik newspapers and announcing his intention of acting against the party, gave Trotsky the excuse to say the soviets were under attack and thereby ensure popular support for the Bolsheviks. Beryl Williams has called this an act of 'unbelievable ineptitude' (*Lenin*, 2000, page 76).

1 Why do you think the Kornilov affair was so damaging to the Provisional Government?
2 How far do you think Kerensky was responsible for the collapse of the Provisional Government in October 1917?
3 Did he hand power to the Bolsheviks?

Before answering these questions, you might like to look back at the material on Kerensky on pages 44–47).

58

WAS THE BOLSHEVIK SEIZURE OF POWER IN OCTOBER 1917 INEVITABLE?

HISTORIOGRAPHY
The study of history writing, talking about the different schools of thought on a historical subject, how the circumstances in which history is written affect what historians say about a subject.

COUP D'ÉTAT
Violent seizure of power, usually by a relatively small number of people.

D Popular revolution or *coup d'état*?

The HISTORIOGRAPHICAL debate about whether the October Revolution was a popular revolution or a *COUP D'ÉTAT* has often been sharp and caustic. This is because it reflects the political views of historians about whether Communism is a good or an evil system.

The range of interpretations and the shades of difference between the two positions stated in Chart 4C are enormous, but we can establish some broad schools of thought.

■ 4C Views of the nature of the October Revolution

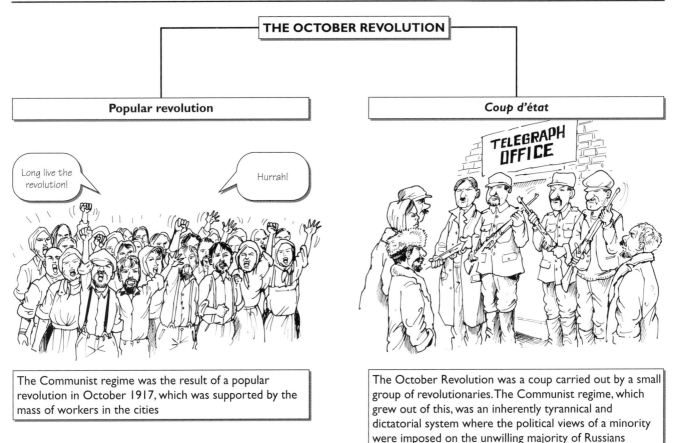

The Communist regime was the result of a popular revolution in October 1917, which was supported by the mass of workers in the cities

The October Revolution was a coup carried out by a small group of revolutionaries. The Communist regime, which grew out of this, was an inherently tyrannical and dictatorial system where the political views of a minority were imposed on the unwilling majority of Russians

The Soviet view (1917–91)

By the Soviet view here we mean the historians and writers who produced their work in Soviet Russia before its collapse in 1991. This view followed the line laid down by the Soviet leadership and writers were not allowed to deviate from it. The Soviet interpretation claims that the October Revolution was a popular uprising which was led and carried out by the working class, supported by the poorer peasants. According to this view, the working class created the soviets, which acted as the power bases through which the revolution was accomplished. They were able to do this because of the weakness of the bourgeoisie in Russia. The Bolshevik Party played a key role in guiding the working classes to success in October. Lenin is given a key role as the leader who directed the party and had the insight to make crucial decisions.

59

WAS THE BOLSHEVIK SEIZURE OF POWER IN OCTOBER 1917 INEVITABLE?

The predominant Western view after 1945

After the Second World War, the West was engaged in a COLD WAR with the Soviet Union. The USA funded a great deal of historical research (called Sovietology) to understand the enemy. The predominant view amongst large numbers of historians was therefore, not surprisingly, hostile to the USSR. They saw a straight line from Bolshevism to Stalinism and totalitarianism. They identified the October Revolution as the starting point for this process, when a 'tiny minority' seized power in a *coup d'état* and then imposed their evil ideology on an unwilling population. In this view, Lenin controlled a well-organised and disciplined revolutionary party who directed the masses. He had the will, the personality and the clear-cut policies that brought about the revolution; the party operated at his command. In recent years, the most vociferous proponent of these views has been Richard Pipes. Other Western historians who have seen the October Revolution as a disaster are Leonard Schapiro and Robert Conquest. This is also called the 'liberal' view, mainly referring to Western liberal historians who took this line during the Cold War when the West feared the aggressive intentions of the Soviet Union.

The revisionists

In the 1970s, a new generation of historians challenged the 'totalitarian' view of the historians they called 'cold warriors'. Influenced by the Vietnam War, they became more critical of American policies. They suspected that the hostile accounts of the October Revolution were part of the Cold War politics of the post-war period. They looked more closely at the role of Lenin and the Bolshevik Party in the revolution. They also wanted to look at history 'from below' as well as 'from above': to put people back into accounts of the October Revolution. Historians like Stephen Smith (*Red Petrograd: Revolution in the Factories 1917–18*, 1983) saw a much more active role for the lower ranks of the Bolshevik Party in pushing forward the revolution. They were not just the instruments of Lenin. Indeed, such historians have suggested that Lenin was not so firmly in control and that the Bolsheviks were not so disciplined as Western historians had previously claimed. Sheila Fitzpatrick went further. In *The Russian Revolution 1917–1932* (1994) she suggested that it was people – workers, soldiers and peasants – who created the circumstances in which the Bolsheviks could operate. They formed soviets and committees before the Bolsheviks were on the scene. This veers back towards the popular view of the October Revolution.

Recent views

Historians in more recent years, such as Robert Service and Chris Read, have acknowledged that there is room to accept the scholarship of the Cold War historians and of the revisionists. They argue that Lenin was a key figure, saying that without his drive and persistence there probably would not have been an October Revolution. They also say that all the hallmarks of a *coup* are present in the way that the Bolsheviks seized power. However, they maintain that there was a lot of independent action at local levels in the party and in the soviets and that the situation greatly facilitated the take-over: the increased radicalism of the workers, soldiers, sailors and peasants cannot be ignored. The extent of their involvement is crucial in assessing whether the events of October 1917 constitute a popular revolution or not.

■ **Learning trouble spot**

Putting historians into camps
Students sometimes want to pigeon-hole historians into particular camps and then assume that within those camps everyone is saying roughly the same thing. Although it is helpful to identify some broad trends of thought in discussing the historiography of this or other topics on Russia, you must be careful about lumping historians together. Historians may take broadly similar positions but take different lines about particular events or developments, that is, their interpretations are varied. For example, there are many differences in interpretation amongst the historians we have grouped together as 'the revisionists'.

TALKING POINT

What do you think are the main issues about the nature of the evidence on which the interpretations are based? Could interpretations change in the future?

60

WAS THE BOLSHEVIK SEIZURE OF POWER IN OCTOBER 1917 INEVITABLE?

LIBERTARIAN
**An interpretation that focuses on the
free will of the people.**

SOURCE 4.5 B. N. Pomomarev, *History of the Communist Party of the Soviet Union*, 1960

*The working class led the struggle of the whole people against the autocracy and
against the dictatorship of the bourgeoisie. The other sections of the working class
had convinced themselves that in the proletariat they had the champion of the
interests of the whole people ... The proletariat were the prime motive force of the
entire social and political development of the country ... The October Revolution
differed from that of all other revolutions in that the workers created their own
organs of power – the Soviets of Workers' Deputies. The Soviets of Workers',
Soldiers' and Peasants' Deputies were organs of alliance of the workers and
peasants under the leadership of the workers.*

SOURCE 4.6 R. Pipes, 'The Great October Revolution as a Clandestine *Coup d'Etat*',
Times Literary Supplement, November 1992

October was not a revolution but a classic coup d'état *planned in the dead of
night on October 10th, and executed two weeks later ... The last thing the
conspirators wanted was to attract attention. The 'masses', so much in evidence
in the bourgeois revolution of February, were not told that they were taking over
until after the event.*

The seizure of power, masterminded by Trotsky, was a model putsch ...
*Conceived and carried out in strictest secrecy, it eschewed barricades and mob
actions in favour of surgical strikes against the organ of the state. It was so
successfully camouflaged as a transfer of power to the All-Russian Congress of
Soviets that virtually no one, including the rank and file of the Bolshevik Party,
had any inkling of what had happened.*

*These facts require emphasis because of the entrenched myth that the
Bolsheviks rose to power in the wake of an explosion of popular fury. No such
explosion is apparent in contemporary sources. Eyewitnesses, including the best
chronicler of 1917, the Menshevik Nicholas Sukhanov, are virtually unanimous in
depicting October as a* coup d'état; *so too are such historians as S. P. Melgunov
who had lived through it.*

SOURCE 4.7 O. Figes, *A People's Tragedy: The Russian Revolution 1891–1924*, 1997,
pp. 460–61

*One of the most basic misconceptions of the Russian Revolution is that the
Bolsheviks were swept to power on a tide of mass support for the party itself. The
October insurrection was a* coup d'état, *actively supported by a small minority of
the population (and indeed opposed by several of the Bolshevik leaders
themselves). But it took place amidst a social revolution, which was centred on
the popular realization of Soviet power ... as the direct self-rule of the people ...
The political vacuum brought about by this social revolution enabled the
Bolsheviks to seize power in the cities ... The slogan 'All Power to the Soviets!'
was a useful tool, a banner of popular legitimation covering the nakedness of
Lenin's ambition ... Later, as the nature of the Bolshevik dictatorship became
apparent, the party faced the growing opposition of precisely those groups in
society who had rallied behind the soviet slogan.*

SOURCE 4.8 A. Berkman's LIBERTARIAN view summarised in E. Acton, *Rethinking the
Russian Revolution*, 1990, p. 177

*The Revolution was truly popular and profoundly democratic. Lenin and his
comrades were the illegitimate beneficiaries of the autonomous action of the
masses. The revolution of 1917 was the product of popular revolt against
oppression. It was accomplished 'not by a political party, but by the people
themselves'. Time and again the self-proclaimed leaders of the revolution were
taken by surprise by the initiative welling up from below – in January 1905, in
February, April and July 1917. The masses were not enticed into revolt by
superior leaders. Their extreme radicalism was not the product of manipulation
or brainwashing by the Bolsheviks, as the liberal view would have it, nor was it
the fruit of enlightenment brought to them by the Bolsheviks as the Soviet view
contends. The goals for which they strove were their own.*

61

WAS THE BOLSHEVIK SEIZURE OF POWER IN OCTOBER 1917 INEVITABLE?

SOURCE 4.9 B. Williams, *The Russian Revolution 1917–1921*, 1987, pp. 46–47

In striking contrast to February and to later film portrayals, this was not a mass uprising. Relatively few people were actively involved. If it were a coup – and Lenin denied this, calling it an armed uprising of the urban masses – it was one enthusiastically supported by the proletariat and accepted by the peasantry.

SOURCE 4.10 E. Acton, *Rethinking the Russian Revolution*, 1990, pp. 203–24

In the light of revisionist research the October revolution emerges as very much more than a conspiratorial coup d'état. By then the central political issue was that of soviet power. It was popular support for this cause which doomed Kerensky and the Provisional Government and explains the ease with which armed resistance to the new order was overcome . . .

The Bolshevik victory in the struggle for power owed less to effective organization and military manoeuvre than Soviet, liberal or libertarian accounts would have it. The party owed its strength to its identification with the cause of Soviet power. By October that cause enjoyed overwhelming support in the cities and the army, and tacit support in the villages. By virtue of its relatively flexible, open and democratic character, its sensitivity to mass opinion, its ability to respond to pressure from below, the party had established itself as the prime vehicle for the achievement of popular goals.

FOCUS ROUTE

Using the information on pages 61–63, collect notes for a short piece of writing (three or four paragraphs) in answer to the question: Do you think the Bolshevik revolution was a popular revolution or a *coup d'état*? In your answer, refer to the views of different historians in Sources 4.5–4.10 on pages 60–61.

What evidence is there for Bolshevik popularity?

You have looked at the ideas of historians, but what about the evidence? The problem is, of course, that it is very difficult to gauge the extent of Bolshevik popularity. This accounts for some of the differences in interpretation. We do not know how many people would have turned out on to the streets for them. But it is clear the party was attracting a great deal of support. The figures in Sources 4.11–4.13 give us some indications.

The November elections (Source 4.13 on page 62) could be interpreted as a disaster for the Bolsheviks because they got less than a quarter of the seats in the Constituent Assembly. However, the Bolsheviks did very well in the cities (as much as 70 per cent of those voting in some working-class districts of Petrograd voted for them). So urban working-class support does seem quite high – look at the figures for the municipal elections in Source 4.12. Also, a lot of the peasants would have been voting for the left wing of the Socialist Revolutionaries who were collaborating closely with the Bolsheviks at this time.

There is a tendency to focus on the political events leading up to the insurrection, but you also need to be aware of the attitudes of the workers and peasants in September and October. The workers had become highly politicised and radicalised in these months when food was very short, wages could not keep pace with rampant inflation and unemployment was rising. Strikes were frequent and militant. Where employers staged lock-outs, workers' committees seized control of the premises. This was usually a desperate attempt to save jobs more than anything else. Employers were assaulted and crowds broke into the houses of the middle classes, accusing them of hoarding food. Hunger was a crucial factor in October. Workers had given up hope of receiving help from the Provisional Government and were tired of the Mensheviks who tried to mediate between them and employers. Only the Bolsheviks offered the chance of real change.

Similarly, in the countryside from September onwards there was an upturn in violence. Estates were raided, land seized, landowners murdered and their houses burned. The peasants would not wait for the Provisional Government any longer. They might not support the Bolsheviks, but they willingly accepted the Bolshevik promise that land would be handed to them, and there was a lot of support for the left wing of the Socialist Revolutionaries who were collaborating with the Bolsheviks.

SOURCE 4.11 Membership of the Bolshevik Party 1917

The bulk of the support came from the industrial proletariat but during the summer cells sprang up in the army and navy. It seems that a high proportion, as much as twenty per cent, of those who joined in 1917 were aged under 21. Accurate figures are unavailable but estimates suggest that membership leaped during the summer:

February   10,000
October   250,000

SOURCE 4.12 Moscow municipal elections 1917 (figures rounded to nearest thousand)

	July	October
Socialist Revolutionaries	375,000 (58%)	54,000 (14%)
Mensheviks	76,000 (12%)	16,000 (4%)
Bolsheviks	75,000 (11%)	198,000 (51%)
Kadets	109,000 (17%)	101,000 (26%)

62

WAS THE BOLSHEVIK SEIZURE OF POWER IN OCTOBER 1917 INEVITABLE?

SOURCE 4.13   Constituent Assembly elections, November 1917. The elections for the Constituent Assembly went ahead in November because the Bolsheviks were not in a position to stop them (see page 74). They seem to have been fairly freely conducted

	Votes cast (in millions)	Number of seats won	Percentage share of the vote
Socialist Revolutionaries	21.8	410*	53
Bolsheviks	10.0	175	24
Kadets	2.1	17	5
Mensheviks	1.4	18	3
Others	6.3	62	15

*includes 40 Left SRs

SOURCE 4.14   Daily bread rations (grams) per person in Petrograd in 1917

	March	April	September	October
Manual workers	675	335	225	110
Others	450	335	225	110

■ **Learning trouble spot**

Soviet power

Many workers and soldiers wanted the soviets to run government locally and nationally. These soviets represented ordinary people, and in October 1917 were not necessarily controlled by the Bolsheviks. Many were run by Mensheviks, Socialist Revolutionaries and other socialists. The Petrograd Soviet had become the most important national soviet and many people were in favour of it taking power from the Provisional Government.

Support for the Bolsheviks or for Soviet power?

One of the problems in deciding whether the Bolshevik take-over was popular or not is working out whom exactly the people (i.e. the 'popular' element in this) were supporting. The historian Beryl Williams makes the point that: 'Workers and soldiers might support October and vote for the Bolsheviks in elections, but this did not necessarily imply support for one-party rule, or indeed for Bolshevik policies once they had become known' (*The Russian Revolution 1917–1921*, 1987, pages 49–50). Sukhanov, in Source 4.15, also expresses this ambiguity of feeling from his contact with the 'masses' at the time.

Workers and soldiers supported the Bolsheviks because they were making the move to soviet power. But they wanted a coalition government of the socialist parties and they did not expect the Bolsheviks to run the state on their own. Some commentators believe that power would have passed to the Soviet anyway without the uprising and that Lenin had hijacked the process to grab power for himself. You can see why this is a complicated issue and why historians can disagree about the 'popular' nature of the revolution.

SOURCE 4.15   J. Carmichael, *A Short History of the Revolution*, 1967, p. 193, quoting N. N. Sukhanov

It may be asked whether the Petersburg proletariat and garrison was ready for dynamic action and bloody sacrifice? ... Was it burning, not only with hate, but with real longing for revolutionary exploits?

There are various answers to this. It is quite fundamental, not because the outcome of the movement depended on it – the success of the overturn was assured because there was nothing to oppose it. But the mood of the masses who were to act is important because in the eyes of history this is what determined the character of the overturn.

Personally, as a witness and participant in the events, I have no single answer. There were various moods. The only common ones were hatred for 'Kerenskyism', fatigue, rage and a desire for peace, bread and land ... During these weeks I made the rounds and spoke to the 'masses'. I had the definite impression that the mood was ambiguous, conditional. The Coalition and the status quo could no longer be endured; but whether it was necessary to come out, or necessary to pass through an uprising, was not clearly known ... On the average, the mood was strongly Bolshevik, but rather slack and wavering with respect to action and rising.

SOURCE 4.16 O. Figes, *A People's Tragedy: The Russian Revolution 1891–1924*, 1997, p. 484

The great October Socialist Revolution, as it came to be called in Soviet mythology, was in reality such a small-scale event, being in effect a military coup, that it passed unnoticed by the vast majority of inhabitants of Petrograd. . . . The whole insurrection could have been completed in six hours, had it not been for the ludicrous incompetence of the insurgents themselves, which made it take an extra fifteen. The legendary storming of the Winter Palace, where Kerensky's cabinet held its final session, was more like a routine house arrest, since most of the forces defending the palace had already left for home, hungry and dejected before the final assault began. The only real damage done to the imperial residence in the whole affair was a chipped cornice and a shattered window on the third floor.

Trotsky himself claimed that 25,000 to 30,000 people 'at the most' were actively involved – about 5 per cent of all the workers and soldiers in the city . . . The few surviving pictures of the October Days . . . depict a handful of Red Guards and sailors standing around in the half-deserted streets. None of the familiar images of a people's revolution – crowds on the streets, barricades and fighting – were in evidence.

ACTIVITY

1 What impression of the October insurrection is suggested in the images in Source 4.17 and in Sources 3 and 4 on page 2?
2 When were these images produced?
3 How do they compare with the account in the text and in Source 4.16?
4 Why would the Bolsheviks want Russians in later years to believe their version of events?

Why did the Bolsheviks present the October Revolution as a mass uprising?

The events of 24–26 October constitute the October Revolution. You have read (on pages 56–57) how on the night of 24–25 October the soldiers and Red Guard had taken key points in Petrograd with no opposition. The next day life went on as normal. On the evening of 25 October, the cruiser *Aurora* fired a blank shot at 9.40pm. This was the signal for the beginning of the attack on the Winter Palace, where the Provisional Government was in emergency session. According to the Bolsheviks, Red Guards, supported by the masses, heroically stormed the Palace, broke in and arrested the ministers. At the beginning of this section, you saw how this event was celebrated in pictures, mainly painted in the 1930s, and in street theatre re-enactments which took place every year (see Sources 3 and 4, page 2). It was also shown graphically in Eisenstein's film *October* (Source 4.17).

In fact, the story was quite different. Bolshevik Red Guards, soldiers and sailors arrived in the square in front of the Winter Palace around noon on 25 October. The palace was defended by cadets from a military school, 200 members of the Women's Death Battalion and two divisions of Cossacks grumbling about having to fight alongside 'women with guns'. Due to Bolshevik inefficiency, no attack took place in the afternoon. The soldiers inside, faced with the prospect of an overwhelming onslaught, began to get panicky and drunk. By the time early evening had arrived, most of the demoralised defenders had left, slipping out of the palace. Meanwhile the members of the Provisional Government in the Palace held emergency meetings and sent out messages for help. When the cruiser *Aurora* fired its shell to signal the beginning of the attack and a few guns were fired, the Women's Battalion became hysterical whereupon it was agreed by everybody that they should be allowed to leave unharmed. The guns of the Peter and Paul Fortress opened up but most of the shots fell short into the River Neva, although one scored a hit. In the next few hours, Bolshevik soldiers filtered into the palace by various entrances and wandered the corridors disarming the few remaining cadets, who put up little resistance. Eventually, a group forced their way into the room where the last members of the Provisional Government were assembled and arrested them. Such was the heroic storming of the Winter Palace.

SOURCE 4.17 The storming of the Winter Palace – a still from Eisenstein's film *October*

E Review: Was the Bolshevik seizure of power inevitable?

■ **4D The ups and downs in support for the Bolshevik Party during 1917**

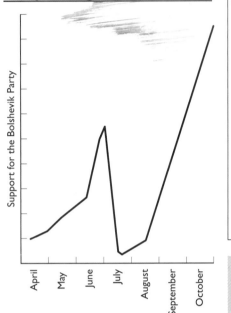

ACTIVITY

If you have completed a graph of Bolshevik fortunes (see the Focus Route on page 49), it might look something like the one shown in Chart 4D.

1 Which of these statements do you think is true? Explain your choice by referring to evidence in this chapter.
   a) The Bolshevik seizure of power was inevitable once they became the only party to provide opposition to the policies of the Provisional Government and the moderate socialists. This was the case from June onwards. They were the only group to express the genuine aspirations of the workers and soldiers.
   b) There were no points at which the Bolshevik seizure of power was inevitable. Right up to the last moment things could have gone wrong. The Bolsheviks were extremely lucky that Kerensky's blunders played into their hands.
   c) Support for the Bolsheviks was growing consistently from May onwards despite the hiccup of the July Days. It looked increasingly likely that they would seize power since they were in tune with the demands of the masses. But there were points at which things could have changed and their bid for power could have been stopped. In the end it was successful because of Lenin's persistence, Trotsky's organisation and Kerensky's mistakes.

TALKING POINT

At the beginning of this section we looked at the question of whether there were two popular revolutions in Russia in 1917. What are your thoughts about this now?

KEY POINTS FROM CHAPTER 4

Was the Bolshevik seizure of power in October 1917 inevitable?

1 The Bolshevik Party and its programme became the focus for all opposition to the Provisional Government and support for them grew rapidly during the summer.
2 The frustration of soldiers and workers exploded in the July Days, partly engineered by middle-ranking Bolsheviks. But the Bolshevik leadership was not ready to take power and the uprising fizzled out.
3 The Bolsheviks were not the tightly disciplined, unified body that some have supposed, although its organisation was better than that of other parties.
4 Kerensky tried to use Kornilov to gain control of Petrograd but Kornilov had his own agenda.
5 The Kornilov affair was disastrous for right-wing forces and the Provisional Government but gave the Bolsheviks a boost.
6 Lenin urged his party leadership to stage an immediate uprising but, initially, they were reluctant.
7 Trotsky persuaded Lenin to put off the uprising until the All-Russian Congress of Soviets so that the Bolsheviks could claim to have taken power in the name of the soviets.
8 Kerensky's inept attempts to ward off the Bolshevik *coup* played into their hands.
9 During 24–26 October, the Bolshevik take-over was carried out successfully.
10 Large numbers of ordinary people supported the idea of the soviets taking power, but not the idea of the Bolsheviks taking power in a one-party state.

Section 1 Review: Why were the Bolsheviks successful in October 1917?

The main focus of Section 1 is the key question: Why were the Bolsheviks successful in October 1917? The two diagrams on pages 65 and 66 summarise the main points relating to this question that have been covered in the last two chapters and add one or two new ideas. You can use these diagrams to help you to write an essay, as suggested on page 66, or for revision in an exam.

■ A The weaknesses and failures of the Provisional Government

The nature of the Provisional Government

- Its scope for action was limited because real power was held by the Soviet.

- It saw itself as a temporary body that could not make binding decisions for the long-term future of Russia; such decisions were to be made by the Constituent Assembly.

- Divisions between socialists and liberals led to a lack of clear policies, as the two groups often blocked each other.

Policies

- The decision to continue the war created a huge amount of opposition, and other problems stemmed from it. If the Provisional Government had made a separate peace with Germany, it might have survived.

  - The failure to legitimise the peasant take-over of land created a rift with the peasants, who were then less willing to supply food to the cities.

    - It lost the support of the national minorities by refusing to give them a degree of autonomy.

      - It did nothing about the deterioration of the economy; together with the lack of social reform this contributed to the radicalisation of the workers.

Mistakes by Kerensky

- He decided to launch a new offensive against Germany in June.

- The Kornilov affair left him discredited. Officers would not fight for him or the Provisional Government because they felt he had betrayed Kornilov and might betray them.

- He underestimated the strength of the Bolsheviks. By moving against them in October, he gave them an excuse for seizing power, thereby increasing their popularity and allowing them to claim that they were seizing power in the name of the Soviet.

Other factors

- Moderate socialists lost contact with their supporters – the workers and peasants.

- The government failed to call the Constituent Assembly early enough.

- Alarmed by violence and the power of the working class, the Kadets moved further to the right and became identified with reactionary military officers, industrialists and landowners.

Summary: By October 1917, the Provisional Government was thoroughly discredited and attracted hatred and contempt.

66

SECTION I REVIEW: WHY WERE THE BOLSHEVIKS SUCCESSFUL IN OCTOBER 1917?

■ B Bolshevik strengths and factors in their favour

Policies

- Bolsheviks opposed the Provisional Government and urged its overthrow. The identification of other socialist parties with the discredited government was fatal for them. It meant that opposition to the Provisional Government became focused around the Bolsheviks.

- The Bolsheviks were the only party that opposed continuing the war – this greatly increased their popularity.

- They secured the tacit, if not active, support of the peasants with the promise of land redistribution.

- Their radical policies were in tune with workers' and soldiers' aspirations; their slogans of 'Peace, Bread and All Power to the Soviets' fitted in perfectly with what the workers and soldiers wanted (even if the Bolsheviks had a different idea about what these policies actually meant).

The party

- The role of Lenin was crucial – his strong, determined leadership and prestige in the party meant he could force through key policy decisions (such as the April Theses) and the October Revolution. There would probably have been no October Revolution without Lenin.

- Although it was probably not the well-disciplined body it was once thought to be, its organisation was better than that of other parties and it broadly followed directives from the party leadership.

- Trotsky's role in persuading Lenin to postpone the date of the uprising and organising the take-over was very important. It was a good tactic to use the All-Russian Congress of Soviets as the vehicle for the seizure of power.

Luck

- The military and economic collapse in September/October offered a unique opportunity that the Bolsheviks seized. The army was not in a position to do much, and hunger was an important factor in October.

- Radicalised workers who favoured soviet power were prepared to support the party that seemed to offer this.

- The Provisional Government, particularly Kerensky, played into the Bolsheviks' hands with its half-hearted attempt to counter the rising.

Other factors

- The Bolsheviks had their greatest number of active supporters, particularly soldiers and sailors, around Petrograd and Moscow, key places in the revolution.

- Whilst only a small minority of the Petrograd garrison actively supported the Bolsheviks, the majority of soldiers remained neutral and refused to oppose them; this guaranteed their success in October.

Summary: By October, the Bolsheviks had become the focus of opposition to the Provisional Government. The people wanted soviet power and the Bolsheviks became identified with this aim. Some historians have suggested that it was not so much what they did as the situation in which they found themselves – the revolution literally fell into their hands because of profound disillusionment with the existing government, the dire economic situation and the radicalised nature of the workers. Nevertheless, it is clear that Lenin played a key role in forcing through the October insurrection.

ACTIVITY

You could use Charts A and B (pages 65 and 66) to help you write an essay:
1 Why were the Bolsheviks successful in October 1917? or
2 It was the weakness of the Provisional Government that brought the October Revolution about rather than the strengths of the Bolsheviks.

Use the points in the charts as a guide. Decide what your main points are and what point could be used to support these main points. Go back to the notes you have made on your Focus Route activities (or the main text) for help in developing your arguments.

Writing an essay

In an essay you have to make a series of main points that answer the essay question. Then you have to support these main points with evidence or further argument. Usually you put one main point in each paragraph, although it is not always convenient to do this. So in an essay you should have:

- main points
- supporting points which explain, back up, and provide evidence for each main point (this is called 'developing your argument')
- an introduction and a conclusion – try not to make them the same.

The consolidation of the Bolshevik state 1917–24

The Bolshevik seizure of power in October was the beginning rather than the end of the revolution. The Bolshevik government had a tenuous grip on power and some observers thought that it would survive only for a few weeks. In this section we look at how the Bolsheviks survived the first months and won the civil war that followed. We examine the impact of this struggle on the emerging state and the problems Soviet Russia faced after seven years of conflict. The final chapter deals with the recovery of the Soviet Union between 1921 and 1924 and considers how centralised and authoritarian the Communist state had become by the time of Lenin's death in 1924.

ACTIVITY

What do Sources 1–7 tell you about:

a) the immediate problems facing the new government
b) the problems the Bolsheviks were likely to have in the longer term?

SOURCE 1 O. Figes, *A People's Tragedy: The Russian Revolution 1891–1924*, 1997, p. 500

Five days after the Bolshevik seizure of power, Alexandra Kollantai, the new People's Commissar of Social Welfare, drove up to the entrance of a large government building on Kazan Street ... she was coming to take possession of it. An old liveried doorman opened the door and examined Kollantai head to foot [but would not let her in] ... Kollontai tried to force her way through, but the doorman blocked her way and closed the doors in her face ... The employees of the Ministry had joined a general Civil Servants' strike in protest at the Bolshevik seizure of power ...

The early weeks of the new regime were frustrated by similar strikes and campaigns in all the major ministries and government departments, the banks, the post and telegraph office, the railway administration, municipal bodies ... and other vital institutions ... Trotsky was greeted with ironic laughter when he arrived at the Ministry of Foreign Affairs and introduced himself to a meeting of officials as their new Minister; when he ordered them back to work, they left the building in protest ... The refusal of the State Bank and the Treasury to honour the new government's cash demands was the most serious threat of all. Without money to pay its supporters, the Bolshevik regime could not hope to survive for long.

SOURCE 2   R. Pipes, *Russia under the Bolshevik Regime 1912–24*, 1994, p. 5

The Bolsheviks were masters only of central Russia, and even there they ruled only the cities and industrial centres. The borderlands of what had been the Russian Empire, inhabited by peoples of other nationalities and religions, had separated themselves and proclaimed independence . . . The Bolsheviks, therefore, had literally to conquer by force of arms the separated borderlands as well as the villages in which lived four-fifths of Russia's population. Their own power base was not very secure, resting on at most 200,000 party members and an army then in the process of dissolution.

SOURCE 3   Striking workers in the Sormovo factory, June 1918

The Soviet regime, having been established in our name, has become completely alien to us. It promised to bring the workers socialism but has brought them empty factories and destitution.

SOURCE 4   C. Read, *From Tsar to Soviets: The Russian People and their Revolution 1917–21*, 1996, p. 178

There was significant opposition to the uprising from within the Soviet itself. No major Soviet leader or group rallied to the Bolsheviks . . . The Menshevik leaders organized forces loyal to themselves to put pressure on the Bolshevik leaders to relinquish their power and to share it more broadly. In particular, through the railwaymen's union, they threatened a paralysing strike.

SOURCE 5   Bolshevik moderates

It is vital to form a socialist government from all parties . . . We consider that a purely Bolshevik government has no choice but to maintain itself by political terror . . . We cannot follow this course.

SOURCE 6   A speech by Lenin, 14 September 1917

Power to the Soviets means the complete transfer of the country's administration and economic control into the hands of workers and peasants, to whom nobody would offer resistance and who, through practice, through their own experience would soon learn how to distribute land, products and grain properly.

SOURCE 7   O. Figes, *A People's Tragedy: The Russian Revolution 1891–1924*, 1997, p. 494, describing what happened when the crowds found thousands of bottles of alcohol in the Tsar's wine cellars in the Winter Palace

The drunken mobs went on the rampage . . . Sailors and soldiers went round the well-to-do districts robbing apartments and killing people for sport . . . The Bolsheviks tried to stem the anarchy by sealing off the liquor supply . . . They posted guards around the cellar – who licensed themselves to sell off the bottles of liquor. They pumped the wine on the street but crowds gathered to drink it from the gutter . . . Machine guns were set up to deter the looters – but still they came. For several weeks the anarchy continued – martial law was even imposed – until, at last, the alcohol ran out with the old year, and the capital woke up with the biggest headache in history.

How did the Bolsheviks survive the first few months in power?

ACTIVITY

What do you think Lenin would do to try to consolidate his position and stay in power in the months immediately following the October Revolution? His opponents thought that he would stay in power for only a few weeks at most.

Decide which of the alternatives in the table below you would expect him to follow. Be prepared to explain your choice.

Issue	Radical option	Cautious option
a) Main instrument of government	Form his own new government	Govern through the Soviet in the name of which he had taken power
b) Elections to Constituent Assembly	Call them off as his party might not be in the majority	Allow them to go ahead
c) Press	Ban newspapers of opposition parties	Allow them to be published
d) Role of other socialist parties in government	Rule alone	Bring other socialist parties into the government
e) Peace with Germany	Agree a separate peace straightaway, whatever the Germans demand	Hold out for a peace deal which would not require giving up too much territory
f) Land	Give land to peasants immediately to parcel out amongst themselves to secure their support	Set up state agencies to allocate land fairly and keep some large estates for government control
g) Political parties	Ban other parties: go for one-party state	Ban Kadets and right-wing parties but allow other socialist parties
h) Trade unions	Ban trade unions	Allow them to continue but with reduced power
i) Army	Democratise army: no ranks, saluting, etc. Power to committees	Keep army structure intact against attacks from outside or inside Russia
j) Women	Introduce full equality immediately	Introduce equal opportunities measures slowly
k) Banks	NATIONALISE banks	Introduce measures to control the banking system but leave banks in private hands
l) Industry	Allow workers' committees to run factories	Give power to workers, eight-hour day, etc., but leave control of factories in private hands
m) National minorities	Grant right of SELF-DETERMINATION to non-Russian groups (Georgians, Ukrainians) in old Russian empire	Retain the boundaries of the old Russian empire but give more rights to non-Russian minorities

NATIONALISE
To take industries and banks out of private ownership and put them under the control of the state.

SELF-DETERMINATION
Principle of nation states ruling themselves.

FOCUS ROUTE

How well did Lenin deal with the problems and threats facing his new government in the early months? As you read through this chapter, fill in a table like the one below or use the headings to make your own notes and evaluation.

Problems	What was the problem?	How did Lenin deal with it?	How effectively did he deal with it? (Give a mark out of ten.)
Getting new government on its feet			
Land ownership			
Running industry			
Opposition			
Other socialist parties			
Peace with Germany			

71

HOW DID THE BOLSHEVIKS SURVIVE THE FIRST FEW MONTHS IN POWER?

A How did Lenin get his new government on its feet?

Lenin had proclaimed Soviet power but he did not exercise power through the Soviet. The Soviet could easily have become the main body of the government and many people expected it to be so. But Lenin formed an entirely new body – the Council of the People's Commissars, or the SOVNARKOM. It was exclusively made up of Bolsheviks (although some left-wing Socialist Revolutionaries were invited to join later). The reason for this was clear: Lenin had no intention of sharing power with the Mensheviks, Socialist Revolutionaries and other socialist groups in the Soviet.

■ 5A Some key posts in the Sovnarkom

Chairman	Lenin
Commissar for Foreign Affairs	Trotsky until February 1918, then Chicherin
Commissar for War	Trotsky from February 1918
Commissar for Internal Affairs	Rykov, later Dzerzhinsky
Commissar for Nationalities	Stalin
Commissar for Social Welfare	Alexandra Kollantai
Commissar for Popular Enlightenment (Education and Culture)	Lunacharsky

The government's position was extremely precarious – one Socialist Revolutionary leader gave it 'no more than a few days', the Menshevik leader Tsereteli gave it three weeks. Its power was strictly limited: many soviets and bodies such as public safety committees were still in the control of Mensheviks, Socialist Revolutionaries or non-socialists, and in the countryside the Bolshevik presence was virtually non-existent. Even in the soviets controlled by the Bolsheviks, there was no guarantee that the central government could get its decisions carried out; some were a law unto themselves. All over the capital, civil servants mounted protest strikes and, even worse, the State Bank refused to hand over any money. It took ten days and armed force to make the bank staff open the vaults so that the government could get its hands on much needed roubles (Russian currency).

So how did Lenin and his government manage to survive the first few months? Lenin could not afford to ignore the tide of popular aspiration that had swept away Kerensky and the Provisional Government, so he gave the workers and peasants what they wanted. Edward Acton says: 'No Russian government had ever been more responsive to pressure from below or less able to impose its will upon society.' Power was thrown out to local soviets to manage their own affairs, even though at this stage they were not, in the main, under central control.

The Sovnarkom ruled by decree without going to the Soviet for approval. The early decrees are summarised in Chart 5B (page 72). In key areas, the Bolsheviks compromised their principles to keep popular support:

- **Land decree** This gave peasants the right to take over the estates of the gentry, without compensation, and to decide for themselves the best way to divide it up (since they were doing this anyway). Land could no longer be bought, sold or rented; it belonged to the 'entire people'. It was not what the Bolsheviks wanted. Privately owned land was not part of their socialist vision.
- **Workers' control decree** Factory committees were given the right to control production and finance in workplaces and to 'supervise' management. This decree did not give direct management to the workers but some committees took it to mean that. This went far beyond what many Bolshevik leaders wanted, but they could not resist the strength of workers' pressure for reform.
- **Rights of the People of Russia decree** This gave the right of self-determination to the national minorities in the former Russian empire. Of course, the Bolsheviks did not have control of the areas in which most of these people lived, so this was nothing more than a paper measure.

SOVNARKOM
Council of the People's Commissars; the Bolshevik governing body (30–40 members) set up after the October Revolution in 1917. It operated until 1941 but became much less influential after the Politburo was formed in 1919 (7–9 members). The Commissars in Sovnarkom ran commissariats.

Yakov Sverdlov (1885–1919)
Another key Bolshevik at this time was Sverdlov, a great organising genius. Born into a working-class Jewish family, he became a Social Democrat in 1905. He was exiled to Siberia with Stalin but they did not get on. He played an important part in organising the October uprising with Trotsky. He was totally loyal to Lenin, who valued Sverdlov's reliability and dependability. After the revolution he was given the job of building up the party secretariat and establishing a network of party officials and local secretariats throughout Russia, all reporting to Moscow. He would almost certainly have been made General Secretary of the party in 1922 – the job which gave Stalin so much power – but he died of flu in 1919.

SOURCE 5.1 Lenin to a delegation of workers and peasants

You are the power – do all you want to do, take all you want. We shall support you.

WHY WOULDN'T LENIN JOIN A SOCIALIST COALITION?

Lenin knew that if a socialist coalition were formed then he would most probably be excluded from it. Other socialist groups would not work with him because of his personality and previous actions. Bolshevik leaders like Kamenev would most probably have taken a major role in a coalition. But there was more to it than this. Lenin saw the revolution as a turning point in world history. He had a vision of a utopian world order that he wanted to make real. He was not prepared to see his vision diluted by compromise with other socialists. He wanted Bolshevik policies carried out.

TALKING POINT

Was Lenin wrong not to enter a coalition? It meant that the new government lost a democratic base of support which might have ensured less dictatorial government and a shorter civil war. Socialist leaders outside Russia criticised Lenin. The leading German socialist Rosa Luxembourg warned that press censorship and the suppression of democratic elections would lead to dictatorship. What do you think about Lenin's actions?

C How did Lenin deal with the threat posed to his government by other socialists?

There was enormous pressure on the Bolsheviks to form a democratic government representing all the socialist parties. Hundreds of resolutions and petitions flooded in from factory committees, army units, and Moscow and provincial towns, demanding that there be co-operation between the parties to avoid factional strife and civil war. A petition from the 35th army division made this clear: 'Among the soldiers there are no Bolsheviks, Mensheviks or Socialist Revolutionaries, only Democrats.' People did not want to lose the gains of the revolution because the socialist parties were fighting amongst each other. They were in favour of Soviet power, not one-party rule.

The railwaymen's union, backed by the post and telegraph union, threatened to cut off communications if the Bolsheviks did not hold talks with other parties. They could paralyse food supplies to Petrograd as well as contact with other cities. This pressure forced Lenin, unwillingly, to send representatives to talks with other parties about a power-sharing government. It also persuaded Lenin, again unwillingly, to allow the planned elections to the Constituent Assembly to go ahead at the end of November. The Bolsheviks knew that there would be an unstoppable backlash if they did not go ahead with the elections, particularly as before October they had attacked Kerensky for postponing them.

Quite a few leading Bolsheviks, including Kamenev and Zinoviev, were in favour of a socialist coalition government. They believed that an isolated Bolshevik Party would have to maintain itself by terror and would almost certainly be destroyed by the civil war that would inevitably follow. So they were happy to be involved in talks with other parties. It seems likely that they were duped by Lenin into thinking he was serious about a coalition, and they temporarily resigned when they found out he was not.

Lenin had always intended the Bolsheviks to rule alone and he engineered the collapse of the talks. He did, however, make an alliance with the Left Socialist Revolutionaries and brought them as junior partners into the Sovnarkom. He saw this as useful because, with them in his government, he could claim to represent a large section of the peasantry. The Left Socialist Revolutionaries had, for some time, been closest to the Bolsheviks, particularly on the land issue; indeed they claimed, with justification, that Lenin had stolen this policy from them.

The Constituent Assembly

The Constituent Assembly posed a bigger threat to Lenin. Elected by the people in the first free elections in centuries, it could claim to be the legitimate body to decide the make-up of the future government of Russia. When the election results became known (see Source 4.13 on page 62), the Bolsheviks found they had won only 175 seats against 410 for the Socialist Revolutionaries (including 40 Left SRs) and nearly 100 for other parties. However, Lenin asserted that his Soviet government represented a higher stage of democracy than an elected assembly containing different political parties. He said that the Constituent Assembly smacked of bourgeois parliamentary democracy and declared it redundant. The Assembly was allowed to meet for one day – 5 January 1918 – then the doors were closed and the deputies told to go home. A crowd which demonstrated in favour of the Assembly was fired on by soldiers loyal to the Sovnarkom, the first time that soldiers had fired in this way on unarmed demonstrators since February 1917.

D How did Lenin deal with the problems posed by ending the war?

The promise that had brought so many people to the Bolshevik banner was the pledge to end the war. The Decree on Peace was signed on 26 October with a plea to other nations for a just peace with 'no annexations, no indemnities'. Lenin was convinced that revolutions in Europe would ensure that equitable peace settlements would be reached.

But the practical resolution proved more difficult. The Russian army at the Front disintegrated rapidly; the soldiers had no desire to die in futile last-minute fighting and wanted to get back home. This represented both good and bad news for the Bolsheviks. The good news was that the army could not be used against them by Russian generals. The bad news was that the German army was free to walk into Russia and take what it wanted. At the peace negotiations held at Brest-Litovsk, the German demands were excessive. Trotsky, the Bolshevik negotiator, withdrew from the negotiations saying that there would be 'neither war nor peace', meaning that the Russians would not fight the Germans but would not sign the treaty either.

Lenin, however, knew that he had to have peace at any price to ensure the survival of the fledgling regime. Opposition to the war had been a key factor in the Bolshevik success in October and he had to honour his promise. Furthermore, there was now no army to fight the Germans, who began to advance into the Ukraine. Lenin even feared that they might move on Petrograd and throw him and his government out. Under pressure from Lenin, representatives of the Bolsheviks reluctantly signed the Treaty of Brest-Litovsk on 3 March 1918. Trotsky refused to go to the final meeting.

■ 5C The terms of the Treaty of Brest-Litovsk

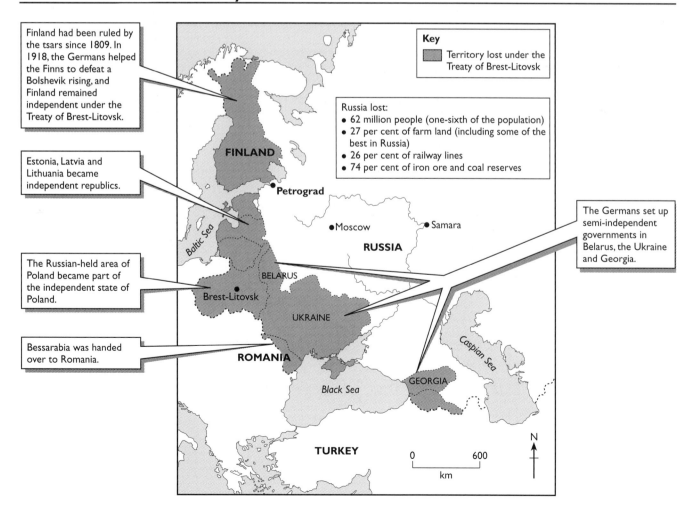

Finland had been ruled by the tsars since 1809. In 1918, the Germans helped the Finns to defeat a Bolshevik rising, and Finland remained independent under the Treaty of Brest-Litovsk.

Estonia, Latvia and Lithuania became independent republics.

The Russian-held area of Poland became part of the independent state of Poland.

Bessarabia was handed over to Romania.

Key
Territory lost under the Treaty of Brest-Litovsk

Russia lost:
- 62 million people (one-sixth of the population)
- 27 per cent of farm land (including some of the best in Russia)
- 26 per cent of railway lines
- 74 per cent of iron ore and coal reserves

The Germans set up semi-independent governments in Belarus, the Ukraine and Georgia.

FINLAND
Petrograd
Baltic Sea
Moscow
Samara
RUSSIA
BELARUS
Brest-Litovsk
UKRAINE
Caspian Sea
ROMANIA
Black Sea
GEORGIA
TURKEY
0   600
km
N

Consequences of the Treaty of Brest-Litovsk

Signing the treaty had serious consequences for the Bolsheviks:

- Patriotic Russians were horrified by the terms. Giving away large chunks of the Russian homeland antagonised many Russians across the class and political spectrum and encouraged them to join anti-Bolshevik forces. It was anathema to the Kadets and conservative forces on the Right.

- It caused more splits in the Bolshevik Party. Bukharin and the left wing of the party wanted to prosecute a revolutionary war to encourage a European socialist revolution. Some thought the international revolution more important than the one in Russia. To them, the Treaty of Brest-Litovsk seemed a shameful peace that helped Germany survive as an imperial power.

- The left wing of the Socialist Revolutionaries, who also wanted to fight a revolutionary war like the Left Bolsheviks, left the Sovnarkom in protest. The Bolsheviks now really were on their own.

All the opposition to Brest-Litovsk made civil war almost inevitable.

■ **Learning trouble spot**

The Bolsheviks and world revolution

The Bolsheviks were sure that other countries in Europe would follow their lead. They believed that the war would collapse into a series of civil wars in European countries as the working class fought with the bourgeoisie. As far as they were concerned, the revolution in Russia could not survive without the support of workers' revolutions in advanced capitalist societies. The Bolsheviks tried to stretch out the negotiations with the Germans as long as they could to give these revolutions time to get started. But they did not materialise. Lenin seems to have made a decision to put the international revolution to one side and save his revolution in Russia.

TALKING POINT

You have seen how difficult it was for the Bolsheviks to negotiate a peace treaty and the unpleasant consequences of signing the treaty. Does this throw a different light on the problems the Provisional Government faced when trying to resolve this issue?

E Review: How did the Bolsheviks stay in power in the first few months?

ACTIVITY

1 Look at the statements in the speech bubbles. Match each comment to one of the people to show how you think the people shown might have responded to the first measures and actions of the new regime.

2 What does this suggest about:
   a) which groups would be likely to support the Bolshevik government
   b) which groups might oppose the Bolsheviks?

(i) Worker at the Putilov engineering works

(ii) Army officer

(iii) Peasant

(iv) Railway worker

(v) Owner of a small factory

(vi) Left-wing Socialist Revolutionary leader

(vii) Moderate socialist leader

(viii) High-ranking civil servant

A I was in favour of the Bolsheviks taking power and I am pleased that we have more power to control our workplaces. No longer will we be humiliated by our employers. Now we are all equal. No more 'bowing and scraping' before our lords and masters. The tables have turned.

B They won't be able to run the country without us; they have no experience of government. They need the middle classes and they shouldn't encourage the mobs to attack us in the streets and plunder our houses.

C I supported the Soviet, not the Bolsheviks. I don't want one party to run everything. I demand that the different socialist parties get together to form a government that represents everybody. I don't want to see a civil war.

D You can't put the workers in control of the factories. They don't have the know-how to buy materials and sell them in the marketplace. Already they are stealing materials and giving themselves huge pay rises. It will all end in disaster.

E The behaviour of the Bolsheviks has been disgraceful. They have closed the newspapers. They have arrested Kadets and Socialist Revolutionaries and fired on demonstrators protesting about the closure of the Constituent Assembly. The Assembly is the legitimate government of Russia. The Bolsheviks are tyrants.

F The Bolsheviks have betrayed the revolution. They have helped the German empire when German workers are crying out for revolution. They have handed over peoples who should have freedom to govern themselves. The Brest-Litovsk Treaty is a shameful peace.

G Now the army really will fall apart. You can't run an army without ranks and discipline. It's happening throughout Russian society. And they have sold Russia to the Germans. Our country must remain 'one and indivisible'. I am off to join the armies forming against the Bolsheviks.

H Now we have what has always been ours. We work the land, it belongs to us. I don't know who the Bolsheviks are and I don't much care, but they have done what we wanted and now they can leave us alone to mind our own affairs.

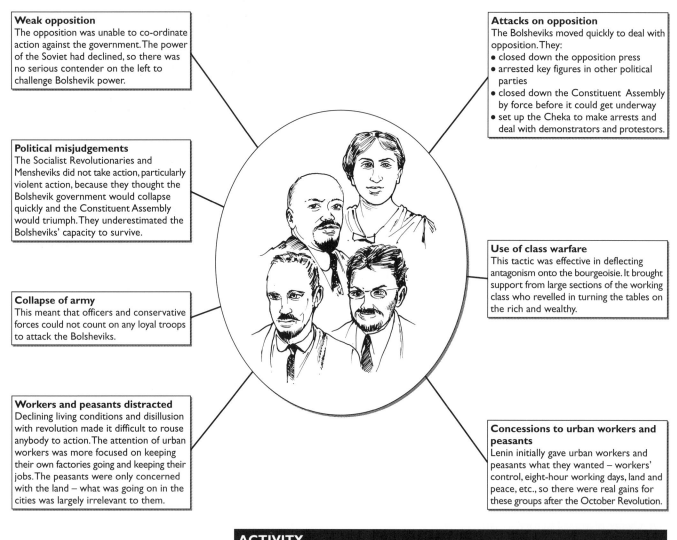

Weak opposition
The opposition was unable to co-ordinate action against the government. The power of the Soviet had declined, so there was no serious contender on the left to challenge Bolshevik power.

Political misjudgements
The Socialist Revolutionaries and Mensheviks did not take action, particularly violent action, because they thought the Bolshevik government would collapse quickly and the Constituent Assembly would triumph. They underestimated the Bolsheviks' capacity to survive.

Collapse of army
This meant that officers and conservative forces could not count on any loyal troops to attack the Bolsheviks.

Workers and peasants distracted
Declining living conditions and disillusion with revolution made it difficult to rouse anybody to action. The attention of urban workers was more focused on keeping their own factories going and keeping their jobs. The peasants were only concerned with the land – what was going on in the cities was largely irrelevant to them.

Attacks on opposition
The Bolsheviks moved quickly to deal with opposition. They:
● closed down the opposition press
● arrested key figures in other political parties
● closed down the Constituent Assembly by force before it could get underway
● set up the Cheka to make arrests and deal with demonstrators and protestors.

Use of class warfare
This tactic was effective in deflecting antagonism onto the bourgeoisie. It brought support from large sections of the working class who revelled in turning the tables on the rich and wealthy.

Concessions to urban workers and peasants
Lenin initially gave urban workers and peasants what they wanted – workers' control, eight-hour working days, land and peace, etc., so there were real gains for these groups after the October Revolution.

ACTIVITY

Look at Chart 5D and the table you have completed for the Focus Route activity on page 70. Write a short essay of four or five paragraphs weighing up how well Lenin dealt with the problems and threats facing him in the first months in power. In each paragraph:

a) identify the problem or threat
b) explain what Lenin did
c) evaluate his performance – did his actions achieve what he wanted and what, if any, were the drawbacks/disadvantages?

KEY POINTS FROM CHAPTER 5

How did the Bolsheviks survive the first few months in power?

1 The Bolshevik government was in a fragile condition in the first few months, facing strikes and protests from other socialists over one-party rule.
2 There were divisions within the party over a proposed socialist coalition. Some leading Bolsheviks temporarily resigned in protest at Lenin's failure to support the coalition idea.
3 Lenin always intended to rule on his own and asserted this in his own party and in government.
4 Lenin's early policies had to be modified in response to pressures from the masses.
5 The Bolsheviks crushed opposition and developed forces of terror and coercion, especially the Cheka.
6 Lenin persuaded the Bolsheviks to sign the unfavourable Treaty of Brest-Litovsk. He knew he had to have peace for his government to survive.

How did the Bolsheviks win the Civil War?

FOCUS ROUTE

1 Draw a spider diagram to show the sides in the Civil War and their different aims.
2 Can you identify any problems you think the Whites are going to have in the war?

■ Learning trouble spot

The sides in the Civil War

If you are confused by the different sides, particularly the Whites, then so were people at the time. When we talk about the White armies, we are mainly referring to Denikin's army in the south, Kolchak's army in the east and Yudenich's army in the north-west. These were largely made up of tsarists, army officers and liberals, with peasants forming a large proportion of the soldiers. The Socialist Revolutionaries and other socialists were involved with White armies at times, but usually operated independently.

A Who was on each side?

The Civil War in Russia from 1918 to 1920 was very complex, as different groups emerged to challenge the Bolsheviks' claim to be the government of Russia. It involved many contestants spread out over an immense area. At one point, there were some eighteen anti-Bolshevik governments in Russia. We can divide the participants in the Civil War into three rather ill-defined sides:

- the Reds – the Bolsheviks
- the Whites
- the Greens.

The Reds – the Bolsheviks

The great strength of the Reds was that they had one clear aim – to stay in power. The 'Workers' and Peasants' Red Army' was formed from Kronstadt sailors and Red Guards, plus workers who volunteered and soldiers from the disintegrating former imperial army.

The Whites

Under this broad banner, there were liberals, former tsarists, nationalists and separatists, Socialist Revolutionaries and other moderate socialists. Few Whites wanted to see the tsar back but many, including liberals, supported military dictatorship until the Bolsheviks were defeated and law and order re-established. Other groups, especially the Socialist Revolutionaries, were keen to see the Constituent Assembly running Russia. Probably the only thing that they all had in common was that they were anti-Bolshevik. The Whites were deeply divided and it was not uncommon for White armies to fight each other. It was very difficult, for instance, for Socialist Revolutionaries to fight alongside former tsarist officers and monarchists (called 'Rightists') who favoured military dictatorship and the return of the land to its former owners. Four White armies were particularly significant (see Chart 6A).

The Greens

The Greens were peasant armies, often made up of deserters from other armies. Some of these armies fought for the Bolsheviks, some against. Most were more concerned with protecting their own area from the ravages of other marauding armies. Some were little more than groups of bandits who did well out of raiding and looting their neighbours. Probably the most famous of the Green armies was that of Nestor Makhno, an anarchist, in the Ukraine. He was a skilled guerrilla leader who at various times fought the Reds, the Whites and the Germans, but became an ally of the Bolsheviks. The Ukrainians, like many of the peasant armies, were fighting for their independence.

■ 6A Main forces of the Whites

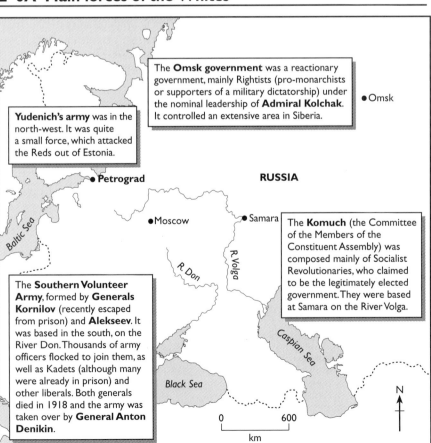

Yudenich's army was in the north-west. It was quite a small force, which attacked the Reds out of Estonia.

The Omsk government was a reactionary government, mainly Rightists (pro-monarchists or supporters of a military dictatorship) under the nominal leadership of Admiral Kolchak. It controlled an extensive area in Siberia.

The Komuch (the Committee of the Members of the Constituent Assembly) was composed mainly of Socialist Revolutionaries, who claimed to be the legitimately elected government. They were based at Samara on the River Volga.

The Southern Volunteer Army, formed by Generals Kornilov (recently escaped from prison) and Alekseev. It was based in the south, on the River Don. Thousands of army officers flocked to join them, as well as Kadets (although many were already in prison) and other liberals. Both generals died in 1918 and the army was taken over by General Anton Denikin.

B The course of the Civil War

FOCUS ROUTE

1 Focus on the geographical position of the forces shown on the map in Chart 6C.
   a) What advantages/disadvantages did the Reds have?
   b) What advantages/disadvantages did the Whites have?
2 What key reasons do the map and text suggest for the defeat of the Whites?

WHAT HAPPENED TO THE CZECH LEGION?

The Czech Legion fought for the Whites for a while, but after the declaration of Czech independence in October 1918 it was weakened by mutinies and desertion and largely withdrew from the fighting.

Although there were some minor clashes in late 1917, the war began in earnest in the spring of 1918. By this time it was clear that the Bolsheviks wanted to run Russia as a one-party state. They had alienated other socialist groups (Socialist Revolutionaries and Mensheviks) as well as the liberals and more conservative right-wing elements in society. It was the Bolsheviks against the rest.

Hostilities were sparked off in the east by the rather bizarre events surrounding the Czech Legion. The Legion had been formed by Czech nationalists hoping to win recognition for an independent Czech state (previously it had been part of the Austrian empire). It had been significantly enlarged by Czech prisoners of war and deserters from the Austrian army. The idea was that it would fight with the Russian army against the Austrians and Germans. When the Treaty of Brest-Litovsk took Russia out of the war, the Legion decided to fight with the Allies on the Western Front. But they did not want to cross enemy lines and it was agreed with the Soviet authorities that they would be transported along the Trans-Siberian railway to Vladivostok, from where they would be taken by ship to Western Europe. The Czechs mistrusted the Bolsheviks and there were clashes with local Bolshevik soviets along the Trans-Siberian railway. When the Bolsheviks tried to disarm them, the Czechs resisted and took control of large sections of this important railway (the main route to the east) and large parts of western Siberia. Substantial White forces then grew up around them.

The full-scale Civil War was underway by the summer of 1918. We shall consider the course of the war by looking at the three White forces that posed the biggest threat to the Bolsheviks. These are shown on the map in Chart 6C on pages 82–83. The Civil War was fought mainly in the east and the south.

■ 6B Key events of the Civil War

1918			July	Denikin advances from the Caucasus and captures Tsaritsyn. Loss of Kharkov and Tsaritsyn leads to criticism of Trotsky. He resigns but his resignation is refused.
Jan	Red Army is established.			
March	Treaty of Brest-Litovsk First British troops land at Murmansk.			
May	Czech Legion rebels and captures a large section of the Trans-Siberian railway. Conscription into Red Army is introduced.		September	Allies evacuate Archangel.
			October	Denikin takes Orel but is forced back later in the month. Yudenich reaches the outskirts of Petrograd.
June	Socialist Revolutionary government is established at Samara. Murder of the Tsar and his family.		November	Yudenich is defeated; Denikin is pushed back.
August	Americans arrive in northern Russia and in the east. British land at Archangel and establish an anti-Bolshevik government.		**1920**	
			February	Kolchak (captured in January) is executed by the Bolsheviks. Red Army invades Georgia.
November	Kolchak assumes control in Omsk.			
December	French land at Odessa.		April	Denikin, having been pursued to the Crimea, is succeeded by Wrangel.
1919			May	Polish army invades Russia and occupies Kiev.
February	Denikin assumes supreme command in the south-east. Red Army occupies Kiev.		July	Tukhachevsky mounts Red Army counter-offensive against Poles.
March	Kolchak's forces cross the Urals but are repulsed by the Red Army. Growing discontent in French and British forces.		August	Red Army defeated by Poles outside Warsaw.
			November	Wrangel, last surviving White general, is defeated in the Crimea.
April	French evacuate Odessa.		**1921**	
June	Denikin and southern army take Kharkov.		March	Treaty of Riga: peace between Poland and Soviet Russia.

Yudenich in the west

General Yudenich's army was the smallest army, only some 15,000 men, but it reached the outskirts of Petrograd in October 1919 before being turned back by larger Bolshevik forces.

Denikin and Wrangel in the south

Denikin's southern army of 150,000 had a large contingent of Don Cossacks. His army made ground across the Don region, intending to join up with Kolchak. By the summer of 1918 it was besieging Tsaritsyn, a key city under the command of Joseph Stalin. The Bolsheviks had to hold this city at all costs to prevent the southern and eastern White armies from linking up, and to protect vital grain supplies that passed through Tsaritsyn en route to Bolshevik-held cities to the north and west. The successful defence of Tsaritsyn became a heroic story in Bolshevik mythology and the city was later renamed Stalingrad in Stalin's honour.

Denikin launched another offensive in the summer of 1919. Spectacularly successful, it came within 320 km of Moscow by October. But Trotsky organised a ferocious counter-attack, forcing a hasty and panic-stricken White retreat. The southern White army was pushed right back into the Crimean peninsula. Denikin was replaced by Wrangel. The Whites held out for much of 1920 but had to be evacuated by British and French ships in November of that year.

Makhno's Insurgent Army

The most dangerous of the Green armies was Makhno's Insurgent Army, which had successfully used guerrilla warfare against Whites and Reds and was strongly supported by the peasant population in the Ukraine. It had encouraged the growth of communes and soviets for peasants to run their own affairs without any central direction – a real challenge to the Bolshevik centralised state. Towards the end of the war, Makhno's army fought as an irregular division for the Reds. But as soon as the war was won, the Bolsheviks crushed his peasant-anarchist movement, although it proved no easy task. Makhno escaped to Romania.

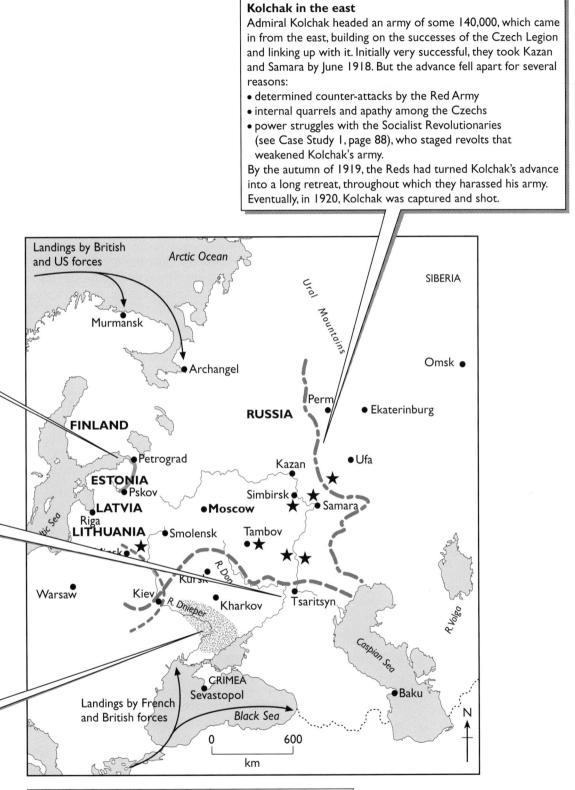

Kolchak in the east

Admiral Kolchak headed an army of some 140,000, which came in from the east, building on the successes of the Czech Legion and linking up with it. Initially very successful, they took Kazan and Samara by June 1918. But the advance fell apart for several reasons:

- determined counter-attacks by the Red Army
- internal quarrels and apathy among the Czechs
- power struggles with the Socialist Revolutionaries (see Case Study 1, page 88), who staged revolts that weakened Kolchak's army.

By the autumn of 1919, the Reds had turned Kolchak's advance into a long retreat, throughout which they harassed his army. Eventually, in 1920, Kolchak was captured and shot.

Landings by British and US forces

Arctic Ocean

SIBERIA

Ural Mountains

Murmansk

Archangel

Omsk

Perm

RUSSIA

Ekaterinburg

FINLAND

Petrograd

Kazan

Ufa

ESTONIA

Pskov

Simbirsk

LATVIA

Riga

Moscow

Samara

LITHUANIA

Minsk

Smolensk

Tambov

R. Don

Warsaw

Kiev

Kursk

R. Dnieper

Kharkov

Tsaritsyn

R. Volga

Caspian Sea

CRIMEA

Sevastopol

Landings by French and British forces

Black Sea

Baku

N

0   600
km

Key

▬▬▬▬	Yudenich offensive against Petrograd
-------	Furthest advance of Polish armies
▬ ▬ ▬	Furthest advance of Denikin and Wrangel's armies
▬ ▬ ▬	Furthest advance of Kolchak's armies
░░░	Area of activity by Makhno's partisans
★	Major peasant uprisings

What was the role of other countries in the Civil War?

ANNEXATION
Taking over the territory of other countries and joining it to own country.

Allied troops were sent to Russia to help to reopen the Eastern Front against Germany. But before they could go into action the war ended, in November 1918. The troops stayed on, ostensibly to guard munitions dumps in Archangel and Murmansk.

Western countries, however, had other objectives. The British, encouraged by Winston Churchill, the War Secretary, were amongst the most active forces. They sent £100-million-worth of supplies to the Whites. Churchill saw the Whites as crusaders against Bolshevism; he dreaded the spread of Bolshevism to other countries in Western Europe. However, within Britain there was substantial opposition to involvement in the Russian Civil War. Lloyd George, the Prime Minister, feared disaffection of war-weary troops, and the small but increasingly influential Labour Party believed Britain should not fight the Russian working class.

A number of other countries sent small forces, but they were there for different reasons. The French were probably the most anti-Bolshevik because French investors had put millions of francs into Russia and the Bolsheviks had nationalised foreign-owned businesses without compensation. But the soldiers were not keen to fight and there were mutinies in the French fleet in the Black Sea. The Japanese sent a sizeable force into Siberia, especially around Vladivostok. But they were more interested in trying to grab some valuable territory than in fighting the Bolsheviks. The USA sent troops to the same area, largely to stop the Japanese ANNEXING any land. Other countries which sent small detachments included Italy, Serbia, Romania, Greece and Canada.

The involvement of the Allies was unenthusiastic and ineffective. The troops had had enough of war and there was no real support from the public in their home countries. The Allies provided the Whites with valuable supplies but that was about all. Allied soldiers got involved in a few skirmishes but took no part in serious military action.

■ 6D The Russo-Polish War, 1919–21

Key
— Poland's established frontiers, June 1920
······ Eastern extent of Poland's conquests in Russia, June 1920
⇐ Russian counter-attacks
▬ Polish line of defence, August 1920
▨ Land annexed by Poland under Treaty of Riga, March 1921
---- Poland's eastern frontier, 1921–39

The Russo-Polish War 1919–21

In 1919, the Poles hoped to take advantage of the chaotic situation in Russia and to take territory which had once been part of the Polish empire. Their troops, under Pilsudski, were initially successful, capturing Kiev in May 1920. But by this time, the Bolsheviks had more or less defeated their Civil War enemies and the Polish invasion brought even non-Bolsheviks to the support of the Red banner – the Poles were an old enemy. In a daring campaign led by Tukhachevsky, the Poles were pushed right back to Warsaw.

Lenin hoped that the success of the Reds might encourage revolution in Germany. In fact this was the sort of revolutionary war – spreading the revolution by force – that left-wing Bolsheviks had wanted much earlier. Germany was unstable and some cities had set up 'red soviets'. However, the Reds had now overstretched their supply lines and, lacking support, were comprehensively defeated by the Poles. A settlement was reached in 1921. Under the Treaty of Riga, the Russians had to surrender large areas of White Russia and the Ukraine to the Poles.

D How important was the role of Trotsky in the Civil War?

When Trotsky was made Commissar for War in 1918, the army was on the point of disintegration. He restored discipline and professionalism to what was now called the 'Worker's and Peasants' Red Army' and turned it into an effective fighting force. He reorganised the army along strict hierarchical lines and brought back thousands of former tsarist officers to train and command army units. Many of these officers, who were unemployed, hungry and poor, seized the opportunity to get back into the world they knew best. To ensure their loyalty, Trotsky had their families held hostage.

The return to a traditional army was resented by other leading Bolsheviks, especially Stalin and Zinoviev. They had a different concept of a revolutionary army – one which was more like a militia and certainly not one that had tsarist officers in charge. Trotsky only managed to get his way with the support of Lenin, who saw that it was the only solution, given the state of the army and the urgency of the situation. To placate the party, and ensure the loyalty of the officers, Trotsky attached a political commissar to each army unit. The job of the commissar (who was often a fanatical Bolshevik) was to watch and report on the actions of the officers and make sure they were politically correct. They also fed back useful information to the central headquarters.

Soldiers' committees (which dominated army units) and the election of officers by soldiers were ended. This did not go down well with the soldiers, who also resented the reintroduction of ranks, saluting and pay differentials. But Trotsky went further – he re-established harsh military discipline, bringing back the death penalty for a range of offences (see Source 6.1). He thought this was essential to make men fight. He also formed labour battalions to help at the Front, comprised of men who could not fight or were seen as unreliable; many of these came from the ranks of the bourgeoisie, or 'former people' as they were now known.

Trotsky's strengths were his energy, passion and organisational abilities. According to Dmitri Volkogonov, a Soviet historian and ex-general, Trotsky was not much of a military strategist and the key military decisions were taken by others. But Trotsky never claimed to be an expert in military matters. His chief contribution was as the person in overall charge, holding things together and making the organisation work effectively; this was no small achievement in Russia between 1918 and 1920.

FOCUS ROUTE

Using Sources 6.1–6.7 and the main text, note down the main ways in which you think Trotsky contributed to the Red victory.

SOURCE 6.1 Orders to the Red Army from Trotsky, 1918

- *Every scoundrel who incites anyone to retreat, to desert, or not to fulfil a military order, will be shot.*
- *Every soldier who voluntarily deserts his post will be shot.*
- *Every soldier who throws away his rifle or sells part of his equipment will be shot.*

SOURCE 6.2 Trotsky used this special train to keep in constant contact with the Front and to take him and his special troops to the points where the fighting was fiercest. The arrival of the train was a great morale booster. It was his general headquarters and was fitted out as a munitions and uniform supply centre, a troop transporter and a radio-communications centre. It also had a garage and his own Rolls-Royce armoured car in which he drove to the Fronts

SOURCE 6.3 Trotsky reviewing troops. He used special forces to back up conventional forces, often marching his special forces, with machine guns, behind the ordinary troops. His special troops were kitted out in black leather and were a macho élite force. Trotsky remarked: 'I issue this warning. If any detachment retreats without orders, the first to be shot will be the commissar, the second will be the commander'

However, this does not mean that Trotsky was just a backroom commander, far behind the front lines. Travelling in a specially equipped train (see Sources 6.2 and 6.5), he rushed to the points where the fighting was fiercest to provide support – although sometimes this involved his special troops making sure that Red forces did not retreat (see Source 6.3). His presence did seem to make a real difference and he genuinely seemed able to inspire men in a way that other leaders, especially White leaders, could not. It was Trotsky who decided to save Petrograd when it was under threat from Yudenich. The capital had been moved to Moscow and Lenin felt that they would have to give up Petrograd, the 'home of the revolution'. Trotsky disagreed, raced off with his train and, after fierce fighting, turned Yudenich's army away

The Red Army

It is easy to overplay the organisation of the Red Army in comparison to the Whites. Once the supply of urban workers ran out, the Reds conscripted peasants. Although they were willing to fight for their lands when the White armies approached, the peasants were generally unwilling conscripts. At harvest time, they would often desert. In protest at the mass conscription by the Reds and the seizure of their best horses and food for the army, the peasants staged uprisings which engulfed whole provinces. Many joined the independent Green armies. Rates of desertion were just as high for the Reds as for the Whites. By the end of 1919, the Red Army had around three million troops; the figure reached around five million by the end of 1920. But it is estimated that one million deserted in 1918 and nearly four million by 1921. The trouble was that when they deserted they took their weapons and uniforms with them, so even in the later stages of the war the Red Army was often poorly equipped (few had good boots), had a ragtag appearance and was short of ammunition. This is why Trotsky's train, which carried uniforms and supplies, was so important.

The Red Army also had its fair share of indiscipline. At worst, this became full-scale mutinies in which *burzhui* officers were murdered and new officers elected. There was festering resentment about *burzhui* officers and a great deal of anti-Semitism. Many of the commissars were Jews, including, of course, Trotsky himself..

SOURCE 6.4 R. Service, *A History of Twentieth-Century Russia*, 1997, pp. 105–6

His [Trotsky's] brilliance had been proved before 1918. What took everyone aback was his organisational capacity and ruthlessness as he transformed the Red Army into a fighting force. He ordered deserters to be shot, and he did not give a damn if some of them were communist party activists; and in this fashion he endeared himself to Imperial Army officers whom he encouraged to join the Reds. He sped from unit to unit, rousing the troops with his revolutionary zeal. . . . His flair too paid dividends. He organised a competition to design a Red Army cap and tunic; he had his own railway carriage equipped with his own map room and printing press. He also had an eye for young talent, bringing on his protégés without regard for length of time and service.

SOURCE 6.5 V. Serge, *Memoirs of a Revolutionary 1901–1941*, translated and edited by P. Sedwick, 1967, p. 92

The news from the other fronts was so bad that Lenin was reluctant to sacrifice the last available forces in the defence of the doomed city [Petrograd]. Trotsky thought otherwise ... He arrived at almost the last moment and his presence changed the atmosphere ... Trotsky arrived with a train, that famous train which had been speeding to and fro along the different fronts ... The train contained excellent motor cars ... a printing shop for propaganda, sanitary squads, and specialists in engineering, provisioning, street fighting, all bound together by friendship and trust, all kept to a strict vigorous discipline by a leader they admired, all dressed in black leather, red stars on their peaked caps, all exhaling energy. It was the nucleus of resolute and efficiently serviced organisers, who hastened wherever danger demanded their presence.

SOURCE 6.6 E. Mawdsley, *The Russian Civil War*, 1987, pp. 277–78

The historian looking at Trotsky's Civil War career must beware of two myths. The first is the Soviet view dominant ever since his disgrace in the late 1920s that he played no beneficial role in the Civil War. ('History,' Comrade Stalin in fact pointed out, 'shows that ... Kolchak and Denikin were beaten by our troops in spite of Trotsky's plans.') The second might be called the 'Trotskyist' myth that exaggerates his importance. The truth lies in between the two, but given the state of Western historiography it is perhaps the second myth that deserves the most attention. Trotsky was, of course, the second best-known Soviet leader. But his career in 1917–1920 was marked by spectacular failures. He made major mistakes in foreign policy in early 1918 and in economic policy in 1920. Even his career in the Red Army had the bitterness of the summer of 1919. Trotsky's vital step was to support the creation of a regular army against much party opposition. He also played an important agitational role, his famous headquarters train covered 65,000 miles, and all this was something that Lenin, as their comrade Lunacharsky pointed out, could not have done. The fighting men needed a figurehead to rally around, and Trotsky played his part effectively. At the same time the other important leaders of the Civil War should not be lost sight of. Sverdlov, who died in early 1919, helped organize the state and the party, and Rykov, disgraced in the 1930s, was the man in charge of the war economy. Smilga, another future oppositionist, was the chief political organizer of the Red Army. Something should be said for Stalin, too, who had a most active career in the Civil War; if he had been killed in 1920 he would certainly be remembered as one of the great activists of the war. And outside the party probably no one was as important as two former Tsarist colonels, Vatsetis and Kamenev.

SOURCE 6.7 Various contemporary images of Trotsky

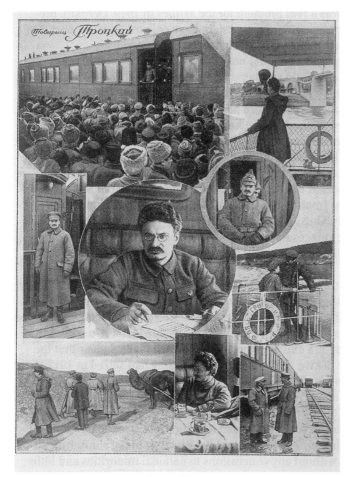

THE PROBLEM OF FOOD SUPPLY

Getting food into the cities had been a problem since 1915 and had contributed significantly to the February and October Revolutions. For some time the peasants had been unco-operative. During 1917 they had been interested only in getting the land and once they had it they wanted to be left alone to farm it. Their main wish was to run their lives without outside interference. They were not really concerned about the problems of the cities, which had little to offer them in return for their grain. Added to this, large peasant households had split themselves into several smaller households to increase their claim for land and consequently the land had been divided up into small parcels. This encouraged a return to subsistence farming rather than production for the market. Yet Lenin had promised to give the workers 'bread' and this was a promise he could not afford to renege on.

SUMMARY OF KEY FEATURES OF WAR COMMUNISM

• Grain requisitioning
• Private trade banned
• State control of industry
• Single managers to replace workers' committees
• Passports to prevent workers leaving the towns
• Rationing

food riots in many cities in early 1918. Workers started to flee from the cities, leaving factories short of workers. The situation was desperate. Lenin was faced with two main problems:

• keeping the workers in the cities to produce munitions, essential war supplies and other desperately needed goods
• feeding the workers.

SOURCE 6.16 B. Williams, *The Russian Revolution 1917–21*, 1987, pp. 62–63

By the end of 1920 the proletariat, the class the revolution was all about, had shrunk to only half its pre-revolutionary size. Petrograd lost 60 per cent of its workforce by April 1918 and one million people had left the city by that June. In Russia as a whole the urban proletariat decreased from 3.6 million in January 1917 to 1.4 million two years later. Starving and unemployed workers left the towns to return to the villages, to join the Red Army, or to enter the ever-growing ranks of the bureaucracy. Hardest hit were the large state-owned metallurgical factories employing the very section of the working class which had provided the Bolsheviks with the core of their support in 1917. The Vyborg district of Petrograd saw its population fall from 69,000 to 5,000 by the summer of 1918.

It was not only economic problems that Lenin faced in the summer of 1918; he was also confronted by the full onslaught of the Civil War. From this point onwards, the Bolsheviks were fighting for their lives. As a result, the whole economy of the Red-held part of Russia was geared towards the needs of the army. The name given to the policies Lenin adopted from 1918 to 1921 is War Communism.

The main features of War Communism

Grain requisitioning
The Bolsheviks had been sending units of Red guards and soldiers out into the countryside to find grain for the hard-pressed cities. In May 1918 a Food-Supplies Dictatorship was set up to establish the forcible requisitioning of grain as the standard policy. Unsurprisingly, the peasants resisted bitterly.

Banning of private trade
All private trade and manufacture were banned. However, the state trading organisation was extremely chaotic and industry was simply not producing enough consumer goods. So an enormous black market developed, without which most people could not have survived.

Nationalisation of industry
All industry was brought under state control and administered by the Supreme Council of National Economy (Vesenkha). Workers' committees were replaced by single managers reporting to central authorities. These were often the old bourgeois managers now called 'specialists'. This was the only way to stop the chaos caused by the factory workers' committees who had voted themselves huge pay rises, intimidated management and stolen materials for illegal goods. Not all workers were against nationalisation: many, faced with the closure of their factory, urged that it be nationalised and kept open. They were desperate to keep their jobs.

Labour discipline
Discipline was brought back to the work place. There were fines for lateness and absenteeism. Internal passports were introduced to stop people fleeing to the countryside. Piece-work rates were brought back, along with bonuses and a work book that was needed to get rations.

Rationing
A class-based system of rationing was introduced. The labour force was given priority along with Red Army soldiers. Smaller rations were given to civil servants and professional people such as doctors. The smallest rations, barely enough to live on, were given to the *burzhui* or middle classes – or as they were now called, 'the former people'.

The Red Terror

Another crucial component of War Communism was the systematic use of terror to back up the new measures and deal with opposition. The Bolsheviks faced increased opposition inside the cities from:

- workers who were angry at their economic plight, low food rations and state violence. There were calls for new Soviet elections, a free press, the restoration of the Constituent Assembly and the overthrow of the Sovnarkom (only six months after the revolution). Signs appeared on city walls saying: 'Down with Lenin and horsemeat! Give us the Tsar and pork!'
- anarchists who rejected the authoritarian control of the government
- left-wing Socialist Revolutionaries who were protesting about the Treaty of Brest-Litovsk. They turned to terrorism, shooting the German ambassador in July 1918 to try to wreck the Russian relationship with the Germans. They captured Dzerzhinsky, the head of the Cheka, in May and managed to shoot Lenin in August 1918. Two other Bolshevik Party leaders were murdered. They put the regime under real pressure.

The assassination attempt on Lenin prompted the Cheka to launch the Red Terror in the summer of 1918, but this was simply an intensification of what was already happening. From June onwards, Socialist Revolutionaries had been arrested in large numbers, along with anarchists and members of other extreme left groups. Mensheviks and Socialist Revolutionaries were excluded from taking part in soviets. Many Kadets were already in prison, others had fled to the south.

The execution of the Tsar and his family

One of the most significant victims in this period was the Tsar. Nicholas, along with his family and servants, was shot on 17 July 1918 in Ekaterinburg in the Urals. Lenin and Sverdlov (Party Secretary 1918–19) claimed that it had been carried out by the local soviet against their wishes, but the weight of evidence now suggests that the order came from the centre. Lenin did not wish to antagonise the Germans at this point so he probably wanted to suggest that it was nothing to do with him. Alexandra, the Tsar's wife, was German and, of course, the Tsar was a blood relation to the other monarchs in Europe – for example, he was cousin to the German Kaiser. The stories about the possible survival of some of the Tsar's children may have been allowed to flourish for similar reasons: the Bolshevik leaders did not wish to accept responsibility in the international community for this horrific act. The truth must have been known to them: that the whole family had been shot and their bodies, having been drenched in acid, had been thrown into a disused mine shaft and later buried.

The Terror intensifies

When the Red Terror got underway, the change was one of scale and intensity. Execution, previously the exception, now became the rule. Prisoners in many cities were shot out of hand. Official records put the figure for deaths at the hands of the Cheka for the years 1918–20 at nearly 13,000, but estimates put the real figure at nearer 300,000. The Cheka fanned the flames of class warfare, as some Bolsheviks talked of wiping out the middle class completely. But the real purpose of the Terror was to terrify all hostile social groups. Its victims included large numbers of workers and peasants as well as princes and priests, prostitutes, judges, merchants, traders, even children (who made up five per cent of the population of Moscow prisons in 1920) – all guilty of 'bourgeois provocation' or counter-revolution. The problem was that no one was really sure who the counter-revolutionaries were.

SOURCE 7.18 Agricultural and industrial production figures, 1913–26, taken from A. Nove, *An Economic History of the USSR, 1917–1991*, 1992, p. 89

	1913	1920	1921	1922	1923	1924	1925	1926
Grain harvest (million tons*)	80.1	46.1	37.6	50.3	56.6	51.4	72.5	76.8
Sown area (million ha.)	105.0	—	90.3	77.7	91.7	98.1	104.3	110.3
Industrial (factory) production (million roubles at 1926–27 values)	10,251	1,410	2,004	2,619	4,005	4,660	7,739	11,083
Coal (million tons)	29.0	8.7	8.9	9.5	13.7	16.1	18.1	27.6
Electricity (million kWhs)	1,945	—	520	775	1,146	1,562	2,925	3,508
Pig iron (thousand tons)	4,216	—	116	188	309	755	1,535	2,441
Steel (thousand tons)	4,231	—	183	392	709	1,140	2,135	3,141
Cotton fabrics (million metres)	2,582	—	105	349	691	963	1,688	2,286
Rail freight carried (million tons)	132.4	—	39.4	39.9	58.0	67.5	83.4	—

N.B. Tons (Imperial Measure) are used throughout. 1 ton = 1.016 tonnes (metric).

ACTIVITY

How successful was the NEP up to 1925?

1 Using Source 7.18 and the text, assemble figures to show the economic recovery up to 1925.
2 Why do you think the economy recovered so quickly after the introduction of NEP? (Refer to the text and Sources 7.15, 7.16 and 7.19.)
3 Describe the 'scissors crisis'.
4 What do you think Communists would find offensive about Nepmen and the NEP (see Source 7.16)?
5 Paragraphs form the building blocks of an essay. Usually a paragraph develops one clear point and provides supporting evidence or further explanation of that point.
   a) Write a paragraph on the economic successes of the NEP, using the evidence you have collected in your answers to questions 1 and 2 above.
   b) Write a second paragraph on the problems associated with the NEP, particularly for the workers and Communists.

TALKING POINT

Does the NEP show that the capitalist economics of the market place are always superior to the centrally planned economy? Discuss this in the light of other developments in the twentieth century, particularly the collapse of the Soviet economy in the 1980s and changes in China.

SOURCE 7.19 A Soviet poster celebrating the electrification of Russia. Lenin saw electrification as a key factor in modernising Russia, bringing even the villages out of the dark ages, and the electrification programme expanded under the NEP. Lenin envisaged a network of power stations powering the large-scale industry that would build socialism. He said, 'Soviet power plus electrification equals Communism'

Did the liberalisation of the economy lead to political liberalisation?

The Bolsheviks had no intention of letting the limited capitalism of the NEP develop into a full-scale restoration of capitalism that might foster the emergence of a political system based on government by a number of political parties (pluralism). Political liberalisation was not on the cards. The NEP was a 'carrot' to buy off the peasants and workers economically, but it was accompanied by the 'stick' of political repression.

■ 7B Political repression during the period of the New Economic Policy

Attacks on political rivals

Political pressure on the rival socialist parties was intensified. The Mensheviks and Socialist Revolutionaries had become much more popular during the strikes and revolts and had played some part in encouraging them. The Bolsheviks used this as an excuse to arrest some 5000 Mensheviks in 1921 for counter-revolutionary activities. The Mensheviks and Socialist Revolutionaries were outlawed as political organisations.

Show trials

The show trial – a classic feature of the later Stalinist terror – made its appearance at the time of the NEP. The Communists rounded up a large number of Socialist Revolutionaries and held a show trial, during which former Socialist Revolutionaries who had collaborated with the secret police accused old colleagues of heinous crimes. Among the accusations was the claim that the Central Committee of the Socialist Revolutionaries had authorised assassination attempts on Lenin or had collaborated with Denikin. Many of those accused were already in jail when the alleged crimes had been committed. Nevertheless, 34 Socialist Revolutionary leaders were condemned as terrorists; eleven were executed.

Censorship

Censorship became more systematic. In the spring of 1922, dozens of outstanding Russian writers and scholars were deported to convince the intelligentsia that it was not a good idea to criticise the government.

In the same year, pre-publication censorship was introduced. Books, articles, poems and other writings had to be submitted to the Main Administration for Affairs of Literature and Publishing Houses (Glavlit) before they could be published.

Establishment of the GPU

The Cheka was renamed the GPU (Main Political Administration) in 1922.

The secret police actually grew in importance during the NEP. Arbitrary imprisonment and the death penalty continued to be applied after 1922 as an instrument of social policy.

The GPU periodically harassed and arrested Nepmen as speculators and class enemies in order to assure left Communists and the urban workers that they were keeping capitalistic tendencies under control.

Crushing of peasant revolts

The peasants who had staged revolts against the government were dealt with harshly.

The Tambov region, for instance, was swamped by Red Army troops in 1922. Whole rebel villages were destroyed in a brutal campaign.

Villages that supported the Reds were rewarded with salt – a vital commodity because it was needed for food preservation – and manufactured goods, and fed propaganda about the benefits that the NEP would bring them.

Attacks on the Church

The Communists also mounted a fierce attack on the Church, which they saw as a rival to their power and which was enjoying something of a revival at the beginning of the NEP.

Previously the war against the Church had mainly taken the form of propaganda, but in 1921 the Union of the Militant Godless was established to challenge the Church more directly.

In 1922, orders were sent out to strip churches of their precious items, ostensibly to help famine victims. When clergy and local people tried to protect their churches, there were violent clashes. Death penalties were handed out to leaders of the Russian Orthodox Church and thousands of priests were imprisoned.

C How did the centralised state develop in Russia between 1918 and 1924?

By 1924, Soviet Russia was governed by a centralised, one-party dictatorship which did not permit anyone to challenge its power. The party organisation dominated government institutions and the main decisions were taken by a Politburo which consisted of seven to nine senior party leaders. A large part of the economy – industry, banking, transport and foreign trade – was controlled by the government. How did this happen?

When the Bolsheviks came to power, they had no blueprint for government and almost no administrative experience. So they had to improvise a system to run the country. The urge to centralise control was clearly present from the beginning. The creation of the Sovnarkom, bypassing the Soviet (see pages 71–72), showed that the main decisions were going to be taken by the Bolshevik centre with little account taken of other political viewpoints. Nationalisation and state control were always part of their plan for the economy (despite having to give way to pressure for workers' control) and, as a step towards this, they had immediately nationalised banking.

However, it seems unlikely that Lenin would have moved so quickly towards a highly centralised state had it not been for the Civil War and the economic chaos in which the country found itself in 1918. Chart 7D (page 115) shows some of the main reasons for the growth of centralisation in this period.

The Bolshevik response to the desperate situation in 1918 was to centralise government control. The Sovnarkom accrued more and more power to itself to direct the course of the war and run the economy. But the centralising tendency did not stop there. Two other distinct trends were taking place during the Civil War:

- The Communist Party began to dominate government.
- The Communist Party itself became more centralised, more bureaucratic and less democratic. Power was concentrated in the hands of a few people at the top.

How did the party come to dominate government bodies?

The Civil War saw the party organisation grow in importance at the expense of government bodies.

- In 1919, the Politburo was created, forming an inner ruling group of around seven people at the top of the Communist Party. The Politburo soon took precedence over the Sovnarkom as the key decision-making body. The Sovnarkom started to meet less frequently and was regarded as less important.
- At district and local level, the local Communist Party organisations took control of soviets across Russia (see the Learning trouble spot on page 116). Party officials ran the soviets and obeyed party orders above all else. So the soviets were now effectively subordinate to the party.
- From 1919 onwards, the Central Committee of the party began to appoint its own 'trusted' nominees to key positions in soviets (previously such positions had been filled by people elected by the members of the soviet). This was done to increase the centre's control over local party apparatus and local government.

There is a tendency, when talking about the growth of centralisation in the Bolshevik regime, to assume that the centre did have control of what was going on. But the Bolsheviks, as you know from the last chapter, were struggling to cope with the chaotic state of government during the Civil War. In Nizhniy-Novgorod, for example, everything was controlled by a local mafia of Bolsheviks and black marketeers who defied Moscow. So it is understandable that the regime should have used the party structure to gain more centralised control of government bodies and bring some sort of order out of the chaos.

Before you read this section you might want to look back at Chapter 5, covering the setting up of the Bolshevik state. As you work through this section, make notes on:

a) the factors that led the Bolshevik state to become more centralised
b) how the Communist Party grew in importance at the expense of government bodies
c) how power became concentrated in the hands of the people at the top of the Communist Party.

■ 7C Politburo membership 1919–24

Name	Full member
V. I. Lenin	1919
L. B. Kamenev	1919
L. D. Trotsky	1919
J. V. Stalin	1919
N. N. Krestinsky	1919
G. A. Zinoviev	1921
A. Y. Rykov	1922
M. M. Tomsky	1922
N. I. Bukharin	1922

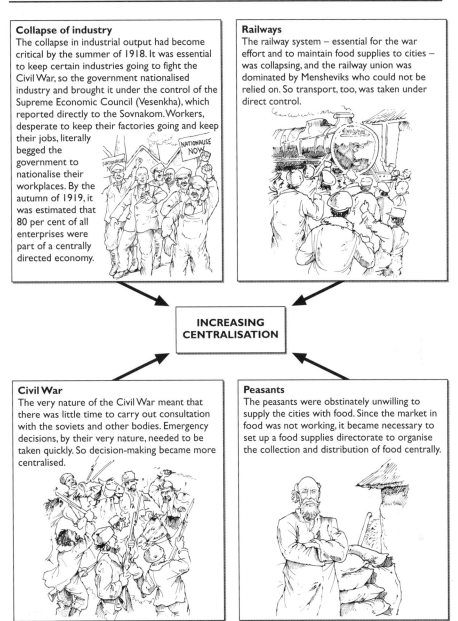

Collapse of industry

The collapse in industrial output had become critical by the summer of 1918. It was essential to keep certain industries going to fight the Civil War, so the government nationalised industry and brought it under the control of the Supreme Economic Council (Vesenkha), which reported directly to the Sovnakom. Workers, desperate to keep their factories going and keep their jobs, literally begged the government to nationalise their workplaces. By the autumn of 1919, it was estimated that 80 per cent of all enterprises were part of a centrally directed economy.

Railways

The railway system – essential for the war effort and to maintain food supplies to cities – was collapsing, and the railway union was dominated by Mensheviks who could not be relied on. So transport, too, was taken under direct control.

INCREASING CENTRALISATION

Civil War

The very nature of the Civil War meant that there was little time to carry out consultation with the soviets and other bodies. Emergency decisions, by their very nature, needed to be taken quickly. So decision-making became more centralised.

Peasants

The peasants were obstinately unwilling to supply the cities with food. Since the market in food was not working, it became necessary to set up a food supplies directorate to organise the collection and distribution of food centrally.

■ **Learning trouble spot**

Pragmatism or ideology?

Left-wing historians tend to see the increasing tendency to centralisation as a practical response to the problems caused by the Civil War. Right-wing historians tend to see it as the result of Communist ideology, which entails central planning and state control. In their view, the Bolsheviks were a small minority who used terror and central control to impose their policies on an unwilling population.

It seems likely that centralisation was a mixture of ideology and pragmatism. The Bolsheviks considered centralised state control to be socialist and this justified War Communism. However, many of their actions were pragmatic responses to the problems the Civil War threw up. For example, they had to take control of the food supply and certain industries because they were collapsing. And at the end of the war, the Bolsheviks were prepared to adopt the pragmatic NEP instead of continuing with War Communism, which some, including Trotsky, believed was the correct ideological line to move towards socialism more quickly.

■ **Learning trouble spot**

Soviets and local Communist Parties

The relationship between the soviets and the Communist Party at local and district level can be confusing. After the revolution, the soviets took over the functions of local government. Many of the soviets were run by elected non-Bolshevik socialists. They often tried to remain independent of the central authorities and ignored instructions from Moscow. The Communists could not tolerate hostile or unco-operative soviets as they sought to marshal their resources to fight the Civil War. So they used ballot rigging or intimidation (in the form of the Cheka) to win soviet elections. They then installed a chairman and executive committee made up of Communists to run the soviet. The chairman of the soviet was often the chairman of the local Communist Party, too. Later on in the 1920s, people who were not Communist Party members were not even allowed to stand for election to the soviets.

■ 7E How did the Civil War make the party more centralised and less democratic?

IMPACT OF CIVIL WAR, 1918–20

The membership had changed. Towards the end of 1919, the party was purged of undesirables. The new members recruited between 1920 and 1922 were mainly of peasant background. Few had any knowledge of Marx and some knew little about 1917. They had joined to improve their life chances. They were more prepared to do as they were told.

The party had lost its base in the proletarian workforce. Many of its earlier urban worker members had gone on to fight in the Civil War or join the party bureaucracy. By 1919, 39 per cent of party members were in the army and the majority of others were workers in offices, not factories.

Discussion and debate declined. In 1917 and in the months afterwards, the party had been characterised by passionate debate, disagreement and splits. But as the Civil War progressed, such debate declined as the need for unity grew.

The party became more centralised and hierarchical. The Politburo, with seven to nine members, took over the decision-making from the much larger and unwieldy Central Committee of around 40 members. Orders were passed out from the centre and party members were expected to carry them out.

The rank and file of the party generally accepted that the crisis caused by the Civil War and the state of the economy justified the increased centralisation and discipline in the party. A large proportion of party members had fought in the Red Army and a military discipline had been instilled in them. The Civil War became for them a heroic period during which they had been linked in camaraderie, and they were used to a pattern of command in which orders replaced consultation.

How did the party become more centralised and less democratic between 1921 and 1924?

This process of centralisation and bureaucratisation did not stop when the Civil War finished; it continued from 1921 to 1924. Two aspects of this are particularly significant.

The ban on factions 1921

The splits in the party during 1920 had angered Lenin. Groups like the Workers' Opposition and the Democratic Centralists (campaigning for more democracy in the party) seemed to him to be an unnecessary distraction given the crises they faced in 1921 (famine, revolts, Kronstadt mutiny). He called for unity and an end to splits and factionalism. As a result, in 1921, the Tenth Party Congress agreed to pass a 'ban on factions'. This meant that once party policy had been agreed by the Central Committee then everybody was expected to accept it and not form 'factions' to challenge the party line. The penalty for factionalism was expulsion from the party.

The *nomenklatura* system

This system was established from 1923 onwards. The Bolshevik leaders wanted to make sure that key personnel in public bodies were drawn from Bolsheviks or pro-Bolshevik workers. So a list of about 5500 designated party and governmental posts – the *nomenklatura* – was drawn up. The holders of these posts could only be appointed by the central party bodies. Overt loyalty counted for more than expertise; people who wanted promotion did what they were told. This tightened the one-party state internally. The people in the *nomenklatura* (key posts) became an elite.

By 1924, the net result of all these changes was a much more authoritarian and centralised Communist Party whose members, on the whole, were less likely to debate issues or challenge the leadership and more likely to carry out instructions through habits of discipline or the chance of promotion. Decision-making was concentrated in an increasingly small number of hands. The party had become more detached from its proletarian base and began to see the workers as 'uncultured' (Lenin) because they did not have the origins, experiences or education of the 1917 revolutionary proletariat. The party began to reinterpret its role: it saw itself as having the exclusive right to lead the people into the light of socialism – the party alone knew the right course to follow.

The government of the Soviet Union

The Russian Soviet Federal Socialist Republic (RSFSR) had been proclaimed in January 1918. Its constitution, introduced in July, defined the state as 'a dictatorship of the urban and rural proletariat'. Its job was to ensure transition to a socialist society. It employed the principle of 'he who does not work shall not eat'. The 'former people' (the middle classes) had no right to vote.

During the Civil War, areas conquered by the Red Army were taken into the RSFSR or, if it was a large area with a history of independence, such as the Ukraine, Belorussia or Georgia, it was made into a separate republic. The RSFSR was regarded as 'Russia' (since the majority of the population was Russian) and was far larger and more powerful than the other republics. The status of the smaller republics in relation to the RSFSR led to an acrimonious debate between Lenin and Stalin, the Commissar for Nationalities (see pages 126–127). Stalin wanted all the republics to be more directly controlled by Moscow. Lenin wanted a federation of soviet republics in which all were on a more or less equal footing. Lenin won the argument and at the end of 1922 the Union of the Soviet Socialist Republics (USSR) was formally established.

RSFSR
The Russian Soviet Federal Socialist Republic, created in 1918 after the Bolsheviks took control. In 1922 it became the main republic in the new USSR and in 1991 remained as the area we now call Russia after the break up of the USSR.

Despite Lenin's victory in the debate, the republics were never really free to govern themselves. The Communist Party organisations in the republics were regarded as regional branches of the Russian Communist Party and the commissariats (governments) of the republics were regarded as regional branches of the Sovnarkom. And, of course, both the Sovnarkom and the Central Committee were controlled by the Politburo.

The Communists were keen to avoid any suggestion that the way they controlled the republics was in any way similar to the tsarist empire, in case this led to national revolts. They tried to establish instead the idea that they were all part of a benign brotherhood of different ethnic groups. They deliberately fostered national consciousness, setting up native language schools and encouraging theatre and cultural events reflecting national traditions. Most members of the Communist Party were Russians, so they tried to bring in people of different ethnic groups to train as party officials and run their local party branches. This was called 'the planting down of roots'.

■ 7F The republics in 1922

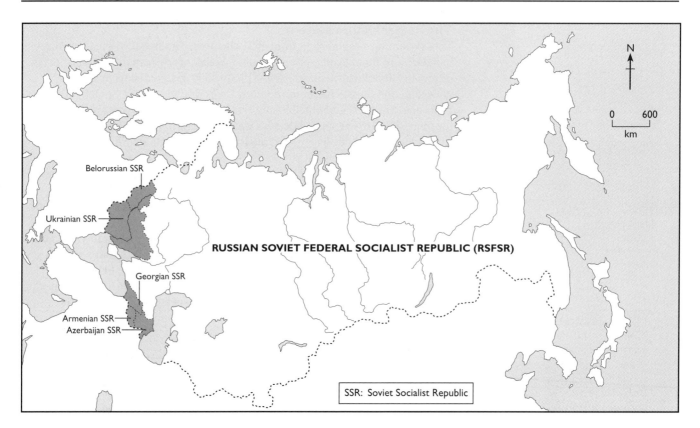

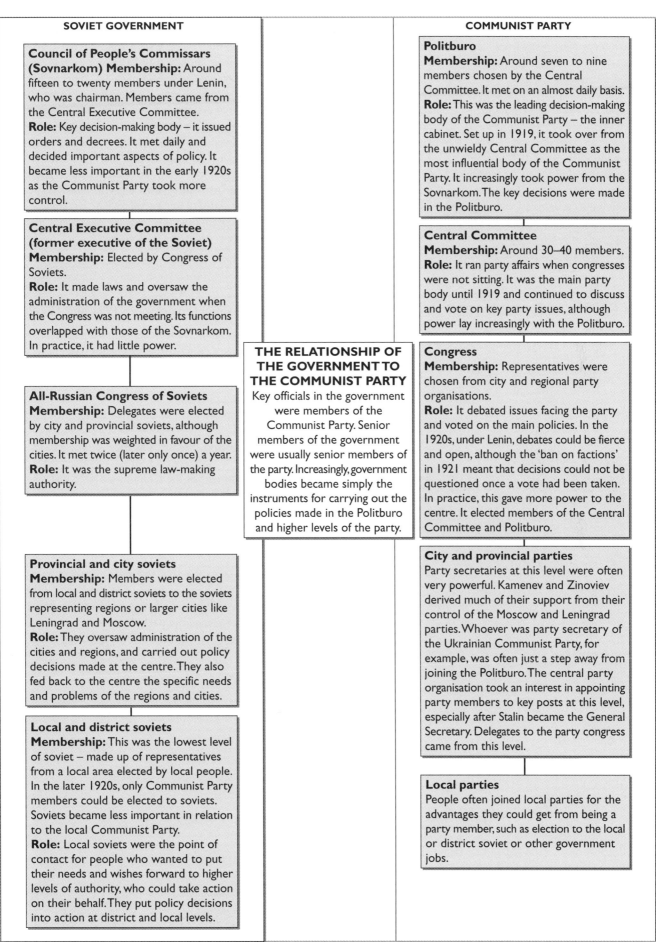

SOVIET GOVERNMENT

Council of People's Commissars (Sovnarkom) Membership: Around fifteen to twenty members under Lenin, who was chairman. Members came from the Central Executive Committee.
Role: Key decision-making body – it issued orders and decrees. It met daily and decided important aspects of policy. It became less important in the early 1920s as the Communist Party took more control.

Central Executive Committee (former executive of the Soviet) Membership: Elected by Congress of Soviets.
Role: It made laws and oversaw the administration of the government when the Congress was not meeting. Its functions overlapped with those of the Sovnarkom. In practice, it had little power.

All-Russian Congress of Soviets Membership: Delegates were elected by city and provincial soviets, although membership was weighted in favour of the cities. It met twice (later only once) a year.
Role: It was the supreme law-making authority.

Provincial and city soviets Membership: Members were elected from local and district soviets to the soviets representing regions or larger cities like Leningrad and Moscow.
Role: They oversaw administration of the cities and regions, and carried out policy decisions made at the centre. They also fed back to the centre the specific needs and problems of the regions and cities.

Local and district soviets Membership: This was the lowest level of soviet – made up of representatives from a local area elected by local people. In the later 1920s, only Communist Party members could be elected to soviets. Soviets became less important in relation to the local Communist Party.
Role: Local soviets were the point of contact for people who wanted to put their needs and wishes forward to higher levels of authority, who could take action on their behalf. They put policy decisions into action at district and local levels.

THE RELATIONSHIP OF THE GOVERNMENT TO THE COMMUNIST PARTY

Key officials in the government were members of the Communist Party. Senior members of the government were usually senior members of the party. Increasingly, government bodies became simply the instruments for carrying out the policies made in the Politburo and higher levels of the party.

COMMUNIST PARTY

**Politburo
Membership:** Around seven to nine members chosen by the Central Committee. It met on an almost daily basis.
Role: This was the leading decision-making body of the Communist Party – the inner cabinet. Set up in 1919, it took over from the unwieldy Central Committee as the most influential body of the Communist Party. It increasingly took power from the Sovnarkom. The key decisions were made in the Politburo.

**Central Committee
Membership:** Around 30–40 members.
Role: It ran party affairs when congresses were not sitting. It was the main party body until 1919 and continued to discuss and vote on key party issues, although power lay increasingly with the Politburo.

**Congress
Membership:** Representatives were chosen from city and regional party organisations.
Role: It debated issues facing the party and voted on the main policies. In the 1920s, under Lenin, debates could be fierce and open, although the 'ban on factions' in 1921 meant that decisions could not be questioned once a vote had been taken. In practice, this gave more power to the centre. It elected members of the Central Committee and Politburo.

City and provincial parties
Party secretaries at this level were often very powerful. Kamenev and Zinoviev derived much of their support from their control of the Moscow and Leningrad parties. Whoever was party secretary of the Ukrainian Communist Party, for example, was often just a step away from joining the Politburo. The central party organisation took an interest in appointing party members to key posts at this level, especially after Stalin became the General Secretary. Delegates to the party congress came from this level.

Local parties
People often joined local parties for the advantages they could get from being a party member, such as election to the local or district soviet or other government jobs.

120

HOW WAS THE BOLSHEVIK STATE CONSOLIDATED BETWEEN 1921 AND 1924?

CENTRE AND PERIPHERY

Although there was a tendency towards the centralisation of power, the further you got away from Moscow, the more district and local party organisations tended to act independently. They would not always carry out orders from the centre. A culture of lying grew up in the lower levels of the party. Local party bodies protected their own areas of power and did not always feed back accurate information to the centre. The relationship between the centre and the 'periphery' (regional and local government) was often strained throughout the 1920s and the 1930s.

DEMOCRATIC CENTRALISM

It was on this idea that the Soviet claim to democracy rested. Town and village soviets were elected by the working people. Day-to-day administration was in the hands of an executive committee appointed by each soviet and directly responsible to it. Delegates were sent from the lower bodies progressively up the different levels to the top. The idea was that the system of soviets represented a real chain from people to government, through which the expressed ideas of the people could be carried to the highest level – this was the 'democratic' element. In this way, the centre could keep in contact with the people. Once decisions had been made at the centre they were passed down through the levels and carried out – the 'centralism' element.

This was how the system was supposed to work in theory. In practice, more and more power was accumulated at the centre during the Civil War. The Sovnarkom made most of the decisions and laws, and sent out its orders. The city and provincial soviets largely carried out the instructions from the centre and there was little democratic input from the lower levels of soviets.

KEY POINTS FROM CHAPTER 7

How was the Bolshevik state consolidated between 1921 and 1924?

1 The Bolsheviks were in serious trouble in 1921, facing massive peasant revolts, strikes and opposition from workers, a rising at the Kronstadt naval base, economic distress and famine. The Bolshevik regime was in jeopardy.

2 There were also factions inside the Communist Party, like the Workers' Opposition, who wanted changes in policy.

3 Lenin made economic concessions in the form of the New Economic Policy to ensure the survival of the regime.

4 The NEP was accompanied by repressive measures as the Communists asserted their control.

5 Between 1918 and 1924, the government of the Communist state became increasingly centralised. This was partly the result of pragmatic responses to fighting the Civil War and coping with an economy in dire circumstances, and partly the result of party ideology.

6 The Communist Party became increasingly important at the expense of government institutions.

7 The Communist Party itself became more centralised and controlled by a smaller number of people at the top. It became more used to obeying orders, there was less open debate and discussion, and a 'ban on factions' meant that party members were less likely to challenge the party leaders.

8 By 1924, the Soviet Union was a highly centralised, one-party state.

Section 2 Review: The consolidation of the Bolshevik state 1917–24

■ A How did the Bolsheviks consolidate their power?

Pragmatic decisions to ensure survival

- They initially gave peasants and workers what they wanted, to get their support in the first months after the October Revolution. They realised they were not able to control the situation so they gave way to popular demands and aspirations. They passed a number of other measures that were popular with workers, for example the abolition of titles and ranks.
- They signed the Treaty of Brest-Litovsk to bring Russia's involvement in the First World War to an end and to honour their peace pledge.
- They employed the tough policy of War Communism to keep the regime afloat. They seized grain from a peasantry reluctant to supply it and took strong measures to keep workers in cities and towns so that they could continue to run industries essential to the war effort.
- They introduced the NEP; this was an economic concession to achieve political survival.

The Bolshevik grip on power tightens

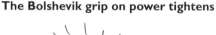

Ruthless methods and terror

- They set up the Cheka (secret police) as an instrument of terror to deal with opposition. They arrested first Kadets, and then Socialist Revolutionary and Menshevik leaders. The Cheka was a formidable force that supported the Bolsheviks at every turn and helped them win the war against 'internal enemies'. Some historians see the Cheka as *the* key factor in the survival of the Bolshevik regime.
- They used force to break the civil service strikes and deal with demonstrations against them.
- Class warfare was used to terrorise the middle classes and all hostile social groups. This played well with workers and soldiers and made it difficult for people to criticise the new government.
- They used repressive measures during the NEP to consolidate their political position.

Staying in control

- They refused to take part in a socialist coalition government and crushed the Constituent Assembly, establishing one-party control.
- They exploited the weakness of the opposition, particularly the Socialist Revolutionaries and Mensheviks, who underestimated them and would not get involved in violent anti-Bolshevik protest.
- They defeated the Whites in the Civil War. People were more inclined to support the Bolsheviks to keep the 'gains of the revolution'.
- They developed a highly centralised state to make sure their policies were carried out.

SOURCE 2   Lenin in his study, a painting by Isaak Brodsky

SOURCE 3   *Lenin on the Tribune*, a painting by Aleksandr Gerasimov

SOURCE 4   *Leader, Teacher, Friend*, a painting by G. Shegal, 1936–37

SOURCE 5   A painting (1926) showing Stalin addressing industrial workers

SOURCE 6   Merkurov's statue of Stalin, displayed at the Great Soviet Exhibition of 1939

SOURCE 7   *An Unforgettable Meeting*, a painting by Vasili Efanov, made in 1936–37

How significant is Lenin's contribution to history?

CHAPTER OVERVIEW

Lenin died in January 1924, although for most of 1923 he was incapacitated by illness. In the last years of his life, he was concerned about the state of the party, the growing bureaucracy and the power of Stalin. His relationship with Stalin deteriorated in 1922 and it seemed likely that Stalin's power would be curtailed. But Lenin died before any changes could take place and it was Stalin who took the lead at his funeral and in developing the Lenin cult. Lenin's contribution to the Russian Revolution from 1917 to 1923 was enormous, but how significant is he in history? Did he really make a difference?

A Lenin's relationship with Stalin at the end of his life (pp. 126–127)

B Lenin's funeral and the Lenin cult (pp. 127–128)

C Summing up Lenin (pp. 129–130)

D Did Lenin make a difference? (pp. 131–134)

A Lenin's relationship with Stalin at the end of his life

Lenin suffered a series of strokes from late 1921 until his death in January 1924. He was able to carry on working during 1922, but a major stroke in March 1923 left him without the power of speech. In 1922, he still had considerable influence but was removed from the onerous work of running the day-to-day business of government. He had time to think about the problems of the party. He became concerned about the extent of the party bureaucracy and increasingly aware of the power that Stalin had accrued to himself. He was particularly worried about the way Stalin had abused his power by intimidating and bullying the Communists who were governing Georgia. Lenin detected a dark side to Stalin that might present a danger to the party. He mounted an investigation into the Georgian affair that confirmed his fears. He also fell out with Stalin over the issue of the Soviet republics (see page 117).

After the second of his strokes in December 1922, Lenin wrote a testament, a 'Letter to the Party Congress' to be read after his death (see Source 8.1 on page 127). In it Lenin warned that Stalin had become too powerful and that he could not be trusted to use his power wisely. From this point onwards, Lenin did not trust the information with which Stalin provided him. How much Stalin knew about this is not certain, but he clearly perceived that relations with Lenin were not good and was anxious about the Georgian investigation.

Stalin's wife worked as a secretary for Lenin, living in his house while he was ill, and she provided a conduit of information about Lenin's contacts. Stalin found out about the increasingly warm correspondence between Trotsky and Lenin. They were working on plans to restore more democracy to the party and there seems little doubt that, if Lenin had survived a little longer, Stalin would have lost some of his key positions in the party. Stalin tried to see Lenin, but Krupskaya, Lenin's wife, would not let him visit. Stalin, in a telephone conversation, insulted her, using crude, abusive language. Lenin was upset by this and added a note to his testament which would have been very damaging to Stalin if made public.

THE GREAT RUSSIAN CHAUVINIST AND THE GEORGIAN AFFAIR

During the Civil War Georgia had been run by Mensheviks. At the end of the war, the Red Army took control by force and Stalin – himself a Georgian – was sent to visit the area and see how the Bolsheviks in Georgia were managing. However, Stalin was insulted and shouted down at meetings by the Mensheviks, and accused of betraying his birthplace. Stalin, who never took kindly to slights and insults, took the Bolsheviks to task for being too weak on opposition groups. He threatened and bullied them to adopt a more aggressive policy. In one incident, a local Bolshevik leader was struck by one of Stalin's henchmen. Stalin believed that Russians should govern the peoples of the USSR from Moscow rather like the tsars had done. This is why Lenin called him the 'Great Russian chauvinist'.

FOCUS ROUTE

Make notes on the relationship between Lenin and Stalin at the end of Lenin's life using these questions to guide you:

a) Why was Lenin concerned about Stalin?
b) What was the Georgian affair?
c) How did Lenin and Stalin's relationship deteriorate?
d) What appears to have been the purpose of Lenin's testament?
e) Who came out of the relationship the worst?

TALKING POINT

Chance or accident can be a significant factor in explaining events.

1 How does chance seem to have played a role in the succession to the Russian leadership?
2 Can you think of other examples when chance may have had a significant impact on historical events?

FOCUS ROUTE

Make notes to explain:

• how Stalin used Lenin's funeral to his advantage
• what the cult of Leninism was and why Stalin encouraged it.

According to the historian Robert Conquest, Lenin was more than upset: 'He was in fact prepared for open hostilities ... One of Lenin's secretaries told Trotsky that Lenin was now preparing "a bomb" against Stalin; and Kamenev learned from another of the secretaries that Lenin had decided "to crush Stalin politically" ' (*Stalin: Breaker of Nations*, 1991, page 104). But before this could happen, Lenin had another stroke on 7 March and never recovered the power of speech.

SOURCE 8.1 Extracts from Lenin's testament, 25 December 1922

Comrade Stalin, having become General Secretary, has immeasurable power concentrated in his hands, and I am not sure that he always knows how to use that power with sufficient caution. Comrade Trotsky, on the other hand ... is distinguished not only by his outstanding ability. He is personally perhaps the most capable man in the present C.C. [Central Committee], but he has displayed excessive self-assurance ... These two qualities of the two outstanding leaders of the present C.C. can inadvertently lead to a split ...

I shall not give further appraisals of the personal qualities of other members of the C.C. but recall that the October episode with Zinoviev and Kamenev was no accident, but neither can the blame for it be laid on them personally, any more than non-Bolshevism can upon Trotsky. Speaking of the young C.C. members I wish to say a few words about Bukharin ... Bukharin is not only a most valuable and major theorist of the Party; he is also rightly considered the favourite of the whole Party; but his theoretical views can only with the very greatest doubt be regarded as fully Marxist.
[Postcript added 4 January 1923]
Stalin is too rude, and this fault ... becomes unacceptable in the office of General Secretary. Therefore, I propose to the comrades that a way be found to remove Stalin from that post and replace him with someone else who differs from Stalin in all respects, someone more patient, more loyal, more polite, more considerate.

B Lenin's funeral and the Lenin cult

The unexpected news of Lenin's death led to widespread displays of public grief. Theatres and shops were closed for a week, while portraits of Lenin draped in red and black were displayed in windows. Over three days, three and a half million people queued for hours to file past his body lying in state. However much they hated the regime the people seemed to have a genuine affection for Lenin, much as they had had for the tsars.

Stalin made the most of Lenin's funeral to advance his position in the party. Just before Lenin's death, Trotsky was ill and had set out to the south of Russia for a rest-holiday. Stalin contacted him and told him that he (Trotsky) would not be able to get back in time for the funeral. So Trotsky did not attend and it looked as though he could not be bothered to turn up. His reputation and political prestige were severely damaged by his non-attendance. Stalin, on the other hand, acted as one of the pallbearers and made a speech in which he appeared to be taking on the mantle of Leninism (see Source 8.2 on page 128). Stalin hoped to transfer to himself the prestige, respect and loyalty associated with Lenin. He set himself up as Lenin's disciple, the person who would carry on Lenin's work. He was already thinking of the looming power struggle.

SOURCE 8.2 J. V. Stalin, *Collected Works*. These are extracts from Stalin's speech at Lenin's funeral

There is nothing higher than the calling of the member of a Party whose founder and leader is Comrade Lenin ... Leaving us, Comrade Lenin ordered us to hold high and keep pure the great title of member of the Party. We vow to thee Comrade Lenin, that we shall honourably fulfil this commandment.... Leaving us, Comrade Lenin enjoined us to keep the unity of the Party like the apple of our eye. We vow to thee, Comrade Lenin. That we will honourably fulfil this, thy commandment ...

SOURCE 8.3 Members of the Central Committee of the Communist Party carrying Lenin's coffin to Red Square on 27 January 1924. Stalin is on the left in the picture

SOURCE 8.4 Extract from a 1918 pamphlet, written by Zinoviev

On the horizon a new figure has appeared. He is the chosen one of millions. He is leader by the grace of God. Such a leader is born once in 500 years in the life of mankind.

SOURCE 8.5 Extract from a poem by V. Mayakovsky written to celebrate Lenin's fiftieth birthday, 1921

I know . . .
It is not the hero
Who precipitates the flow of revolution.
The story of heroes
Is the nonsense of the intelligentsia!
But who can restrain himself
And not sing
Of the glory of Il'ich?
Kindling the lands with fire
Everywhere . . .
Lenin! Lenin! Lenin!
I glorify in Lenin.

SOURCE 8.6 I. Deutscher, *Stalin*, rev. edn 1966, pp. 270–71. Deutscher demonstrates that Stalin's own 'Biographical Chronicle' shows how he orchestrated Lenin's funeral and put himself in the central role

21 January – *6.50a.m. Lenin dies at Gorky. 9.30a.m. Stalin and other members of Politburo arrive at Gorky.*
23 January – *9a.m. Stalin and other leaders carry coffin with Lenin's body from Lenin's home at Gorky . . . (they travel on by train) . . . to the House of Trade Unions in Moscow where Lenin lay in state for the next four days; 6.10p.m. Stalin stands in the guard of honour at the bier.*
25 January – *Stalin calls upon the party to collect relics of Lenin for the newly founded Lenin Institute.*
26 January – *At the second congress of the Soviets, Stalin reads an oath of allegiance to Lenin.*
27 January – *9a.m. Stalin and others carry the coffin out of the House of Trade Unions; 4p.m. End of the funeral procession at the Red Square – Stalin and others carry the coffin into the future mausoleum.*
28 January – *Stalin addresses a memorial meeting.*

The cult of Leninism

The Lenin cult had begun just after the attempt on his life in 1918 (see page 97). Stalin gave it new momentum at Lenin's funeral. The Lenin cult was a sort of quasi-religion in which Lenin's name could be invoked like a deity or his words trotted out, much as the Bible is used to justify actions. At least, Stalin used it this way. Lenin made it clear before he died that he did not want this kind of adulation. His wife, Krupskaya, publicly asked that there should be 'no external reverence for his person'. But under pressure from Stalin, Lenin was embalmed and his tomb turned into a shrine. Lenin's brain was sliced into 30,000 segments and stored so that scientists in the future could discover the secrets of his genius.

All sorts of Lenin memorabilia, from posters to matchboxes, were produced. Statues of Lenin appeared all over the Soviet Union. Petrograd was renamed Leningrad and many streets and institutions were named after him. Trotsky was sickened by the whole business, but it was difficult to speak out against it without being accused of disloyalty and disrespect.

C Summing up Lenin

Lenin had many qualities that proved invaluable in pushing through the October uprising in 1917 and ruling Russia in the post-revolutionary period. He had great organisational abilities and leadership skills, together with a strong personality to force through decisions in the Politburo and Central Committee. He was tough, hard and calculating, totally dedicated to politics and revolution. From October 1917 until his last major stroke in March 1923, he spent up to sixteen hours or more a day, running the Bolshevik government, making sure that the revolution survived.

Lenin was a good orator, though not brilliant in the way that Trotsky was. He did not bring his speeches to life with metaphors and well-crafted phrases. Rather his skill lay in his ability to express ideas simply and make his audience understand complicated political concepts. He was good in argument, bringing people around to his views, an essential quality in a leader. He was forceful and persuasive.

Lenin did not look for personal gain from the Revolution. He did not seek the pleasures of life like some other Bolshevik leaders. His one diversion was his romantic friendship with Inessa Armand. He lived simply with Krupskaya, whom he called 'comrade', and his sister in a three-bedroomed apartment in the Kremlin and often slept in a small room behind his offices. They ate their meals in the cafeteria. He continued the austere life of the revolutionary that he was used to. He liked things to be orderly and tidy with fixed hours for meals, sleep and work. He had little private life: his life was the Revolution.

Politics also dominated his personal friendships. He would cut off personal connections with people with whom he fell out over politics. Martov, who was a close personal friend in the early days of the Social Democratic Party, was cast off when he became a Menshevik and Lenin poured scorn upon him, something he regretted when Martov died. Lenin's attitude to political opponents was vitriolic. According to the Russian writer Maxim Gorky in 1918, Lenin's attitude was that 'who is not with us is against us'.

Lenin had a strong streak of ruthlessness and cruelty. In the late 1980s and 1990s, Soviet archives were opened up as the Communist regime came to an end. These revealed a much harder, more ruthless Lenin than the 'softer' image he had enjoyed amongst left-wing historians and groups. For instance, a memorandum, first published in 1990, reveals his ordering the extermination of the clergy in a place called Shuya after people there fought off officials who had come to raid the church. The Politburo voted to stop further raids on churches but Lenin countermanded them (see page 286). Similarly, he was vitriolic about the peasants, ordering the hanging of a hundred kulaks as a lesson to others (see page 98).

Lenin believed that revolutionaries had to be hard to carry out their role, which would inevitably involve spilling the blood of their opponents. Although hard and tough on others, it seems that Lenin was not personally brave. He was not a revolutionary who rushed to the barricades. He left the fighting to others. According to Valentinov, a revolutionary who knew him well, Lenin's rule was to 'get away while the going was good'.

Lenin's domination of the party is one of the key factors in his success. There were many disputes and splits in the party, such as the serious split over the Treaty of Brest-Litovsk, right into the 1920s. But in the end he always managed to bring the party behind him and keep it united. According to Beryl Williams (*Lenin*, 2000, page 13), Lenin's contemporaries attested to his 'hypnoptic influence'. His personal magnetism and charisma are not in doubt. But he also had tremendous political skills – of knowing when to persuade, when to cajole, when to give in, when to threaten to resign and when to get really tough and demanding. Above all, Lenin was convinced of his role and his destiny (see Source 8.8 on page 130). He never had any doubt that he knew the right path and could lead the party along it.

LENIN – THE ABSENT REVOLUTIONARY

It is strange to think that Lenin had been absent from Russia for seventeen years (apart from six months in 1905–6) before his return in April 1917. He was a professional revolutionary who knew very little about the people he had come to lead to revolution, and they knew virtually nothing about him. After the July Days he went into exile again and was not seen again until he returned secretly in October. Most people did not recognise him even in the period after the Bolsheviks took power. Trotsky was much better known and much more popular. Commentators have said that Lenin had no real knowledge of ordinary Russian people and no experience of their everyday working lives (he had only had a paid job for two years). Maxim Gorky said that his ignorance bred contempt for ordinary people and the suffering they endured.

Joseph Stalin

Joseph Dzhugashvili was born in Gori in Georgia in 1878 or 1879. He is one of the few leading revolutionaries who had a genuine working-class/peasant background. His mother was the daughter of serfs and very devout in her religious beliefs. His father was a shoemaker who worked mainly in Tiflis, some distance away. Stalin's mother brought him up virtually on her own, working hard as a seamstress and laundress to support Joseph. They were poor and he had a hard upbringing as she beat him severely for acts of disobedience. However, he did well at school and gained a place at a seminary in Tiflis to train as a priest. But the young Joseph found Marxism rather than God. He was drawn into the underground world of the revolutionaries, writing pamphlets and attending secret meetings. He particularly admired the writings of Lenin. He soon graduated to the full-time role of revolutionary, organising strikes and possibly becoming engaged in raiding banks to fill the Bolshevik Party coffers. The name he used as his first revolutionary pseudonym was Koba.

Between 1902 and 1913, he was arrested frequently and exiled to Siberia, escaping on five occasions. He was placed in a number of prisons where he gained a reputation for toughness. He became hardened, particularly after the death of his first wife in 1907. He later took on the pseudonym 'Stalin' which means 'man of steel'. In 1912, he was invited onto the Central Committee of the Bolshevik Party because they were short of working-class, leading members and Stalin remained in Russia as a point of contact, while most of the others were in exile in European countries. When the February Revolution broke in 1917, he was one of the first to arrive on the scene in Petrograd.

Stalin had not played a key role in the events of 1917. He was made editor of *Pravda*, the party newspaper, and given a seat on the Executive Committee of the Petrograd Soviet. Initially, he followed a pro-war line in accordance with the Soviet and other socialists. He changed his line when Lenin appeared on the scene and seems to have followed Lenin slavishly thereafter. Whilst close to the centre of the Party, he does not seem to have been given any discernible role. There is no evidence of Stalin taking charge of any of the events during the October Revolution. Sverdlov and Trotsky were the main organisers and Sverdlov did not like Stalin.

After the October Revolution, Stalin was made Commissar for Nationalities in the new government. His offices were close to Lenin's and it is likely that at this time he gained Lenin's trust as a devoted Bolshevik operator. In the Civil War, he was sent to Tsaritsyn (later renamed Stalingrad) to organise food supplies and defend this very important strategic position from the Whites. It was in doing this job that he came into conflict with Trotsky: Stalin did not like having to carry out Trotsky's orders and was removed from his military post for disobedience. On several occasions during the Civil War he had shown a tendency to disobey orders from the centre, even Lenin's, because he wanted to do things his own way. Lenin, however, set these 'mistakes' aside because he had other work for Stalin.

Good luck helped Stalin in his next advancements. In March 1919, Sverdlov, who had shown himself to be a great organiser, died of Spanish flu. Lenin was left with few top administrators and looked to Stalin. He appointed Stalin head of the Workers' and Peasants' Inspectorate, through which he became familiar with the work of different government departments. In May 1919, Lenin put him in charge of the Orgburo which controlled aspects of the party organisation. Stalin was also elected to the new Politburo, which from now on became the main organ of power. This was followed in 1922 by his appointment as the party's first General Secretary in charge of general organisation.

Stalin's appointment to these key positions showed how much his reputation had grown and how much trust Lenin placed in him. He gained a reputation for 'industrious mediocrity'. Other Bolsheviks saw these jobs as part of the dull routine of party bureaucracy. They were soon to find out otherwise.

Sukhanov, the diarist of the revolution, made this comment about Stalin in 1917: 'The Bolshevik Party … includes a whole series of great figures and able leaders in its general staff. Stalin, however, during the course of his modest activity in the Executive Committee gave me the impression – and I was not alone in this view – of a grey blur which flickered obscurely and left no trace. There is really nothing more to be said about him.' Stalin had his revenge. Sukhanov died in the camps in 1940.

FOCUS ROUTE

As you work through this chapter, compile a table like the one below to record information about the factors working for Stalin and against his opponents. You will be able to use this in the essay at the end of the chapter.

Factors that favoured Stalin	Weaknesses of Stalin's opponents

FOCUS ROUTE

Make brief notes on each of the leadership contenders, identifying their strengths and weaknesses as potential leaders.

A Who were the contenders?

In retrospect, it is clear that the contest for the leadership was really between Trotsky and Stalin. But this was not apparent at the time. At first, Stalin was regarded as a minor player, with the chief contenders being Trotsky on the one hand and Zinoviev and Kamenev on the other. Also, in the early stages the power struggle was more about stopping others getting to the top rather than trying to come out on top oneself.

It is useful to place the contenders for party leadership in terms of their political position in the party of 1924. There was a clear split between the radical left wing led by Trotsky and the right wing headed by Bukharin. The majority of party members lay somewhere in between. Stalin fell into this group. The men shown in Chart 9A were in the Politburo elected in June 1924.

■ 9A Contenders for leadership of the Communist Party

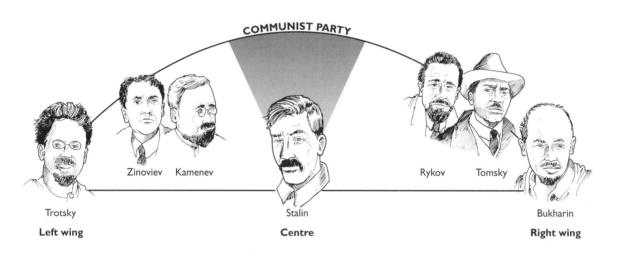

COMMUNIST PARTY

Trotsky | Zinoviev | Kamenev | Stalin | Rykov | Tomsky | Bukharin

Left wing | **Centre** | **Right wing**

Contenders

Leon Trotsky

Trotsky was the only member of the Communist Party who could rival Lenin in intellect and in his writings on Marxist theory. He was one of the Bolshevik's best orators, able to work crowds and bring them around to his point of view. He was particularly popular with the younger, more radical elements in the party. His contribution in the years 1917–24 had been second, if not equal, to that of Lenin himself. He had planned the October Revolution, persuading Lenin to wait until the end of October. His organisation of the Red Army and his drive and determination had played a significant part in bringing victory in the Civil War. His position as Commissar for War gave him a strong base in the army.

Working against him were his arrogance and aloofness. He seemed dismissive of other leading Bolsheviks, sometimes treating them with disdain and lack of respect. He was short and brusque with people who seemed to be wasting his time and he never went out of his way to endear himself to his colleagues. They felt his uncompromising views might lead to splits in the party. Many old Bolsheviks regarded Trotsky as an outsider since he had only joined the Bolshevik Party in 1917 and other party members were not convinced of his loyalty to the party. This perception was wrong: he was loyal, perhaps too loyal, and accepted decisions that he did not agree with because he did not want to damage the party.

Two other important factors worked against Trotsky in the power struggle. First, he did not like the business of political in-fighting, making deals and alliances. He preferred to work on a level where arguments were hammered out in debate or by the pen, where he was convinced of his natural superiority. This high-minded approach left him vulnerable to less scrupulous colleagues. Second, for three years from late 1923 Trotsky suffered attacks of an undiagnosed fever. This sapped his strength and left him less able to deal with the continuous political attacks mounted on him by his enemies. It also meant that he was absent for crucial votes in the Politburo, although meetings were sometimes held at his bedside.

Gregory Zinoviev

Zinoviev was an old Bolshevik, active in the party as early as 1903. He had worked closely with Lenin before the Revolution and was with Lenin on the train that pulled into Petrograd's Finland Station in 1917. However, Zinoviev opposed the armed uprising in October and fell out with Lenin about the construction of the new government; he favoured a socialist coalition. As a result, he was not given a major post in the Sovnarkom but he was made Party Secretary in Leningrad. This was an important position, allowing him to build up a strong power base. In 1919, he was made Chairman of the Comintern (see page 241) and became a full member of the Politburo in 1921. He was a good orator but not an intellectual. He was not popular, being seen by others as vain, incompetent and cowardly, making himself scarce when things got dangerous. No one seemed to like him. Victor Serge said he gave 'an impression of flabbiness ... irresolution' and was 'simply a demagogue'. The historian E. H. Carr said he was 'weak, vain, ambitious [and] only too eager to occupy the empty throne' (*The Russian Revolution from Lenin to Stalin*, 1979, page 64).

Lev Kamenev

Kamenev was an active Bolshevik and full-time revolutionary from 1905. He was a close collaborator with Lenin abroad from 1907 to 1917. He was a major contributor to party doctrine and had heated debates with Lenin, who regarded him as able and reliable. In 1917, he opposed Lenin's April Theses on ideological grounds. With Zinoviev, he opposed the armed uprising in October 1917 and wanted a socialist coalition government. This lost him influence in the party but he was made Party Secretary in Moscow and later Commissar for Foreign Trade. This brought him into the Politburo and into a position to challenge for the leadership. He was a moderate, liked and well regarded. But he was much too soft to become a real leader. In his book *Socialism in One Country* (1958), E. H. Carr describes Kamenev as intellectually superior to Stalin and Zinoviev but 'by far the least effective of the three ... Kamenev had neither the desire nor the capacity to lead men; he lacked any clear vision of a goal towards which he might have led them' (pages 161, 162).

Nikolai Bukharin

Bukharin was one of the younger generation of Bolsheviks. Born in 1888, the son of a schoolmaster, he was nearly a decade younger than Stalin. He had joined the Bolshevik Party in 1906, was arrested in 1912, and then escaped to Germany. He had become a major figure in the party before 1917, close to Lenin. He was an important theorist who argued with Lenin about political strategy. He took a leading role on *Pravda*, the party newspaper, during 1917. He led the left-wing opposition to the signing of the Treaty of Brest-Litovsk and between 1920 and 1921 criticised Trotsky and Lenin in the 'trade-union' controversy (see page 105). He did not become a full member of the Politburo until 1922.

Bukharin was intellectually inquisitive. He did not accept that only Marxists could contribute to knowledge about history and politics. He loved poetry and novels and was a talented painter. He liked to enjoy life and was very popular. Even his opponents found it hard to dislike him. Lenin called him 'the golden boy' of the Bolshevik Party. He was not a saint and could argue his points fiercely, especially on the NEP. He did not have the skills and political cunning of Stalin. In his testament, Lenin called Bukharin 'the biggest and most valuable theoretician in the Party' and 'the favourite of the whole Party'.

Alexei Rykov

Alexei Rykov, born in 1881 into a peasant family, became chairman of Vesenhka (Supreme Economic Council) in 1918 and later succeeded Lenin as Chairman of the Sovnarkom, having been his deputy from 1921. He was outspoken, frank and direct, not always endearing himself to his colleagues. He was a strong supporter of the NEP and opposed any return to War Communism. He was more statesmanlike than many of his colleagues but a notorious drinker: in some circles, vodka was known as Rykova.

Mikhail Tomsky

Mikhail Tomsky, born in 1880, was an important figure in the trade union movement, being an active member of the metalworkers' union before 1917. In 1918, he was made Chairman of the Central Council of Trade Unions. He was one of the few genuine workers in the party leadership. He fought hard for workers to have trade union rights and was dismayed by the reduction of trade unions to an 'appendage of the state'. He opposed Lenin in the trade union debate of 1920.

ACTIVITY

Stage 2
You have now read about the main contenders for the leadership of the Communist state. Which of them best meets the criteria that you drew up in Stage 1 of this Activity on page 135? Do you now wish to change your mind about the key characteristics/qualities the new leader should have?

TROTSKY – A DICTATOR?

Trotsky had no intention of becoming a dictator and had always been aware of the tendency for this to happen after a revolution. In 1904, he had warned that if a small party seized power, then: 'The organisation of the Party takes the place of the Party itself; the Central Committee takes the place of the organisation; and finally the dictator takes the place of the Central Committee.' He did not attempt to use the Red Army to secure his position. He was to argue for more democracy and openness in the party in the mid-1920s. However, some commentators have suggested that, whatever he said, he was dictatorial in style and may have acted accordingly if he had become leader.

B What were the main issues in the leadership struggle?

When we study power struggles in history we, quite naturally, focus on the personalities involved, their strengths and weaknesses, and why one emerged stronger than others. We see the struggle as a sort of contest of wills in which the contestants possess or do not possess certain qualities that allow one of them to come out on top. Whilst this is certainly important, we also have to look at the issues that were uppermost in people's minds when the struggle was taking place. These may be just as important in persuading people to support one candidate rather than another. This is particularly the case in the Soviet Union where there was a very real and contentious debate about government policy and the road to socialism. The key issues here were to do with leadership, industrialisation and party policy.

1 The nature of the leadership

Many party members did not want to see one person running the party and the government; they favoured 'collective leadership' or rule by committee. During the Civil War, the state had become highly centralised, with Lenin taking executive decisions. Now that the situation was more settled, it was thought that a collective leadership would be a more socialist way of running the state.

Party members feared that a 'dictator' could emerge to take control of the centralised state that had developed by 1924. This fear affected the decisions party members took between 1924 and 1926 – and the man they feared was Trotsky. As commander of the Red Army, he was in a strong position to crush opposition. His arrogant manner and conviction that he knew the direction the party should take seemed to confirm such fears.

Party members were also worried about the unity of the party after Lenin's death. They knew it was essential that the party stick together if it were to accomplish the huge task of transforming an unwilling population into good socialists. They therefore did not want a leader who might cause divisions among the different wings of the party and split it into warring factions. Again, it was Trotsky they feared.

2 The NEP and the industrialisation debate

The issue that dominated party conferences in the mid-1920s was the NEP and how the economy should be run. Everybody agreed on the need to industrialise. Industrialisation was the key to creating a large class of proletarian workers to build socialism. The question was how to do this in the most effective way. As the 1920s progressed, the NEP became increasingly unattractive to party members and they were deeply disturbed by its outward manifestations – the growth of a rich superclass, property dealing, land speculation, gambling and prostitution. These did not have any place in a socialist state. Also, after 1925 serious problems began to emerge:

- By 1925–26, industry had recovered to its pre-1913 levels. Some new impetus was needed to take it on but there was argument about where the resources to do this were going to come from.
- There was a high level of unemployment amongst workers. Wages for those in work did not keep pace with the rising prices of consumer goods, always in short supply. So many workers remained relatively poor and many could not get jobs – in the workers' society!
- Food shortages started to reappear. Peasants held on to their produce because they could not buy much for their money.

It was against this backdrop that the power struggle took place. It was a question not so much of whether party members supported the NEP – they had only accepted it as a stop-gap measure – but of when and how it should be ended. It was on this point that the two wings of the party diverged.

- The left wing of the party, led by Trotsky, Zinoviev and Kamenev, wanted to end the NEP and go for rapid industrialisation. This entailed the militarisation of labour, breaking the stranglehold the peasants had on the economy and squeezing more grain out of them to pay for industrialisation.
- The right wing, led by Bukharin, wanted to keep the NEP going and to encourage the peasants to become richer, so that they would spend more on consumer goods, which would, in turn, lead to the growth of manufacturing industry. They believed that conflict with the peasants might lead to economic collapse and endanger the Communist state.

(You can find out more about this debate and how it was resolved in Chapter 10.)

FOCUS ROUTE

1 Make notes summarising the key issues facing the party in the 1920s.
2 Which contender would be most hindered by the leadership issue?
3 How do you think the divisive NEP debate would affect the chances of particular contenders?
4 Which policy – 'Permanent Revolution' or 'Socialism in One Country' – do you think would most appeal to party members after so many years of conflict? Which contender would this help most?
5 Add any relevant information to the table you started on page 136.

ACTIVITY

Study Source 9.1.

1 What does the horse represent?
2 Who are the people on the sledge?
3 Why do you think the artist used the image of a horse and sledge?
4 How does this cartoon reveal the stance of Kamenev and the Left towards the NEP?

SOURCE 9.1 A 1924 cartoon showing Kamenev's stance on the NEP. The horse has the letters NEP on its collar

Why was the NEP so crucial to discussions in the party in the 1920s?

a) The NEP was crucial because economic policy was at the centre of the debate about the nature of the society the Communists were trying to create. It was a passionate issue. How long should they allow rich traders and peasants effectively to control the new workers' society? When could they push forward to industrialisation?

b) Attitudes in the party towards the NEP changed during the 1920s because economic circumstances were changing. In 1924, the NEP was still delivering economic recovery, but after 1925 problems started mounting. A threat of war in 1928 provided an added spur to industrialise more quickly, as did food shortages in the cities after 1927. So, party members, who had been prepared to go along with the NEP in the mid-1920s, might have adopted a different position in the late 1920s. The positions that the contenders took on this issue during the 1920s would therefore influence the amount of support they got from different sections of the party.

3 'Permanent Revolution' versus 'Socialism in One Country'

Another important issue in the 1920s was the overall policy that the party should develop for the future, now that the USSR was the only Communist state in the world and world revolution had not taken place. Trotsky and Stalin developed different lines on this.

Permanent Revolution

Trotsky believed in 'Permanent Revolution'. He was convinced that the Communist revolution in Russia could not really succeed because the Russian working class was too small and the economy underdeveloped; it needed the support of the working class in the more industrialised countries of Europe. Trotsky felt therefore that the Russians should put energy and money into helping the working class in other countries to stage their own revolutions. He believed that the Russians should go on fighting a 'permanent revolution' until a world Communist revolution had been achieved.

Trotsky also wanted to subject the USSR to a continuing revolutionary process that would move society in the direction of socialism. He believed that measures such as compulsory labour units organised along military lines and forcing peasants into collective farms might be necessary to squeeze out old attitudes and create the economic base on which a socialist society could be built.

Socialism in One Country

Towards the end of 1924, Stalin put forward a different policy line that he called 'Socialism in One Country'. He said that the Communists had to accept that the world revolution had not happened and was not likely to take place in the immediate future. He proposed that the Russians build a socialist state in the USSR without the help of people from outside. Appealing to nationalism and patriotism, he said that they were in a unique position to show the world what socialism meant. They would solve their own problems and create a workers' society that was vastly superior to the capitalist West. They would be world leaders. It was also a very flexible doctrine because it meant that the leaders of the Communist Party could say what was the best way to achieve socialism at any particular moment in time.

Stage 3

Having looked at the issues which divided the party, delete from the list you produced for the Activity on page 135 any characteristics/qualities that you think would **not** be useful in a new leader. Add new ones (or ones from the original list) that you now think would be helpful. In small groups, discuss your final lists and then compare them with other groups to see if you have reached any consensus.

■ 9B Summary: Three key issues affecting the power struggle

1 **LEADERSHIP**

Collective?   Single person (danger of dictatorship)?

2 **NEP**

End now?   Keep going?

3 **PARTY POLICY ABOUT DIRECTION OF REVOLUTION**

Permanent Revolution?   Socialism in One Country?

BEFORE THE BOUT BEGINS
- The positions Stalin held in the party administration – General Secretary from 1922, and member of the Orgburo and Secretariat – gave him enormous power over the policy and personnel of the party. This was the case even before Lenin died, but his rivals did not realise it and underestimated him.
- The ban on factions in 1921 was potentially a devastating weapon in the hands of the man who could control votes at party congresses.

Round 1: Stalin ahead on points
Stalin struck two significant blows at Lenin's funeral:
- He tricked Trotsky into not turning up for the funeral, severely damaging Trotsky's reputation and political prestige (see page 127).
- He made the most of the funeral, setting himself up as Lenin's disciple, the person who would carry on Lenin's work (see page 127).

Round 2: Stalin dodges a knock-out blow
Krupskaya gave Lenin's secret testament (see page 127) to the Central Committee in May 1924 just before the Thirteenth Party Congress. If read out to the congress, it would have spelt the end of Stalin's career. But Zinoviev and Kamenev urged that it should not become general knowledge, probably because
- it was not very flattering about them because of their opposition to Lenin in 1917; this was not something they wanted to bring to the congress's attention when they hoped to become its leading lights
- they thought that Stalin presented no real threat to them or the party and they wanted Stalin's help in defeating Trotsky
- they thought the testament might help Trotsky.
Trotsky remained silent, unwilling to become involved. This was a major mistake on his part and was to cost him dearly later.

Round 3: Trotsky on the ropes
The Thirteenth Congress in 1924 saw hostilities out in the open. Zinoviev, Kamenev and Stalin, now effectively a triumvirate leading the party, presented party policy at the congress. Trotsky criticised the party for becoming bureaucratic and less democratic. Despite making brilliant speeches, Trotsky was easily defeated in the votes because the congress was packed with 'well-instructed Stalinist delegates' as well as the powerful blocs controlled by Zinoviev and Kamenev. Trotsky could have appealed to supporters inside and outside the party, but he had approved the 'ban on factions' in 1921 and was unwilling to cause splits in the party.

Round 5: Knockout blow for the left

In 1925, Stalin's policy of 'Socialism in One Country' proved very popular with party members, attracting the right wing of the party because it seemed to fit in with the NEP – their own route to socialism. A new alliance emerged between Stalin in the centre of the party and Bukharin on the right, supporting NEP and co-operation with the peasants. At the Fourteenth Party Congress in 1925, Zinoviev and Kamenev attacked Stalin, calling for a vote of no confidence in him, the ending of the NEP and a tough line against the peasants. But Stalin's control of the party machine was now so complete that they gave him little trouble. They lost every vote because Stalin had control of the delegates.

In 1926, they joined Trotsky, their old enemy, to form a 'United Opposition' and made a direct appeal to the party masses and the workers, trying to organise demonstrations in Moscow. This was a mistake because they could now be accused of 'factionalism'. As a result, all three lost their positions of power (see page 143) and in 1927 were expelled from the party.

The winner

In December 1929, Stalin celebrated his fiftieth birthday. He was now the undisputed leader of the USSR.

Round 4: The left slugs it out

In 1924, Zinoviev and Kamenev mounted a vicious campaign against Trotsky, questioning his loyalty and raising his opposition to Lenin before 1917. Trotsky retaliated by attacking them in *Lessons of October*, in which he criticised their unwillingness to back Lenin in the 1917 revolution. Stalin stayed in the background, happy to see the left wing tearing itself apart while he continued to build his power base. He seemed to be the moderate peacemaker, anxious to maintain party unity. Zinoviev and Kamenev, still frightened of Trotsky, allowed Stalin to bring more of his supporters into key positions in the party organisation, forming the majorities on committees and at conferences.

Round 6: Knockout blow for the right

In 1928, Stalin turned against the NEP and attacked the right wing of the party. He now advocated rapid industrialisation and the use of force to make the peasants co-operate – the very policies of the left that he had just smashed! Bukharin mounted a strong defence of the NEP but at the congress of 1929 found himself outvoted by Stalin's supporters, who were joined by those on the left who supported the anti-NEP line. Bukharin and the other right-wing leaders, Rykov and Tomsky, were removed from the Politburo and other party bodies (Rykov had been Premier since Lenin's death and Bukharin had been head of the Comintern).

D Why did Stalin become party leader?

ACTIVITY

1 You will already have developed your own ideas about why Stalin emerged as the leader of Soviet Russia by 1929. The writers of Sources 9.3–9.10 indicate some of the key reasons why they think Stalin won the power struggle and whether this was to do with his skills or the weaknesses of his opponents. Read the sources carefully. Decide which column of the table below they would fit into.

Importance of control of party organisation	Policies	Stalin's personal characteristics and political skills	Weaknesses of opponents, especially Trotsky	Luck

2 How do these sources suggest that perceptions of Stalin changed considerably between 1924 and 1928?
3 What does this tell us about how Stalin conducted his campaign for the leadership?
4 Add new information from these sources to the table of factors which helped Stalin and worked against his opponents (page 136).

SOURCE 9.3 G. Hosking, *A History of the Soviet Union*, 1985, p. 140

To his comrades in the Party leadership he [Stalin] was known, rather condescendingly, as 'Comrade Card-Index' (Tovarishch Kartotekov): they were content to leave him to assemble and classify the personnel files, not yet realising what power was accumulating therein. Most of them, being well read in the history of past revolutions, were obsessed by a very different danger: that of finding the revolutions hijacked by another Bonaparte.
[Note: Bolsheviks were very knowledgeable about the French Revolution and expected, after the initial period of violent revolution, that a Napoleon Bonaparte figure would emerge as a dictator in Russia.]

SOURCE 9.4 I. Deutscher, *The Prophet Unarmed: Trotsky 1921–29*, 1959, p. 93

The truth is that Trotsky refrained from attacking Stalin because he felt secure. No contemporary, and he least of all, saw in the Stalin of 1923 the menacing and towering figure he was to become. It seemed to Trotsky almost a bad joke that Stalin, the wilful and sly but shabby and inarticulate man in the background, should be his rival.

SOURCE 9.5 E. H. Carr, *Socialism in One Country*, 1958, p. 151

[Trotsky] ... the great intellectual, the great administrator, the great orator lacked one quality essential – at any rate in the conditions of the Russian Revolution – to the great political leader. Trotsky could fire masses of men to acclaim and follow him. But he had no talent for leadership among equals. He could not establish his authority among colleagues by the modest arts of persuasion or by sympathetic attention to the views of men of lesser intellectual calibre than himself.

SOURCE 9.6 Bukharin, at a secret meeting with Kamenev in July 1928

Stalin is a Genghis Khan, an unscrupulous intriguer, who sacrifices everything else to the preservation of power ... He changes his theories according to whom he needs to get rid of next.

SOURCE 9.7 I. Deutscher, *Stalin*, rev. edn, 1966, p. 277

In the Politburo, when matters of high policy were under debate, he [Stalin] never seemed to impose his views on his colleagues. He carefully followed the course of debate to see what way the wind was blowing and invariably voted with the majority, unless he had assured his majority beforehand. He was therefore always agreeable to the majority. To Party audiences he appeared as a man without personal grudge and rancour, as a detached Leninist, a guardian of the doctrine who criticised others only for the sake of the cause.

SOURCE 9.8 C. Ward, *Stalin's Russia*, 1993, pp. 35–36

All Bolshevik leaders were trying to find their feet in an unfamiliar and unanticipated world, and the doctrine of socialism in one country at least had the merit of describing things as they really were ... The theory evoked a sympathetic response from two groups: the new sub-elites advanced by the crises of the immediate post-evolutionary years and workers sickened by the manifold injustices and inequalities of the NEP. The latter were men and women indifferent to factional squabbles and impatient for socialist reconstruction; the former were people ... for whom the Revolution was primarily a Russian achievement – Soviet patriotism sat easily with the enjoyment of the fruits of offices. A Stalinist constituency was in the process of formation and Stalin's 'left turn' (rapid industrialisation and collectivisation) brought most of them round to his way of thinking.

SOURCE 9.9 R. Conquest, *Stalin: Breaker of Nations*, 1991, pp. 129–30

In 1923 Stalin had been on the point of political ruin. In 1924 he was one among equals, but without any outright supporters in the full membership of the Politburo. Six years later he would be in unchallenged power ... In six years Stalin outmanoeuvred a series of opponents; first in alliance with the rest of his colleagues, he opposed and demoted Trotsky. Then in alliance with the Bukharin–Rykov 'Right' he defeated the Zinoviev–Kamenev 'Left' bloc ... and finally he and his own following attacked their hitherto allies, the 'Rightists'.

SOURCE 9.10 M. McCauley, *Russia 1917–41*, 1997, p. 78

Stalin had luck on his side. Had Lenin not died Stalin would probably have been sent to the provinces to work for the Party. Dzerzhinsky, the head of the Cheka, from its inception to his death in 1926, was never one of Stalin's fans. His death allowed Stalin to infiltrate his supporters into the political police and eventually use them against his opponents.

ACTIVITY

Write an essay entitled: Why did Stalin rather than Trotsky emerge as the leader of the USSR in 1929?

You will have collected a lot of information to help you to answer this question as part of the Focus Route activity on page 136 but how are you going to structure your essay and deploy the information? The twenty-one cards on page 148 can help you to do this. Five of the cards are paragraph headings. They represent the **main points** which directly answer the essay question. The other cards represent points which **support** the main points.

1 Using your own copy of the cards and working in groups of three or four, find the **main points** and arrange them in a row. Then find the **supporting points** that go with each main point and put them in the correct column. The columns are not evenly balanced. Some main points have three cards, others have only two.

2 But how much weight should you give to each of the different explanations – which are the most important reasons? Try this: choose **nine** cards that you think are the most important in answering this question. Arrange them in the shape of a diamond like the one shown here. Put the one you think is the most important at the top, the next two most important on the second line and so on. (N.B. We have **not** shown a correct answer in the example.)

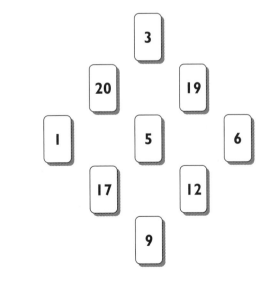

3 Discuss the cards you chose and the order you put them in with other members of the class. Argue the case for your ordering compared with theirs.

4 Now write your essay. Don't just use the information given on the cards. Use the rest of the information in this chapter to develop your points fully. You don't have to stick to our paragraph headings. The important thing is that you decide what your main points are to answer the question and how you are going to explain/support these main points.

1	2	3	4
Stalin had control of the party machine through his key positions in the Politburo and Orgburo and as General Secretary.	Stalin stayed in the background pretending to be a moderate peacemaker. So no one realised he was a serious power player. He outmanoeuvred his opponents, playing them off against each other.	Luck favoured Stalin rather than Trotsky.	Socialism in One Country was more appealing to most party members than Permanent Revolution. It gave Russians a special historic role.
5	**6**	**7**	**8**
Stalin made full use of Lenin's funeral to advance his position. He tricked Trotsky into not attending the funeral. He took on the mantle of Leninism to transfer Lenin's prestige to himself.	Stalin's personal characteristics and qualities helped him become leader of the party.	Stalin was able to appoint his own supporters to key positions in the party. He controlled the membership of the party, using his power to expel members likely to support Trotsky and bring in new members likely to support him.	Stalin was politically very skilful and cunning.
9	**10**	**11**	**12**
Stalin was perceived as dull and mediocre – the 'grey blur'. So no one saw him as a threat until it was too late. He was tough and ruthless. He was determined to protect his power base and make sure that he was not ousted.	Trotsky himself was responsible for his own downfall. He had weaknesses that made him unfit for the power struggle.	Lenin and Sverdlov died at the right time for Stalin.	Trotsky had only joined the Bolsheviks in August 1917 and was not seen as a loyal member of the party. Many Bolsheviks did not trust him. They thought he might try to become a dictator.
13	**14**	**15**	**16**
Stalin's different positions on the NEP during the mid to late 1920s and his decision to go for rapid industrialisation at the end of the 1920s were supported by the majority of party members.	Less high-minded, more down to earth and practical than other leading Bolsheviks, Stalin was ideally suited to managing the bureaucratic and centralised party that had developed.	Trotsky was too high-minded and arrogant, dismissive of his colleagues. He was respected but did not engender affection or personal loyalty. He was seen as the person most likely to cause splits in the party.	Stalin's control of appointments and the membership made him a useful ally. Other contenders wanted him on their side because he could deliver votes in the congresses.
17	**18**	**19**	**20**
Trotsky did not go out of his way to develop or build up his power base in the party and allowed Stalin to erode the one he already had. Like the other contenders, he underestimated Stalin and was outmanoeuvred by him.	Stalin was a very loyal party member who was one of the few leaders with proletarian roots. It seemed he would not cause splits in the party.	Stalin adopted policies that were broadly approved by the majority of the Communist Party. He was responsive to the mood of the times.	Trotsky did not like getting involved in the 'drudgery of politics'. He was no good at political intrigue, making alliances and trade-offs.
			21
			It was lucky for Stalin that Lenin's testament was not read out and that Trotsky was ill for most of the power struggle.

What happened to Trotsky and the other leadership contenders?

In January 1925, Trotsky lost his position as Commissar for Military Affairs; in December of the same year he lost his Politburo seat. Zinoviev was sacked as Leningrad Soviet Chairman in January 1926 and was ousted from the Politburo in July. Kamenev lost his Politburo seat at the same time and in October was removed as leader of the Comintern. In 1927, all three were expelled from the party because of their role in the United Opposition, when they campaigned for more democracy and openness in the party. Factionalism had been banned in 1921.

Kamenev and Zinoviev, demoralised, recanted their views and petitioned to be allowed to rejoin the party. They were readmitted in June 1928. Trotsky refused to recant and in 1928, on Stalin's orders, found himself being bundled in his pyjamas into a train heading for central Asia. He was allowed to go with his secretaries and around 30 other oppositionists to Alma-ata, almost 5000 km from Moscow. The following year he was deported to Turkey, where he started to write his account of the Russian Revolution and to mount what turned out to be a continuous attack on Stalin over the next decade. In 1933, he moved to France and then on to Norway, but his political activities did not make him welcome in Europe and in 1937 he went to live in Mexico. He was always under threat from Stalin's agents and in August 1940 was murdered by a hit man with an ice-pick.

Bukharin, Rykov and Tomsky suffered a similar fate. Accused of 'right deviation', in 1929 they lost their posts. Bukharin was ousted from the Politburo and lost his posts as editor of *Pravda* and President of the Comintern. All three later recanted their views and were allowed to remain in the party. Bukharin made a major contribution in writing the Soviet constitution of 1936 but this did not save him from trial and execution later in the 1930s (see Chapter 13).

KEY POINTS FROM CHAPTER 9   **How did Stalin emerge as the sole leader of Russia?**

1 The main protagonists in the power struggle were Stalin and Trotsky. Zinoviev, Kamenev and Bukharin were also contenders.
2 Key issues – leadership, the NEP, policies – were as important as the personalities involved.
3 It was a struggle *over* power rather than a struggle *for* power. The contenders were anxious to prevent rivals from coming to power and pursuing policies with which they did not agree.
4 On the whole, party members tended to support Stalin's changes of policy line. They supported Socialism in One Country and his line on the peasants at the end of the 1920s.
5 Stalin's control of the party machine was a crucial factor in his success.
6 Stalin was a skilful politician who outmanoeuvred his opponents, but he was also lucky.
7 Trotsky's weaknesses and errors of judgement were important factors in his defeat.
8 All Stalin's opponents vastly underestimated him.

How did Stalin transform the economy of the USSR in the 1930s?

4

SOURCE 1 S. Fitzpatrick, *The Russian Revolution 1917–1932*, 1994, pp. 9–10

In theory, industrialization and economic modernization were only means to an end for Russian Marxists, the end being socialism. But the more clearly and single-mindedly the Bolsheviks focused on the means, the more foggy, distant and unreal the end became. When the term 'building socialism' came into common use in the 1930s, its meaning was hard to distinguish from the actual building of new factories and towns currently in progress.

SOURCE 3 R. W. Davies, 'Stalin and Soviet Industrialization', *History Sixth*, March 1991

This was the first attempt at the comprehensive planning of a major economy, and was thus an important turning point not only for Russian history, but also for the history of world industrialization ... In 1929, Stalin launched the so-called 'socialist offensive', which combined rapid industrialization with the forcible collectivization of peasant agriculture.

At the end of the 1920s, Stalin launched radical economic policies that literally changed the face of Russia, creating a new industrial and agricultural landscape. In Russia this was called the 'Great Turn'. Historians have talked about a second revolution (1917 being the first) and a 'revolution from above' since it was instigated by Stalin and the Communist leadership. The NEP was cast aside and Stalin introduced Five-Year Plans for industry and agriculture. Chapter 10 examines the reasons for the Great Turn. Chapter 11 looks at the collectivisation of Soviet agriculture and Chapter 12 looks at Stalin's programme for rapid industrialisation. A cultural revolution accompanied the Great Turn and this is covered later, in Chapter 18.

SOURCE 2 Stalin, writing in *Pravda*, 5 February 1931

To lower the tempo [of industrialisation] means falling behind and those who fall behind get beaten. But we don't want to be beaten ... The history of old Russia consisted, amongst other things, in her being beaten continually for her backwardness. She was beaten by the Mongol khans. She was beaten by the Turkish beys ... She was beaten by the Polish and Lithuanian gentry. She was beaten by the Anglo-French capitalists. She was beaten by the Japanese barons. She was beaten by all of them because of her backwardness, her military backwardness, cultural backwardness, political backwardness, industrial backwardness, agricultural backwardness ... We are fifty or a hundred years behind the advanced countries. We must make good this distance in ten years. Either we do it, or we shall be crushed.

SOURCE 4 Stalin, in an article entitled 'Year of the Great Breakthrough', *Pravda*, 7 November 1929

From small, backward, individual farming to large-scale, advanced, collective farming. The new and decisive feature of the peasant collective farm movement is that the peasants are joining the collective farms not in separate groups, but in whole villages, whole regions, whole districts, and even whole provinces ... We are becoming a country of metal, an automobilised country, a tractorised country. And when we have put the USSR on an automobile, and the muzhik [peasant] on a tractor, let the esteemed capitalists, who boast their 'civilisation', try to overtake us.

151

HOW DID STALIN TRANSFORM THE ECONOMY OF THE USSR IN THE 1930S?

SOURCE 5 Uzbek peasants in Samarkand crowd around a tractor for a lesson in the new farming methods. The tractor came to symbolise the changes taking place in the countryside; children were even named 'Tractor' in honour of the new machines

SOURCE 6 Workers looking at a board showing production plans and targets

SOURCE 7 A propaganda poster, made during the First Five-Year Plan, showing Stalin marching alongside miners

SOURCE 8 Workers digging in Magnitogorsk, an industrial centre that expanded rapidly in the early 1930s

SOURCE 9 A women's construction brigade, whose job was to build a factory in Moscow, 1931

10

Why did Stalin make the Great Turn?

CHAPTER OVERVIEW Under the NEP the Soviet Union had recovered from seven years of warfare (1914–21), but by 1927 it had not developed its industry much beyond the pre-1914 level and its agriculture was still backward. Also, by the late 1920s the NEP was presenting the Communists with a variety of economic and social problems. Stalin, with the support of the majority of the party, felt that the NEP was not delivering the economic performance or the type of society they had envisaged. They wanted to press ahead with rapid industrialisation to build a socialist society. In this chapter we look at the reasons for the Great Turn.

A What were the driving forces behind Stalin's economic policies? (pp. 152–153)

B Was the NEP working at the end of the 1920s? (pp. 154–156)

C The Great Turn (pp. 156–157)

A What were the driving forces behind Stalin's economic policies?

FOCUS ROUTE

Make notes on the reasons why Stalin wanted to industrialise the USSR as rapidly as possible.

The overriding aim of Stalin's policies was to industrialise and modernise the USSR as quickly as possible. He wanted backward Russia to become the 'Soviet America'. The Russians would beat the capitalists at their own game and become a force in the world to be reckoned with. Stalin had a number of reasons – practical and ideological – for wanting to force the pace.

Why did Stalin want to industrialise the USSR so quickly?

1 To increase military strength
Stalin knew that a country that was not industrialised was a weak country. To fight a modern war, a country had to have a well-developed industrial base to manufacture the huge quantities of weapons and munitions that would be required. There was a war scare in the late 1920s, and during the 1930s Stalin became increasingly convinced that the USSR would be attacked.

2 To achieve self-sufficiency
Stalin wanted to make the USSR much less dependent on Western manufactured goods, especially the heavy industrial plant that was needed for industrial production. It was important that the USSR had a strong industrial base to produce the goods its people needed. This would make it self-sufficient and more independent in the world.

3 To increase grain supplies
Stalin wanted to end the dependence of the economy on a backward agricultural system. In the past, this had created major problems whenever there was a bad harvest or the peasants did not produce enough food. He did not want the new socialist state to be at the mercy of the peasantry.

4 To move towards a socialist society

According to Marxist theoreticians, socialism could only be created in a highly industrialised state where the overwhelming majority of the population were workers. In 1928, only about twenty per cent of the population of the USSR were workers.

5 To establish his credentials

Stalin needed to prove to himself and other leading Bolsheviks that he was the successor and equal of Lenin. His economic policies were central to this. The economic transformation of the USSR, taking the revolution forward in a giant leap towards socialism, would establish him as a leader of historic importance.

6 To improve standards of living

Stalin wanted to catch up with the West, not just militarily, but also in terms of the standard of living that people enjoyed. Industrialisation created wealth for a society. The Communist life should be a good life and people in other parts of the world should appreciate what it had to offer working people.

■ **Learning trouble spot**

Why did industrialisation depend on agriculture in the USSR?

To industrialise a country you need to spend money on factories, machinery and equipment to produce goods. This is called capital investment. Initially, the machinery and equipment have to be bought from foreign countries. The USSR had gold, furs, timber, oil and a range of products to export, but these could not generate the sums of money needed to pay for heavy industrial equipment on the scale Stalin required.

The Soviet Union was not in a position to obtain loans from abroad (as the tsars had done); few Western capitalists would invest in a Communist state. The only source which could generate enough wealth was agriculture. Surplus grain could be exported to earn foreign currency to buy industrial capital equipment. On top of this, the peasants were required to produce extra grain to feed a growing workforce in the cities. This meant that every year the state had to obtain from the peasants food for the cities as well as grain for export. The problem for the Communist government was that agricultural production was in the hands of the millions of peasants who could hold the great socialist experiment to ransom. If they did not yield up sufficient grain, the push to industrialisation could not move forward.

COMMUNISTS AND PEASANTS

Lenin, Stalin and other leading Communists had never had much time for the peasants. The conservative tendencies of the peasants and their petty-bourgeois attitudes had no place in the new state. Lenin looked forward to huge factory farms where the agricultural workers would be no different from their industrial brothers, all part of the socialist utopia. The party never really managed to secure any real hold on the mass of the peasantry and the peasants, for their part, returned the hostility.

Was the NEP working at the end of the 1920s?

FOCUS ROUTE

Why did the majority of the party think a new approach to the peasantry was required?

ACTIVITY

Work in groups of three. Each person takes on one of the roles below and has a minute to clearly explain one of the following:

a) as a bureaucrat – why more grain is needed and why it isn't reaching the markets

b) as a government official – how you are going to persuade the peasants to get more grain to the markets

c) as a peasant – how and why you will avoid supplying more grain to the markets.

After each explanation, the other two members of the group summarise what they have heard by choosing two or three key points.

THE URALS–SIBERIAN METHOD

Stalin's visit to the Urals, in January 1928, lasted for only three weeks. It is said that this is the only time he visited an agricultural area in his life. During this period, the so-called 'Urals–Siberian method' was developed. This involved encouraging poor and middle-income peasants to denounce kulaks who were 'hoarding grain'. The grain would then be seized and the kulaks arrested. The Urals–Siberian method was identified with the coercion of the peasants.

The 1926 Party Congress had charged the leadership with 'the transformation of our country from an agrarian into an industrial one, capable by its own efforts of producing the necessary means'. The push for industrialisation was on. However, at the end of the 1920s it seemed that the NEP had run out of 'push'. By 1926, the excess capacity in industry had been used up. This meant that all the factories, machinery and equipment that had existed pre-1914 had been put back into use as far as this was possible. A massive injection of capital investment was now needed to move the industrialisation process forward. To make matters worse, the economy was facing serious difficulties at the end of the 1920s.

The NEP and the peasants

Although the grain supply had increased enormously under the NEP and the fear of famine had receded, the peasants were not producing the quantities of grain the government needed for its industrialisation plans. In 1913, Russia exported twelve million tons of grain; in the best years of the NEP the amount never exceeded three million. This was having a devastating effect on foreign trade: in 1926–27 exports were at 33 per cent and imports at 38 per cent of their 1913 levels due to the decline in grain exports. So the Soviet Union could not bring in the technology (machinery, etc.) it needed for industrial expansion.

The grain was simply not reaching the market. There were a number of reasons for this:

- Agriculture was still very backward, relying on traditional methods of farming. For example, in 1927 over five million inefficient wooden ploughs were still in use.
- When the land was shared out after the revolution, peasant landholdings had tended to become smaller than before 1917. The large estates and large farms which supplied the cities had disappeared. They had been divided up amongst the land-hungry peasants. On the majority of these smaller holdings, people ate most of what they produced.
- The relationship between the government and the peasants deteriorated towards the end of the 1920s (you will find out more about this in Chapter 11).

The government tried a new tactic to encourage the peasants to put more grain on the market. It stopped collecting taxes from the peasants in the form of grain and made them pay a money tax. At the same time, the government clamped down on private traders who were paying the peasants around twice the price that the state was paying for grain. So the peasants had to sell at lower prices to the state and had to sell more than before to pay their taxes.

This worked initially, but the peasants soon got wise to the government's ploy. Since meat prices were still going up, they started to feed grain to their animals rather than sell it at low prices. Also, they found that there was not much point in having surplus money because there was little they could buy with it, since industrial consumer goods were still in short supply. So peasants started to hold back their grain from the market, hoping for the price to rise. As a result, the grain procured by the state at the end of 1927 was about three-quarters of what it had been in 1926.

Stalin sent out officials, backed by the police, to seize grain. In January 1928, he himself went to the Urals and Western Siberia on a requisitioning campaign. He got more grain, but the relationship between the peasants and the government was breaking down and there was substantial resistance to Stalin's actions. Despite resistance in the party to Stalin's methods, he used them again the following year after the poor harvest in 1928 forced the government to ration bread in the cities.

Was the NEP working for the urban workers?

The NEP had not brought great rewards for the urban workers. Although they were better off than at any time before the revolution, real wages had, by 1928, only just passed their pre-war level. True, they had an eight-hour working day and other social benefits, and in state-run factories they had some power: local trade-union representatives often sat on a panel running the factory alongside the specialist director (usually an old bourgeois manager). But most industrial organisations were still hierarchical and the trade unions tended to support government-appointed managers rather than their own members. Lenin himself had favoured schemes from the USA which used time and motion studies to speed up production.

Worse than this, thousands of workers did not have jobs at all. High unemployment persisted throughout the NEP. The workers complained bitterly about the gap between themselves and the better off. They complained about the high prices charged for food by the peasants and market traders and about the bourgeois specialists and officials who were paid so much more than they were.

Women had been particularly hard hit by the NEP. Many had been forced out of their jobs when the Red Army was demobilised or been forced to move from skilled to unskilled work. So large numbers of jobless, unsupported women ended up on the streets.

Housing was still a major problem and most workers lived in overcrowded, poor-quality houses and flats. For instance, in Smolensk in 1929, the factory committee of a cement works reported: 'Every day there are many complaints about apartments: many workers have families of six and seven people, and live in one room.' There was also a mounting crime problem in the cities. As a result of the turmoil of the war and civil war, thousands of young people were parentless and rootless, forming gangs which roamed the streets to find their victims. It was hardly the workers' paradise that the revolution had promised.

ACTIVITY

What would you advise?

You are one of Stalin's advisers. Everyone agrees on the need for industrialisation but you have to help him decide how to carry it out. Decide which policy you think is the better one for Stalin to follow. Give your reasons for choosing that policy and identify three points which would make the other policy less acceptable. You must take into account the circumstances at the end of the 1920s.

Policy 1

- Carry on with the NEP policies with some modifications. In particular, increase the price of grain to encourage the peasants, especially the best farmers, to produce more.
- This will give the peasants more money to spend on consumer goods, which will encourage growth in industry. This will increase employment and gradually improve wages.
- The state will be able to procure more grain for export and for the workers. However, in the short term there will not be so much money for investment, so industrialisation will have to proceed more slowly.
- Provide a programme of agricultural help, encouraging peasants to work together and share machinery, and even to join collective farms. The state will provide help with mechanisation, especially tractors, to increase grain production. Develop model farms for peasants to visit and educate them in modern agricultural methods.
- This is the only way to avoid a return to the days of War Communism and the conflict with the peasants that had such disastrous results in 1921. Workers will benefit in the long term.

Policy 2

- Go all out for rapid industrialisation because time is running out. Russia needs to move towards socialism and be able to defend itself. Organise workers into 'shock brigades' to achieve higher production, and keep their wages low so that all available resources can be invested in industry.
- Squeeze the peasants hard: keep the price the state pays for grain low and tax the peasants heavily. This will provide extra money to invest in industry, and grain for export in order to buy industrial machinery.
- If the peasants do not offer the grain for sale voluntarily, wring it out of them by force as in 1918.
- Encourage peasants to work on large collective farms which can be farmed more efficiently and productively. The government will provide tractors and other mechanised equipment. This will also release surplus labour to go to the cities to work in the new developing industries. Collective farms will socialise the peasants.
- Fast industrialisation will actually help the peasants because it will produce the tractors and equipment they need.

FOCUS ROUTE

Draw up a chart. On one side, make the case for continuing the NEP. On the other, put the case for a more direct, forced approach.

Continuing the NEP	Ending the NEP/rapid industrialisation

Discussion and review

The policies that you have considered in the Activity on page 155 broadly represent the positions of different groups in the Communist Party at the end of the 1920s, although they have been adapted for the purposes of this exercise.

Policy 1

The first policy is close to that of Bukharin and the right. Bukharin accepted that industrialisation was the main goal but believed that the best way to achieve this was with the co-operation of the peasantry. He thought that the 1905 Revolution had failed because there was no link between the workers and the peasants – 'the supreme lesson for us all' – and that they had been successful in 1917 because of the combination of '*a peasant war* against the landlord and a *proletarian revolution*'. It was not that he particularly liked the peasants. But he had been impressed by their fierce independence during 1920–21 and believed that trying to force the peasants to supply more grain might lead to the collapse of Soviet Russia and the end of all their revolutionary hopes.

The right, which included most of the party's agricultural experts, were prepared to take more time to achieve the desired ends. They believed it would take time to prepare Soviet agriculture for collectivisation and were not keen on Stalin's 'War Communist'-style methods of seizing grain.

Policy 2

The second policy is close to the ideas of Eugene Preobrazensky, a leading left-wing economist. He argued that the USSR had to pass through a stage of 'primitive socialist accumulation' similar to the 'primitive accumulation' that Marx identified as a stage in the development of industrialised societies. In developing capitalist societies, workers had been exploited (for example, by low wages and poor conditions) and colonies had been raided (for cheap raw materials) to provide the capital for industrial growth. In the USSR, it was the peasantry who had to be exploited through taxation and prices so that the wealth they generated could be transferred to industrial investment. For example, if the government bought cheap grain from the peasants and sold it for higher prices, the surplus money that resulted could be 'pumped' into industry. The implication of this policy was that industrial development could be funded only at the expense of the peasants. However, Preobrazensky did not advocate violence, confiscation or forced collectivisation.

C The Great Turn

At the Fifteenth Party Congress in December 1927, the announcement of the First Five-Year Plan marked the end of the NEP. The plan demanded more rapid industrialisation, setting high targets for industry to achieve. In agriculture, the plan called for collectivisation – some fifteen per cent of peasant households were to be collectivised.

The NEP had provided a 'breathing space' while industry and agriculture recovered from the dismal depths of War Communism. But it was not developing an industrial, urban, proletarian, socialist society. From the Bolsheviks' point of view, it was creating the wrong type of society. The NEP encouraged private markets, private enterprise and Nepmen. The peasants, still the great mass of the population, showed no signs of becoming good socialists and could not be relied upon to produce the grain that the state needed for its industrialisation programme.

The majority of party members had accepted the constraints of the NEP but they had never liked it. They were itching to move forward towards the establishment of a socialist society. This could only, in their eyes, be achieved with the support of a largely proletarian workforce in a highly developed industrialised society. So they warmly welcomed Stalin's 'left turn' (adopting the ideas of the left wing of the party) in his policies for the modernisation and industrialisation of the USSR. The Five-Year Plans represented a significant step towards achieving the goals of the revolution.

There was also another factor which encouraged the party to support more rapid industrialisation – the fear of invasion. By 1927, relations with France and Poland had deteriorated, Britain had broken off diplomatic relations and there were suspicions about Japanese intentions. The USSR needed an industrial base to build armaments.

The change from the NEP to Five-Year Plans is called the Great Turn because it marks a major shift in the direction of the Soviet economy towards central planning – the 'command economy'. The land was to be socialised through collectivisation; no longer would it be owned by individual peasants. Industrialisation would lead to the growth of the proletariat, along with new cities and new wealth – the 'good society' that workers aspired to – and would build a strong, self-sufficient state. This was to be the big step forward towards the new socialist society. It indicated a significant cultural shift, in the process of which 'New Soviet Man' would emerge. You can read about this in Chapter 18.

Stalin's policies were not new. Planning by the centre had been an important feature of the Soviet economy since the revolution. Lenin had assumed direct control of industry after 1917 and had kept control of the 'commanding heights' of industry (large-scale industries, banking, etc.) under the NEP. It was the way Stalin carried out his policies that was new. He was to take the planning to a level unimaginable at the time of Lenin's death in 1924 and to implement his policies in a way that few could have foreseen.

Another reason why the Great Turn is significant is that these policies also wrought great changes in the Communist Party and the relationship between the party and the people. Some historians maintain that it is at this point that the Soviet Union 'went wrong' – that it now followed a path that led to totalitarianism, tyranny and inhumanity. These historians suggest that the USSR would have done better to have continued with the NEP (see page 197).

ACTIVITY

Use the information collected in your Focus Route activities to answer the following questions.

Either:

1 Write three or four paragraphs setting out the reasons why Stalin made the Great Turn. Each paragraph should make a key point and be backed up with further explanation or supporting evidence for the key point.

Or:

2 Draw a large annotated diagram showing the issues and debates surrounding the NEP and why Stalin and the Communist Party opted for the Five-Year Plans.

KEY POINTS FROM CHAPTER 10   **Why did Stalin make the Great Turn?**

1 The NEP was not producing the sort of society that many Communists wanted by the end of the 1920s.

2 There was a continuing debate about the NEP in the Communist Party throughout the 1920s: the right wing of the party wanted to keep it and the left wing wanted to end it.

3 No Communists liked the outward manifestations of the NEP – the Nepmen and the strength of the private market. Nor did they like being held to ransom by the peasants.

4 Urban workers and Communist Party members wanted to move forward to take the revolution on and build a socialist society.

5 The workers were suffering high unemployment rates and low wages.

6 The peasantry were starting to hold back food from the market and food shortages were serious in 1928 and 1929.

7 There was a war scare in 1928 that increased fears about the Soviet Union's vulnerability to attack and made the need to produce armaments more urgent.

8 In 1928, the decision was taken to end the NEP and to embark on a massive industrialisation programme in the Five-Year Plans.

9 This has been called the Great Turn and it marked a significant shift – economic, political and cultural – in the history of the Soviet Union.

11

Was collectivisation a success?

CHAPTER OVERVIEW Stalin forced through collectivisation at an incredibly rapid pace. This caused chaos in agriculture as well as suffering and misery on a huge scale. At the end of the first wave of collectivisation, he appeared to relent and called a halt. But the next year he restarted the programme with increased vigour. Peasant attempts to resist the process proved futile. By 1932, collectivisation had resulted in an enormous drop in agricultural production and created a famine in which millions died. However, Stalin secured the surplus food he needed to feed the industrial workforce and, to some extent, to pay for industrialisation.

A Why collectivise? (pp. 158–161)

B Why was collectivisation carried out so rapidly? (p. 162)

C How was collectivisation carried out? (pp. 163–164)

D What impact did collectivisation have on the peasants? (pp. 164–170)

E Was collectivisation a success? (pp. 171–172)

A Why collectivise?

In mid-1929, less than five per cent of peasants were on collective or state farms. In January 1930, Stalin announced that around 25 per cent of the grain-producing areas were to be collectivised by the end of the year. This announcement took even his own officials by surprise. Most party members had assumed that collectivisation would be carried out on a voluntary basis and had not anticipated the speed at which it was going to take place. Some were horrified.

SOURCE 11.1 A mechanised harvester at work. The government promised that collective farms would bring modern agricultural machinery and methods to the peasants

SOURCE 11.2 Babies are settled into an outdoor nursery as their mothers march off to work in the fields of the collective farm

SOURCE 11.3 A literacy class on a collective farm

SOURCE 11.4 The slogan on this poster reads 'Come and join our kolkhoz, comrade!'

ACTIVITY

Examine Sources 11.1–11.4. They are examples of propaganda published to persuade peasants of the advantages of collectivisation. What messages do they contain about why the Communists thought collectivisation was a good thing?

FOCUS ROUTE

Make notes explaining:

a) why the Communists saw collectivisation as the solution to the problems facing Soviet agriculture

b) how a KOLKHOZ worked and its relationship with the towns and with machine and tractor stations (MTS).

KOLKHOZ
Collective farm.

What was a collective farm?

There were three main types of collective farm:

- the toz, where peasants owned their own land but shared machinery and co-operated in activities like sowing and harvesting. This type was more common before 1930
- the sovkhoz, which was owned and run by the state. The peasants who worked on this state farm were paid a regular wage, very much like factory workers
- the kolkhoz, where all the land was held in common and run by an elected committee. To form a kolkhoz, between 50 and 100 households were put together. All land, tools and livestock had to be pooled. Under the direction of the committee, the peasants farmed the land as one unit. However, each household was allowed to keep its own private plot of up to one acre. They could use this to grow vegetables and keep a cow, a pig and fowl.

The original aim of collectivisation was to create more sovkhozes, but the kolkhoz with private plots became the type most favoured by the Communists in the collectivisation process of the 1930s.

Why did the Communists think collectivisation was the solution to the USSR's agricultural problems?

1 Larger units of land could be farmed more efficiently through the use of mechanisation. Tractors and other machinery would be supplied by the state through huge machine and tractor stations (MTS). Experts could help peasants to farm in more modern ways using metal ploughs and fertilisers. The net result would be much higher food production.

2 Mechanised agriculture would require fewer peasants to work the land. This would release labour for the new industries.

3 It would be much easier for the state to procure the grain it needed for the cities and for export. There would be fewer collection points and each farm would have Communist supporters who would know how much had been produced.

4 Collectivisation was the socialist solution for agriculture. You could not build a socialist state when the majority of the population were private landholders who sold their products on the market. Collectivisation would socialise the peasantry. They would live in 'socialist agrotowns': living in apartment blocks instead of wooden huts, leaving their children in crèches, eating in restaurants, and visiting libraries and gymnasiums. They would be bussed out to the fields to work. They would learn to work together co-operatively and to live communally.

B   Why was collectivisation carried out so rapidly?

The answer to this question lies in the grain procurement crisis of 1928–29. We saw on page 154 that Stalin had visited the Urals and sent officials into the countryside to seize grain in 1928. In 1929, even though the harvest was much better, the state was still finding it difficult to get grain out of the peasants. The peasants were resisting the government's policies and were not marketing their food. Matters were so bad that meat as well as bread had to be rationed in the cities. The cities were hungry. Stalin blamed kulaks (rich peasants) for hoarding grain (see Source 11.5). Large numbers were arrested and deported to Siberia.

MTS stations

There were 2500 machine and tractor stations (MTS). Established to support collective farms, they maintained and hired out machinery. Typically, peasants had to hand over twenty per cent of their produce for this service. But the MTS stations were also used to control the countryside. Each MTS had a political department. Its job was to root out anti-soviet elements and troublemakers, and establish party cells in local areas. It was also there to ensure that every kolkhoz handed over its quota of grain.

Relationship of the collective farm to the towns

The first priority of the collective farm was to deliver quotas of grain and other food products to the state. The state paid very low prices, then sold the produce to the towns at slightly higher prices. Once the state quota had been met, peasants could sell any surplus at the local market. This came mostly from the peasants' private plots and was the main source of milk, butter, eggs, etc., for the urban population.

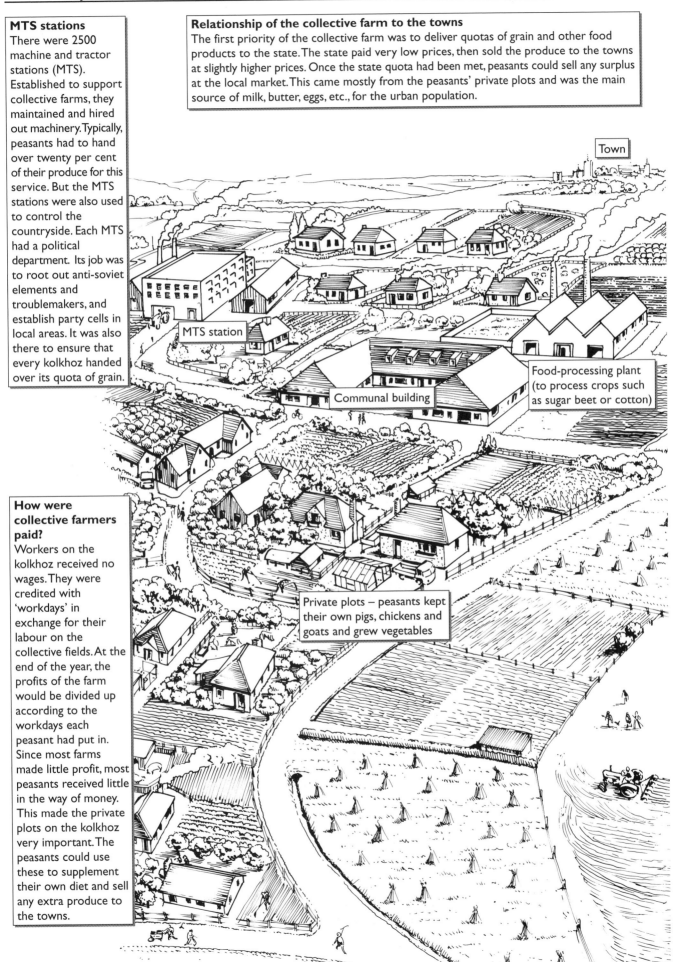

Town

MTS station

Communal building

Food-processing plant (to process crops such as sugar beet or cotton)

Private plots – peasants kept their own pigs, chickens and goats and grew vegetables

How were collective farmers paid?

Workers on the kolkhoz received no wages. They were credited with 'workdays' in exchange for their labour on the collective fields. At the end of the year, the profits of the farm would be divided up according to the workdays each peasant had put in. Since most farms made little profit, most peasants received little in the way of money. This made the private plots on the kolkhoz very important. The peasants could use these to supplement their own diet and sell any extra produce to the towns.

FOCUS ROUTE

1 How can you explain why Stalin decided to collectivise so rapidly?
2 Why was his policy so actively resisted by Bukharin and the right wing of the party?
3 What other pressures was Stalin under at the time when the decision to collectivise rapidly was taken?
4 Why is it difficult to explain the reasons for Stalin's decision?

SOURCE 11.5 J. V. Stalin, *Collected Works*, Vol. 11, 1955. Visiting Siberia in January 1928, Stalin is reported to have said the following to administrators

You have had a bumper harvest . . . Your grain surpluses this year are bigger than ever before. Yet the plan for grain procurement is not being fulfilled. Why? . . . Look at the kulak farms: their barns and sheds are crammed with grain . . . You say that the kulaks are unwilling to deliver grain, that they are waiting for prices to rise, and prefer to engage in unbridled speculation. That is true. But the kulaks . . . are demanding an increase in prices to three times those fixed by the government . . .

But there is no guarantee that the kulaks will not again sabotage the grain procurements next year. More, it may be said with certainty that so long as there are kulaks, so long will there be sabotage of grain procurements.

Bukharin and the right wing of the party were worried that Stalin's methods would lead to the return of War Communism – a cycle of violence and rural unrest, shortages of bread and other foods, and rationing. Under pressure from the right, Stalin agreed to stop grain seizures in 1928 and to try raising the price of grain to encourage peasants to put more on the market. But with continuing food shortages in 1929, the party swung behind Stalin, and Bukharin and the rightists were removed from key posts. Shortly afterwards, Stalin announced a policy of forced mass collectivisation. He had decided to break the peasants' stranglehold on the economy.

It seems likely therefore that the decision to collectivise rapidly was an emergency decision taken to solve the procurement crisis of 1928–29 and to crack down on the resistance of the peasants. This conclusion is supported by the lack of preparation and planning for a revolution in Soviet agriculture. There were simply not enough tractors, combine harvesters, agricultural experts or supplies of fertiliser to carry out a high-speed collectivisation programme.

However, this decision should be seen in the context of the other factors mentioned at the end of Chapter 10. Stalin, the party and many others wanted to move forward. There was a genuine sense of crisis in urban Russia at the end of the 1920s. The 1927 war scare had made the perceived need for industrialisation all the more urgent and that meant getting more grain out of the peasants. The party broadly supported Stalin and wanted to force the pace of industrialisation and solve the peasant problem.

Historians have also shown that there was a lot of support for collectivisation among the urban working class. It was not only that they were hungry and angry at what they saw as the deliberate actions of peasants in holding back food. Many saw the socialisation of the land as a key part of the revolution and the way out of poverty towards the great society. Whether they, or indeed Stalin, had any idea of what this would entail is a different matter.

■ **Learning trouble spot**

Complicated explanations

It is sometimes difficult to explain the actions of politicians because they have to cope with a range of interrelated issues at any given time and under different political and economic pressures. When Stalin was deciding whether or not to opt for rapid forced collectivisation, he was also:
- trying to push forward rapid industrialisation plans upon which his credibility as a leader was staked
- dealing with the problem of feeding the workers, his natural supporters
- engaged in a power struggle to become leader of the party
- fighting a political battle with Bukharin and the right about the pace of industrialisation and how they should handle the peasants

- looking at the results of the Urals–Siberian method in 1929, which appeared to have been a successful way of getting grain from the peasants
- thinking about a long-term solution to allow the development of agriculture, which for Communists had always been collectivisation and agrotowns.

So when Stalin made his decision, he was playing with a range of factors. And it might also be the case that he decided he had had enough of the peasants and was going to break their resistance. His personality also has a role to play here and he had a history of taking revenge on people who thwarted him.

C How was collectivisation carried out?

WHO WERE THE KULAKS?

Soviet writers divided the peasants into three classes:

- kulaks, or better-off peasants
- middle peasants (those on moderate incomes)
- poor peasants and landless labourers.

An examination of Soviet data shows that the so-called kulak might own one or two horses, hire labour at times during the year and produce a small surplus for the market. There was no separate rich peasant stratum. Indeed, once the attack on kulaks began, many got rid of some of their animals and other resources so that they would be classed as middle peasants.

In practice, a kulak was anyone officials decided was one. Often the people they identified were the most enterprising peasants in a village, the better farmers, the ones who had a little machinery and a few animals. So, in getting rid of them, they were destroying the best chance for more successful agriculture.

Force, terror and propaganda were the main methods employed in carrying through collectivisation. Stalin returned to the familiar ideological weapon of the 'class enemy' as the mechanism to achieve his ends. It was not difficult to find a class enemy in the countryside – the kulak! In December 1929, he announced the 'liquidation of the kulaks as a class'. Molotov, one of Stalin's leading supporters, said that they would hit the kulaks so hard that the so-called 'middle peasants' would 'snap to attention before us'.

The aim of identifying the kulak as a class enemy was to frighten the middle and poor peasants into joining the kolkhozes. But villagers were often unwilling to identify kulaks, many of whom were relatives or friends, people who might have helped them out in difficult times or lent them animals to plough their land. Even if the kulaks were not liked, they were part of a village community in which the ties to fellow peasants were much stronger than those to the Communist state. In some villages, poor peasants wrote letters in support of their richer neighbours. Meanwhile, richer peasants quickly sold their animals and stopped hiring labourers so that they could slip into the ranks of the middle peasants.

Many local party officials opposed the policy of forced collectivisation, knowing that it was unworkable. They were unwilling to identify as kulaks good farmers who were valuable to the community. They also knew that collectivisation would tear the countryside apart. So Stalin enlisted an army of 25,000 urban party activists to help to revolutionise the countryside. After a two-week course, they were sent out in brigades to oversee the collectivisation process, backed by the local police, the OGPU (secret police) and the military. Their task was to root out the kulaks and persuade the middle and poor peasants to sign a register demanding to be collectivised. The land, animals, tools, equipment and buildings would be taken from the kulaks and used as the basis for the new collective farm, the creation of which the activists would then oversee.

The so-called 'Twenty-five Thousanders' had no real knowledge of how to organise or run a collective farm, but they did know how to wage class warfare. 'Dekulakisation' went ahead at full speed. Each region was given a number of kulaks to find and they found them whether they existed or not. The kulaks were divided into three categories: counter-revolutionaries who were to be shot or sent to forced-labour settlements; active opponents of collectivisation who were to be deported to other areas of the Soviet Union, often to Siberia; and those who were expelled from their farms and settled on poor land.

A decree of 1 February 1930 gave local party organisations the power to use 'necessary measures' against the kulaks. Whole families and sometimes whole villages were rounded up and deported. The head of the household might be shot and his family put on a train for Siberia or some distant part of Russia. Others would be sent off to the Gulag labour camps or to work in punishment brigades building canals, roads or the new industrial centres. Up to ten million people had been deported to Siberia or labour camps by the end of the collectivisation process.

The Communists also mounted a huge propaganda campaign to extol the advantages of collective farms and to inflame class hatred. In some areas this was effective. Many poorer peasants did denounce their neighbours as kulaks. Sometimes this was an act of revenge for past grievances but, of course, it was to the advantage of the poor peasants to get their hands on their neighbours' animals and equipment for the new collective. Children were encouraged to inform on their neighbours and even on their parents. One thirteen-year-old girl denounced her mother for stealing grain.

Peasant resistance

The peasants resisted collectivisation bitterly despite the mass deportations. There were riots and armed resistance. One riot lasted for five days and armoured cars had to be brought in to restore order. In many instances troops had to be brought in. Peasants burned crops, tools and houses rather than hand them over to the state. Raids were mounted to recapture animals that had already been taken into the collectives. Action by women often proved the most effective form of opposition. Women's revolts were reported in the press. Kaganovich, a member of the Politburo, recognised that 'women had played the most advanced role in the reaction against the collective farm'. The women's protests were carefully organised, with specific goals such as stopping grain requisitioning or retrieving collectivised horses. They reckoned, sometimes correctly, that it would be more difficult for troops to take action against all-women protests. The government found their tactics difficult to deal with.

One of the main forms of resistance was to slaughter animals and eat or sell the meat rather than hand over the beasts to the kolkhoz. Mikhail Sholokhov described this graphically in his novel *Virgin Soil Upturned* (1935):

'Kill, it's not ours any more . . . Kill, they'll take it for meat anyway . . . Kill, you won't get meat on the collective farm . . . And they killed. They ate until they could eat no more. Young and old suffered from stomach ache. At dinner-time tables groaned under boiled and roasted meat. At dinner-time every one had a greasy mouth . . . everyone blinked like an owl, as if drunk from eating.'

ACTIVITY

Imagine you are a party activist. Use Sources 11.1–11.4 on pages 158–159 to write a speech explaining to peasants the advantages of joining a collective farm and encouraging them to take part in the great experiment of 'socialist construction'.

D What impact did collectivisation have on the peasants?

By the end of February 1930, the party claimed that half of all peasant households had been collectivised – a stunning success. In reality, it was an agricultural disaster on a huge scale. The most enterprising peasants had been shot or deported, agricultural production disrupted, and a huge number of animals slaughtered – around 25–30 per cent of all the cattle, pigs and sheep in the USSR (mostly eaten by the peasants). Peasants who had been forced into collectives were in no mood to begin the sowing season and the level of resistance was high. This was fed by rumours in some areas that women were about to be 'socialised' and that there were special machines to burn up old people.

Knowing that further peasant resistance could lead to the collapse of grain production, Stalin backtracked. He wrote an article for *Pravda* in March 1930 saying that his officials had moved too far too fast. They had, he said, become 'dizzy with success'. This was probably not far from the truth. Young, ferocious and militant urban activists had got carried away, competing with each other to see who could get the most households into collectives. Central government seemed to have little direct control over what was happening in the provinces. Stalin called for a return to the voluntary principle and an end to coercion. Given the choice, a huge number of peasants abandoned the new collective farms and went back to farming for themselves.

But once the harvest had been gathered in, Stalin restarted the campaign and it was just as vicious as before. Throughout 1931 peasants were forced back into the collectives they had left, so that by the end of the year large areas of the USSR had been collectivised, taking in over 50 per cent of peasant households. The peasants had already paid a terrible price for their resistance and lack of co-operation. But worse was to come.

FOCUS ROUTE

Make notes on:

a) why Stalin halted and then restarted the collectivisation process in 1930–31

b) the consequences of collectivisation

c) what happened in agriculture after 1934.

The famine of 1932–34

While collectivisation proceeded apace, the state continued to requisition grain. The state had collected 22.8 million tons of grain by the end of 1931, enough to feed the cities and to export to finance the industrialisation drive. However, this had taken place against a huge drop in grain production, largely caused by the chaos and upheaval of collectivisation (see Source 11.16 on page 166). This was partly due to the activists' lack of farming knowledge and the skills to run collectives properly, but there were other reasons. For instance, there were not enough animals to pull the ploughs (because the peasants had eaten them) and tractors had not arrived in sufficient numbers to fill the gap. To make matters worse, there was a drought over a large area of the USSR during 1931.

By the spring of 1932, famine had appeared in parts of the Ukraine and, after a temporary respite following the harvest of 1932, it spread to other areas. From late 1932 until well into 1934, the USSR was subject to a famine which killed millions of peasants. In his exhaustive study *The Harvest of Sorrow* (1986), Robert Conquest puts the figure as high as seven million although other historians have suggested it was much lower. But all historians accept that the scale of human suffering was enormous. One reason why it is difficult to give exact numbers is that the scale of the famine was largely unacknowledged by the Soviet regime. It did not want to admit that collectivisation had failed to deliver. But it seemed to go further than this. According to Conquest, collectivisation had become the weapon to break peasant resistance and to deal once and for all with the 'accursed problem' as Communists called the peasant question.

Conquest cites the example of the Ukraine which was, he believes, singled out for special treatment because of the strength of Ukrainian nationalism and opposition to collectivisation. As the 'breadbasket' of Russia, the Ukraine had been set high targets for grain procurement in 1931 and 1932 (over seven million tons each year), even though the total amount being produced was falling rapidly. Thousands of extra officials, backed by detachments of OGPU, were drafted in to root out hidden stocks of grain held by peasants – and root it out they did, in brutal requisitioning gangs (see Source 11.14 on page 168). This condemned hundreds of thousands to starvation. Worse than this, Conquest claims that requisitioned grain was left rotting in huge dumps or in railway sidings while starving people could not get access to it. In some areas, groups did make attacks on grain dumps, only to be punished later. Many were shot while others were rounded up and deported to labour camps.

While other historians do not see the famine as being directly sought by Stalin, most acknowledge that the Communist government was determined to procure grain at any cost. This is borne out by the continued export of grain to other countries – 1.73 million tons in 1932 and only slightly less the following year – during the worst period of the famine.

The government brought in strict laws to ensure that grain was handed over. A law of 7 August 1932, which became known to many peasants as the Law of the Seventh-Eighths (passed on the seventh day of the eighth month), prescribed a ten-year sentence for stealing 'socialised' property, which could mean a few ears of corn. This was later changed to the death sentence. Decrees in August and December laid down prison sentences of up to ten years for peasants selling meat and grain before quotas were fulfilled. Peasants tried to escape famine-hit areas by fleeing to the cities and other areas. The Soviet government brought in internal passports to control the vast movement of people.

The net result of the government's policy was the death of millions of peasants in the Ukraine, the north Caucasus, Kazakhstan and other parts of the USSR. It is difficult to reach any other conclusion than that the famine of 1932–34 was man-made. It was the direct result of the upheaval caused by collectivisation – the purging of the peasants who had the best farming expertise, the poor organisation of the new collective farms, the lack of machinery and fertilisers, the lack of know-how, and the resistance of peasants who slaughtered animals and refused to work hard on the land. This was compounded by government policy which continued to take excessive amounts of grain from the worst-hit areas and export it abroad to pay for industrial equipment.

SOURCE 11.6 V. Kravchenko, *I Chose Freedom: The Personal and Political Life of a Soviet Official*, 1947, p. 104. Kravchenko was a Communist who later fled the Soviet Union. Here he is an eyewitness to a round-up of kulaks

'What's happening?' I asked the constable.

'Another round-up of kulaks,' he replied. 'Seems the dirty business will never end. The OGPU and District Committee came this morning.'

A large crowd was gathered outside the building.... A number of women were weeping hysterically and calling the names of husbands and fathers. It was like a scene out of a nightmare ... In the background, guarded by the OGPU soldiers with drawn revolvers, stood about twenty peasants, young and old, with bundles on their backs. A few were weeping. The others stood there sullen, resigned, hopeless. So this was 'Liquidation of the kulaks as a class!' A lot of simple peasants being torn from their native soil, stripped of their worldly goods and shipped to some distant labour camps. Their outcries filled the air ... As I stood there, distressed, ashamed, helpless, I heard a woman shouting in an unearthly voice ... The woman, her hair streaming, held a flaming sheaf of grain in her hands. Before anyone could reach her, she had tossed the burning sheaf into the thatched roof of the house, which burst into flames instantaneously.

'Infidels! murderers!' the distraught woman was shrieking. 'We worked all our lives for our house. You won't have it. The flames will have it!' Her cries turned suddenly into bitter laughter. For some reason, on this occasion, most of the families were being left behind.

SOURCE 11.7 Peasants protesting against the kulaks. The Soviet version of the collectivisation process was that the poorer peasants themselves demanded that the kulaks be forced out and asked to be collectivised

SOURCE 11.8 V. Serge, *Memoirs of a Revolutionary 1901–1941*, translated and edited by P. Sedwick, 1967, p. 247

In a Kuban market town whose entire population was deported, the women undressed in their houses, thinking that no one would dare make them go out naked; they were driven out as they were to the cattle trucks, beaten with rifle butts ... Trainloads of deported peasants left for the icy north, the forests, the steppes, the deserts. These were whole populations, denuded of everything; the old folk starved to death in mid-journey, newborn babes were buried on the banks of the roadside, and each wilderness had its crop of little crosses.

ACTIVITY

Use Sources 11.6–11.14 on pages 166–168 to answer these questions.

1 What impression do you get of the dekulakisation and collectivisation process from Sources 11.6–11.11?
2 Given Sholokhov's background (Source 11.12), how valuable do you think his novel is as historical evidence?
3 Look at Sources 11.13 and 11.14. Do they change your answer?
4 What justification or explanation of the process is provided by Communists in Sources 11.12–11.14?
5 What value, if any, does a novel like Sholokhov's have for historians looking at collectivisation?

SOURCE 11.9 Peasants signing up to join a collective farm. Typically, party activists would call a village meeting and invite the villagers to set up and join a collective farm. They would offer inducements such as machinery, or make threats of increased taxes or forced exile

SOURCE 11.10 A famine victim, 1932

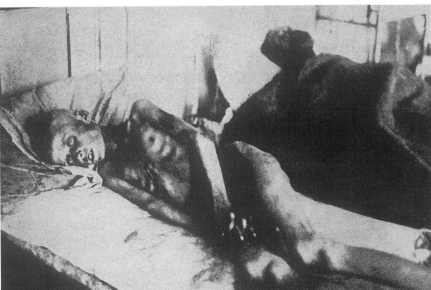

SOURCE 11.11 An OGPU colonel speaking to the historian I. Deutscher as they travelled to Kharkov, quoted in *Stalin*, rev. edn 1966, pp. 324–25

'I am an old Bolshevik,' he said almost sobbing, 'I worked in the underground against the Tsar and I fought in the civil war. Did I do all that in order that I should now surround villages with machine-guns and order my men to fire indiscriminately into crowds of peasants? Oh, no, no!'

SOURCE 11.12 M. Sholokhov, *Virgin Soil Upturned*, 1935, pp. 71–73. Sholokhov was an active Communist who wrote this pro-collectivisation novel. But he was horrified by what he saw of dekulakisation and wrote a letter to Stalin condemning the 'disgusting methods' that officials used. In his reply Stalin acknowledged that officials were guilty of crimes but claimed that Sholokhov did not appreciate the other side of the picture, that the peasants were engaged in sabotage and 'waging what was in essence a "quiet war" against the Soviet power – a war of starvation, Comrade Sholokhov'. In this extract from Sholokhov's novel, one of the main activists of the local soviet, Razmiotnov, at a meeting with other activists where they are adding up the totals of grain they have confiscated from kulaks, is making a surprise announcement

'*I'm not going on.*'

'*What do you mean? "Not going on."* ' *Nagulnov pushed the abacus to one side. . . .*

'*I've not been trained! I've not been trained to fight against children! At the front was another matter. There you could cut down who you liked with your sword or what you liked . . . And you can all go to the devil! I'm not going on! . . . Do you call it right? What am I? An executioner? Or is my heart made of stone? I had enough at the war . . . Gayev's [a kulak] got eleven children. How they howled when we arrived! You'd have clutched your head. It made my hair stand on end. We began to drive them out of the kitchen . . . I screwed up my eyes, stopped my ears and ran into the yard. The women were all in a dead fright . . . the children . . . Oh, by God, you . . .*'

. . . '*Snake!*' *[Nagulnov] gasped out in a penetrating whisper, clenching his fist.* '*How are you serving the revolution? Having pity on them? Yes . . . You could line up thousands of old men, women and children, and tell me they'd got to be crushed into the dust for the sake of the revolution, and I'd shoot them all down with a machine gun.*' *Suddenly he screamed savagely, a frenzy glittered in his great, dilated pupils, and the foam seethed at the corners of his lips.*

SOURCE 11.13 V. Kravchenko, *I Chose Freedom: The Personal and Political Life of a Soviet Official*, 1947, p. 130. Kravchenko, a party activist in the Ukraine, quotes the secretary of the Ukrainian Central Committee

A ruthless struggle is going on between the peasantry and our regime. It's a struggle to the death. This year was a test of our strength and their endurance. It took a famine to show them who is master here. It has cost millions of lives, but the collective farm system is here to stay. We've won the war.

SOURCE 11.14 L. Kopelev, an activist who later went into exile, quoted in R. Conquest, *The Harvest of Sorrow*, 1986, p. 233

With the rest of my generation, I firmly believed that the ends justified the means. Our great goal was the universal triumph of Communism . . .

I saw what 'total collectivisation' meant – how they mercilessly stripped the peasants in the winter of 1932–33. I took part in it myself, scouring the countryside . . . testing the earth with an iron rod for loose spots that might lead to buried grain. With the others, I emptied out the old folks' storage chests, stopping my ears to the children's crying and the women's wails. For I was convinced that I was accomplishing the great and necessary transformation of the countryside; that in the days to come the people who lived there would be better off . . .

In the terrible spring of 1933 I saw people dying of hunger. I saw women and children with distended bellies, turning blue, still breathing but with vacant lifeless eyes. And corpses – corpses in ragged sheepskin coats and cheap felt boots; corpses in the peasant huts . . . I saw all this and did not go out of my mind or commit suicide . . . Nor did I lose my faith. As before, I believed because I wanted to believe.

Collectivisation after 1934

At the end of 1934, it was announced that 70 per cent of peasant households were in collectives, rising to 90 per cent in 1936. Individual peasant landholdings were gradually squeezed out. Grain production began to recover slowly but did not exceed pre-collectivisation levels until 1935 (1930 being an exceptional year). Meat production did not pass pre-collectivisation levels until after 1953. Grain procurement continued at a high level throughout the 1930s, whatever the harvest.

The problem was lack of incentive – the peasants had nothing to work for. They were supposed to get a share in the profits of the farm at the end of the year but there never were any profits. They practised a form of passive resistance shown in apathy, neglect and petty insubordination on the newly created kolkhozes. The state could do little about it. On many farms the chairman (usually a Communist) was changed regularly because he could not get the peasants to perform.

This made the private plots on collectives very important. It was the only way peasants could earn something for themselves. Peasants could sell their products on the local market. The state did not hinder them because the economy desperately needed food. It has been estimated that these private plots provided 52 per cent of vegetables, 57 per cent of fruit, 70 per cent of meat and 71 per cent of milk as well as butter, honey and wool to Soviet consumers.

The peasants referred to collectivisation as the 'second serfdom'. They were tied to land they did not own. They could not leave the farms without the permission of the authorities. Draconian laws would punish them if they stepped out of line. However, Sheila Fitzpatrick in her book *Stalin's Peasants* (1994) maintains that the peasants developed all sorts of ways of subverting the farms and turning matters to their advantage. The peasants had been broken by collectivisation but they had not been totally crushed.

SOURCE 11.15 Extracts from peasants' letters to *Our Village*, a peasant newspaper, concerning the first collectivisation drive, 1929–30. These letters were not actually published in the newspaper

Ivan Trofimovitch

I am a poor peasant. I have one hut, one barn, one horse, three dessyatins *of land ... Isn't it true that all the poor peasants and middle peasants do not want to go into the kolkhoz at all, but you drive them in by force? ... [In my village] poor peasants came out against it ... they did not want serfdom.*

Pyotr Gorky

Every day they send us lecturers asking us to sign up for such-and-such a kolkhoz for eternal slavery, but we don't want to leave our good homes. It may be a poor little hut, but it's mine, a poor horse, but it's mine. Among us, he who works more has something to eat ... Let the peasant own property. Then we assure you that everyone will be able to put more surpluses on the market.

Unnamed peasant

Comrades, you write that all the middle peasants and poor peasants join the kolkhoz voluntarily, but it is not true. For example, in our village of Podbuzhye, all do not enter the kolkhoz willingly. When the register made the rounds, only 25 per cent signed it, while 75 per cent did not ... If anyone spoke out against it, he was threatened with arrest and forced labour ... Collective life can be created when the entire mass of the peasants goes voluntarily, and not by force ... I beg you not to divulge my name, because the Party people will be angry.

COLLECTIVISATION CASE STUDY: SMOLENSK

The Smolensk Archive was seized from the Nazis by US troops in 1945, having been abandoned by Soviet forces in 1941. It contains a lot of information about changes in agriculture in the province of Smolensk. It tells the story of how collectivisation was carried out and how the peasants responded to it. The following account is a summary of the findings from the Smolensk Archive. Source 11.15 contains extracts from the archive.

Before collectivisation, 90 per cent of the population lived on the land. In 1927, five per cent of households were classified as kulaks, 70 per cent middle peasants and 25 per cent as poor peasants. During 1927–28, increasing pressure was applied to the kulaks. They were made to pay heavier taxes and higher wages for hired labourers; they were prosecuted for grain speculation and concealment.

After September 1929, activists were sent to the area to intensify the campaign against the kulaks and to speed up grain deliveries. But they found it difficult to get local support. Often the 'kulaks' were respected village leaders linked by blood ties to poor and middle peasants. The villagers maintained their solidarity against the Soviet authorities. Even more problematically, the activists found that local soviet members and party workers sided with the peasants.

As the activists could get little co-operation, they took harsher measures. All peasant households were required to deliver fixed quotas of grain, with penalties or even prison sentences for failure to do so. If households failed to deliver their quota, 'workers' brigades' would descend and seize their grain. The peasants responded by hiding grain and attacking activists. In October 1929, ten chairmen and eight party secretaries of village soviets were murdered. The OGPU were called in to support the activists and a 'pall of terror' enveloped the villages. In court cases it was found that almost half of the offenders were middle and poor peasants; they were condemned as ideological kulaks.

Shortly after this, Smolensk was hit by the first collectivisation drive (1929–30) characterised by 'storm' tactics. The local soviets and party workers could not be trusted to carry out effective dekulakisation or organise the kolkhozes, so brigades of urban workers, the 'Twenty-five Thousanders' (see page 163), were used.

OGPU reports reveal a picture of chaos and confusion.

There was a wave of panic in the villages. Kulaks were dekulakising themselves – selling all they owned, leaving their property to relatives and friends, even just abandoning their fields and homes. Growing numbers were fleeing east to Moscow and the Urals. There was a reported wave of suicides amongst richer households with well-to-do peasants killing their wives and children as well as themselves. While some poor peasants were pleased to see the attacks on the kulaks, other poor and middle peasants colluded with kulak friends to protect their lives and property. Petitions were collected testifying to the good character of kulaks who were on the lists.

There was also a lot of antagonism towards the kolkhozes, as the extracts from the letters in Source 11.15 show. In one incident in September 1929, 200 peasants attacked a kolkhoz, destroying equipment and clothes. The majority of the attackers were women armed with pitchforks, spades and axes. There were numerous instances of burned barns, haystacks and houses. The OGPU noted the heavy involvement of women in these outbursts against the collectives.

Generally, the halt to collectivisation in March 1930, after Stalin's 'dizzy with success' article in *Pravda* (see page 164), was well received. The archives show how the local officials and activists were really out of control, arresting whomever they pleased, including many middle peasants, often on the basis of vicious rumour. There were cases of activists blackmailing kulaks to take their names off the confiscation and deportation lists.

But by March 1931, Smolensk was again the subject of intense dekulakisation. Lists of kulaks were collected by village soviets. Activists set about liquidating kulak households and deporting whole families. The OGPU reported that there was much sympathy in the villages for the deported. Nevertheless, the process of collectivisation went ahead with over 90 per cent of peasant households in kolkhozes by the end of the 1930s.

Although there are gaps in the Smolensk Archive about how the collective farms operated, it is full of complaints about inefficiency, poor chairmen, lax working practices, drunkenness, thievery and worse abuses. The picture is one of apathy from the ordinary kolkhoz members and lack of enthusiasm for life on a collective farm.

ACTIVITY

1 Compare the material from the Smolensk Archive with what you have already read about collectivisation. List the points where the specific detail here agrees with the general picture and the points where it disagrees.
2 What does the archive tell us about the kulak response to the pre-collectivisation grain seizures?
3 What does the archive show us about the behaviour and actions of the activists and their relations with the kulaks?
4 Think about the value of the archive to historians. Remember, it was collected by the Soviet authorities.
   a) Do you think we can trust the general picture it presents of collectivisation?
   b) What view of the peasant response is clear from the unpublished letters?
   c) Do you think these letters are useful and reliable evidence for historians?

E Was collectivisation a success?

Assessing collectivisation

Draw up a table to make notes on your assessment of collectivisation. You can use the table shown here or make notes under your own headings. You might also like to design a more interesting way of setting out your notes, for example, in a flow diagram or spider diagram.

Use the sources and information which follow to complete your table or diagram. At the end of this section you are going to use these notes in an essay which considers the overall successes and failures of Stalin's economic policies in the 1930s.

Ways in which collectivisation was economically successful for the government	Ways in which collectivisation was politically successful for the government
Ways in which collectivisation was an economic failure	**The human cost of collectivisation**

Study the figures in Source 11.16 and answer the following questions.

1 How can you explain the figures for grain harvests from 1928 to 1935?
2 What is the significance of the state procurement of grain in relation to the overall grain harvest over the same period?
3 Why are the grain export figures significant?
4 Analyse and explain the figures for animals over this period.

SOURCE 11.16 Agricultural output and state procurement of grain, 1928–35, from A. Nove, *An Economic History of the USSR, 1917–91*, 1992, pp. 180, 186

	1928	1929	1930	1931	1932	1933	1934	1935
Grain harvest (million tons)	73.3	71.7	83.5	69.5	69.6	68.4	67.6	75.0
State procurement of grain (million tons)	10.8	16.1	22.1	22.8	18.5	22.6		
Grain exports (million tons)	0.03	0.18	4.76	5.06	1.73	1.69		
Cattle (million head)	70.5	67.1	52.3	47.9	40.1	38.4	42.4	49.3
Pigs (million head)	26.0	20.4	13.6	14.4	11.6	12.1	17.4	22.6
Sheep and goats (million head)	146.7	147.0	108.8	77.7	52.1	50.2	51.9	61.1

Any assessment of collectivisation reveals a very mixed picture. Economically, it appears to have been a disaster. The fact that grain harvests dropped dramatically in the early 1930s when grain was most needed and did not recover to their 1928 level (apart from 1930 which was an exceptional year) until the latter half of the 1930s is a damning indictment. This is an even worse performance when you compare the figures with the last harvest of tsarist Russia in 1913 (see Source 7.18 on page 112). The Soviet Union also lost a huge proportion of the animal population, a loss from which it did not really recover until after the Second World War.

However, although the overall grain harvest declined in the early 1930s, state procurements did not. The state collected the grain it needed to feed the rapidly growing workforce and to sell abroad to pay for industrial equipment. What is more, dispossessed peasants from the overpopulated countryside fled to the towns, so providing labour for the new factories. Collectivisation had succeeded in its main purpose – to provide the resources for industrialisation.

This view, however, has been challenged by several historians. They believe that valuable resources had to be diverted to agriculture: because of the need to build large numbers of tractors, for example, and to send out agronomists and large numbers of activists and secret police. Furthermore, the USSR did not get as much foreign money for its grain as it had hoped because the GREAT DEPRESSION had forced down world grain prices.

GREAT DEPRESSION
A world economic slump that began in 1929 with the Wall Street Crash and lasted until the beginning of the Second World War.

On top of this, the human costs were horrendous. The suffering cannot be quantified, particularly for those who not only lost their homes but ended up in the Gulag prison camps. Roy Medvedev estimates that some ten million peasants were dispossessed between 1929 and 1932, of whom around two or three million lost their lives. Then we must add the cost of the famine. Robert Conquest estimates around seven million died, five million of them in the Ukraine alone. Whatever the actual figure, it represents an inexcusable episode in Soviet history.

For the party, collectivisation was an essential part of its modernisation drive. The party did not want a sizeable sector of the economy to be dominated by the private market or to be at the mercy of the peasants who hoarded grain. In this sense, collectivisation was a political success. The party gained control of the villages and did not have to bargain with the peasants any more. It had established a system, using local soviets and MTS, of controlling the countryside and making agriculture serve the towns and workers.

SOURCE 11.17 C. Ward, *Stalin's Russia*, 1993, p. 47

What happened between November 1929 and December 1931 cannot be grasped merely by reciting statistics ... a socio-economic system in existence for five hundred years vanished for ever. But the whirlwind which swept across the countryside destroyed the way of life of the vast majority of the Soviet people, not just the Russians ... Early in 1930, countless individuals and families in entire regions and republics – the Russian, Ukrainian and Caucasian grain districts – were stigmatized as kulaks, driven from their land, forced into collectives, exiled or shot. Central Asian cotton growers and sugar beet farmers in the Central Black Earth region suffered the same fate in 1931.

SOURCE 11.18 R. Service, *A History of Twentieth-Century Russia*, 1997, pp. 181–82

With the exception of 1930, mass collectivisation meant that not until the mid-1950s did agriculture regain the level of output achieved in the last years before the Great War. Conditions in the countryside were so dire that the state had to pump additional resources into the country in order to maintain the new agrarian order ... to agronomists, surveyors, and farm chairmen but also to soldiers, policemen and informers. Moreover, 'machine-tractor stations' had to be built from 1929 to provide equipment for the introduction of technology.

Yet Stalin could draw up a balance sheet that, from his standpoint, was favourable. From collectivisation he acquired a reservoir of terrified peasants who would supply him with cheap industrial labour. To some extent, too, he secured his ability to export Soviet raw materials in order to pay for imports of industrial machinery ... Above all, he put an end to the recurrent crises faced by the state in relation to urban food supplies as the state's grain collections rose from 10.8 million tons in 1928–9 to 22.8 million tons in 1931–2. After collectivisation it was the countryside, not the towns, which went hungry if the harvest was bad.

TALKING POINT

Use the information and sources on pages 171–172 to discuss the statement: 'Collectivisation was a political success but an economic failure and a human disaster.'

KEY POINTS FOR CHAPTER 11

Was collectivisation a success?

1 Collective farms were the socialist solution for agriculture, changing individualistic peasants with capitalist tendencies into agroworkers.
2 Stalin also wanted to bring the peasants under control and ensure the food supply needed for his plans to industrialise the Soviet Union.
3 There was a lot of support for his programme amongst the urban working classes but a high level of resistance from the peasantry.
4 Stalin used force, terror and propaganda to collectivise Soviet agriculture at high speed. Brutal methods were used, including mass arrests, mass murder and the deportation of hundreds of thousands of peasants.
5 Peasants resisted by slaughtering and eating their animals and fighting the activists who carried out collectivisation.
6 The impact on agriculture was disastrous. Grain production fell and there was a tremendous drop in the number of animals.
7 In 1932–34 a famine, largely the result of government policies, killed millions of peasants.
8 Vast numbers of peasants fled the countryside to become industrial workers in the new booming industrial centres.

How well planned were the Five-Year Plans?

CHAPTER OVERVIEW

The Five-Year Plans for industry were ambitious and far-reaching. They envisaged nothing less than the transformation of the Soviet Union into a great industrial power. Central planning would replace the capitalist market as the main device for managing the economy.

   The plans soon hit problems as the central planning system found it could not cope with the demands it had imposed on itself. The First Five-Year Plan was marked by its outrageous targets for INDUSTRIAL ENTERPRISES. The workers suffered as their needs were pushed to the bottom of the scale of priorities. Yet, despite all the problems, the plans were successful in many respects.

> INDUSTRIAL ENTERPRISE
> Large factory, mine, etc. or collection of factories, mines, etc. run as one unit.

A How were the Five-Year Plans organised? (pp. 176–178)

B What did the Five-Year Plans achieve? (pp. 179–183)

C How did the workers fare under the plans? (pp. 184–193)

D Did urban living standards improve during the plans? (pp. 194–195)

E How successful were the Five-Year Plans for industry? (pp. 196–198)

ACTIVITY

What do Sources 12.1–12.7 below suggest about:
a) the attitudes of certain groups towards the big push for industrialisation
b) the scale and vision of the venture
c) the idea of socialism in comparison to capitalism in the 1930s?

SOURCE 12.1 S. Kotkin, *Magnetic Mountain: Stalinism as a Civilisation*, 1995, p. 35

The transformation of the old Russia into the USSR was viewed as tantamount to the discovery of a new continent by one contemporary geographer... To the majority of people who participated in building it, socialism in the USSR afforded the means to acquire a niche, as well as a sense of pride, in a society that did seem to be qualitatively different – in comparison with capitalism, which was then synonymous not with wealth and freedom but poverty and exploitation, as well as imperialism and war.

SOURCE 12.2 A. Bullock, *Hitler and Stalin: Parallel Lives*, 1991, p. 298

A young Komsomol [Young Communist League] member leaped at the opportunity to organise a shock brigade [see page 181] in 1929. 'When we went to work in the factories, we lamented that nothing would be left for us to do, because the revolution was over, because the severe [but] romantic years of civil war would not come back, and because the older generation had left to our lot a boring, prosaic life that was devoid of struggle and excitement.'

SOURCE 12.3 A. Nove, *An Economic History of the USSR, 1917–91*, 1992, p. 193

There were, in the later years, all too many examples of phoney official superlatives, which gave rise to widespread cynicism. So it is all the more necessary to stress that thousands (of young people in particular) participated in the 'great construction projects of socialism' with a will to self-sacrifice, accepting hardship with a real sense of comradeship. Statistics will also be cited to show that others had very different attitudes to their work, not only prisoners and deportees but also peasants fleeing collectives.

SOURCE 12.4 S. Kotkin, *Magnetic Mountain: Stalinism as a Civilisation*, 1995, p. 93

A group of young enthusiasts, working double shifts, whole days without rest and with little food, met to discuss the work on blast furnace no. 2, 'their' furnace, the Komolska. One of them opened the meeting by asking, 'Does anybody have any suggestions?' Someone else was quoted as saying, 'What kind of suggestions could there be – everybody straight to the site for a subbotnik [any time extra time was performed without compensation].' If we are to believe the credible account from which this conversation is taken, the youths 'worked till dawn'. Such pathos was genuine and it was widespread. 'Everyone, even the labourers, felt that Magnitogorsk [steel works] was making history, and that he, personally, had a considerable part in it,' wrote John Scott [see case study, page 175], himself deeply affected by the enthusiasm of the crusade. 'This feeling was shared to some extent even by the exiled kulaks.'

SOURCE 12.5 The Dnieprostroi Dam, built in the 1930s, increased Soviet electric power output fivefold when it began operating

SOURCE 12.7 The Magnitogorsk steel works, 1932. Magnitogorsk rapidly developed into a major industrial centre in the early 1930s

SOURCE 12.6 The Moscow metro, built in the 1930s, was a showpiece of Soviet construction

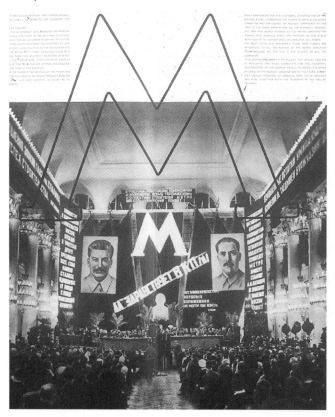

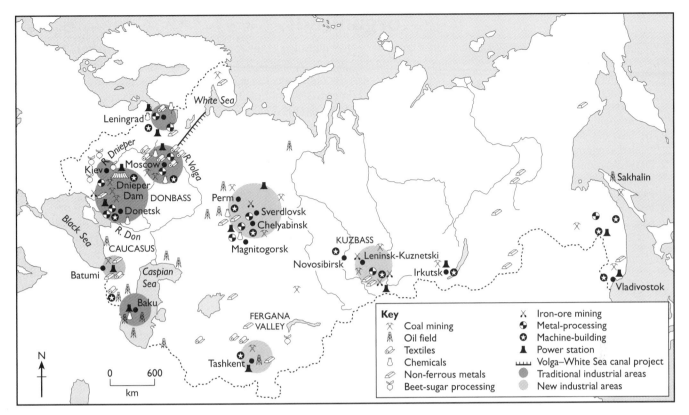

MAGNITOGORSK CASE STUDY

Throughout this chapter the development of the industrial centre at Magnitogorsk in the Urals, 'the most celebrated of the new, superior industrial age' (S. Kotkin, *Magnetic Mountain: Stalinism as a Civilisation*, 1995, pages 34–35), is used as a case study to show what general policies involved when translated into practice. Magnitogorsk was designed to be the socialist city of the future, inhabited by Soviet Socialist Man (*Homo Sovieticus*). Two main sources are used for the case study:

- Stephen Kotkin, *Magnetic Mountain: Stalinism as a Civilisation*, 1995. This outstanding study is an example of the recent trend among some Western historians of focusing on the experiences of the Russian people. Kotkin looks at the relationship between the authorities and the inhabitants of Magnitogorsk. The latter were not mere passive clay in the hands of the authorities; they knew how to make the best of their situation and which rules could be bent. So the people and the authorities influenced each other in the creation of the new city and the attempt to create new socialist citizens. He gives a vivid picture of the life of the newly urbanised Soviet workers of the 1930s that emphasises chaos and population movement. Thus the reintroduction of the tsarist internal passport system appears not as the culmination of a premeditated policy designed to establish total control over the populace, but rather as a typically heavy-handed Communist improvisation to combat a problem their policies had done so much to create.

- John Scott, *Behind the Urals*, 1942. Scott was an American college student who left the Depression-hit USA in 1932 to take part in the great experiment. He became a member of the Communist Party and spent several years as a volunteer worker at Magnitogorsk. Sympathetic to the aims of the socialist authorities, he nevertheless reveals the problems and hardships of life in the front-line of the industrial expansion. His book is regarded as the best eyewitness account by a Westerner.

The idea that the Soviet Union was at last on the road to socialism, via industrialisation, inspired party members and urban workers alike. There was a feeling that they were creating a new type of society that would be far superior to that of their capitalist neighbours. After the compromises of the NEP, there was a return to the war imagery of the Civil War and War Communism. There was talk of a 'socialist offensive', and of 'mobilising forces on all fronts'. There were 'campaigns' and 'breakthroughs', 'ambushes' by 'class enemies'. People who opposed or criticised the regime's policies thus became guilty of treachery.

The creation of this state of psychological warfare, with appeals to patriotism, was a useful device to push through policies, particularly since mistakes and failures could be blamed on the enemy. But many Communists did see the struggle as a war against backwardness and enemies inside and outside the Soviet Union. Industrialisation was the way to break through to socialism and to protect themselves from the hostile forces that appeared to be surrounding them.

■ **Learning trouble spot**

What is the difference between central planning and capitalism?

In a capitalist market economy, the production of goods and the allocation of resources and investment in industry are largely determined by supply and demand working through prices, that is, by the operation of the market. The demand for a product pushes up the price of that product. This encourages producers to enter the market to supply the product and make a profit. They bring the necessary investment in industrial plant and make decisions about the methods and techniques used to produce and distribute the goods. In this way, resources – raw materials, land and labour – flow to this particular industrial activity.

In a centrally planned system, state agencies co-ordinate the activities of the different branches of production. They make the decisions about the allocation of resources, where investment should be targeted, what methods of production should be used and what economic strategies should be followed.

  # **A** **How were the Five-Year Plans organised?**

The plans put central planning at the forefront of the Soviet economy. The state decided what was produced, where it was produced and when it was produced. The key feature of the plans was the setting of production and output targets which industrial enterprises had to achieve. Five-Year Plans set down broad directions and could be changed as they went along. There were also shorter one-year or even quarterly plans which set more specific targets for individual enterprises. The targets were backed by law, so failure to meet targets could be treated as a criminal offence. Bonuses were paid to enterprises that exceeded their plan target.

The party, acting through the government, set the priorities for the plans and the targets for key industries. The People's Commissariats (ministries or government departments) were responsible for working out more detailed plans for different regions and the enterprises under their control. Although there were varying numbers of industrial commissariats during the 1930s, four major ones had developed by 1934: heavy industry, light industry, timber and food. The most important of these was the Commissariat of Heavy Industry, which headed the industrialisation drive. By 1939, there were twenty commissariats.

In theory, industrial enterprises could have a say in formulating the plan but, in practice, instructions would be passed down through various bureaucratic layers to the managers of the enterprises. Chart 12B shows a simplified diagram of how the system worked using heavy industry as an example. However, this system emerged only as the plans developed and was not in place at the beginning. The planning of the First Five-Year Plan was much more chaotic.

■ **12B How the Five-Year Plans were administered using changes to heavy industry as an example**

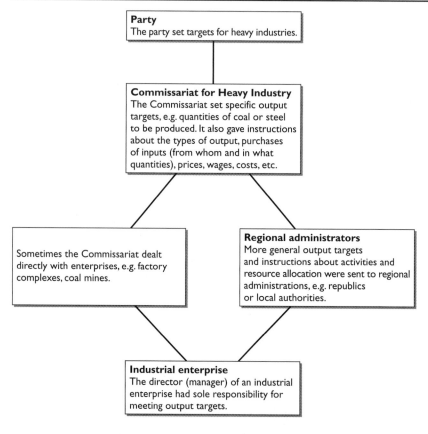

WHAT HAPPENED TO PRIVATE INDUSTRY?

The state already had control of large-scale industry (run by trusts) under the NEP, so these were brought into the new system. But there were quite a lot of small-scale private industries supplying consumer goods such as shoes and textiles. These were starved of supplies and resources and most collapsed during the First Five-Year Plan. This was a disaster for the Russian consumer who found it very hard to get clothing, shoes and other products. The situation was compounded by the collapse of cottage industries in the countryside due to collectivisation. Peasants had traditionally made clothes, tools and other products for a domestic market and these were swept away in the collectivisation upheaval. Most industrial enterprises of any size were under state control by the end of the 1930s.

Sergei Ordzhonikidze

'Sergo' had joined the Bolshevik Party in 1903 and became active in the underground political scene where he became friends with Stalin. Elected to the Central Committee, he played a prominent role in the revolution and the Civil War. He worked with Stalin in Georgia and it was he who struck the Bolshevik official in the incident which upset Lenin so much (see page 127). He was one of Stalin's staunchest supporters in the Politburo during the First Five-Year Plan. His key position as head of the Commissariat of Heavy Industry put him in the driving seat of the push for rapid industrialisation. He was reasonably popular in the party and was a moderating influence in the Politburo.

It was a top-down method of management which applied in the workplace as well. The principle of one-person management was established right at the beginning. The director of an industrial enterprise (for example, a large factory or several units of production) was in sole charge and responsible for seeing that the targets were achieved. The trade unions were told not to interfere and to focus on increasing worker productivity. Workers' control and influence over the factory floor, such as it had ever existed, receded as the plans progressed.

All this begs the question: who co-ordinated the activities of the different branches of industry to balance the system and make it work? For instance, if you decide to expand the railway, then you need to plan for enough steel to make the rails. Gosplan (the State Planning Commission), which had originally been set up in 1921 as a forecasting agency, was given the job of working out the figures – the inputs each industry would need and the output each had to produce – to meet overall targets for the plan (see the example in Chart 12C).

The party not only laid down basic priorities but interfered in the day-to-day running of enterprises. It had a grip on the economy at all levels. Senior party officials appointed and dismissed planners and senior managers, often for political rather than economic reasons. From 1930 to 1937, the Commissariat for Heavy Industry was led by Sergei Ordzhonikidze, who had a direct line to different factories and moved around people and resources as he wished. At the local level, the party got involved in checking whether enterprises were fulfilling the plans; party secretaries were held responsible if industrial enterprises in their area did badly.

■ 12C Planning required to achieve targets

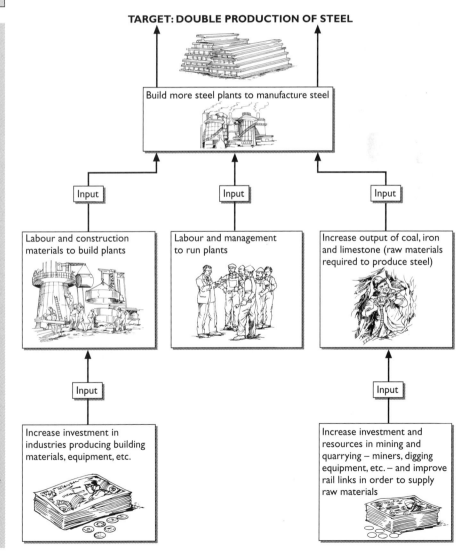

Features of the plans

The plans in the 1930s were dominated by an emphasis on the development of heavy industry. Stalin and the Supreme Economic Council (Vesenkha) agreed that the lion's share of investment should go into coal, iron, steel and other heavy industries. These would provide the power, capital equipment and machine tools that could be used to manufacture other products. The Soviet Union would then be less dependent on the West for these goods and could move towards self-sufficiency or 'autarky'. This decision meant that consumer industries producing clothes, shoes and similar products would be downgraded. Soviet citizens were asked to sacrifice their standard of living for longer-term objectives. There were two main reasons behind this:

1 It seemed to the Stalinists that Western industrial revolutions had been underpinned by the initial development in coal, iron and steel.
2 They were driven by the need to develop the sort of industries that could protect the Soviet Union should it be attacked from the West.

Three other features of the plans are worthy of note:

- The plans were always declared complete a year ahead of schedule. This denoted the superiority of Soviet planning over the Western capitalist economies which were, at this time, going through the worst throes of the Great Depression. It was also a psychological device to encourage the already hard-pressed workforce to even greater achievements.
- Huge new industrial centres were constructed virtually from nothing, for example at Magnitogorsk in the Urals and Kuznetz in western Siberia. Most of these were located east of the Ural mountains, a strategic decision to make them less vulnerable to attack from the West.
- Spectacular projects were conceived to demonstrate the might of the new Soviet industrial machine. This has been called 'gigantomania'. The Dnieprostroi Dam in eastern Russia (Source 12.5 on page 174) was, for two years, the world's largest construction site and it increased Soviet electric power output fivefold when it came on stream. Other projects included the Moscow–Volga canal and the prestigious Moscow metro with its elaborate stations and high vaulted ceilings (see Source 12.6 on page 174).

Foreign participation

A significant aspect of the industrial development of the USSR in the early 1930s was the involvement of foreign companies and individuals. A large number of companies sent specialists, engineers and skilled workers to help to erect new factories or exploit new resources. Henry Ford helped the Russians to develop a car industry. Russian engineers were trained by Ford in the USA and it was Ford-designed cars that were produced at the car plant in Gorky. Colonel Hugh Cooper, the engineer in charge of the Dnieprostroi Dam project, was an American. So was A. Ruckseyer, the man behind the huge growth in the asbestos industry at a remote place in the Urals called Asbest. Thousands of skilled workers – British, American and many other nationalities – came for a variety of reasons, some ideological and some because of unemployment in the West. The Great Depression convinced many people that capitalism was in its death throes and that the dynamic Soviet Union offered hope for the future of working people.

AT MAGNITOGORSK

Iron and steel were at the heart of Soviet industrialisation so the development of Magnitogorsk, with its huge reserves of iron ore, was at the forefront of the labour offensive. One contemporary Soviet pamphlet stated: 'Near Magnetic Mountain the steppe has been turned into a battlefield, the steppe is retreating.' The object of the battle was to build a gigantic steel plant capable of challenging the best in the capitalist world. In March 1929, 25 settlers arrived on horseback at the snow-covered site. By June 1930, the first train arrived with the banners 'The Steel Horse Breathes Life into the Magnitogorsk Giant. Long Live the Bolshevik Party!'

B What did the Five-Year Plans achieve?

■ **12D The achievements and weaknesses of the Five-Year Plans in the 1930s**

FIRST FIVE-YEAR PLAN
October 1928 to December 1932
The emphasis was on heavy industries – coal, oil, iron and steel, electricity, cement, metals, timber. This accounted for 80 per cent of total investment; 1500 enterprises were opened.

Successful sectors
- Electricity – production trebled.
- Coal and iron – output doubled.
- Steel production – increased by one-third.
- Engineering industry developed and increased output of machine-tools, turbines, etc.
- Huge new industrial complexes were built or were in the process of being built.
- Huge new tractor works were built in Stalingrad, Kharkov and other places to meet the needs of mechanised agriculture.

Weaknesses
- There was very little growth, and even a decline, in consumer industries such as house-building, fertilisers, food processing and woollen textiles.
- Small workshops were squeezed out, partly because of the drive against Nepmen and partly because of shortages of materials and fuel.
- Chemicals targets were not fulfilled.
- The lack of skilled workers created major problems. Workers were constantly changing jobs, which created instability.

Comment
In reality, many targets were not met. The Great Depression had driven down the price of grain and raw materials, so the USSR could not earn enough from exports to pay for all the machinery it needed. Also, a good deal of investment had to go into agriculture because of the forced collectivisation programme. However, the Soviet economy was kick-started: there was impressive growth in certain sectors of the economy and there were substantial achievements.

SECOND FIVE-YEAR PLAN
January 1933 to December 1937
Heavy industries still featured strongly but new industries opened up and there was greater emphasis on communications, especially railways to link cities and industrial centres. Four and a half thousand enterprises opened. The plan benefited from some big projects, such as the Dnieprostroi Dam, coming into use.

Successful sectors
- Heavy industries benefited from plants which had been set up during the first plan and now came on stream. Electricity production expanded rapidly.
- By 1937, the USSR was virtually self-sufficient in machine-making and metal-working.
- Transport and communications grew rapidly.
- Chemical industries, such as fertiliser production, were growing.
- Metallurgy developed – minerals such as copper, zinc and tin were mined for the first time.

Weaknesses
- Consumer goods industries were still lagging, although they were showing signs of recovery. There was growth in footwear and food processing – modern bakeries, ice-cream production and meat-packing plants – but not enough.
- Oil production did not make the expected advances.

Comment
There was a feeling in the party that Stalin had overreached himself in the First Five-Year Plan, that targets had been too high. The second plan was more one of consolidation. The years 1934–36 were known as the 'three good years' since the pressure was not so intense, food rationing was ended and families had more disposable income.

THIRD FIVE-YEAR PLAN
January 1938 to June 1941
The third plan ran for only three and a half years because of the USSR's entry into the Second World War. Once again, heavy industry was emphasised as the need for armaments became increasingly urgent.

Successful sectors
- Heavy industry continued to grow, for example, machinery and engineering, but the picture was uneven and some areas did poorly.
- Defence and armaments grew rapidly as resources were diverted to them.

Weaknesses
- Steel output grew insignificantly.
- Oil production failed to meet targets and led to a fuel crisis.
- Consumer industries once again took a back seat.
- Many factories ran short of materials.

Comment
The third plan ran into difficulties at the beginning of 1938 due to an exceptionally hard winter and the diversion of materials to the military. Gosplan was thrown into chaos when the purges (see Chapter 13) created shortages of qualified personnel, such as important managers, engineers and officials, who linked industries and government.

FOCUS ROUTE

1 As you work through pages 179–183, collect evidence about the planning system and its effectiveness and record it in a table like the one shown here.

Evidence of success and achievements	Evidence of failures and weaknesses	Evidence that the Five-Year Plans were not well planned

2 Who were the 'bourgeois specialists' and why were they attacked by the party?
3 Why were officials and managers reluctant to admit to problems in the plans?

SOURCE 12.8 Industrial output 1913–40, from R. W. Davies, M. Harrison and S. G. Wheatcroft (eds), *The Economic Transformation of the Soviet Union, 1913–1945*, 1994

	1913	1928	1932	1933	1936	1937	1940
Electric power (billion kWh)	1.9	5.0	13.5	16.4	32.8	36.2	48.3
Crude oil (million tons)	9.2	11.6	21.4	21.5	27.4	28.5	31.1
Coal (million tons)	29.1	35.5	64.4	76.3	126.8	128.0	165.9
Pig-iron (million tons)	4.2	3.3	6.2	7.1	14.4	14.5	14.9
Rolled steel (million tons)	3.5	3.4	4.4	5.1	12.5	13.0	13.1
Quality steel (million tons)	0.04	0.09	0.68	0.89	2.06	2.39	2.79
Copper (thousand tons)	31.1	30.0	45.0	44.3	100.8	97.5	160.9
Cement (million tons)	1.52	1.85	3.48	2.71	5.87	5.45	5.68
Mineral fertilisers (million tons)	0.07	0.14	0.92	1.03	2.84	3.24	3.24
Sulphuric acid (million tons)	0.12	0.21	0.55	0.63	1.20	1.37	1.59
Metal-cutting machine tools (thousands)	1.5	2.0	19.7	21.0	44.4	48.5	58.4
Locomotives (standard units)	265	478	828	941	1566	1582	1220
Generators (thousand kW)	–	75	1085	587	–	561	468
Electric motors (thousand kW)	–	259	1658	1385	1653	1833	1848
Tractors (thousand 15 hp units)	–	1.8	50.8	79.9	173.2	66.5	66.2
Lorries (thousands)	–	0.7	23.7	39.1	131.5	180.3	136.0
Raw sugar (million tons)	1.35	1.28	0.83	1.00	2.00	2.42	2.17
Cigarettes (billions)	22.1	49.5	57.9	62.7	85.9	89.2	100.4
Vodka (million decalitres)	118.9	55.5	72.0	–	89.7	92.5	44.3
Cotton fabrics (million linear metres)	2582	2678	2694	2732	3270	3448	3954
Woollen fabrics (million linear metres)	105	101	89	86	102	108	120

SOURCE 12.9 A comparison of pig-iron and steel production in the USSR and in Magnitogorsk

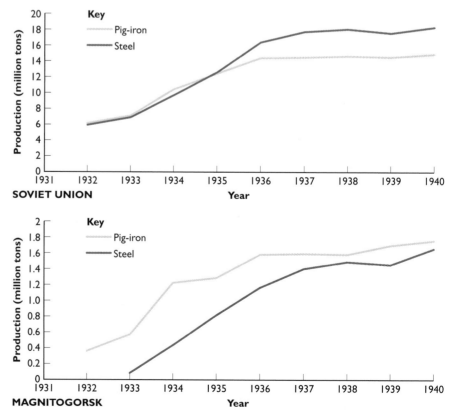

ACTIVITY

Compare the two graphs in Source 12.9. The similarities in their pattern are striking. Study Source 12.8 also, and consider why there was a slowdown in production between 1936 and 1938.

AT MAGNITOGORSK

SOURCE 12.10 Changing production targets for pig-iron during the First Five-Year Plan

		Tons per year
	1928	656,000
Summer	1929	850,000
Late	1929	1,100,000
Early	1930	2,500,000

Raw materials Firms routinely requested far more than they required because they were never sure what they would be allocated. Interruptions in deliveries were so regular that firms hoarded what they could, while at the same time bombarding the centre with requests for more of everything. Coal supplies were often found to be short on arrival, having been pilfered on the way. The plant therefore had to request more coal than it needed and probably ended up buying the 'lost coal' on the black market.
Quality Significant amounts of pig-iron and steel were found to be unusable when the time came to count up output. But even if it was declared defective, it was still sent to metal-starved firms that had little choice but to use it.

SOURCE 12.12 A. Nove, *An Economic History of the USSR, 1917–91*, 1992, p. 191. Nove recounts a story told by Isaac Babel

'One old oil expert, given what he regarded as an absurd order to increase production, is said to have written to the Central Committee as follows: "I cease to be responsible for the planning department. The [plan] figure of 40 million tons I consider to be purely arbitrary. Over a third of the oil must come from unexplored areas ... Furthermore the three cracking plants which now exist are to be turned into 120 plants by the end of the five-year plan. This despite the huge shortage of metal ... and so on."'...
Needless to say the new targets were far beyond practical possibility. The rush, strain, shortages, pressures became intolerable, and caused great disorganization. Naturally, supplies of materials, fuels, goods wagons, fell short of requirements.

The First Five-Year Plan

As the First Five-Year Plan got underway, there was a wave of planning fervour or 'target mania'. There was a sort of competition between Gosplan and Vesenkha (the Supreme Economic Council), who were bidding each other up with higher targets. The original targets set in the first plan were optimistic, but almost before it was begun targets were revised upwards. In April 1929, two versions of the plan were produced – a 'basic' and a much higher 'optimum' version. The latter was chosen. This envisaged targets being increased by astonishing amounts, for instance, coal up from 35 to 75 million tons and iron ore from six to nineteen million tons. To many, these seemed hopelessly unachievable.

Some historians have suggested that planning was more in the realms of socialist fantasy than rational calculation. In *The Russian Revolution 1917–1932* (1994, pages 129–34), Sheila Fitzpatrick talks of this period as one in which the 'spirit of a Cultural Revolution' swept people along. Party leaders and members had a millennial vision of a country that would be transformed. They believed that in two or three years they would have a socialist rather than a market economy and money would be abandoned as the main means of rewarding workers. In this sense, the First Five-Year Plan can be seen more as a propaganda device to drive Soviet citizens forward and create a sense of urgency.

Setting targets is one thing; detailed planning, which involves the complex co-ordination of different branches of industry over a huge area, is something else. And this sort of detailed planning seemed to be notably absent from the First Five-Year Plan. The party handed out broad directives and priorities and it was left to officials and managers at regional and local levels to work out ways to achieve the production targets they had been set. This was bound to lead to problems.

SOURCE 12.11 Output targets for the First Five-Year Plan, from A. Nove, *An Economic History of the USSR, 1917–91*, 1992, p. 145

	Actual output in 1927–28	1932–33 targets in first version of plan	1932–33 targets in 'optimum' version of plan
Coal (million tons)	35	68	75
Iron ore (million tons)	6	15	19
Steel (million tons)	4	8	10

The high targets placed enormous strain on the economy. Materials of all sorts were in short supply and there was intense competition to get hold of them. At higher levels, powerful people in industrial commissariats pulled strings to make sure that their pet projects got the resources they needed for completion. Materials and workers – shock brigades – were rushed into key industries to do certain jobs, often on the order of a senior party official, despite the fact that this left other areas short and waiting for supplies. At the regional and local levels, factories competed with each other for scarce resources. Bribery and corruption were rife. Managers made illegal deals in their desperation to get the parts or supplies they needed to fulfil their targets. Some were known to hijack lorries and ambush trains to get supplies intended for other plants. Bottlenecks appeared everywhere due to shortages of materials and the inadequacy of the transport system. The railways could not cope with what they were expected to transport: it soon became clear that the planners had not invested enough in track or rolling stock.

The net result of this was twofold:

1 In some parts of the economy there was underproduction because factories were held up by shortages of materials. In other parts there was overproduction as factories rushed to exceed their targets.
2 There was a great deal of wastage because:
   a) overproduction created thousands of parts that other industries did not want
   b) much of the output was sub-standard, such as lorry tyres that lasted for only a few weeks.

What made matters worse was that few managers or officials were prepared to admit anything was wrong. They did not want to be accused of sabotaging the plans or criticising the party. So mistakes were covered up and problems were left unresolved. It was all buried in the colossal amount of paperwork that flowed around the USSR. All that mattered to managers and officials at different levels was that they could show they had achieved their targets, whether this was real or invented. In fact, there were extravagant claims of over-fulfilment in many areas. This seemed to confirm that the system was working and discouraged others from speaking out about problems.

Of course, not all the mistakes could be covered up and somebody had to be blamed. Class enemies were ready to hand and Stalin was not slow to use this political tool in the same way as he had in the collectivisation drive. The industrial equivalent of the kulak was the 'bourgeois specialist'. These were the old pre-1917 managers, engineers and technical staff who had survived the NEP in important jobs because of their skills and abilities. Now they were identified as saboteurs who were deliberately causing hold-ups, breakdowns and general problems in the supply industries. They were uncovered and imprisoned. Show trials were held to hammer home the point to other managers.

The attack on the bourgeois specialists was not just a cynical tool to frighten others and find a convenient scapegoat for errors and miscalculations. Many party members believed that this group did harbour bourgeois, anti-socialist attitudes that would scupper their revolution: they wanted proletarians in key technical positions. Unfortunately, the loss of valuable personnel so quickly caused so many problems that by 1931 the offensive against them was quietly dropped.

In the First Five-Year Plan, consumer goods industries, such as textiles, were sacrificed to the needs of heavy industry. Other areas suffered from the closure of small-scale enterprises and workshops. These were squeezed out for two main reasons:

• They had been largely run by Nepmen.
• They could not get supplies of raw materials.

These small-scale operations might have been able to respond to consumer demand but there was no room for them in a centrally organised system.

WHY WERE OFFICIALS AND MANAGERS TOO FRIGHTENED TO ACKNOWLEDGE THE PROBLEMS OF THE PLANNING SYSTEM?

In March 1928, managerial and technical staff were accused of counter-revolutionary activities at the Shakhty coal mine in the Don Basin. Stalin was closely involved in the proceedings. The staff were forced to confess to subversive activities in a 'show trial' for all of the public to see. Five were executed and the rest were given long prison sentences.

The aim of this was clear – to intimidate managers and party officials who did not go along with the pace of industrialisation. The Shakhty trial created shock waves throughout the planning system. Gosplan was purged of pessimists and non-party members at the end of the 1920s. Statisticians who presented low targets were replaced by those who could paint a more optimistic picture.

In the early 1930s, trials of professionals and specialists were held in cities throughout the Soviet Union. In November 1930, the 'Industrial Party' show trial was held. This was a party of professionals who were supposedly organising the sabotage and wrecking of the Five-Year Plan. But this party was invented by Stalin. The accused were mainly industrialists, Mensheviks and Socialist Revolutionaries who worked for the government. In 1933, in the Metro-Vickers trial, British specialists were found guilty of sabotage.

It is therefore not surprising that managers were unwilling to admit to mistakes when it could lead to investigation and criminal charges.

The Second and Third Five-Year Plans

By the beginning of the Second Five-Year Plan, party leaders were prepared to acknowledge the problems that had resulted from the breakneck speed of industrialisation from 1929 to 1932. The severe shortages, disruptions in transport, lack of skilled workers and slower growth rates for certain industries were sufficient evidence of this. In 1932, the great leap forward seemed to be on the verge of collapse.

The second plan was revised and targets were scaled back. The emphasis was more on consolidation. The plan was worked out in greater detail for each industry and region. The People's Commissariats, which were more organised and clearly defined by 1934, gave specific targets for the enterprises under their control as well as estimates of costs, labour, prices, and so on. Investment was ploughed into the railway system, thus increasing enormously the amount of freight it was able to carry. There were new training schemes that encouraged workers to learn skills and master techniques to tackle the problem of skills shortages. There were still plenty of rough edges to the planning system – shortages, waste, and under/over-production continued – but not on the scale of the first plan.

Many of the schemes started in the first plan now came on stream, boosting industrial growth enormously. For instance, the USSR was almost self-sufficient in the production of machine tools and far less dependent on foreign imports of machinery. The Soviet Union enjoyed the 'three good years' of 1934–36 and the achievements by 1937 were impressive. The Second Five-Year Plan envisaged more resources going into consumer industries, since leaders had realised how badly the workers had suffered during the early 1930s through lack of goods and basic commodities. There were improvements in some areas, like footwear production and food processing, but as the plan progressed, resources were again diverted into other areas.

After 1937, the USSR witnessed an economic slowdown. Although there was a general increase in industrial output during the Third Five-Year Plan, some areas like iron and steel virtually stopped growing. There was a fuel crisis when the oil industry failed to meet its modest targets. As Europe moved towards war, resources were channelled into the armaments industry and this created shortages elsewhere. Alec Nove (Source 12.13) places much of the blame for this slowdown on the Great Purges that were in full swing in 1936 and 1937 (see Chapter 13). Nove claims the purges deprived the economy of valuable personnel and paralysed the ability of administrators and party officials to take the initiative and solve problems. Also, many planners were purged with the result that the planning system was thrown into confusion.

The picture at the end of the Third Five-Year Plan shows planning once more in a confused and even chaotic state, with shortages, waste and bottlenecks as growing features of the economy. Indeed, looking back over the plans it is sometimes difficult to see where the word 'planned' fits into the 'planned economy' of the 1930s. Yet this rough-and-ready system worked and, by 1941, the USSR had succeeded in creating the industrial base for a powerful arms industry.

SOURCE 12.13 A. Nove, *An Economic History of the USSR, 1917–1991*, 1992, p. 239

[The purge] swept away ... managers, technicians, statisticians, planners, even foremen. Everywhere there were said to be spies, wreckers, diversionists. There was a grave shortage of qualified personnel, so the deportation of many thousands of engineers and technologists to distant concentration camps represented a severe loss. But perhaps equally serious was the psychological effect of this terror on the survivors. With any error or accident likely to be attributable to treasonable activities, the simplest thing to do was to avoid responsibility, to seek approval from one's superiors for any act, to obey mechanically any order received, regardless of local conditions.

C How did the workers fare under the plans?

Did the workers support the plans?

The urban working classes and young people in general were enthusiastic at the beginning of the plans. They were carried forward by the spirit of cultural revolution and wanted to move forward to a better society. Evidence of this enthusiasm can be found in the actions of the thousands of young people who volunteered to go and work on distant projects, often labouring in the most primitive of conditions. They were prepared to make sacrifices to build a new world which would probably bring real benefits only for their children. They were participating in the great construction projects of socialism (see Sources 12.5–12.7 on page 174).

On a more practical note, workers believed they would be better off. Their real wages had risen only slowly under the NEP and unemployment had been high in the late 1920s. Social historians have found evidence suggesting that shop-floor workers in the main supported the party hierarchy in its industrialisation push. They also approved of the attack on the bourgeois specialists. Young workers were tired of their 'old' managers still strutting around giving orders and engineers enjoying privileges while they slaved away.

The party had envisaged the creation of a proletarian intelligentsia with highly developed technical skills ('red specialists') who would fill the role of the old specialists and become loyal to the regime. To some extent this succeeded. The cohort of industrial workers of the late 1920s, possessing highly valued skills, quickly advanced to supervisory posts or became managers or party officials. There were great strides in higher technical education for more able and intelligent proletarians. This group did well on the whole when wage differentials were introduced and their standard of living was significantly higher than that of the broad mass of workers.

Workers who stayed in their jobs and observed labour discipline could do well in the 1930s. Training courses meant they could improve their qualifications and position, pay and prospects. Those who exceeded their targets were rewarded with higher pay, better working conditions and, with luck, better housing. They were celebrated in newspapers and on notice boards where they worked.

Women in the labour force

One of the most important sources of new labour was women. Some ten million women entered the workforce. Women dominated some professions, particularly medicine and school teaching. The less well educated, especially tough ex-peasant women, became labourers or factory workers. Generally, women were paid less and found it more difficult to gain advancement than men. However women were working in jobs that they had not done before, as Source 12.14 on page 185 shows.

Sarah Davies' survey of women workers in Leningrad in 1935 (*Popular Opinion in Stalin's Russia: Terror, Propaganda and Dissent 1934–41*, 1997) showed that women workers in the city made up 44 per cent of the workforce but were likely to be less well paid, less literate and less involved in political

---

■ **Learning trouble spot**

Proletarianisation

Some students have difficulty understanding why the Communist Party was so anxious to 'proletarianise' the mass of the Russian people, that is, turn them into industrial workers. The Communists believed that the vast majority of the population had to be proletarians with the right attitudes before you could create a socialist state and then move on to establish Communism – the ultimate Marxist goal. This meant that you had to get rid of the old bourgeois capitalist attitudes connected to the selfishness of the free market economy – the notion of working for one's own self-interest with profit as the main incentive for economic activities. The people who held these attitudes were class enemies. Only when you got rid of these people could you proceed to the co-operation and sharing envisaged in the higher form of socialism.

To push forward proletarianisation, the party believed it had to:

- get rid of bourgeois specialists who made up the majority of the managers and engineers in industry and replace them with proletarians (red specialists)
- turn peasants flooding into the towns into good proletarians
- turn peasants remaining in the countryside into agricultural proletarians, hence the vision of factory farms and agrotowns.

and technical education than their male counterparts. The issues that were most important to them were their children's needs, queues and fluctuating prices, not surprising as women had to look after the home as well as work. Their chances of reaching the top were limited. Of 328 factory directors, only twenty were women and seventeen of these were in textile and sewing factories where well over three-quarters of the workforce were women. There were only four women head doctors in hospitals, even though 50–60 per cent of all doctors were women.

SOURCE 12.14 Soviet women pilots in the 1930s

AT MAGNITOGORSK

Almost half of the workers in January 1932 were under 24 and typically ex-peasant, male, unskilled and illiterate. In 1933, about one-fifth (40,000) of the population were exiled peasants. John Scott (*Behind the Urals*, 1942) estimates that between 1928 and 1932 about three-quarters of new arrivals came of their own free will seeking work and the rest came under compulsion. Few of the engineers had real engineering experience. A colony of several hundred foreign engineers and specialists arrived to advise and direct the work.

SOURCE 12.15 S. Kotkin, *Magnetic Mountain: Stalinism as a Civilisation*, 1995, p. 95, writing about the fluidity of labour

By early 1934 almost ten times as many workers had passed through the site than were at hand. Indeed, who had not been to Magnitogorsk! You tell someone you're going to Magnitogorsk and everywhere you hear: 'Magnita, I'm going there,' or 'I just came from there.' Somebody says he has a brother there, somebody else is waiting for a letter from his son. You get the impression that the whole country either was there or is going there. Many people in fact came and left several times in the course of one year. In 1931 the average length of stay for a worker was 82 calendar days. Magnitogorsk became a revolving door.

The quicksand society

The First Five-Year Plan required an enormous expansion of the labour force. The majority of the new workers were peasants who had been forced off the land by collectivisation. Around half the labour force by the end of the First Five-Year Plan was made up of peasants. They wandered in from the countryside, bemused and bewildered, looking for work, lodgings and adequate food. If they could find a better deal elsewhere, they moved on. There was a phenomenal turnover of labour. In the coal industry in 1930, the average worker moved jobs three times a year. These ex-peasants lacked the most elementary disciplines of time-keeping and punctuality. Their normal working pattern was entirely different from that required in a factory and they found it difficult to adapt to the monotonous hours of machine-based work. Many were resentful about being forced into industrial work anyway. This led to a high rate of absenteeism.

This turnover was not restricted to the peasants. Skilled and semi-skilled workers soon found that skills were at a premium and that managers, desperate to fulfil their targets, were anxious to attract them. They began to compete for skilled workers by offering higher wages or additional perks, such as extra food rations. These workers were able to move easily between jobs and this contributed to the destabilising effect of high labour turnover on industrial enterprises. One Communist leader talked of Russia being like a huge 'nomadic gypsy camp' and Moshe Lewin likened it to a 'quicksand society' (see Source 12.19 on page 187).

The skills shortage was one of the biggest problems the planners faced. In 1931, it was estimated that less than seven per cent of the workforce were skilled. A survey in 1933 showed that only seventeen per cent of those recruited to industry had any skills. In Elektrozavod, a $25,000 lathe from the USA lay unused for want of a minor repair which workers were unable to perform. Untrained, clumsy workers were doing an astonishing amount of damage to expensive imported machinery and were turning out poor-quality goods. Machines were not properly oiled and maintained. There were stories of whole production runs being ruined by ill-educated and untrained ex-peasants.

ACTIVITY

1 Use the information in Sources 12.16 and 12.17 and a graph-drawing program to produce bar graphs illustrating the following:
   a) net gains or losses in the Magnitogorsk labour force for each month in 1931
   b) the overall pattern of gains and losses between 1930 and 1933.
2 Using ICT, produce a bar graph which shows:
   a) total number of workers on 1 January 1931
   b) total arrivals for 1931
   c) total departures for 1931
   d) total number of workers on 31 December 1931.
3 What do these graphs reveal about the turnover of labour in Magnitogorsk in 1931?

SOURCE 12.16 Labour turnover at Magnitogorsk, 1931

1st of month	Total workers	Arrived during the month	Left during the month
January	18,865	3,597	3,853
February	18,609	4,398	3,402
March	19,605	8,570	5,934
April	22,241	9,391	7,166
May	24,446	17,640	9,826
June	32,280	17,292	10,825
July	38,747	10,983	12,694
August	37,006	8,693	11,447
September	34,252	10,381	9,421
October	35,162	8,003	10,072
November	33,093	10,350	10,797
December	32,666	7,440	7,835

SOURCE 12.17 Workers arriving at and departing from Magnitogorsk, 1930–33

	Arrived	Left
1930	67,000*	45,000
1931	111,000	97,000
1932	62,000	70,000
1933	53,000	53,000
Total	**293,000**	**265,000**

* It is possible that the figure of 67,000 for 1930 is a typographical error and should have read 57,000

SOURCE 12.18 A. Nove, *An Economic History of the USSR, 1917–91*, 1992, p. 192. Nove quotes a future minister, talking about the birth of the Stalingrad tractor works

a) *A worker ... came to the Volga from a Moscow factory. Even he was full of wonder at the American lathes without belt transmission, with their own motors. He could not handle them. What is one to say of peasants fresh from the fields? They were sometimes illiterate.*
b) *The first director of the factory, Ivanov, wrote as follows: 'In the assembly shop I talked to a young man who was grinding sockets. I asked him how he measured, and he showed me how he used his fingers. We had no measuring instruments!'*

ACTIVITY

You are advisers to the Politburo. Working in groups of three, suggest at least one solution for each of the problems identified below. Then compare your solutions with those of other groups.
   Are you going to:

• use methods of intimidation to force the most out of the workers?
• find ways to encourage them to perform more satisfactorily?

Problems

1 Continuing shortage of labour – where can you get more workers for the ever-expanding factories?
2 Skills shortage – what can you do about the lack of technical skills?
3 Poor work habits amongst the ex-peasants – poor discipline and clumsiness.
4 Keeping the workforce stable – it is very hard to establish good practices if your workforce is constantly changing and moving to other places.
5 Absenteeism.
6 Motivating the workers to increase their productivity.
7 Keeping the existing skilled working class happy.

How did the party respond to its labour problems?

FOCUS ROUTE

1 Draw a diagram to record the main ways in which the Soviet government tried to deal with the problems it faced).
2 Compare these with the solutions you suggested in the Activity on page 186.
3 What surprises you about some of the methods adopted by the Communists?

Wage differentials and incentives

To stop workers 'flitting' from job to job, wage differentials (i.e. paying some people more than others) were introduced to reward those who stayed put and acquired skills. Managers were allowed to pay bonuses. Other incentives were also used, such as awarding honours to outstanding workers; these were not just moral rewards but could bring perks and privileges such as access to closed shops, better housing and better clothes. Egalitarianism in wages was abandoned as early as 1931.

Piece work

Payment according to the pieces of work completed became common across industry, to try to drive up productivity.

Training

A massive training programme was brought into being. But many of the training programmes were poor and trainees were rushed through by poor instructors. The situation improved in the Second Five-Year Plan with fewer but better training schemes made available.

Tough measures

A series of measures were brought in between 1930 and 1933 to deal with absentees. These included dismissal, eviction from factory-owned homes or loss of various benefits. Causing damage or leaving a job without permission could lead to a prison sentence. The intimidation and terror applied to the bourgeois specialists were also applied to the workers.

The degree of control increased during the Second and Third Five-Year Plans. In 1938, labour books were issued, along with internal passports. The labour book gave details of a worker's labour history, qualifications and any misdemeanours. It was very difficult to survive without one of these. In 1940, absenteeism became a crime, with two offences bringing a prison sentence.

Forced labour

Some labour shortages were solved by using forced labour, especially for the worst jobs in the worst conditions. Around 300,000 prisoners worked on the Baltic–White Sea Canal, many of them kulaks arrested during the collectivisation drive. After April 1930 all criminals sentenced to more than three years were sent to labour camps to provide cheap labour. The government decreed that these camps should be self-supporting. Lumber camps were set up in the forests of the frozen north and the timber produced was exported to help earn money for industrial investment. The number of forced labourers increased when the Great Purges got into full swing in the mid-1930s.

Propaganda and encouragement

A huge propaganda campaign was mounted to encourage workers to raise their productivity, which was outstandingly low during the First Five-Year Plan (see Sources 12.19 and 12.21). Shock-brigade campaigns (mounting intensive efforts to build structures such as dams) and 'socialist competition' were tried to raise work norms but they enjoyed only limited success. Probably the most significant propaganda initiative was the Stakhanovite movement (see pages 190–192). Although this caused some problems in the economy, productivity rates did improve.

SOURCE 12.19 S. Kotkin, *Magnetic Mountain: Stalinism as a Civilisation*, 1995, pp. 90–92

In 1930 work began on a dam on the Ural River to supply the steel factory with water. Shock work began: 'Everyone to the dam! Everything for the dam!' There was socialist competition between left and right banks. The target date moved forward but the dam was built in a record 74 days, well ahead of schedule. One contemporary writer wrote: 'The Magnitogorsk dam was the school at which people began to respect Bolshevik miracles.' But it was not deep enough and the water froze, there was a chronic shortage of water, and a new dam five times as big was started almost immediately. When it was completed the first dam was submerged.

SOURCE 12.20 M. Lewin, 'Society, State and Ideology during the First Five-Year Plan', 1976, in C. Ward (ed.), *The Stalinist Dictatorship*, 1998, pp. 178–79. Lewin has an interesting background. Born in Poland in 1921, he became active in left-wing politics, escaping from the Nazis to work in the Soviet Union on a kolkhoz and in a mill. He was an officer in the Red Army for a brief time. After the Second World War he spent ten years in a kibbutz in Israel before holding academic positions in France, Britain and the USA

One of the results of this [mass influx of peasants to the cities] was the breakdown of labour discipline, which saddled the state with an enormous problem of education and disciplining the mass of the crude labour force. The battle against absenteeism, shirking, drinking in factories during working hours, and breaking tools was long, and the Soviet government played no 'humanistic' games in this fight. Very soon, methods such as denial of ration cards, eviction from lodgings, and even penal sentences for undisciplined workers were introduced.

Factories and mines in these years were transformed into railway stations – or as Ordzhonikidze [see page 177] exclaimed in despair – into one huge 'nomadic gypsy camp'. The cost of the turnover was incredible. Before they had managed to learn their job, people had already given their notice or done something in order to get fired. But the same process, and on a large scale, was going on among managers and administrators, specialists and officials. At all levels of the local administration and party apparat, *people adopted the habit of leaving in good time, before they were penalized, recalled, brought in for questioning, downgraded, fired or arrested.*

Thus workers, administrators, specialists, officials, party apparatus men, and, in great masses, peasants were all moving around and changing jobs, creating unwanted surpluses in some places and dearths in others, losing skills or failing to acquire them, creating streams and floods in which families were destroyed, children lost, and morality dissolved. Social, administrative, industrial and political structures were all in flux. The mighty dictatorial government found itself, as a result of its impetuous activity during those early years of accelerated industrialisation, presiding over a 'quicksand' society.

SOURCE 12.21 A Soviet propaganda poster, *In the Struggle for Fuel and Metal*, produced in 1933 with the aim of spurring on the workers to fulfil the Five-Year Plan. Gustav Klutsis, the creator of this poster, was a master of photo-montage techniques, and his posters were reproduced thousands of times. A party member since 1920, he was a loyal Stalinist, but neither this nor his work for the party could save him when he was denounced by a jealous rival during the purges; he was shot in 1938

SOURCE 12.22 J. Scott, *Behind the Urals*, 1942, p. 49. Scott describes aspects of the attempts to motivate workers in Magnitogorsk

In 1933 wage differentials were approximately as follows: the average monthly wage for an unskilled worker in Magnitogorsk was something in the neighbourhood of 100 roubles; a skilled workers' apprentice 200, a skilled worker, 300; an engineer with experience 600 to 800; administrators, directors etc., anywhere from 800 to 3000. The heavy differentiation plus the absence of unemployment and the consequent assurance of being able without difficulty to get any job in any profession learned, supplemented and stimulated the intellectual curiosity of the people. The two together were so potent that they created a student body in the Magnitogorsk night schools of 1933 willing to work eight, ten or even twelve hours on the job under the severest conditions, and then come back to night school, sometimes on an empty stomach and, sitting on a backless wooden bench, in a room so cold that you could see your breath a yard in front of you, study mathematics four hours straight....

... Competition between individuals, brigades and whole departments was encouraged ... The Stakhanov movement [see pages 190–192] hit Magnitogorsk in the autumn of 1935. Brigade and shop competition was intensified. Banners were awarded to the brigades who worked best, and monetary remuneration accompanied banners ... Wages rose. Production rose ...

SOURCE 12.23 Extracts from a letter preserved in the Magnitogorsk archives, from Anna Kovaleva to Marfa Gidzia, and quoted in S. Kotkin, *Magnetic Mountain: Stalinism as a Civilisation*, 1995, pp. 218–19

Dear Marfa!
We are both wives of locomotive drivers of the rail transport of Magnitka. You probably know that the rail transport workers of the MMK (Magnitogorsk Metallurgical Complex) are not fulfilling the plan, that they are disrupting the supply of the blast furnaces, open hearths and rolling shops ... All the workers of Magnita accuse our husbands ... Every day there are stoppages and breakdowns in rail transport ... [To fulfil the plan] it is necessary to work like the best workers of our country work. Among such shock workers is my husband, Aleksandr Panteleevich Kovalev. He always works like a shock worker, exceeding his norms, while economising on oil and lubricants ... My husband receives prizes every month ... My husband's locomotive is always clean and well taken care of....

Your husband, Iakov Stepanovich, does not fulfil the plan. He has frequent breakdowns on his locomotive, his locomotive is dirty, and he always overconsumes fuel ... all the rail workers of Magnita know him, for the wrong reasons, as the worst driver. By contrast, my husband is known as a shock worker. He is written up and praised in the newspapers ... He and I are honoured everywhere as shock workers. At the store we get everything without having to wait in queues. We moved to the building for shock workers. We get an apartment with rugs, a gramophone, a radio and other comforts ...

Therefore, I ask you, Marfa, to talk to your husband ... Persuade him that he must work honourably, conscientiously, like a shock worker. Teach him to understand the words of comrade Stalin, that work is a matter of honour, glory, valour and heroism....

ACTIVITY

Use the information in Sources 12.19–12.23 on pages 188–189 to answer the following questions.

1 Which of the measures the Soviet government brought in do not fit well with socialism and would be more at home in a capitalist system?
2 a) What does Moshe Lewin (Source 12.20) reveal about the problems facing the Soviet authorities and the actions they took?
  b) How reliable do you think Moshe Lewin's account is as a historical source?
3 What do Sources 12.19–12.22 tell you about the methods used to motivate workers?
4 a) Does John Scott's account (Source 12.22) suggest these were successful?
  b) How reliable do you think his account is?
5 a) Do you think the 'Dear Marfa' letter (Source 12.23) is solely the work of the author?
  b) Why did she write this letter or allow her name to be attached to it?
  c) What arguments does Anna use to persuade Marfa to reform her husband?
  d) Marfa was illiterate but the letter could have been read to her. How effective do you think it was?

STAKHANOVITES
Named after Alexei Stakhanov who produced an enormous amount of coal in one shift in 1935; the Stakhanovite movement was part of a government campaign to make workers produce more and put pressure on managers to make their operations more efficient; workers who gained the accolade 'Stakhanovite' enjoyed better food, accommodation and other privileges such as holidays.

ACTIVITY

You are going to take part in a STAKHANOVITE simulation. To do this you need to split your class into groups of four or five. Each group takes on one of the roles below. The crucial characters are starred.

• The manager*
• Assistant manager
• Would-be Stakhanovite*
• Local party secretary*
• At least one, but not more than three, ordinary workers

The scenario

A worker in a factory producing steel wants to make an attempt to gain Stakhanovite status by raising his production rate enormously. You have to decide whether your character will support this attempt. To do this you need to think about:

a) your position at the moment:
   • your aims
   • what you have to do to achieve these aims and be successful
   • the problems you face.

b) what the implications of a successful attempt will be for you and others.

Then decide whether you will or will not support the attempt, setting out your reasons clearly.

How to proceed

1 Read the material on pages 191–193 about Stakhanovites, working conditions and the pressures on a manager in 1936 in industry. Different members of your group can read different parts and then you can pool your knowledge.
2 Discuss in your group how your character will respond by considering the points in a) and b) above. Decide on your response (if possible, the whole group should agree) and prepare your case for a meeting of all the characters, to be held in the next lesson. Some groups may wish to consult with others before the meeting, for example the groups playing the workers or the groups playing the manager and assistant manager.
3 Hold the meeting of all the characters to decide if the attempt should go ahead. The characters should be prepared to argue their cases aggressively in an open meeting.
4 Come out of role and discuss the following questions:
   a) What decisions were made and why were they made?
   b) What does the simulation tell you about the tensions in Soviet society?
   c) What were the advantages/disadvantages of Stakhanovism for:
      i) the individual
      ii) the factory/mine/workplace?
   d) How effective was the Stakhanov movement as a mechanism for driving up productivity?
   e) What can we learn about the relationship between politics and economics in the USSR in the 1930s?

The Stakhanov record

SOURCE 12.24 Alexei Stakhanov, the coal miner whose astonishing output inspired countless other workers to copy his example

At ten o'clock on 30 August 1935, Alexei Stakhanov, a pneumatic-pick operator, began his special shift. After five hours of uninterrupted work he had cut 102 tons of coal, almost sixteen times the norm of 6.5 tons per shift. How was this done?

The idea came from Konstantin Petrov, party organiser at Central Ormino in the Don Basin. Central Ormino lagged behind its plan quota and Petrov wanted to do something about it. He knew Stakhanov usually produced above the norm results on his shift. Ideal conditions were set up: an uninterrupted supply of compressed air, a good pick, two carefully selected proppers (to prop up the roof as Stakhanov cut away the coal) and ample supplies of timber. Hauliers were on hand to take the coal away. Petrov was there, holding a lamp on the coal face. Normally, the miners working on the face that Stakhanov cut produced around 52 tons in total per shift, but they did their own propping. Stakhanov with his support team cut twice the amount that the eight miners would have produced.

Barely two hours after Stakhanov had finished, Petrov assembled a party committee at which Stakhanov was acclaimed for his world record for productivity – the correct path to 'guarantee the fulfilment of the annual plan ahead of schedule'. Stakhanov received 200 roubles (instead of the normal 30 roubles), a bonus equal to a month's wages, an apartment reserved for technical personnel with a telephone and comfortable furniture, passes to the cinema and live performances at the local workers' club, and places at a holiday resort. He also had his name prominently displayed on the mine's honour board.

A special meeting of coal hewers was called, with compulsory attendance of local party, union and managerial leaders. Sectional competitions were set up for miners to emulate Stakhanov's achievements. The party got the response it wanted. Several miners demanded the chance to beat the record, and by 5 September two had done so. Others were warned: 'All those who try to slander Stakhanov and his record will be considered by the party committee as the most vile enemies of the people.'

Ordzhinikidze, the Commissar for Heavy Industry, had Stakhanov, the 'Soviet Hercules', put on the front page of *Pravda*. He said, 'In our country, under socialism, heroes of labour must become the most famous.' On 11 September, *Pravda* used the term 'Stakhanovite movement' for the first time and in November Stalin called for Stakhanovism to spread 'widely and deeply' across the entire Soviet Union. Recordmania swept the country: by December 1935, the records achieved in heavy industry alone filled two volumes.

The Stakhanovite movement was seen as a way of compelling management to adopt new production methods and increase rates of production. Those reluctant to do so were branded as saboteurs, with the warning 'Such pseudo leaders must be removed immediately'. With pressure from above to meet increased targets and from below from workers wanting to be Stakhanovites, who would have wanted to be a manager in Soviet Russia at that time?

A MAGNITOGORSK STAKHANOVITE

V. P. Ogorodnikov was the son of a peasant from Smolensk. His name features four times in a list of eight record-breaking shifts in a Magnitogorsk steel mill between September 1935 and January 1936. The second-highest-earning worker in Magnitogorsk, he was rewarded with a brand-new motor cycle and an individual house with its own garden, 70 per cent paid for by the factory. Before the revolution perhaps only a factory owner could have afforded such a house. He became a household name.

SOURCE 12.25   A cartoon showing the leading 'Stakhanovite' blooming mill operators, featured in the Magnitogorsk newspaper. Left to right: Ogorodnikov, Chernysh, Bogatyrenko and Tishchenko

SOURCE 12.26   The output of the leading 'Stakhanovite' blooming mill operators in Magnitogorsk, 1935–36 *(In a blooming mill, melted metal is formed into steel ingots or bars.)*

Date/shift	Name	Steel ingots produced per shift
12 September 1935	Ogorodnikov	211
22 September	Tishchenko	214
25 September	Bogatyrenko	219
9 October	Ogorodnikov	230
? October	Bogatyrenko	239
29 October	Ogorodnikov	243
11 January 1936	Ogordnikov	251
11 January (next shift)	Chernysh	264

PARTY SECRETARIES

Party Secretaries were charged with overseeing the implementation of Moscow's orders. They were judged by the output of major industrial enterprises in their areas – over fulfilment of plan targets was demanded at any cost, and health and safety issues came a poor second. They would use their influence to help managers secure scarce supplies in competition with factories from other areas. Failure to meet a target might have serious consequences.

The Stakhanovite campaign gave them the chance to overcome inertia in industry and put pressure on managers to improve productivity and raise output.

WORKERS

Workers were anxious to improve their position. But they could not strike; the NKVD saw to that. They wanted to take advantage of any wage differentials in order to secure a better standard of living. Also, they tried to avoid harsh punishments for absenteeism or poor quality work – they did not want to be accused of wrecking. One way to get higher wages and to avoid accumulating a poor record was to move from one job to another so that the authorities could not keep track of them.

When Stakhanovism started, workers resented the increased norms (these went up by around 30 per cent in some enterprises) and there was increased tension between managers and workers. Some workers demanded to become Stakhanovites in order to gain increased pay and privileges. For example, they demanded good tools, but other workers resented that the would-be Stakhanovites got the best equipment.

MANAGERS

Managers had to fulfil their targets and would do anything, including bribery and corruption, to do it. They could only fulfil their targets with the co-operation of the workers. Managers were especially desperate to keep skilled workers: some managers registered non-existent workers on the payroll and distributed their ration cards to favoured workers. Harsh laws on absenteeism were not enforced, payments were made for work that had never been done and bonuses were paid wherever possible. Moscow attacked the overpayment of wages but managers were more worried about failing to meet production targets. They made up success stories to keep Moscow happy. Soviet managers had a saying: 'It's necessary not to work well but to account well.'

Stakhanovism presented managers with problems. Workers put them under a lot of pressure to be classified as Stakhanovites and wanted good tools to do the job more efficiently, but there were not enough of these to go around. Such shortages frustrated workers and could lead to them charging managers with wrecking by 'hindering us from working in a Stakhanovite fashion'. Managers also had to deal with other problems arising from Stakhanovism, such as:
- resentment from workers who did not want production norms to increase
- distortions in the production process caused by resources being focused on Stakhanovite workers. Managers were judged on total output, not output from specific areas within the enterprise.

■ 12E Pressures on a manager in 1936

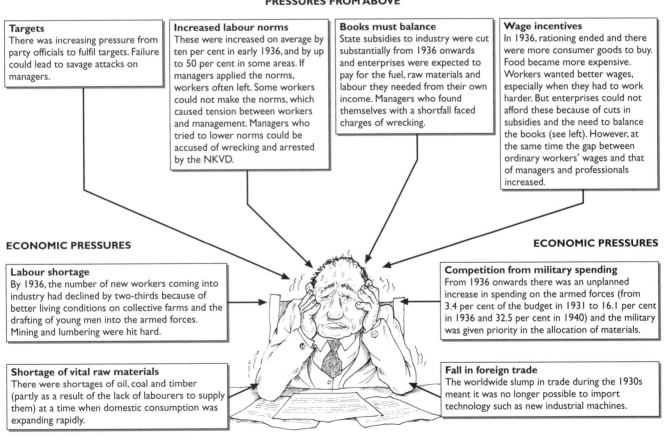

PRESSURES FROM ABOVE

Targets
There was increasing pressure from party officials to fulfil targets. Failure could lead to savage attacks on managers.

Increased labour norms
These were increased on average by ten per cent in early 1936, and by up to 50 per cent in some areas. If managers applied the norms, workers often left. Some workers could not make the norms, which caused tension between workers and management. Managers who tried to lower norms could be accused of wrecking and arrested by the NKVD.

Books must balance
State subsidies to industry were cut substantially from 1936 onwards and enterprises were expected to pay for the fuel, raw materials and labour they needed from their own income. Managers who found themselves with a shortfall faced charges of wrecking.

Wage incentives
In 1936, rationing ended and there were more consumer goods to buy. Food became more expensive. Workers wanted better wages, especially when they had to work harder. But enterprises could not afford these because of cuts in subsidies and the need to balance the books (see left). However, at the same time the gap between ordinary workers' wages and that of managers and professionals increased.

ECONOMIC PRESSURES

Labour shortage
By 1936, the number of new workers coming into industry had declined by two-thirds because of better living conditions on collective farms and the drafting of young men into the armed forces. Mining and lumbering were hit hard.

Shortage of vital raw materials
There were shortages of oil, coal and timber (partly as a result of the lack of labourers to supply them) at a time when domestic consumption was expanding rapidly.

ECONOMIC PRESSURES

Competition from military spending
From 1936 onwards there was an unplanned increase in spending on the armed forces (from 3.4 per cent of the budget in 1931 to 16.1 per cent in 1936 and 32.5 per cent in 1940) and the military was given priority in the allocation of materials.

Fall in foreign trade
The worldwide slump in trade during the 1930s meant it was no longer possible to import technology such as new industrial machines.

D Did urban living standards improve during the plans?

Throughout the 1930s, the central planning system never managed to improve the standard of living of the very citizens for whom the plans were ostensibly designed. During the First Five-Year Plan, in particular, the workers suffered very badly. There was a profound lack of consumer goods, and food was rationed. It is estimated that in Leningrad and Moscow between 1928 and 1933 meat, milk and fruit consumption declined by two-thirds.

The pressures created by the expanding urban population were phenomenal. It is estimated that cities and towns were growing at a rate of 200,000 every month and there was very little provision for this wave of humanity pouring in from the countryside. The newcomers were mainly peasants who had suffered from the psychological upheaval of being uprooted from their rural lifestyle. Some of the towns in more remote areas were akin to frontier towns, with no paved roads and inadequate sanitary arrangements. They had been turned into huge construction sites, surrounded by a sea of mud. Workers lived in barracks in appalling conditions. Overcrowding was intense, and with it came its usual bedfellows – dirt and squalor. There was very little control and life was brutish, violent and crime-ridden.

In 1935, Stalin announced that 'Life has become better, comrades, life has become more joyous.' Just how joyous is open to question. The planners were not able to meet the needs of urban dwellers. Housing, in particular, remained abysmal; there was intense overcrowding in sub-standard accommodation as building materials were diverted to factory building. Town transport, mainly trams, was also invariably packed. There was a shortage of water, shops and catering facilities. Most workers ate in their factory canteens. There was some expansion of shops during the Second Five-Year Plan but the centralised distribution system was poor and the shops often lacked basic commodities. Long queues, seemingly a permanent feature of Russian life, had as much to do with the scarcity of shops as with lack of products. However, some industrial enterprises set up their own shops, bringing in food from farms, and the peasants supplied towns with milk, eggs, vegetables and meat from their private plots. It is difficult to generalise for all sections of society and some workers certainly became better off during this period.

AT MAGNITOGORSK

Only 15 per cent of Magnitogorsk's population lived in permanent brick apartment buildings, taking up 33 per cent of the city's space. Twenty-five per cent lived in mud huts they had built for themselves. Virtually everybody had at some time lived in the huge barrack-like workers' housing. By 1939, there were enough public bath-houses to allow every inhabitant to have seven baths a year. In *Behind the Urals* (1942, pages 184–88), John Scott records that there were different levels of housing: directors and top managers had houses with several rooms and gardens; skilled workers had small houses or apartments with basic facilities; unskilled workers had poor-quality housing or mud huts.

SOURCE 12.27 M. Lewin, 'Society, State and Ideology during the First Five-Year Plan', 1976, in C. Ward (ed.), *The Stalinist Dictatorship*, 1998, p. 177

In the cities, the inordinate and unanticipated growth transformed a strained housing situation into an appalling one, creating the specifically Soviet [or Stalinist] reality of chronically overcrowded lodgings, with consequent attrition of human relations, strained family life, destruction of privacy and personal life, and various forms of psychological strain. All this provided a propitious hunting ground for the ruthless, the primitive, the blackmailer, the hooligan, and the informer. The courts dealt with an incredible mass of cases testifying to the human destruction caused by this congestion of dwellings. The falling standards of living, the lines outside stores, and the proliferation of speculators suggest the depths of the tensions and hardships.

SOURCE 12.28 M. Fainsod, *Smolensk under Soviet Rule*, 1958, p. 322, describing living conditions for unskilled workers in 1937

The workers' barracks were described as overcrowded and in a state of extreme disrepair with water streaming from the ceiling 'straight on to workers' beds'. Heat was rarely provided in the barracks; bedding went unchanged; and sanitary work was almost non-existent. There were no kitchens and eating halls on the construction sites; hot food could not be obtained until the evening when workers had to walk a long distance to reach the dining hall. 'Many of the women', one female Party member reported, 'live practically on the street. No one pays any attention to them; some of those defenceless creatures threaten to commit suicide.' In addition, cases where wages were not paid on time were on the increase. All this 'neglect of the elementary needs of workers' as well as 'lack of care for them as human beings' resulted in 'fully justified dissatisfaction' and bitterness on the part of the workers.

SOURCE 12.29 H. Eekman, a Belgian diplomat, saw ordinary families in Moscow in the late 1930s cramped into small, shared living accommodation

They made pathetic efforts to isolate from their neighbours the few square feet of floor space allotted to their use. Every piece of furniture, every stick they owned, every ragged remnant saved from old curtains, was pressed into service to build some sort of fence or stockade around their cramped refuge.

SOURCE 12.30 N. Mandelstam, *Hope Against Hope*, 1971. Nadezhda Mandelstam was the wife of one of Russia's greatest poets of the twentieth century, Osip Mandelstam, and a victim of Stalin's repression. She survived and wrote two volumes of memoirs: *Hope Against Hope* and *Hope Abandoned*

At the end of the twenties and in the thirties our authorities, making no concessions to 'egalitarianism', started to raise the living standard of those who had proved their usefulness. The resulting differentiation was very noticeable, and everybody was concerned to keep the material benefits he had worked so hard to earn – particularly now that the wretched poverty of the first post-revolutionary years was a thing of the past. Nobody wanted to go through that again, and a thin layer of privileged people gradually came into being – with 'packets', country villas, and cars. They realized only later how precarious it all was: in the period of the great purges they found they could be stripped of everything in a flash, and without any explanation. But in the meantime those who had been granted a share of the cake eagerly did everything demanded of them.

SOURCE 12.31 J. Scott, *Behind the Urals*, 1942, pp. 122–23. John Scott was an American volunteer working in Magnitogorsk (see page 175). Here, he writes about Masha the daughter of illiterate, poor peasants. Masha did not receive her first pair of shoes until she was fourteen years old. Her parents were very supportive and Masha studied at school, in a higher education institute in Moscow and at Magnitogorsk Teachers' College. She then taught adults in a party higher education college

From the incredible poverty and suffering of the civil-war period, the Russian people were working their way up to a higher standard. All Masha's family were enthusiastic. Several of the children joined the Komsomol, and after years of argument, the mother succumbed to the pressures of her children and took down the icons from the walls of the hut. Then she too decided to study. Masha's mother learned to read and write at the age of fifty-five. She was taught by her youngest daughter.

Masha went to the capital in 1929. At that time the industrialization of the country was just beginning. Russia's rapidly expanding economy was crying for every kind of professional skill, for engineers, chemists, teachers, economists, and doctors. The higher schools paid stipends to their students, and aided them in every way to get through their courses and out to factory and laboratory. Masha finished up her preparatory work, and then entered the Mendelyeyev Institute, where she worked part time as laboratory assistant to make a few roubles for bread.

Masha was very happy in Magnitogorsk. She felt that the world was at her feet. She slept on the divan of her sister and brother-in-law's tiny hotel room, she had two or three dresses, two pairs of shoes and one coat. In two more years, she would graduate from the teachers' college. Then she would teach, or perhaps take graduate work. Not only this, she was living in a town which had grown up from nothing just as she herself had. Living conditions were improving as the pig-iron production of the mill increased. She felt herself a part of a going concern. Hence her spontaneous pity for me, whom she first saw as a cast-off from a bankrupt and degenerating society.

ACTIVITY

Life in Stalin's Russia makes a good AS coursework unit of which Chapters 11 and 12 on economic policy are an important part. Coursework units can be assessed by source work (see Sources 12.27–12.31) and an essay (see page 199).

The five sources here could be used for the source work. **Part 2** appears on page 199.

Part 1
How do the sources confirm Stalin's claim of 1935 that 'Life has become better comrades, life has become more joyous'.
Note: This activity requires you to interpret, evaluate and use source material in relation to its historical context.

1 Carefully analyse both the content and the provenance of the sources. Notice the differences in content and what this says about the experience of different sections of Soviet society and how experiences change in different parts of the country.

2 Examine the origins and purpose of the sources so you can judge their reliability and value.

3 Think about the different perspectives of the writers, for example, Lewin is a professional historian (see Source 12.19, p. 188), and N. Mandelstam was a victim of Stalin's repression.

E How successful were the Five-Year Plans for industry?

Conclusions

Despite the problems with the statistics, all commentators agree that there was substantial growth in heavy industry during this period, that there were impressive achievements, and that the Soviet Union was transformed on the industrial front. The command economy clearly had major weaknesses – unrealistic targets; the use of bribery, corruption and crooked deals to achieve targets; major shortages; and products of dubious quality. At best, the economy was ill-organised and badly co-ordinated, at worst it was chaotic. There were imbalances in the economy, with heavy industry taking priority over chemicals and transport and consumer goods being neglected throughout. The Russian people still spent an enormous amount of their time queuing and went short of essential commodities. Living conditions remained abysmal.

However, this has to be set against the state of Soviet Russia in 1928 and the massive steps forward that industry took in the 1930s. In a sense, the plans were trying to do the impossible in conditions of appalling backwardness. The targets were always unrealisable but they were designed to drive people forward to achieve the impossible. Resources were directed towards the areas of key priority and in a rough and crude way progress was made. Given the results, some historians have concluded that the type of command economy that emerged, with clearly set priorities, seemed reasonably well suited to the circumstances of the USSR in the 1930s. It got the Soviet industrial juggernaut rolling and that was no mean achievement.

SOURCE 12.32 C. Ward, *Stalin's Russia*, 1993, p. 81

When the first piateletka *(Five-Year Plan) was declared complete in December 1932 no major targets had been reached, but there were some dramatic advances. In these four or five years the Soviet economy was fundamentally transformed. In the Urals, the Kuzbass, the Volga district and the Ukraine hundreds of mining, engineering and metallurgical enterprises were in the making. New factories materialised in the empty lands of the non-Russian republics scarcely touched by the modern world. More than half the machine tools on stream in the USSR by 1932 were fabricated or installed after 1928. Gigantic schemes like the Magnitogorsk combine (part of the Ural–Kuznetsk iron and steel complex) were built from scratch, the Truksib railway line opened in 1930 and the first of the Dnieprostroi's new turbines began to turn in 1932.*

SOURCE 12.33 A. Bullock, *Hitler and Stalin: Parallel Lives*, 1991, pp. 295–96

After the grey compromises of the NEP, the Plan revived the flagging faith of the party. Here at last was the chance to pour their enthusiasm into building the New Jerusalem they had been promised. The boldness of the targets, the sacrifices demanded and the vision of what 'backward' Russia might achieve provided an inspiring contrast with an 'advanced' West with millions unemployed and resources left to waste because of the Slump. None of Stalin's targets might be achieved, but in every case output was raised: 6 million tons of steel was little more than half the 10 million allowed for, but 50 per cent up on the starting figure.

TALKING POINT

How well planned do you think the plans for industry were?

■ **Learning trouble spot**

Examining the statistics

The production figures for the Five-Year Plans can be seen in Source 12.8 on page 180. All of the figures are based on Soviet estimates. There are several ways in which the figures could be inaccurate:

- Managers of enterprises and factories had plenty of opportunity to manipulate the paperwork in order to inflate their successes and cover up their failures. It was not only their jobs that were on the line if they could not show that they had fulfilled their targets.
- Officials at regional levels also did not want to be seen to be failing to meet the targets set by the central administration. So they were likely to cover up failures and to accept good figures given to them by enterprises.
- Top officials did not want to be seen to be failing to achieve the key targets set for their industry. They wanted to show Stalin that they had been successful.

Western analysts, such as R. W. Davies, Alec Nove and Eugene Zaleski, have looked carefully at the Soviet figures and used different ways of calculating growth. Others have concluded that the Soviet statistics are often so contradictory that it is impossible to give an accurate picture of the achievements of the plans in the 1930s.

Would the Soviet Union have done better if it had continued with the NEP?

One question remains: would the Soviet Union have done better if it had continued with the NEP as Bukharin and the right wing of the party had wanted it to?

Some historians believe that the Soviet government could have avoided the human suffering and done just as well, probably better, by sticking with the NEP. Roy Medvedev (*Let History Judge*, 1972) and Stephen Cohen (*Bukharin and the Bolshevik Revolution*, 1974) were among the first historians to put forward this case. They contend that the modernisation of Russia could have been achieved by the continuation of the limited market economy of the 1920s. They accept that the pace would have been slower but maintain that the waste of resources would have been far less.

R. W. Davies, a leading British expert on the Russian economy, has a mixed view (*Soviet Economic Development From Lenin to Khrushchev*, 1998, pages 36–37). According to him, the NEP had delivered rapid recovery after the Civil War and the economy probably could have continued to expand at a moderate rate. But he acknowledges that the NEP had limitations for the Communists: serious unemployment and an unfavourable effect on other sectors of the economy, such as education and the railways. Also, Soviet officials were worried about the defence and armaments industries. He accepts that there were powerful arguments in favour of rapid industrialisation. He believes that in the end it is a political judgement of how essential it was for the USSR to establish a powerful heavy industry sector and an armaments industry in the space of a few years and whether the NEP was capable of doing that.

Alec Nove, in *Was Stalin Really Necessary?* (1964, page 23), argues that the party had reached an impasse at the end of the 1920s: the economy was stagnant and they needed to find a way forward. This was heightened by the sense of crisis caused by war threats. The policy of Bukharin – sometimes called 'riding towards socialism on a peasant nag' – was ideologically and politically unacceptable to the party. They could not base their industrialisation plans on the development of a prosperous peasantry who would voluntarily supply food. Rapid industrialisation and collectivisation were the way out of the impasse.

In his *An Economic History of the USSR, 1917–91* (1992), Alec Nove admits that there were colossal mistakes and disasters, but asserts that these should be seen in the context of the 1930s, when capitalism was in crisis in the rest of the world (this was the period of the Great Depression) and there were no models to follow. The command economy was inefficient but it concentrated resources in key areas and got the job done. Nove accepts there was a high price to pay for this, particularly the human suffering involved in collectivisation, and accepts that there might have been other ways of doing it. But he thinks that for Stalin and the Communist Party there was no real alternative. Without this 'leap forward', however crudely it took place, Nove doubts that the Russians would have created the sort of industrial base that helped them to win the Second World War.

TALKING POINT

Historians call the 'what if . . .?' approach counterfactual history. What do you think are the advantages and problems of asking 'what if . . .?' about the past. Can you suggest other topics where a counterfactual approach would be useful?

FOCUS ROUTE

In your Focus Route activities (pages 179 and 184), you should have collected information about the plans under these headings:

Evidence of success and achievements
Evidence of failures and weaknesses
Evidence that the Five-Year Plans were not well planned
Ways in which the plans benefited the workers
Ways in which the workers suffered or did not do well

1 Look back over the chapter and add any further information that you think should go in these categories.
2 Read pages 196–197, assessing the plans, then:
  a) add any more details
  b) note down any final comments.

KEY POINTS FROM CHAPTER 12   How well planned were the Five-Year Plans?

1 The party was convinced that the route to socialism was through industrialisation and the proletarianisation of the Russian people.
2 Although this was a 'revolution from above', there was a great deal of active support for the plans and for socialist construction from young urban workers.
3 The changes were administered through a 'command economy' which relied on centralised planning and control by government commissariats overseen by the Communist Party.
4 The mechanism chosen to deliver industrialisation was the Five-Year Plans, which set broad targets for all branches of industry. Most operational targets were contained in plans covering shorter periods such as one year.
5 Extremely ambitious targets were set to drive people to huge efforts. These had little to do with rational planning and more to do with propaganda.
6 Fulfilment and over-fulfilment of the plan targets became the overriding force driving the managers of industrial enterprises and officials.
7 Intimidation and fear permeated the system as managers strove to fulfil their targets. They, together with party officials, were evaluated on their target performance. This led to the falsification of figures and corruption.
8 The First Five-Year Plan was chaotic. There was an enormous amount of waste and many products were unusable. At the same time, remarkable progress was made in key heavy industries and huge-scale projects were undertaken.
9 Some workers did well out of the plans, particularly skilled urban workers. Other workers, particularly ex-peasants forced into cities by collectivisation, found themselves part of a 'quicksand society' trying to make a better living and avoiding harsh punishments by constantly moving from place to place and job to job.
10 The Second Five-Year Plan saw more developed planning and more reasonable targets. Workers enjoyed 'three good years' with more food and consumer goods but these were ended by the purges. The third plan saw a return to shortages and chaotic planning as resources were diverted to the military.
11 Generally, the standard of living for most workers during the plans was poor and improved marginally; housing standards remained abysmal.

Section 4 Review: How did Stalin transform the economy of the USSR in the 1930s?

This essay could also be **Part 2** of the coursework activity started on page 195.

ACTIVITY

Use the results of the Focus Route activities that you have completed in Chapters 11 and 12 to write the essay: How successful were Stalin's economic policies?

Work in groups to draw up a plan for the essay, using the skills you have learned in preceding essay-writing activities in this book.

a) Decide what the key points are and form these into your main paragraphs. Each point should directly answer the question posed in the essay title.

b) Work out what you are going to use as supporting points for each key point. These can be evidence that supports the key point or you can develop the argument around the key point.

In this essay, you have to weigh up the evidence for both sides of the argument. There is a debate about the economic issues and there is also a human dimension to take into account. You have to decide what line you are going to take. You could:

• deal with collectivisation first and then consider industrial policies
• deal with the economic aspects of agriculture and industry first and then look at the human dimension
• look at the successes of the agricultural and industrial plans first and then look at ways in which they were not successful
• take a different line altogether.

At the end, you need to write a concluding paragraph which draws the key points together and makes an overall assessment. Make sure that this is not a repetition of what you wrote in the introductory paragraph.

This essay could also be **Part 2** of the coursework activity started on page 195. It fulfils your ICT key skills requirements. To satisfy these you have to provide evidence that you can find information, develop it and present it.

1 **Finding information** – provide evidence, e.g. annotated photocopies, to show that you have searched websites and the library for relevant articles and books. You must include a bibliography.

2 **Developing information** – show that you have used or changed information to construct your essay on a word processor, for instance, you could provide a draft copy that you have amended. You could show that you have changed figures into graphs, e.g. the Magnitogorsk labour turnover figures, and you could re-size graphs to fit.

3 **Presenting information** – present the essay in word-processed form, using headers and footers and spell check. The proper use of footnotes should also be shown.

How did Stalin control the USSR?

During the 1930s, Stalin extended his control of the Communist Party and of the people of the Soviet Union. The machinery of state terror had been put in place in the early 1930s to push through the industrialisation and collectivisation drives. In the mid-1930s Stalin instituted the **Great Purges**, which for the first time applied terror to the **Communist Party** itself. Stalin removed the old **Bolsheviks** from power and repressed other potential sources of opposition in the party, replacing them with an élite, the *nomenklatura*, who had a vested interest in supporting him. Terror was also applied to other sections of the population: anyone who showed signs of dissent or was critical of the regime was liable to arrest and imprisonment in the **Gulag**, the vast system of labour camps throughout the **USSR**.

At the same time Stalin, through the cult of the personality, was projected as a god-like leader. He alone could lead the people through present troubles to a glorious society – a socialist society – in the not too distant future. Stalin was feared but he was also loved. Chapter 13 looks at the causes of the **Great Purges** in the 1930s and considers Stalin's responsibility for the huge numbers who were killed. Chapter 14 examines the cult of the personality.

ACTIVITY

Terror, secret police and labour camps provide us with some of the most dramatic and enduring images of the Soviet Union in the 1930s: the knock on the door in the middle of the night ... sleep deprivation and interrogation ... show trials ... hard labour in freezing conditions, or execution. A human tragedy on a huge scale lies behind these images. Read the case studies on pages 201–202.

1 For each case study explain:
   a) who the subject of the case study is
   b) what happened to him or her
   c) why you might be surprised that they were treated in the way they were.
2 What do you think these case studies show about what was happening in the USSR in the 1930s?
3 Draw up a list of questions that you would like to find the answers to – for example, how could it be that a party leader was purged?

PARTY LEADER

You have already met Nikolai Bukharin, the leading theorist of the right and the 'favourite of the whole party'. Although ousted by Stalin in the power struggle of 1929, he continued to work hard for the party. He edited *Isvestia* and was a major contributor to the 'Stalin Constitution' of 1936. But he was not safe. Arrested in February 1937, he was imprisoned for a year before becoming the 'star' of the third great show trial in March 1938. According to Sir Fitzroy McLean, a British diplomat, Bukharin dominated the proceedings in a most extraordinary way. Although forced to plead guilty, he showed his intellectual and moral superiority over Vyshinsky, the chief prosecutor. McLean adds that, by mistake, a flashlight revealed that Stalin was watching the proceedings from behind dark glass.

Before he was arrested, Bukharin wrote a 'last letter' dedicated to the future generation of party members, insisting that his young wife Anna Larina memorise it. In it he denounced the NKVD as the 'hellish machine [which] can transform any Party member into a terrorist or spy' and protested his innocence. He told Anna Larina that she was young and would live to see history clear his name. She did, but she had to wait 50 years: Bukharin was not REHABILITATED until 1988. Anna Larina herself spent twenty years in labour camps and in exile and did not see her baby son again until he was 21. Bukharin's disabled first wife was arrested in 1938 and interrogated at intervals until March 1940, when she was shot. Other members of her family were shot, disappeared or died in prison.

NKVD
The name of the secret police from 1934 to 1943.

REHABILITATED
Reputation restored. No longer treated as a traitor.

SOURCE 1 'Koba, why do you need me to die?' Bukharin wrote in a note to Stalin after the death sentence was pronounced on him. (Koba, meaning 'the Indomitable', was Stalin's revolutionary pseudonym. Its use here is a sign of how close Bukharin and Stalin had once been.) Two days later, Bukharin was shot

SOURCE 2 Anna Larina, Bukharin's wife

DAUGHTER OF A PARTY OFFICIAL

Seven-year-old Engelsina Cheshkova was bored, sitting with her bunch of flowers at a party meeting in 1936. So she got up and wandered towards the platform. Stalin picked her up, cameras clicked, and Engelsina became famous. A statue was erected in Moscow based on the picture: 'Thank you, Comrade Stalin, for my happy childhood.' But it did not turn out to be so happy. In December 1937, her father, a minor party official, disappeared. Engelsina, who was now 'the daughter of an enemy of the people', wrote a letter, dictated by her mother, to Stalin asking for help; she did not link her father's arrest with Stalin. The letter led to the arrest of her mother, who died in exile in Turkestan. Engelsina never saw her father again. Despite this, the adult Engelsina cried when she heard of Stalin's death because her eight-month-old daughter would never see Stalin alive – such was the effect of the cult of Stalin in the Soviet Union.

SOURCE 3 Stalin with Engelsina Cheshkova, 1936

WORKER AND MANAGER

You have already met the Stakhanovite Ogorodnikov, who worked in the steel mill in Magnitogorsk and had been praised as a hero of socialist labour. He had been refused entry to the party on the basis of his ex-kulak past and was soon to find himself caught up in the purges of the late 1930s. His boss at the mill, Golubitsky, seems to have resisted the scapegoating of subordinates when there were regular machine breakdowns at the plant, which were probably caused by Stakhanovites trying to break work norms. However, in doing so (or for other reasons), he incurred the resentment of the Procurator (Head of Justice in Magnitogorsk) who used the breakdowns to accuse Golubitsky of wrecking. Testimony from those below Golubitsky was needed and Ogorodnikov and two others were arrested and tortured in 1937. Golubitsky was arrested in March 1938, convicted in July 1938 and shot. Ogorodnikov was executed too, going from hero to villain in just two years.

SOURCE 4   A cartoon published in the *Magnitogorsk Worker*, the city newspaper, in September 1936. It shows factory bosses, including Golubitsky (top left), with piles of unusable products

How far was Stalin responsible for the Great Purges?

CHAPTER OVERVIEW   At the end of the First Five-Year Plan there was a great deal of hostility towards the Communist government and concerns within the party about the breakneck speed of industrialisation. There were growing signs of opposition to Stalin and a possibility that he would be replaced as leader. Then, in December 1934, Sergei Kirov, a leading member of the Politburo, was murdered. This triggered the wave of terror known as the Great Purges, which reached its peak in 1937 and 1938. Thousands of members of the Communist Party were accused of being involved in conspiracies against Stalin and the party leadership. They were arrested and imprisoned or executed. The purges also engulfed other sections of the population, notably the armed forces. Historians disagree about the causes of the purges and the extent to which Stalin was personally responsible for them.

What do we mean by the purges?

FOCUS ROUTE

Make notes on the different sorts of purge. Make sure that you understand the differences between them.

The word 'purge' refers to 'cleaning out' or 'cleansing' an organism of impurities. The first purge of the Communist Party took place in 1918 and there were periodic purges or *chistki* (cleansings) throughout the 1920s. These usually took place at times when the leaders were seeking to exercise more control over the party or reshape it, as in the Lenin Enrolment of 1924 (see page 142). The party often took in more members (lowering entry standards) during periods of crisis such as the Civil War and collectivisation, and shed what it saw as undesirable elements when the crisis was over. But a *chistka* was, by and large, a non-violent process. Party members were required to exchange their party cards for new ones or to verify their party documents. In this process, people were refused new cards: they were expelled but not usually arrested.

After the murder of Sergei Kirov at the end of 1934 this changed. From 1936 and particularly in 1937–38, many old Bolshevik leaders were disposed of, the party was purged ruthlessly and violently, and other groups in society were swept up in the 'cleansing' process. This later period is called the Great Purges. According to Sheila Fitzpatrick, in *The Russian Revolution 1917–1932*, the term 'Great Purges' is a Western term, not a Soviet one. There was no acceptable public way to refer to it at the time; in private it was referred to as '1937'. Robert Conquest calls this period 'The Great Terror'.

We can identify three phases in the purges of the 1930s:

1 The *chistka* of 1932–35 in which over twenty per cent of the party were expelled non-violently as part of a clearing-out process after collectivisation.
2 The show trials which saw prominent old Bolsheviks publicly tried and executed.
3 The Yezhovshchina, named after Yezhov, the head of the NKVD, which was a period of mass terror from 1937 to 1938 when thousands of party members, state officials, members of the armed forces, industrial directors, professionals and other sections of society were denounced, arrested and imprisoned. Many were executed; many more died in Soviet labour camps.

TERROR AND THE PURGES

Lenin used terror and class warfare to crush opposition. Stalin extended the use of terror and class warfare in the early 1930s to push through the Five-Year Plans. Millions of kulaks or 'class enemies' were killed or sent to labour camps. Many workers and engineers, accused of sabotage and wrecking, were sent to the growing Gulag. Government organisations, like Gosplan, were purged of ex-Mensheviks and the old bourgeois intelligentsia.

But Lenin and other Communists made a distinction between the methods to be used against opposition from outside the party and those for dealing with disagreements and opposition inside the party. There was a clear understanding that terror should not be used on party comrades. In the Great Purges, Stalin unleashed terror *inside* the party, which then engulfed people in the wider society in a further wave of terror.

■ **Learning trouble spot**

Why join the Communist Party?
Many Russians joined the party not for ideological reasons but for the considerable advantages and privileges that came with the party card. Party members could often get larger rations and access to scarce consumer goods. In some areas, belonging to the party gave members power over other groups. People were expelled from the party for all sorts of reasons such as drunkenness, corruption and not being an active member.

1932	Signs of opposition to Stalin's leadership. Ryutin, who had denounced Stalin as the 'evil genius of the Russian Revolution', was expelled from the party but not executed.
1932–34	Purge of 'undesirable elements' – mainly the more illiterate and inactive of the new working class and peasant recruits: 22 per cent of the party were expelled.
1934 February	Seventeenth Party Congress. Several provincial delegates urged Kirov to take over as General Secretary.
July	OGPU replaced by NKVD.
1 December	Murder of Kirov.
1935–36	Purge of the party resumed, with the focus now shifting to men who held more important posts. An 'exchange of party cards' led to half a million members being expelled.
1935 January	Zinoviev and Kamenev were arrested and accused of instigating terrorist activities.
June	The death penalty was extended not only to spies and parasites but also to all those who were aware of such activities.
1936 August	The first show trial, involving Zinoviev, Kamenev and fourteen others.
September	Yezhov replaced Yagoda as head of the NKVD.
December	The new Constitution was adopted.
1937 January	The second show trial, involving Radek, Pyatakov and fifteen others.
May	The purge of the Red Army began.
June	Tukhachevsky and leading army officers were shot.
1938 March	The third show trial involving Bukharin, Rykov, Yagoda and eighteen others.
December	Beria replaced Yezhov as head of the NKVD.
1939 March	Eighteenth Party Congress. Stalin declared an end to the 'mass purges'.
1940 February	Yezhov was shot.

THE STALIN CONSTITUTION OF 1936

As one of the worst periods of political repression in the history of the USSR was initiated, Stalin published the most 'democratic' constitution in the world (passed 5 December 1936). The rights it enshrined included:

*   freedom from arbitrary arrest
*   freedom of speech and the press
*   the right to demonstrate
*   respect for privacy of the home and personal correspondence
*   employment for all
*   universal suffrage for over-eighteens, free elections and secret ballots.

It was a hollow and cynical piece of propaganda since at that very time such rights were being systematically abused. However, the Constitution made it clear that all these rights were subordinate to the interests of the working classes and it was the role of the Communist Party to decide what those interests were. Also, only Communists could be put up for elections. So one-party dominance was assured.

The Constitution was written by a team headed by

Bukharin and Radek, who were both to perish shortly afterwards in the purges. It was intended largely for international consumption, to show Communist sympathisers that the Soviet state was a democratic one at heart and provided the chief hope for the future of the world. Other important sections of the Constitution proclaimed that:

*   the Soviet Union was a federal state with eleven autonomous republics
*   ethnic groups would have local autonomy within the republics
*   the old Congresses of Soviets were to be replaced by the Supreme Soviet, a single legislative body, filled by elected representatives from the Soviet republics
*   the Council of the People's Commissars would continue as the chief executive authority
*   the Soviet state embraced equality for all and joint ownership of the means of production.

Stalin claimed that his constitution was 'proof that socialism and democracy are invincible'.

B What sort of opposition to Stalin had developed before 1934?

By 1933, the Communist Party was extremely unpopular. Rapid industrialisation had created tension and stress in Soviet society which was putting a strain on relations between the party and the people. The violence of forced collectivisation and the famine of 1932–33 had alienated the peasantry, making the murder of rural Communists a regular event. Many urban workers were antagonised by the low wages, strict controls and harsh punishments in the workplace. There was upheaval and unrest in the overcrowded, insanitary and often violent cities with their constantly changing populations. Hatred was particularly high among the 'former people' such as priests, industrialists, traders and 'bourgeois specialists'. Russian society was unstable and volatile.

The majority of party members had supported the drive for industrialisation, but some had been deeply disturbed by the methods employed to push it through and were worried by the disaffection in the cities. Many were horrified by the terror methods used to collectivise agriculture, and the waging of a virtual war against the peasants. This was not the road to socialist construction that they had envisaged. Some, in despair at the events of these years, had committed suicide. Among these was Stalin's own wife, Nadezda Allilueva, who shot herself in November 1932. She was deeply depressed by the excesses of collectivisation, agreeing with Bukharin that the ravages of the countryside had gone too far.

FOCUS ROUTE

Make notes under these headings:

- why the Communist Party was unpopular with the people
- why many Communists were distressed by Stalin's policies
- what opposition Stalin faced in the regions
- the *chistka* of 1932–35
- opposition to Stalin at higher levels of the party
- Stalin's difficulties at the Seventeenth Party Congress.

SOURCE 13.1 Popular ditties expressed opposition to the regime in the early 1930s. The following examples are included in the Russian State Archive of Literature and Art (RGALI)

*Stalin stands on a coffin
Gnawing meat from a cat's bones
Well, Soviet cows
are such disgusting creatures*

*How the collective farm had become prosperous
There used to be thirty-three farms
and now there are five*

*We fulfilled the Five Year Plan
and are eating well
We ate all the horses
And are now chasing the dogs*

*O commune, O commune
You Commune of Satan
You seized everything
All in the soviet cause*

STALIN'S WIFE

The story of Stalin's relationship with his wife is important because some historians suggest that it may have had an impact on the terror that was about to unfold. It is alleged that Stalin treated his wife badly, and that he was cold and impersonal. There have been allegations that he had affairs with other women; in *Stalin* (1997) Edward Radzinsky says 'he was unfaithful more and more frequently simply to hurt her'. According to Khrushchev, on the night of Nadezda's  suicide it is claimed that Stalin was so outrageously rude to his wife that she stormed out, knowing that he was with another woman, and that this finally prompted her to take her own life.

There are different interpretations of the significance of her suicide. Some writers say that Stalin showed little remorse and little interest in her funeral, and that he never visited her grave. They suggest that he saw her suicide as an act of betrayal. Other writers maintain that there is evidence to prove he loved his wife, despite a stormy relationship, and never got over her death. Radzinsky uses as evidence Bukharin's wife Anna, who said that Stalin asked for the lid of the coffin to stay open and sat by it for hours, and one of his bodyguards who recalled that Stalin spent hours by her graveside.

Most historians (including Bullock, Tucker and Medvedev) agree that the suicide made him draw more into himself and become more paranoid, less likely to trust those around him. In *Twenty Letters to a Friend* (1968), Svetlana Allilueva, Stalin's daughter, says inwardly things had changed catastrophically: 'something had snapped inside my father'. Robert Thurston suggests in *Life and Terror in Stalin's Russia 1934–41* (1996) that Nadezda's death, occurring at the same time that other groups were opposing him, may have filled him with hatred, suspicion and a desire to project his guilt over her death onto others.

TALKING POINT

Do you think that a personal event, such as the suicide of Stalin's wife, can play an important role in deciding the future history of a country?

Breakneck industrialisation and forced collectivisation brought dissension in the party at large. Throughout the First Five-Year Plan the central party in Moscow had had difficulties in getting local party secretaries and members to implement central policies and orders. They were unwilling to push forward, argued about high grain collection targets, were unwilling to identify kulaks and were reluctant to get rid of specialists and managers who might help them achieve their industrial production targets. Some were reluctant to implement the degree of terror the centre demanded.

This caused anger and some panic among party leaders who valued discipline above all else. So, in December 1932, Moscow launched a chistka to root out passive elements, violators of party and state discipline 'who do not carry out decisions, but cast doubt upon the decisions by calling them unrealistic and unrealisable' and 'turncoats who have allied themselves with bourgeois elements'. By 1935, around 22 per cent of members had lost their party cards. This was an attempt to re-establish control of the party in the regions, but it was also used to expel members critical of the party line laid down by Stalin.

And it was not just in the local party organisations that there were problems. In the early 1930s there were signs of growing opposition to Stalin's leadership at much higher levels. In 1932, a former Moscow party secretary, Ryutin, circulated to the Central Committee a 200-page document highly critical of Stalin. He called Stalin 'the evil genius of the Russian revolution'. Referring to his 'personal dictatorship', he urged Stalin's removal. This became known as the Ryutin platform.

Stalin wanted the death penalty for Ryutin. But other members of the Politburo, including Kirov and his friend Ordzhonikidze, opposed him. Ryutin was not executed. This was a blow to Stalin and a reminder that he was still subject to the majority of the Politburo.

Ryutin was not alone. The old Bolshevik A. P. Smirnov (a party member since 1896) was charged with forming an opposition group with several others looking to moderate the pace of industrialisation, make trade unions more independent and bring OGPU (the secret police) under party control. Again, Stalin wished to treat these oppositionists inside the party in the same way as those outside – to imprison or execute them – but again the majority of the Politburo would not support the execution of party members for purely political offences.

SOURCE 13.2 An extract from the Ryutin platform or memorandum

The rule of terror in the party and in the country under the clearly ruinous policy of Stalin has led to a situation where hypocrisy and two-facedness have become common phenomena . . .

The most evil counter-revolutionary and provocateur could not have carried out the work of destroying the party and socialist construction better than Stalin has done. Stalin and his clique will not and cannot voluntarily give up their positions, so they must be removed by force.

KIROV TOPS POLL

There is evidence to suggest that provincial delegates asked Kirov to take over as General Secretary and that Stalin did badly in elections to the Central Committee: Kirov was supposed to have polled all but three of the 1225 votes, whereas 300 did not vote for Stalin. The result, it seems, was hushed up by Kaganovich, a staunch Stalinist, perhaps with the help of other senior party members.

The Seventeenth Party Congress

In January 1934, the front page of *Pravda* announced 'Socialism in Our Country has Won'. The Seventeenth Party Congress, which opened on 26 February 1934, was hailed as the 'Congress of Victors'. There was a feeling that the economic groundwork had been accomplished and it was now possible to slow down, stabilise, reduce the tensions caused by the breakneck pace of change, and give the workers some rewards – more food, more clothing and better living conditions. This seemed to have been recognised in the Second Five-Year Plan, which had been redrafted in 1933 with lower targets.

However, it became clear at the beginning of the congress that Stalin wished to push ahead energetically and not slacken the pace of industrialisation. A split opened between Stalin and other leading members of the Politburo. The popular, handsome Sergei Kirov, the Leningrad party boss, pointedly said 'The fundamental difficulties are behind us' and went on to talk about stopping forcible grain seizure from peasants and increasing rations for workers. He received long standing ovations from the congress, as long as those received by Stalin.

The title of General Secretary was done away with and Stalin and Kirov were both given the title of Secretary of Equal Rank. Stalin was by no means secure as leader. He commanded the unswerving loyalty of only two of the Politburo – Kaganovich and Molotov. He could be removed or demoted. On the sidelines stood Bukharin, who had always supported a more moderate line.

It was at this key point in the history of the Communist Party that Sergei Kirov was murdered.

C   The Kirov murder mystery

The murder of Sergei Kirov is one of the great mysteries of Russian history in the 1930s. And it is an important murder. Robert Conquest argues in *The Great Terror: A Reassessment* (1990, page 37) that it was a turning point in history, which not only unleashed a terror that killed millions but also determined the future of Soviet Russia. But it is a strange mystery because we know who the murderer was. The mystery surrounds the motives for the murder and who, if anybody, arranged it.

SOURCE 13.3   Leading Communists attended Kirov's funeral. Many of them, including Stalin, were seen to weep

ACTIVITY

You are going to play the detective. Your job is to examine the evidence and make your own judgements. Then you will be asked to reconsider your preliminary judgements in the light of other evidence. Read the account on pages 208–209, which is based on Robert Conquest's book *Stalin and the Kirov Murder* (1989), and answer the following questions.

1   In what circumstances did the assassin carry out the murder?
2   What strange coincidences surround the murder?
3   Is there any evidence to link Stalin to the murder?
4   Is there any evidence to suggest that the NKVD was involved in the murder?
5   Who had the best motive for the murder?
6   What theories can you suggest about who was responsible – was it the assassin alone or were others involved?

The murder

Just after 4pm on 1 December 1934, Sergei Kirov entered party headquarters in Leningrad – the Smolny Institute from where seventeen years previously Lenin and Trotsky had directed the October uprising. He left his personal bodyguard, Borisov, downstairs and went up to his offices on his own. He did not notice that the usual guards were absent from the corridors. Waiting, probably in a nearby toilet, was the assassin. As Kirov passed him in the corridor, he emerged from the shadows and shot Kirov in the back of the neck. He then fainted beside the body. Kirov died soon afterwards and the assassin was arrested.

The assassin

Leonid Nikolayev, aged 30, was a nervous man whose health was poor. He had joined the Communist Party in 1920 at the age of sixteen. After a troubled time in the party, he was expelled in March 1934 for a breach of discipline but later reinstated. He had never been linked to the left opposition of Trotsky, Zinoviev and others but had developed a hatred of the party bureaucracy which had not, he felt, recognised his worth and given him his due.

Nikolayev was married to Milde Draule who was a secretary at party headquarters and may have been having an affair with Kirov. A diary found in Nikolayev's briefcase showed he had planned the murder. A further statement found there claimed that the murder was 'a personal act of desperation and dissatisfaction arising out of his straitened material circumstances and as a protest against the unjust attitude of certain members of the government towards a live person'.

SOURCE 13.4 G. Lyushkov, deputy head of the NKVD Secret Political Department, one of Nikolayev's interrogators

Nikolayev lacked balance, he had many problems ... He was convinced that he was capable of any work ... and did not get on with people easily ... all his efforts led to him losing his official positions ... This drove him to the belief that the problem was not in his personal faults but in the institutions. This discontent in turn drove him into his scheme to assassinate some important figures in the Party.

DRAMATIS PERSONAE

Kirov – the victim
Nikolayev – the assassin
Yagoda – head of the NKVD
Medved – head of the NKVD in Leningrad
Zaporozhets – Yagoda's deputy
Stalin – the leader

Just before the murder

- Kirov had received a great deal of support at the Seventeenth Party Congress and more people had voted for him than for Stalin. He had opposed Stalin over the Ryutin affair and over the pace of industrialisation. He now wanted a relaxation of the terror and reconciliation with the peasantry. (This would have downgraded the role of the NKVD and reduced its profile and status.) By the summer of 1934, Kirov and Stalin had fallen out over a number of issues.
- The head of the NKVD in Leningrad was Medved; his deputy was Zaporozhets. It is alleged (but not proven) that just before the murder Zaporozhets brought in some personnel from Moscow and put them in key posts without Medved's permission, presumably on the orders of some higher authority. Medved wanted them removed and got Kirov's backing. When Kirov asked Stalin to have them removed, Stalin refused. Zaporozhets had previously worked with Yagoda, overall head of the NKVD.
- Prior to the murder, Nikolayev had twice been arrested in Kirov's neighbourhood and released both times on the order of Zaporozhets. It was also alleged that an NKVD man had posed earlier as a friend of Nikolayev and practised shooting his revolver with him.

What happened after the murder?

- Stalin came to Leningrad and carried out an interrogation of Nikolayev. When asked why he had murdered Kirov, Nikolayev pointed to the NKVD men, saying that Stalin should ask 'them' that question.
- A key witness was going to be Borisov, Kirov's bodyguard. But on the way to be questioned at the Smolny Institute, in a truck with several NKVD men, there was an accident in which he was killed and nobody else was hurt. The NKVD men were killed later.
- Very shortly afterwards, the first arrests were made on Stalin's instructions. Thousands in the Leningrad party were purged. This was the beginning of the Great Purges.
- The leading Leningrad NKVD men accused of negligence for not protecting Kirov were sentenced to labour camps but were given only short sentences. They were sent to the camps in special railway carriages and received privileged treatment, including regular gifts and the status of 'assistants' which gave them power over other prisoners. They were shot in the late 1930s.
- In the third show trial in 1938, Yagoda (by now the ex-head of the NKVD) was accused of involvement in the murder by making it easy for Nikolayev to get to Kirov. He pleaded guilty.

Sergei Kirov (1886–1934)
Born into a lower middle-class family, Kirov lost his parents early. He went to a vocational school to train as a mechanic, where he met radical activists from a nearby university. He moved to Tomsk in Siberia and joined the Social Democratic Party. In the 1905 Revolution he organised railway strikes, and was arrested in 1906. Released in 1909, he went to the Caucasus, worked on a newspaper and became committed to the Bolshevik wing of the party. He played an active part in the 1917 Revolution and in the Civil War as head of the Military Revolutionary Committee in Astrakhan. Later he was involved in bringing the Caucasus under Bolshevik control. After 1921 he became Secretary of the Azerbaijan Central Committee and in 1923 a member of the Central Committee.

When Zinoviev was ousted from his power base in Leningrad, Kirov became Party Secretary in Leningrad, which put him in a powerful position. He had not been particularly keen on forced collectivisation or on attacking Bukharin and the right, but in the end he threw in his lot with Stalin and was firmly committed to the rapid industrialisation policy. He was an excellent orator, the best in the party after Trotsky, and seemed to be popular in the party.

ACTIVITY

Conquest's account of the murder (summarised on pages 208–209) is based on evidence he has collected, much of it from memoirs and personal conversations. Not all of it is established fact, including exactly where everybody was at the time of the murder. Conquest also makes some inferences from the evidence that may or may not be true.

You are now going to consider a range of evidence from historians and other sources. You will have to judge whether you think their evidence is helpful, convincing and/or reliable. At the end you have to decide whether you think the murder was:

- carried out by Nikolayev alone
- carried out by Nikolayev with the help of the NKVD but without Stalin's knowledge
- ordered by Stalin, arranged by the NKVD and carried out by Nikolayev.

Write a paragraph explaining your decision. Say what you think is 'certain', 'highly likely', 'likely', 'probable', 'uncertain' or 'open to question'.
You should bear these points in mind:

- Everyone agrees that Nikolayev did the murder and that he was a disgruntled and unstable man.
- So far no published evidence has been unearthed that directly links Stalin to the murder. Most of the evidence is second or third hand and has particular biases, for example, some of it is memoirs from people fleeing the USSR during the Cold War.

SOURCE 13.5 R. W. Thurston, *Life and Terror in Stalin's Russia 1934–41*, 1996, p. 20

There are many problems with the idea that he [Stalin] had Kirov killed. Evidence recently released from Russia shows that, contrary to many accounts, the police did not detain Nikolayev three times near Kirov, on each occasion mysteriously releasing him despite the fact that he was carrying a gun. He was stopped only once, and the circumstances were not suspicious. He had not received the gun from a Leningrad NKVD officer, as is typically claimed, but he had owned it since 1918 and had registered it legally in 1924 and 1930 (evidence from Pravda, *4 November 1991).*

Nikolayev had a diary with him at the Smolny, but instead of showing that the party's enemies helped him in his attack, it indicated that he had acted alone. Kirov's bodyguard was not present at the fatal moment because his boss had called to say he would stay at home that day. Kirov went to his office anyway, only to meet Nikolayev by chance. The latter, who had a party card that would automatically admit him to the building, had gone there to ask for a pass to an upcoming conference.

SOURCE 13.6 J. Lewis and P. Whitehead, *Stalin: A Time for Judgement*, 1990, p. 63. A commission to look into the murder was held under Khrushchev, the Soviet leader after Stalin. This took place at a time when Stalin's record and reputation were being attacked. The commission did not produce a public report but one of its members, Olga Shatunovskaya, recalled events as follows

The NKVD latched on to this, that he [Nikolayev] was dissatisfied, and he wrote them a letter saying: 'I am ready for anything now. I hate Kirov' and they organised it. At the inquiry before Stalin he said: 'For four months the NKVD prepared me and convinced me that it was necessary for the Party and the country.'
[On the question of the motive, she said:]
When Stalin found out [that some delegates had approached Kirov to ask him to become General Secretary in Stalin's place] he decided to remove him and Kirov realised this. When he came back from the Seventeenth Congress he told his friends and family: 'My head is now on the block.' I had all these testimonies from his friends and family and now they have been destroyed ... It has been irrefutably proved that the murder of Kirov was organised by Stalin, through Yagoda and the NKVD.

SOURCE 13.7 R. W. Thurston, *Life and Terror in Stalin's Russia 1934–41*, 1996, p. 22, quoting the opinion in 1991 of A. Iakoviev, a Russian scholar and politician, who studied the available archives

L. V. Nikolayev planned and perpetrated the murder alone. [Files on the case] contain no information implicating J. V. Stalin and agencies of the NKVD. [Stalin] did not know of and had no relation to the attack on Kirov.

SOURCE 13.8 R. C. Tucker, *Stalin in Power: The Revolution from Above, 1928–1941*, 1992, p. 301

A young woman journalist then living and working in Rostov, Vera Panova, recalls in a posthumously published memoir that her husband, Boris Vakhtin, managing editor on another local paper, telephoned her late on 1 December and said: ' "Vera! In Leningrad they've killed Kirov!" Who killed him? I ask, no answer comes, but I know what will happen now: after all I've written about the burning of the Reichstag. And that night I have a dream but I don't dare tell it even to Boris: they themselves have killed Kirov so as to start a new terror. Against whom? Against the "lefts", against the "rights", against anyone they want. But I can't keep this dream from Boris for long. After vacillating, I tell it to him. He gives me a strange look and is silent.'

Even among ordinary Leningrad workers, a ditty was making its whispered rounds [and this might help explain the savage repressions soon to be visited upon the Leningrad working class]:

Oh cucumber, oh pomidor
Stalin killed Kirov
In the corridor.

SOURCE 13.9 J. Arch Getty and O. V. Naumov, *The Road to Terror: Stalin and the Self-Destruction of the Bolsheviks, 1932–39*, 1999

Yagoda (through whom Stalin presumably worked to kill Kirov) was produced in open court and in front of the world press before his execution in 1938. Knowing that he was about to be shot in any event, he could have brought Stalin's entire house down with a single remark about the Kirov killing . . . such a risk would appear to be unacceptable for a complicit Stalin . . .

The Stalinists seemed unprepared for the assassination and panicked by it. Indeed it took them more than eighteen months after the assassination to frame their supposed targets – members of the anti-Stalin old Bolshevik opposition – for the killing.

POSSIBLE MOTIVES

- Stalin's motives are clear: to get rid of a rival and to use murder to get rid of opposition.
- Nikolayev, by all accounts, was disgruntled with the party but there is also a story that Kirov was having an affair with Nikolayev's wife, a secretary at party headquarters. This may have led him to transfer his disillusionment with the party onto Kirov.
- The motives of the NKVD are more difficult to identify. Conquest suggests there is no clear motive. Suggestions are:
  - they thought, or had been told, that Stalin wanted Kirov murdered
  - Kirov wanted to relax the terror, but the NKVD did not want to see this happen and did not want to see Kirov replace Stalin
  - they did not intend Nikolayev actually to kill Kirov; they intended to stop him before he could carry out the attack and use the attempted assassination as justification for their continuing role against enemies of the state.

ENEMY OF THE PEOPLE
This vague term now came into everyday use. It could be applied to anybody, covering any supposed offence that the authorities chose. Being identified as an enemy of the people meant arrest and imprisonment.

D The Great Purges

The show trials – getting rid of the old Bolsheviks

The Stalinist leadership used Kirov's murder as a pretext and justification for the Great Purges, which took place over the next four years. The murder was seen as evidence of a widespread conspiracy against the Soviet state and its leaders. There were enemies everywhere and they needed to be rooted out.

Within a few weeks there was an extensive purge of the Leningrad party, Kirov's power base. A 'Leningrad centre', plotting terrorist acts against the Soviet state, was uncovered. Thousands more, many outside the party, were soon accused of being Trotskyites involved in the plot to murder Kirov and other leading Communists. Kamenev and Zinoviev were arrested and put on trial in January 1935. Although no direct evidence could be produced against them, they were found guilty and given prison sentences.

It seems that few of those close to Stalin were demanding an extension of the terror at this point. But Stalin found out about communications between Trotsky and members of oppositionist groups in the party. He retaliated by sending out a Central Committee circular in June 1936 on the 'terrorist activities of the Trotskyist counter-revolutionary bloc'. This contained the crucial words 'the inalienable quality of every Bolshevik under present conditions should be the ability to recognise an ENEMY OF THE PEOPLE no matter how well he may be masked'. This was the sign that old Bolsheviks were going to be 'unmasked'.

Zinoviev and Kamenev were pulled out of prison and in August 1936 were put on trial in the full glare of the public. With them were fourteen others who had previously been members of the oppositionist groups in the party. These show trials were elaborately staged events in which the state prosecutor, Vyshinsky, proved the accused guilty of spying for foreign powers, as well as of being part of a counter-revolutionary bloc involved in Kirov's murder, with Stalin as the intended next victim. The idea of a show trial was not new. It was used in 1928 in the Shakhty trial (see page 182). It was an effective way to create an atmosphere of intimidation, a sense of danger and the feeling that there were enemies, spies and wreckers around. At the time, many accepted that such trials were genuine.

The accused confessed and were executed the next day. Zinoviev, according to police gossip, became so hysterical that his executioner panicked and shot him in a cell. These executions were significant because they were the first

SOURCE 13.10 A gallery of Stalin's victims put together by Trotsky's supporters. It shows what happened to leading Bolsheviks who had worked with Lenin

LEFT-WING OPPOSITION

The Bolsheviks in the first two major show trials were those who had formed the left-wing opposition in the 1920s. Many had supported Trotsky and had opposed Stalin's 'Socialism in One Country'. However, after their defeat in 1927 most had recanted and supported Stalin when he made his left turn to pursue what were, to all intents and purposes, their policies. Trotsky, in exile in the 1930s, was writing articles condemning Stalin as the 'grave digger of the revolution', claiming that his policies had brought the Soviet Union to ruin. Stalin was incensed by this. This is why he was so angry when he found out that Trotsky had been trying to communicate with members of the old left-wing opposition.

THE RIGHTISTS

The last big show trial featured the right wing of the Communist Party, people who had supported the NEP and opposed rapid industrialisation and forced collectivisation. Bukharin had recanted his views and worked on producing the 1936 Constitution. Tomsky, the other leading member of the right, did not wait for the show trial; once it was announced he was going to be investigated he committed suicide.

executions of people who had belonged to the Central Committee. The line had been crossed and many more executions were to follow. A second show trial took place in January 1937 in which Karl Radek, a well-known Trotskyite, and Pyatakov, a deputy in the Commissariat of Heavy Industry, were the main defendants. Needless to say they confessed and were found guilty.

The third and last great show trial was staged in March 1938. It was possibly the most dramatic because it involved Bukharin and he was able to make a more spirited defence of his actions. But in the end, he – along with twenty others, including old Bolsheviks like Rykov as well as the former head of the NKVD, Yagoda – confessed and was sentenced. Most were shot within a few hours, Bukharin and Rykov cursing Stalin as they died.

SOURCE 13.11   A show trial from the 1930s

SOURCE 13.12   J. Arch Getty and O. V. Naumov, *The Road to Terror: Stalin and the Self-Destruction of the Bolsheviks, 1932–39*, 1999, p. 301. The authors quote this letter, which provides a good example of the sort of denunciations that flowed in after Bukharin had been named as a suspect

11 August 1936
Dear Comrade Yezhov
I would like to call your attention to the following:
Comrade N. I. Bukharin has been travelling to Leningrad frequently. While there, he has been staying at the apartment of Busygin, a former Trotskyite and now a counter-revolutionary. Comrade Bukharin has maintained a close relationship with him, both in person and by correspondence ... The fact was uncovered at a party meeting of this institute and reported by Zubkov, who was expelled from the party as a White Guard and abetter of counter-revolutionary work.

I consider it my duty to report this to you in view of the fact that a simple friendship with a sworn counter-revolutionary is hardly possible. It is my suspicion that Comrade Bukharin was aware of Busygin's work and, in particular, of his counter-revolutionary activities at the Institute of the Academy of Sciences.
With Communist greetings,
I. Kuchkin,
Official of the Vasileostrovsky Party District Committee, Leningrad

ACTIVITY

Read Source 13.12 and answer the following questions.

1 In what way are Bukharin's actions considered suspicious?
2 Why is Busygin identified as a counter-revolutionary?
3 What is interesting about Zubkov, the reporter of the association?
4 What does this letter tell you about denunciations and the way the purges spread?

ACTIVITY

Read the poem extract in Source 13.14 and answer the following questions.

1 Who is the hated Judas?
2 What crimes are they accused of?
3 Who do they seem to be serving?
4 How is Stalin portrayed?
5 Do you think this poem is useful historical evidence of the era of the show trials in Russia?

SOURCE 13.13   A speech by Vyshinsky, the prosecutor at the third show trial, March 1938

Our whole country is awaiting and demanding one thing. The traitors and spies who were selling our country must be shot like dirty dogs. Our people are demanding one thing. Crush the accursed reptile. Time will pass. The graves of the hateful traitors will grow over with weeds and thistles. But over us, over our happy country our sun will shine bright and luminous as before. Over the road cleared of the last scum and filth of the past, we, with our beloved leader and teacher, the great Stalin at our head, will march as before onwards and onwards towards communism.

SOURCE 13.14   The party poet was commissioned to write a poem for *Pravda* two days after the first show trial had started, although it was not published. Here is an extract:

*Like flies stuck in glue
They carried out their villainous policies
And finally found
The place their villainy deserved . . .
Fascists . . . Himmler . . . how do you like that?
The incredible suddenly became clear fact,
Recorded in the transcript of the trial:
Betrayers of the Soviet motherland,
Pseudoparty traitors, liars,
Devoted clients of hostile offices,
Underground enemies, Fascist agents,
Murderers of Kirov . . .
Here are the ones who murdered Kirov!
They are going for Stalin! But they failed . . .
WE HAVE GUARDED STALIN
WE ARE UNABLE NOT TO GUARD HIM!
WE GUARD HIM AS OUR HEAD
WE GUARD HIM AS OUR HEART!
Where is Trotsky? Without him . . .
Your foredoomed group
Is lacking, empty,
But proletarian justice will pursue
The hated Judas everywhere . . .*

STALIN'S FALCONS

Today's spin doctors would have had little to teach Stalin. It was important to contrast the good and heroic with the evil traitors. In 1933, he had challenged his pilots to fly 'farther than anyone, faster than anyone, higher than anyone'. At the time of the show trials, pioneering flights were being made by Soviet aviators over the Arctic. The first was greeted with a triumphal parade in Moscow on 15 August 1936, four days before the first show trial started. The second flight took place at the same time as the trial and execution of Tukhachevsky, the army general. And before the third great show trial, an Arctic explorer was literally kept on ice (on an Arctic ice-floe for nine months) so that he could arrive home to a mass welcome just after Bukharin and the others had been executed.

SOURCE 13.15   Stalin greets Valery Chkalov after a record-breaking flight in 1936

SOURCE 13.16 W. G. Krivitsky, *I Was Stalin's Agent*, 1939, p. 211

They made [their confessions] in the sincere conviction that this was their sole remaining service to the Party and the Revolution. They sacrificed honour as well as life to defend the hated regime of Stalin, because it contained the last gleam of hope for the better world to which they had consecrated themselves in early youth.

Why did they confess?

The show trials were a grotesque sham, although many inside and some outside the Soviet Union believed that the defendants were guilty. Some of the charges were ludicrous: plotting to assassinate Kirov, Stalin and even Lenin and the novelist Maxim Gorky; espionage on behalf of foreign powers; conspiring with Trotskyites, Mensheviks, rightists and other opposition groups; planning to restore capitalism and overthrow socialism. The evidence was clearly faked and some of it did not stand up: for example, one of the hotels the conspirators were supposed to have met at did not even exist; one of the accused was in prison when he was supposed to have committed an offence. So why did these tough and battle-hardened Bolsheviks confess?

The most obvious answer is that they were worn down by torture and interrogation (see pages 217–218) and this undoubtedly played a part. It is also clear that they agreed to confess as part of a deal in which their families would be spared. This is true of Bukharin, who wrote a last loving testament to his wife, and probably of Zinoviev and Kamenev. In the event, few of the family members escaped. But another clue is given by W. G. Krivitsky in Source 13.16.

The Yezhovshchina

Just after the first great show trial had ended in September 1936, Nicolai Yezhov replaced Yagoda as head of the NKVD (secret police). Yagoda was criticised for not finding enemies of the state quickly enough. This was a clear sign from Stalin that he wanted to advance the terror. Yezhov was about to initiate a period of terror – called the Yezhovshchina – which reached its height in mid-1937 and lasted until late 1938.

Nicolai Yezhov (1895–1939)

Yezhov (left) and Stalin in conversation

Yezhov had joined the party in 1917. Stalin brought him into the Central Committee in 1927 and gave him an investigative role before he made him head of the NKVD. He was responsible for the deaths of thousands of people. Only about 1.5 m tall, he was known as the 'Bloodthirsty Dwarf' or the 'Iron Hedgehog'. One old Communist remarked, 'In the whole of my long life I have never seen a more repellent personality than Yezhov's.' A Soviet account in 1988 in *Komsomolskaya Pravda* talks of Yezhov's 'low moral qualities' and 'sadistic inclinations'; that 'women working in the NKVD were frightened of meeting him even in the corridors' and that he lacked 'any trace of conscience or moral principles'. (All quoted in Robert Conquest, *The Great Terror: A Reassessment*, 1990, pages 14–15.)

THE STRANGE DEATH OF ORDZHONIKIDZE

SOURCE 13.17 Ordzhonikidze lies dead and high-ranking party members pay their respects. Left to right around the bed are his widow, Molotov, Yezhov, Stalin, Zhdanov, Kaganovich and Voroshilov

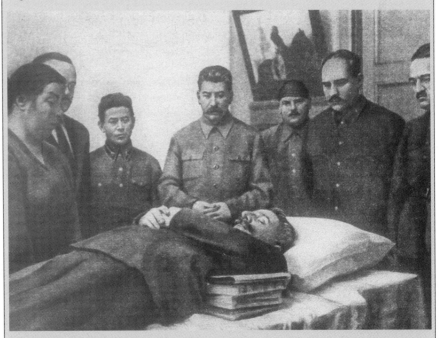

In February 1937, Sergei Ordzhonikidze died, after an angry confrontation with Stalin in which he pleaded for an end to the terror. He was particularly upset by the proceedings against Pyatakov who had worked closely with him at the Commissariat of Heavy Industry. Apparently, Ordzhonikidze was given the choice of suicide and a state funeral or being shot with no state funeral. He chose the former and Stalin said that it must be reported that he died of heart failure. Ordzhonikidze was buried with full honours. He was the last leading Politburo member to resist Stalin's policies. After this, the Great Terror of 1937–38 was unleashed.

SOURCE 13.18 R. Conquest, *The Great Terror: A Reassessment*, 1990, p. 257

It was not only this process of association that gave the Purge its increasingly mass character. In the 1930s, there were still hundreds of thousands who had been members of non-Bolshevik parties, the masses who had served in the White armies, nationalist elements in local intelligentsias, and so on. The increasingly virulent campaign for vigilance against the hidden enemy blanketed the whole country, not merely the Party, in a press and radio campaign. And while the destruction of hostile elements in the party was going forward, it must have seemed natural to use the occasion to break all remaining elements suspected of not being reconciled with the regime.

TALKING POINT

Khrushchev, who led Russia after Stalin's death, once said, 'historians are dangerous people'. Why would leaders of totalitarian regimes regard historians as dangerous?

Purging the party

In the spring of 1937, Stalin made it clear that he thought traitors and spies had infiltrated the party at all levels in every locality. He encouraged lower-ranking party members to criticise and denounce those in higher positions. This resulted in a flood of accusations. Party members were 'unmasked' by colleagues for 'being part of the Bukharin Right in the 1920s' or 'authorising concessions to the peasants in 1925'. They were usually invited to confess before mass meetings and were then arrested. The flood turned into a torrent as more and more party members were dragged in. Some denounced fellow members in order to get their jobs or settle old scores, others to deflect criticism from themselves.

Denunciations were not directed only from the bottom of the party towards the top. Party secretaries and higher officials were anxious to find the counter-revolutionaries and 'fascist spies' in their local party network, if only to show how loyal they were to the regime. So they denounced people below them. Yezhov and the NKVD pursued top party members.

Widening the terror

The purges were not restricted to the party. They took in all areas of society and all institutions (see Chart 13B on page 220). There had been deportations of social groups hostile to Communism after Kirov's murder but arrests of oppositionists, economic officials and administrators increased dramatically from spring 1937 onwards.

In July 1937, the Politburo passed a resolution condemning 'Anti-Soviet Elements' in Russian society. Yezhov drew up an arrest list of over 250,000 of these 'elements', including scientists, artists, writers and musicians, as well as managers and administrators. The historian Chris Ward writes: 'An avalanche of monstrous charges, nightmarish allegations, incredible scenarios and random arrests overwhelmed swathes of the population while terrified, vindictive or simple-minded *apparatchiki* [party officials] flung denunciations at all and sundry ... [for example] Boris Numerov, a distinguished scientist, supposedly organised a "counter-revolutionary astronomers' group" which engaged in wrecking, espionage and terror' (*Stalin's Russia*, 1993, pages 120–21). Historians were particularly vulnerable and many were accused of leading terrorist groups. One leading Bolshevik mentioned at his trial that 'arrests had begun among the historians'.

In practice, anybody could be arrested as an oppositionist. A quota system was applied to geographical areas and to public bodies. It went further than this: in July 1937, the proportion to be shot was fixed at 28 per cent, with the rest being sentenced to up to ten years' hard labour – and this was before the oppositionists had actually been arrested!

A huge media campaign was started, encouraging ordinary people to criticise party officials, bureaucrats and managers – to seek out the 'hidden enemies'. This harnessed popular dissatisfaction with officialdom and resulted in a huge number of denunciations and arrests. People were also encouraged to denounce workers and saboteurs in the workplace, so the rest of the population did not escape either. In *Let History Judge* (1972), Roy Medvedev mentions that over 1000 were arrested in a single factory. Conquest contends, in *The Great Terror: A Reassessment* (1990, page 258), that thousands of peasants, factory workers, shop girls and office clerks were swept up in the purges, although he accepts that the main target was 'officialdom, the intelligentsia'.

Once suspects had been arrested and subjected to interrogation by the NKVD, they always came up with names of accomplices. Workmates, friends, husbands and wives, sons and daughters – all could find themselves arrested because they had connections with someone who had been accused. The victims of the terror increased exponentially.

SOURCE 13.19 G. Gill, *Stalinism*, 1990, p. 32

People hoped to gain leniency for themselves or their families by co-operating with the NKVD, and were therefore willing to denounce others to the security organs. The circle of victims thereby widened.

SOURCE 13.20 Georgi Tsialadee, NKVD member

I asked him, Christopher Sergevich ... tell me honestly, how many people were executed in Georgia? I can tell you he said 80,000 ... we overfulfilled our plan.

SOURCE 13.21 R. Conquest, *The Great Terror: A Reassessment*, 1990, p. 253

Individual denouncers operated on an extraordinary scale. In one district in Kiev, 69 persons were denounced by one man, in another 100. In Odessa a single Communist denounced 230 people. In Poltava, a party member denounced his entire organisation.

ACTIVITY

Did the purges gain a momentum of their own?

1 Examine Sources 13.19–13.24. Explain what evidence each source provides to show how the purges gained their own momentum.

2 How do these sources agree/disagree with Conquest's suggestion, in Source 13.18, of the way that the mass terror spread?

SOURCE 13.22 J. Arch Getty, *The Origins of the Great Purges*, 1985, p. 178

Members denounced leaders [and each other] for dubious class origins, long-forgotten sins, and current misdeeds. Secretaries defended themselves and proved their vigilance by expelling and denouncing batches of rank and file members. Spetseedstvo [attacks on bourgeois specialists], antibureaucratism and class hatred re-emerged in strength against the backdrop of a full-blown spy scare. Panic-stricken local party officials even resorted to filling administrative positions with politically 'safe' employees of the NKVD.

SOURCE 13.23 A. Weissberg, *Conspiracy of Silence*, 1952, p.364. The physicist Alexander Weissberg, himself a victim of the purges, wrote of repeated purges of directors of the big foundries of the Ukraine

It was only the third or fourth batch who managed to keep their seats. They had not even the normal advantages of youth in their favour, for the choosing had been a very negative one. They were the men who had denounced others on innumerable occasions. They had bowed the knee whenever they had come up against higher authority. They were morally and intellectually crippled.

SOURCE 13.24 W. G. Krivitsky, *I Was Stalin's Agent*, 1939, p. 247. Krivitsky sheds some light on why Stalin purged the army

Stalin knew that Tukhachevsky and the other ranking generals could never be broken into the state of unquestioning obedience which he now required of all those about him. They were men of personal courage, and he remembered [that in] the days when his own prestige was at the lowest, these generals had enjoyed enormous popularity ... He remembered too that at every critical stage of his rule – forcible collectivisation, hunger, rebellion – the generals had supported him reluctantly, had put difficulties in his path, had forced deals upon him. He felt no certainty now that ... they would continue to recognise his totalitarian authority.

Purging the armed forces

In 1937 it was the turn of the armed forces. Stalin was convinced that he could not count on the army to follow his policies. The leaders of the army were tough and difficult to intimidate. Marshall Tukhachevsky was the hero of the Civil War, but during this period he had come into conflict with Stalin. Stalin claimed that the army was plotting to overthrow him. Tukhachevsky and other generals had confessions beaten out of them (Tukhachevsky's written confession actually had blood stains on it) and were then executed. The NKVD then worked its way through the rest of the armed forces to devastating effect (see Chart 13B on page 220). That Stalin should risk wiping out his best commanders when the prospect of war loomed is a powerful indication of how far the terror had gone.

Arrest and interrogation

Many of the arrests came at night between 11pm and 3am. NKVD officers drove around in black vehicles called 'ravens', collecting their unwilling passengers. A knock at the door in the middle of the night inspired fear; some people kept a packed bag ready in case the knock was for them. In Moscow a sort of black humour developed during the purges. One joke told of a husband and wife being woken in the night by a loud noise. Terrified, the husband opened the door, then cheerfully called out to his wife: 'Don't worry, it's only bandits come to rob us.' A similar joke tells of a household being woken by bangs on the door. Eventually, one brave occupant opened it, calling up to the others: 'Don't worry comrades, it's just the fire brigade come to tell us the house is on fire.'

The reasons for arrest were arbitrary: criticising Stalin, telling a joke about Stalin, being a friend of someone who was arrested. Arrests were followed by the inevitable interrogation in which the victims were urged to confess their opposition to Stalin and involvement with counter-revolutionary groups. The theatre director Meyerhold, a prominent member of the avant-garde movement in the early Soviet Union, was forced to drink his own urine and then sign his confession with his left hand because his right arm had been broken.

Despite the pressure put on them, many Russians did refuse to confess and were executed quietly. Ryutin (see page 208) was brought from prison and tortured, but he refused to take part in a show trial and so he was executed. His wife and sons were also killed.

Confessions were important. They legitimised the arrests and proved that the state was right. It was a logical strategy when there was no real evidence to prove the accused guilty. The state prosecutor, Vyshinsky, thought a confession written by the accused looked more 'voluntary'. He said: 'I personally prefer a half confession in the defendant's own handwriting to a full confession in the investigator's writing' (see Sources 13.25 and 13.26).

Many Soviet citizens died in prison, either shot or dying from torture. Vans marked 'Meat' regularly arrived at Moscow cemeteries to deliver their loads – the naked bodies which filled the mass graves. People always knew when the female victims were Communist Party members because they had short hair. Those who did not die were sent to the Gulag, the network of labour camps that infested the USSR. Some of the most feared were in the north, in the Kolyma area, where the freezing weather made life intolerable. Relentless hard work and inadequate food and clothing killed many. Forced labour was also used on large building projects like the White Sea Canal, where it has been estimated that over 100,000 died because of the appalling conditions.

SOURCE 13.25 Mikhail Mindlin (arrested 1937), quoted in *The People's Century*, BBC TV, 1996

When the interrogation began, I was asked to sign some lies about myself and some good comrades from my region. They handed me a list of 47 people. They wanted me to sign a statement – I wouldn't. They kept me standing for five days, day and night. My legs were so swollen.

SOURCE 13.26 D. J. Dallin and B. I. Nicolaevsky, *Forced Labour in Soviet Russia*, 1948, p. 459

The basic mechanism and chief reliance of the extortion artists were physical torture . . . several basic techniques were common . . .

The 'parilka' or sweat room . . . several hundred men and women, standing close packed in a small room where all ventilation has been shut off, in heat that chokes and suffocates, in stink that asphyxiates . . . Many have stood thus two days . . . their feet are swollen, their bodies numb . . . they are not allowed to squat or sit. Every now and then, those who faint are dragged out into the corridor, revived and thrown back in the sweat room.

The so-called conveyor belt . . . examiners sit at desks in a long series of rooms, strung out along corridors, up and down stairs, back to the starting point: a sort of circle of OGPU agents. The victims run at a trot from one desk to the next, cursed, threatened, insulted, bullied, questioned by each agent in turn, round and round hour after hour. They weep and plead and deny and keep on running . . . If they fall they are kicked and beaten on their shins, stagger to their feet and resume the hellish relay. The agents, relieved at frequent intervals, are always fresh and keen while the victims grow weaker, more terrorised and degraded.

From the parilka to the conveyor, from the conveyor to the parilka, then periods in ugly cells when uncertainty and fear for one's loved ones outside demoralise the prisoner.

SOURCE 13.27 a Baldeyev cartoon of corpses in a mass grave in a labour camp

SOURCE 13.27 b Baldeyev cartoon of labour camp prisoners

SOURCE 13.28 D. Volkogonov, *Stalin*, 1988, p. 339. This is the testimony of Stepan Ivanovich Semenov, a Muscovite, who spent fifteen years in the camps. Two of his brothers were shot and his wife died in prison. He is now an old man without children or grandchildren

The worst thing is when you have no one waiting for you, when no one needs you. I and my brothers might have had children and grandchildren, families. The accursed Tamerlaine [Stalin] smashed and trampled everything. He took the future away from citizens who were not born because he killed their mothers and fathers. I'm living out my life alone and I still can't understand how it was that we didn't see that 'our' leader was a monster, how the people could let it happen.

The end of the purges

Stalin called a halt to the terror towards the end of 1938. By this time, Yezhov had been replaced by Beria. Arrests slowed down, although Central Committee members and army officers were purged well into 1939. The purges were destabilising Russian society. Administrative systems were falling apart with key personnel missing and this was having a negative impact on industrial production. Stalin blamed Yezhov and the NKVD for the excesses of the terror, which was probably true. In 1940, a hitman, on Stalin's orders, murdered Trotsky. Now indeed virtually all of the old Bolsheviks had been wiped out. However, the purges continued in a much-reduced form into the Second World War. For the victims, the purges never really ended, as Source 13.28 shows.

Osip Mandelstam

With a few notable exceptions, writers and artists suffered greatly during the purges. It was easy to step out of line and fall foul of the NKVD. In 1933 the poet Osip Mandelstam composed a sixteen-line poetic epigram about Stalin. It ran as follows:

We live, deaf to the land beneath us,
Ten steps away no one hears our speeches,

But where there's so much as half a conversation
The Kremlin's mountaineer will get his mention,

His fingers are as fat as grubs
And the words, final as lead weights, fall from his lips,

His cockroach whiskers leer
And his boot tops gleam.

Around him a rabble of thin necked leaders – fawning
half men for him to play with.

They whinny, purr or whine
As he prates and points a finger,

One by one forging his laws, to be flung
Like horseshoes at the head, the eye or groin.

And every killing is a treat
for the broad-chested Ossete.

The oral composition travelled from Muscovite mouth to mouth until it reached the police in a verse whose second stanza ran:

All we hear is the Kremlin mountaineer,
the murderer and peasant slayer.

Mandelstam read his poem to half a dozen friends, one of whom informed on him. Yagoda was so struck by the poem that he could recite it by heart and he did – to Stalin. Mandelstam was arrested and interrogated. Luckily, he was defended by Bukharin and exiled for three years rather than being shot or sent to a labour camp. When he returned, he tried to write a poem praising Stalin but it was never published. He was arrested in 1938 and his wife never saw him again. She later found out that he died in December 1938 of typhus: 'Silently, in pain, lying in the filth of a prison camp, Russia's greatest poet of the twentieth century died' (E. Radzinsky, *Stalin*, 1997, page 406).

■ **13B Who were the victims?**

Leading party members

Khrushchev states that 98 out of 139 (70 per cent) members of the Central Committee elected at the Seventeenth Party Congress were arrested and shot. Of the 1966 delegates to the Congress, 1108 were arrested. This was the congress which favoured Kirov over Stalin.

Senior military officers

These included:

- Tukhachevsky, Chief of the General Staff, and seven other generals – all heroes of the Civil War
- all eleven war commissars and three out of five marshals of the USSR
- all admirals commanding fleets and their replacements
- all but one of the senior commanders of the air force.

In all, 35,000 officers were either imprisoned or shot – although over 11,000 were reinstated by the middle of 1940.

Managers, engineers and scientists

A high proportion of managers at all levels were purged. The railways were particularly hard hit. Leading physicists and biologists were arrested.

People related to those who had been purged

This was probably the largest category of all – colleagues, subordinates, relatives, wives, children, friends and associates.

Party and state leaders

In every national republic within the USSR, party and state leaders were charged with treason or bourgeois nationalism. In Georgia, two state prime ministers, four out of five of the regional party secretaries and thousands of lesser officials lost their posts.

NKVD

Yagoda, head of the NKVD, was arrested in 1937. According to figures given by D. Volkogonov in *Stalin* (1988, p. xxiv) more than 23,000 NKVD men perished at the end of the 1930s.

Other groups

- Anyone with contacts abroad, such as Comintern agents, diplomats, foreign trade officials, intelligence agents, railwaymen, sportsmen
- Former Mensheviks and Socialist Revolutionaries
- Priests, members of religious groups and people holding unorthodox views of any sort
- People in the media, artists and historians.

Peasants and industrial workers

Members of these groups were arrested, imprisoned or shot in huge numbers, although most peasants died during collectivisation and the famine.

Why is it so difficult to give an accurate figure for the number of people who were killed in the purges?

How many were killed in the purges?

It is notoriously difficult to calculate the number of people killed in the purges when the evidence is full of gaps and inconsistencies. For instance, the results of a census taken in the Soviet Union in January 1937 were suppressed and the census organisers were shot as 'a serpent's nest of traitors in the apparatus of Soviet Statistics' who had exerted themselves to diminish the numbers of the population of the USSR. Also, the NKVD burned much of their archive as the Germans approached Moscow in 1941. Another problem is that historians calculate the number of victims over different periods of time and include peasants and workers repressed during collectivisation and the industrialisation drive of the early 1930s.

■ **13C Estimates of the number of victims of the Stalinist regime**

Wheatcroft and Davies (1994) estimate that 10 million people died between 1927 and 1938. They believe that around 8.5 million of these died between 1927 and 1936, mostly from famine.

Dmitri Volkogonov claims that around 7 million people were executed between 1929 and 1953, with another 16.5 million imprisoned.

Estimates of victims
of the Great Terror 1937–38
by **Robert Conquest** (1990):

	Arrests	7–8 million
	Executions	1–1.5 million
	Population of camps	7–8 million
	Died in camps	2 million
1932–1933:	Famine	7 million
1929–1953:	Deaths (total)	20 million

E Interpretations of the Great Purges

FOCUS ROUTE

Draw spider diagrams to represent the position of different historians on the purges. You could call one diagram the 'totalitarian view' and another 'revisionist views'. But do look carefully at the Learning trouble spot below.

There has been a vigorous debate between historians over the explanation of the Great Purges. The process that led to so many arrests and executions – what we might call the mechanism of the purges – is not clear. Few documents were released under the Soviet regime and certain key archives, such as those of the KGB, have still not been opened. Those archives that have recently become available have provided a vast amount of information reflecting different experiences in different parts of the former USSR. So views might change as more archive material is examined and more becomes available.

Much of the debate between historians centres around:

- the role of Stalin in the purges and the extent of his personal control of the process
- the extent to which his actual personality shaped the purges.

The debate has been dominated by two broad approaches, outlined in Charts 13E and 13F (page 222).

Why do historians disagree about the purges?

The purges are a very political topic. It is not surprising that the 'totalitarian' view of the purges – that they were masterminded by an evil puppet master – should have been predominant in the Cold War period. Historians in the West wanted to demonstrate that it was a system where the leadership exercised totalitarian control over an unwilling population. However, the emergence of a new generation of historians in the 1970s and 1980s, who were not so anti-Soviet, and changes within the USSR itself, led to the totalitarian view being challenged. There are a number of reasons why historians disagree about the purges and these are summarised in Chart 13D. In the context of the purges there has been an acrimonious debate over the use of sources.

■ 13D Why do historians disagree about the purges?

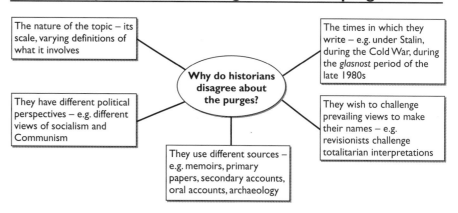

The nature of the topic – its scale, varying definitions of what it involves

The times in which they write – e.g. under Stalin, during the Cold War, during the *glasnost* period of the late 1980s

They have different political perspectives – e.g. different views of socialism and Communism

Why do historians disagree about the purges?

They wish to challenge prevailing views to make their names – e.g. revisionists challenge totalitarian interpretations

They use different sources – e.g. memoirs, primary papers, secondary accounts, oral accounts, archaeology

■ Learning trouble spot

A word of warning: pigeon-holing historians

As we have mentioned in earlier sections of this book, you should be very careful about putting historians into pigeon-holes and thinking that certain groups of historians all hold the same views on a particular topic. The two lines of thought identified in Charts 13E and 13F represent the broad positions in this debate, but there is a great deal of variation and many different views, especially among the revisionists. Some revisionists ascribe a great deal of importance to the influence of Stalin's personality on the purges.

Debate over sources

In the context of the purges there has been an acrimonious debate over the use of sources. J. Arch Getty has criticised Western accounts that have relied on sources such as memoirs and accounts by people who fled the Soviet Union. He says they have a political bias that makes them unreliable and they are bound to attack Stalin as the central agent of terror. He places his emphasis on the use of archival records and official documents.

Other historians, including Alec Nove and Robert Conquest, accept that personal accounts should be treated with caution but make the point that archival materials and official reports can also be unreliable; officials simply reported what their superiors wanted them to hear. They maintain that oral history and memoirs are indeed valuable sources.

■ 13E The totalitarian line

The totalitarian view has predominated in the West since the Second World War. It is sometimes called:

- the 'top down' view of the terror, because instructions were given by those at the top and carried out by those below, or
- the 'intentionalist' interpretation, because Stalin intended to kill his opponents and increase his personal power.

The prime exponent of this line in the West is Robert Conquest whose book, *The Great Terror: A Reassessment* (1990) sets out the case clearly with much supporting evidence. This view is also shared by liberal historians who were dissidents in the old Soviet regime, such as Roy Medvedev and Alexander Solzhenitsyn. But while Medvedev distinguishes between Lenin and Stalin, seeing the latter as the evil director of the terror, Solzhenitsyn sees a direct connection to the methods used by Lenin. He sees the terror of the 1930s as an escalation of the institutions (secret police, labour camps) put in place by Lenin.

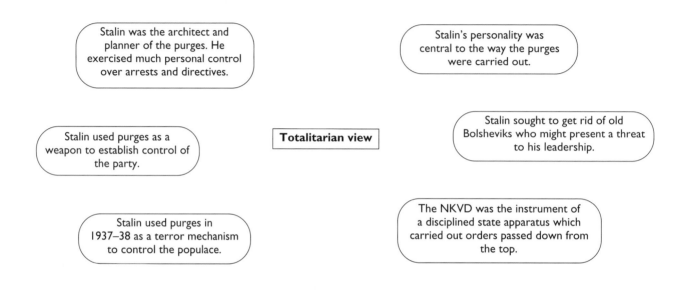

Stalin was the architect and planner of the purges. He exercised much personal control over arrests and directives.

Stalin's personality was central to the way the purges were carried out.

Stalin used purges as a weapon to establish control of the party.

Totalitarian view

Stalin sought to get rid of old Bolsheviks who might present a threat to his leadership.

Stalin used purges in 1937–38 as a terror mechanism to control the populace.

The NKVD was the instrument of a disciplined state apparatus which carried out orders passed down from the top.

■ 13F The revisionist line

The totalitarian view has been challenged by revisionist historians from the 1970s onwards. This view is sometimes called 'decisionist' because it sees the purges as the result of decisions made by the Communist leadership in reaction to a series of crises in the mid-1930s. J. Arch Getty, in his book *The Origins of the Great Purges* (1985), put the most extreme case of the revisionists, seeming to take a lot of responsibility for the purges away from Stalin. He argues that focusing on Stalin alone has, for too long, provided simple and convenient interpretations when the real story is much more complicated. Other historians who have taken a revisionist or decisionist line on the purges are Sheila Fitzpatrick, Graeme Gill and Roberta Manning.

Stalin is responsible for the terror and set it in process, but his personality alone is not a sufficient explanation for the scale and form of the purges.

Stalin did not have a masterplan for the purges.

Stalin did not exercise the personal control of the process ascribed to him and he himself had little idea about what was going on in some areas.

Revisionist view

The machinery of terror was not well organised. Many people were selected at random, denounced or implicated by their colleagues or other people. Terror was generated from below as well as from above.

The Soviet state was chaotic in the mid-1930s. There was confusion and conflict between Moscow and the rest of the USSR. The centre used the purges to try to get control but they spiralled out of control and gained a momentum of their own.

The NKVD was riven by internal divisions. Units within the organisation often acted on their own initiative.

F How far was Stalin's personality responsible for the Great Purges?

ACTIVITY

You are going to use this activity to help you to prepare for a major essay with the title 'How far was Stalin's personality responsible for the Great Purges?'

1 Read Sources 13.29–13.35. Decide how important each historian feels that Stalin's personality was to the Great Purges and where each of them fits on the five-point scale below. Justify your choice by a brief reference to each source.

Absolutely central		Important		One of a number of factors
1	2	3	4	5

2 Make a list of the factors mentioned as causes of the purges or of specific episodes in the purges.
3 Choose two sources which show markedly different interpretations of the purges. Explain how they are different.

SOURCE 13.29 R. Conquest, *The Great Terror: A Reassessment*, 1990, pp. 69–70

The one fundamental drive that can be found throughout is the strengthening of his own position. To this, for practical purposes, all else was subordinate. It led him to absolute power . . .

He carried out a revolution which completely transformed the Party and the whole of society. Far more than the Bolshevik Revolution itself, this period marks the major gulf between modern Russia and the past . . . It is true that only against the peculiar background of the Soviet past, and the extraordinary traditions of the All-Union Communist Party, could so radical a turn be put through. The totalitarian machinery, already in existence, was the fulcrum without which the world could not be moved. But the revolution of the Purges still remains, however we judge it, above all Stalin's personal achievement.

SOURCE 13.30 J. Arch Getty, *The Origins of the Great Purges*, 1985, p. 205

Western scholars have remained hypnotised by Stalin's cult of personality, and their obsession with him has led to studies of the Great Purges period that provide no detailed investigation of the political and institutional context. Rather than placing these events in these contexts, scholars have often discussed the Great Purges only against the background of Stalin's personality and categorised Stalinism simply as the undisputed rule of an omniscient [all-knowing] and omnipotent [all-powerful] dictator. Contradictions and confusion are seen as manifestations of Stalin's caprice, and too often the political history of the Stalin period has merely been the story of Stalin's supposed activities.

SOURCE 13.31 A. Nove (ed.), *The Stalin Phenomenon*, 1993, p. 32

No doubt there were rivalries and conflicts within the apparatus, and it is certainly useful to try to examine the relationships between elements of the apparatus and segments of society. But how can one avoid the conclusion that it was Stalin's decision to purge the party and society of what he regarded as suspect and unstable elements – even if one can accept that orders might have been distorted by [those who carried them out]? One is struck by the number of references to arrest plans, which zealous locals sought to fulfil or overfulfil. However, the whole process was set in motion from the top, and we do have the known telegram sent by Stalin and Zhdanov demanding the appointment of Yezhov to replace the apparently too lenient Yagoda.

SOURCE 13.32 R. Manning, 'The Soviet Economic Crisis of 1936–40 and the Great Purges', in J. Arch Getty and R. Manning (eds), *Stalinist Terror – New Perspectives*, 1993, pp. 140–41

In this way, the economic problems of 1936–41 and the Great Purges appear to be inexorably linked. The industrial showdown, which set in at a time when the USSR could least afford it, when a two-front war without allies seemed to be the Soviets' inevitable fate, shaped the course of the Great Purges at least as much, if not more so, as the terror in turn influenced the operation of the economy. When plans went awry, when deprivations, instead of disappearing, became more severe, when promised improvements in food supply did not materialise, the subconscious temptation to seek scapegoats became irresistible.

ASSESSING THE DIFFERENT INTERPRETATIONS

Source 13.29 Robert Conquest is the British author of *The Great Terror*, first published in 1968, with a second edition, *The Great Terror: A Reassessment*, published in 1990. This is a standard work on the subject. Conquest is regarded by some as a 'cold warrior'. He follows the 'totalitarian' line.

Source 13.30 J. Arch Getty, an American, is the leading revisionist historian on this topic – he attacks the 'totalitarian' view. He is a decisionist historian who concentrates on institutional rather than ideological, personal or social factors.

Source 13.31 Alec Nove (1915–94) was Russian-born – his father was a Menshevik. His family left the USSR for Britain in 1924. An expert on Soviet economic policy, he wrote extensively on Stalin and Stalinism.

Source 13.32 Roberta Manning, an American, is the mentor of J. Arch Getty with whom she worked closely and edited *Stalinist Terror – New Perspectives* (1993). She is a revisionist historian on Stalin.

Source 13.33 Stephen Cohen, a revisionist historian and biographer of Bukharin, sees a marked difference between the Leninist state and the Stalinist state. He suggests that Stalin led Soviet Russia along the wrong path and feels they would have done better to stick with Bukharin and the right.

Source 13.34 Isaac Deutscher (1907–67), a Polish Communist, was expelled from the party in 1932 because he was the leader of the anti-Stalinist group. He moved to England and became a journalist and historian. As well as his biography of Stalin, he wrote a three-volume biography of his hero, Trotsky.

Source 13.35 Alan Bullock is a distinguished liberal British historian, the author of *Hitler and Stalin: Parallel Lives* (1991).

SOURCE 13.33   S. Cohen, quoted in Thames TV documentary *Stalin*, 1990

Ultimately you cannot explain the great terror against the Party without focusing on Stalin's personality. For some reason Stalin had a need to rid himself of the old Bolshevik Party, the Party that remembered everything of Bolshevik history and knew in its heart of hearts that Stalin was not the Lenin of today. He had to rid himself of this party and he did. By the end of the thirties, it was a completely different party demographically, most of its members had joined since 1929. The older league had gone, there were a few tokens left but almost to a man/woman they were dead.

SOURCE 13.34   I. Deutscher, *Stalin*, rev. edn 1966, pp. 372–74

But why did Stalin need the abominable spectacle [in 1936]? It has been suggested that he sent the men of the old guard to their deaths as scapegoats for his economic failures. There is a grain of truth in this but no more. For one thing, there was a very marked improvement in the economic conditions of the country in the years of the trials. He certainly had no need for so many scapegoats; and, if he had needed them, penal servitude would have been enough – Stalin's real and much wider motive was to destroy the men who represented the potentiality of alternative government.

The question that must now be answered is why he set out to reach this objective in 1936? Considerations of domestic policy can hardly explain his timing. Widespread though popular dissatisfaction may have been, it was too amorphous [lacking focus] to constitute any immediate threat to his position. The opposition was pulverised, downtrodden, incapable of action. Only some sudden shock . . . involving the whole machine of power might have enabled it to rally its scattered and disheartened troops. A danger of that kind was just then taking shape; and it threatened from abroad. The first of the great show trials, that of Zinoviev and Kamenev, took place a few months after Hitler's army had marched into the Rhineland . . .

. . . In the supreme crisis of war, the leaders of opposition, if they had been alive, might indeed have been driven to action by a conviction, right or wrong, that Stalin's conduct of the war was incompetent and ruinous. At an earlier stage they might have been opposed to his deal with Hitler . . . It is possible they would have then attempted to overthrow Stalin. Stalin was determined not to allow things to come to this . . . It is not necessary to assume that he acted from sheer cruelty or lust for power. He may be given the dubious credit of the sincere conviction that what he did served the interests of the revolution and that he alone interpreted those interests aright . . .

SOURCE 13.35   A. Bullock, *Hitler and Stalin: Parallel Lives*, 1991, pp. 496–97

I have already suggested the two most important features of Stalin's psychology. The first was his narcissistic personality, characterised by his total self absorption . . . and his conviction that he was a genius marked out to play a unique historical role. The second was the paranoid tendency which led him to picture himself as a great man facing a hostile world peopled with jealous and treacherous enemies engaged in a conspiracy to pull him down, if he did not strike and destroy them first . . .

Throughout his life Stalin had a psychological need to confirm and reassure himself about both those beliefs – about his historic mission and about the truth of the picture he had formed of himself in relation to the external world . . . The same obsession which had provided the drive to defeat his rivals and match Lenin's revolution with his own now nerved him to outdo his predecessor by freeing himself from the constraints of the party and becoming the sole ruler of the Soviet state.

Even more striking is the coincidence between Stalin's second psychological need . . . and his political aim, in the years 1934–9, to destroy the original Bolshevik Party created by Lenin and replace it with a new one, maintaining a façade of continuity but in fact remaking it in his own image.

TWO STORIES ABOUT STALIN

1 He was supposed to have said: 'To choose one's victims, to prepare one's plans minutely, to slake an implacable vengeance, and then to go to bed … there is nothing sweeter in the world.'

2 There was a caged parrot in the room in the Kremlin where Stalin often paced back and forth, smoking his pipe while he thought things out and spitting from time to time. Once, the parrot imitated him spitting. Stalin was furious, reached into the cage and killed the parrot with one blow to the head from his pipe.

SOURCE 13.36 Stalin in a photograph believed to show him signing death warrants

SOURCE 13.37 Two of Stalin's sayings

One death is a tragedy, a million is a statistic.

If there is a person, there is a problem; no person no problem.

What reasons have been put forward for the purges?

In this section we look at Stalin's personality and motives, and also at other reasons that have been put forward to explain the form the purges took.

The vast majority of historians accept Stalin's responsibility for the terror. He was at the centre of the decision-making process and cannot be absolved. However, some revisionists argue that focusing on Stalin alone has for too long provided simple interpretations when the real story is more complicated.

The role played by Stalin

A number of historians argue that Stalin's personality was the driving force behind the terror, and that without him there would have been no Great Purges in the form they took – for example, old Bolsheviks would not have been humiliated and executed. Chart 13G outlines the role that they think his personality played in the terror.

■ 13G What role did Stalin's personality play?

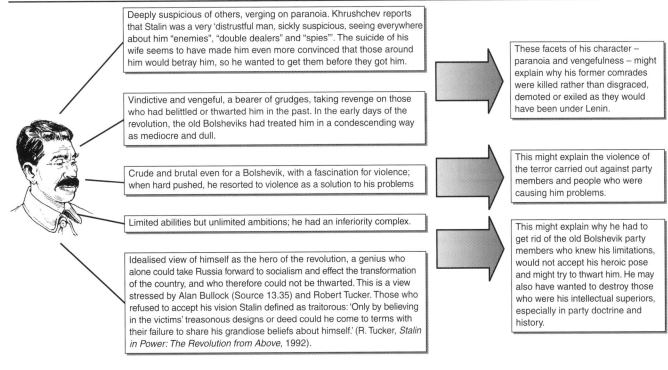

Deeply suspicious of others, verging on paranoia. Khrushchev reports that Stalin was a very 'distrustful man, sickly suspicious, seeing everywhere about him "enemies", "double dealers" and "spies"'. The suicide of his wife seems to have made him even more convinced that those around him would betray him, so he wanted to get them before they got him.

Vindictive and vengeful, a bearer of grudges, taking revenge on those who had belittled or thwarted him in the past. In the early days of the revolution, the old Bolsheviks had treated him in a condescending way as mediocre and dull.

Crude and brutal even for a Bolshevik, with a fascination for violence; when hard pushed, he resorted to violence as a solution to his problems

Limited abilities but unlimited ambitions; he had an inferiority complex.

Idealised view of himself as the hero of the revolution, a genius who alone could take Russia forward to socialism and effect the transformation of the country, and who therefore could not be thwarted. This is a view stressed by Alan Bullock (Source 13.35) and Robert Tucker. Those who refused to accept his vision Stalin defined as traitorous: 'Only by believing in the victims' treasonous designs or deed could he come to terms with their failure to share his grandiose beliefs about himself.' (R. Tucker, *Stalin in Power: The Revolution from Above*, 1992).

These facets of his character – paranoia and vengefulness – might explain why his former comrades were killed rather than disgraced, demoted or exiled as they would have been under Lenin.

This might explain the violence of the terror carried out against party members and people who were causing him problems.

This might explain why he had to get rid of the old Bolshevik party members who knew his limitations, would not accept his heroic pose and might try to thwart him. He may also have wanted to destroy those who were his intellectual superiors, especially in party doctrine and history.

CASE STUDY: THE PURGES IN SVERDLOVSK

This case study is based on the work of James Harris ('The purging of local cliques in the Urals region 1936-7', in S. Fitzpatrick (ed.) *Stalinism: New Directions*, 2000, pages 267-71). He examined new archive material on Sverdlovsk, a large industrial centre and showed that the purges did not have a uniform cause.

Members of the regional party leadership had ensured an excellent standard of living for the ruling clique – large apartments, special access to consumer goods, high salaries – provided they remained loyal. Those who caused trouble or would not carry out instructions would lose these privileges. By 1935, all key positions were in their control; even the local NKVD man was a member of their inner circle. When faced with problems in fulfilling excessively high economic targets for the First Five-Year Plan, they manipulated the production figures, hid deficiencies in projects under construction, and found scapegoats outside the clique to explain underfulfilment.

But when it came to the Second Five-Year Plan, with more realistic targets, deficiencies could not be hidden because all the enterprises were supposed to be up and working. Poor management and machine breakdowns meant that there was serious underfulfilment as production fell. To make matters worse, a new NKVD man replaced the old one as the Great Purges got underway and there were demands to search for 'enemies everywhere'. The cosy coping mechanism had broken down.

The result was an avalanche of accusations, denunciations and incriminating information as members of the clique tried to save themselves. But each arrest led to further arrests as the NKVD followed the threads of the conspiracy. The use of terror grew in momentum and ferocity.

He now acknowledges that the 'fingerprints of Stalin' are all over the purges and that he played a central role in planning and executing them, although he still maintains that they did not happen as part of a master plan but rather as the response by Stalin and the Soviet élite to changing circumstances in Russia (see Source 13.39). However, there are many historians who continue to lay the main blame for the purges clearly at Stalin's door, believing them to be the intended outcome of his ideas and his personality. So the debate goes on.

SOURCE 13.38   R. Service, *A History of Twentieth Century Russia*, 1997, pp. 210–11

The Great Terror would not have taken place but for Stalin's personality and ideas. He it was who directed the state's punitive machinery against all those whom he identified as 'anti-Soviet elements' and 'enemies of the people'. Among his purposes was a desire to use his victims as scapegoats for the country's pain; and in order to sustain his mode of industrialisation he also needed to keep his mines, timber forests and construction sites constantly supplied with slave labour. It was probably also his intention to take pre-emptive measures against any 'fifth column' [internal dissidents] operating against him in the case of war. These considerations, furthermore, fitted into a larger scheme to build an efficient Soviet state subservient to his personal dictatorship – and to secure the state's total control over society. Such was the guiding rationale of the Great Terrorist.

SOURCE 13.39   J. Arch Getty and O. V. Naumov, *The Road to Terror: Stalin and the Self-Destruction of the Bolsheviks, 1932–39*, 1999

In spite of some misreadings and misunderstandings of earlier work, Stalin's guilt for the terror was never in question. We can now see his fingermarks all over the archives. Although he approved suggestions and draft documents from others as often as he launched his own initiatives, he played the leading role in the terror. But even with the new documents, the role remains problematic and hard to specify . . . Stalin worked assiduously toward the goal of enhancing his power and centralizing authority in Moscow . . . But even in Stalin's office, there were too many twists and turns, too many false starts and subsequent embarrassing backtrackings to support the idea that the terror was the culmination of a well-prepared and long-standing master design. Stalin was not sure exactly what kind of repression he wanted or how to get it until rather late in the story. He seems not to have decided on wholesale massacre until early in 1937.

ACTIVITY

Write an essay to answer the following question: Was Stalin's personality much the most important factor in explaining the Great Purges?

This kind of essay invites a number of responses:

a) a 'Yes' answer in which you argue that Stalin's personality was central to the purges and set out the evidence that supports your view

b) a 'Yes but . . . ' answer in which you argue his personality was important but suggest there were other reasons

c) a 'No' answer in which you suggest there were a variety of reasons for the purges. This answer does not exclude Stalin as a central player in the purges: you are saying that his other motives were more important than motives of personal vengeance, fuelled by paranoia and his own self-image. Or, you might want to argue that Stalin's role in the purges has been exaggerated.

You may wish to distinguish between the treatment of the old Bolsheviks in the show trials and the wider purges that drew in many thousands. You will probably want to give more weight to some factors than others. The diagram below may help.

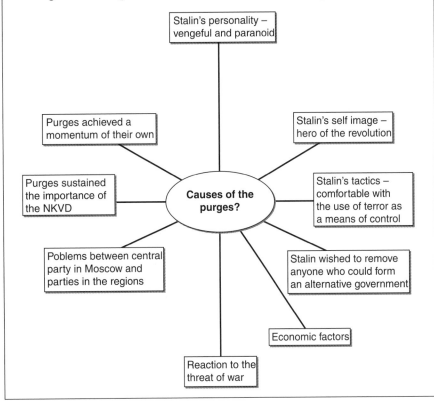

KEY POINTS FROM CHAPTER 13   **How far was Stalin responsible for the Great Purges?**

1 There was a difference between the earlier purges (*chistki*), which were non-violent, and the Great Purges, which used terror against the party.

2 Terror had been a consistent feature of the Stalinist regime from its beginning.

3 There was marked opposition to Stalin before 1934 and at the Seventeenth Party Congress.

4 The murder of Sergei Kirov triggered the Great Purges.

5 Old Bolsheviks from both the left and the right wings of the party were disposed of in a series of show trials.

6 The party was purged from above and from below when members were encouraged to criticise and denounce others.

7 The terror engulfed other sections of the population, notably the armed forces. Millions died or were imprisoned.

8 At the end of the process, Stalin emerged as dictator of the USSR with supreme control of a party that had been moulded by him and a populace that was, in the main, subservient to the leader and the party.

The cult of the personality

CHAPTER OVERVIEW This chapter looks at the growth of the cult of the personality from the 1920s through to the end of the 1940s, when it was at its height. Stalin's image dominated the Soviet Union and he was seen as an omnipotent leader whom people should love and revere. The cult was not just about personal adulation of Stalin. It was also a response to a rapid period of change in the Soviet Union when many Russians were bewildered and confused about what was going on. The Stalin cult provided an image of purpose and solidity, giving people confidence and faith that someone could lead them out of their troubles to the good society.

A How did the cult of the personality develop? (pp. 230–233)

B Rewriting history (pp. 234–235)

C How did Russians react to the cult? (pp. 236–238)

A How did the cult of the personality develop?

ACTIVITY

1 The images in Sources 14.1–14.6 each carry a different message about Stalin. For each one, explain:
   a) the message it is designed to convey to the Russian people
   b) how you reached your interpretation.
2 **a)** What impression of Soviet Russia and of Stalin does Prokofiev's ode (Source 14.7) create?
   b) What are the religious overtones of this ode?
3 Does the fact that images of Stalin appeared everywhere, as described by Steinbeck in Source 14.8, prove that Stalin attracted genuine adulation?

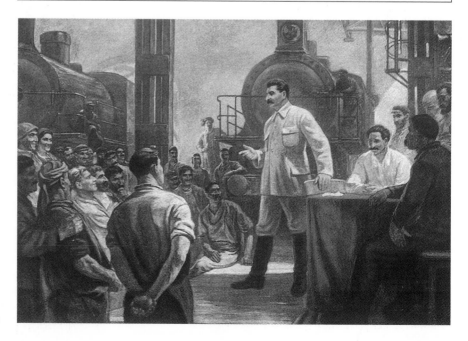

SOURCE 14.1 A painting from 1926 showing Stalin addressing industrial workers

SOURCE 14.2 Stalin at the Helm, a poster from 1933

SOURCE 14.3 A 1937 photomontage of Stalin surrounded by a sea of children's faces

SOURCE 14.4 Grzelishvili's painting, *Comrade Stalin in his Early Years*, 1939

SOURCE 14.6 A painting by Kibrik: *On 24 October Lenin Arrived at Smolny During the Night*. In *Totalitarian Art* (1990), I. Golomstock points out that Lenin is motioning Stalin to go ahead of him, symbolically showing him the way to the bright future

SOURCE 14.5 The cover of *Ogonyok* magazine, December 1949, showing Stalin's godlike image projected into the sky, as part of the celebrations for his seventieth birthday

SOURCE 14.7 Ode to Stalin on his sixtieth birthday by the composer Prokofiev, 1939

Never have our fertile fields such a harvest shown,
Never have our villages such contentment known.
Never life has been so fair, spirits been so high,
Never to the present day grew so green the rye.
O'er the earth the rising sun sheds a warmer light,
Since it looked on Stalin's face it has grown more bright.
I am singing to my baby sleeping in my arms,
Grow like flowers in the meadow free from all alarm.
On your lips the name of Stalin will protect from harm.
You will learn the source of sunshine bathing all the land.
You will copy Stalin's portrait with your little hand.

SOURCE 14.8 John Steinbeck, the American novelist, visited the Soviet Union in 1947 and wrote the following entry in his diary (quoted in M. Cullerne Brown, *Art Under Stalin,* 1991, p. 175)

Everything in the Soviet Union takes place under the fixed stare of the plaster, bronze, drawn or embroidered eye of Stalin. His portrait does not just hang in every museum but in a museum's every room. Statues of him dignify the façade of every public building. His bust stands in front of all airports, railway and bus stations. A bust of Stalin stands in every classroom, and often his portrait hangs directly opposite. In parks he sits on plaster benches and discusses something or other with Lenin. In shops they sell million upon million of images of him, and in every home there is at least one portrait of him ... He is everywhere, he sees everything ... we doubt whether Caesar Augustus enjoyed during his life the prestige, the worship and the godlike power over the people of which Stalin disposes.

The personality cult and the adulation Stalin received are two of the most striking features of Soviet propaganda. By the end of the 1940s, Stalin dominated the USSR physically as well as politically. His image was literally everywhere, as Source 14.8 indicates. He was presented as the heir of Lenin and the sole infallible interpreter of party ideology. He acquired an almost god-like status. The unique position Stalin attained and the power he possessed to shape the Communist state and the lives of the people of the Soviet Union are called the 'cult of the personality'.

The origins of the cult can be seen in the late 1920s, but in this period the leadership was usually portrayed as an anonymous collective body making joint decisions; few pictures of the leaders appeared in the press. In 1929, Stalin was perceived as rather cold and distant. The full-blown cult really got going around 1933–34. Praise was heaped on Stalin personally and his link with Lenin and his role in the achievements of the First Five-Year Plan were emphasised. From 1935 onwards, it was possible to speak of Stalin only in glowing terms. He was portrayed as the *vozhd* (the leader), a genius with great wisdom and even prophetic powers.

The most likely explanation for the development of the cult lay in the economic and political circumstances of Soviet Russia in the mid-1930s. The disruption and disorientation brought about by the First Five-Year Plan and the purges meant that this was a bewildering and confusing time. Former heroes were revealed as traitors; wreckers and saboteurs were everywhere. The image of Stalin reassured the people that they had a strong leader to take them through these difficult and momentous times. There was a firm hand at the helm steering the ship, someone who knew where they were going. The cult of the personality was useful in holding Soviet society together.

Paintings, poetry and sculpture all served the cult. At the beginning of the cult the regime did not want people to be alienated by a remote leader, so they deliberately cultivated a more popular image of Stalin. Paintings and posters stressed Stalin's humanity and his active participation in the lives of ordinary people. He is seen marching alongside workers or in the fields with the peasants, or inspecting great projects. Stalin's relationship with children was emphasised: no nursery was without a 'Thank you, Stalin, for my happy childhood' painting. As the cult developed, operas and films glorified his role in the revolution or as the chief hero of the Civil War. By the end of the 1930s, paintings show him more detached and superior. Statues show him as more monumental, an all-powerful leader; this image could not be clearer than in the statue of Stalin at the Great Soviet Exhibition in 1939. Also in 1939, an exhibition entitled 'Stalin and the Soviet People' contained pictures of his childhood showing him as a natural leader or like a young Christ explaining the scriptures (see Source 14.4, page 231).

Success in the Second World War and the defeat of the Nazis enhanced Stalin's position and fed the cult, which reached its height at the end of the 1940s. Paintings show him in god-like solitude or with Lenin, sometimes even appearing to tell Lenin what to do. Stalin had lost his role as a disciple, now he was an equal or even the master. The omnipresent images of Stalin said to the Soviet people: 'Stalin is everywhere present and watching over you; he understands your hopes and has your best interests at heart.' During the celebrations of his seventieth birthday, a giant portrait of Stalin was suspended over Moscow and lit up at night by a battery of searchlights (see Source 14.5).

FOCUS ROUTE

1 Use the information on pages 230–233 and Chart 14A on page 233 to produce a diagram, mapping out the development of the cult.
2 Make brief notes describing the devices used to establish and spread the cult.
3 Why do you think the cult was used by the Soviet leadership when individual adulation was against their collective code?

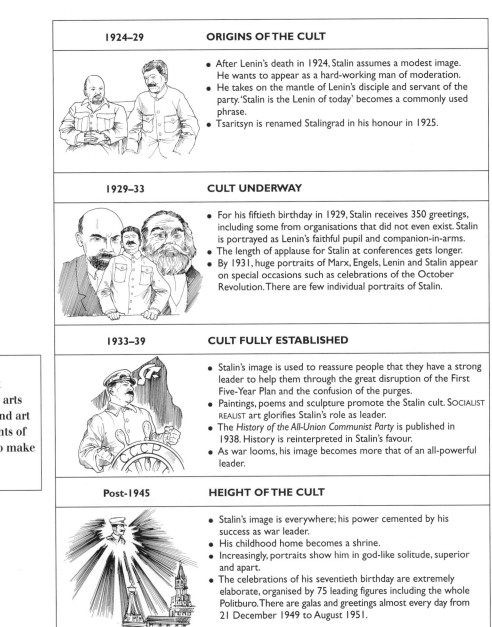

1924–29	ORIGINS OF THE CULT
	• After Lenin's death in 1924, Stalin assumes a modest image. He wants to appear as a hard-working man of moderation. • He takes on the mantle of Lenin's disciple and servant of the party. 'Stalin is the Lenin of today' becomes a commonly used phrase. • Tsaritsyn is renamed Stalingrad in his honour in 1925.

1929–33	CULT UNDERWAY
	• For his fiftieth birthday in 1929, Stalin receives 350 greetings, including some from organisations that did not even exist. Stalin is portrayed as Lenin's faithful pupil and companion-in-arms. • The length of applause for Stalin at conferences gets longer. • By 1931, huge portraits of Marx, Engels, Lenin and Stalin appear on special occasions such as celebrations of the October Revolution. There are few individual portraits of Stalin.

1933–39	CULT FULLY ESTABLISHED
	• Stalin's image is used to reassure people that they have a strong leader to help them through the great disruption of the First Five-Year Plan and the confusion of the purges. • Paintings, poems and sculpture promote the Stalin cult. SOCIALIST REALIST art glorifies Stalin's role as leader. • The *History of the All-Union Communist Party* is published in 1938. History is reinterpreted in Stalin's favour. • As war looms, his image becomes more that of an all-powerful leader.

Post-1945	HEIGHT OF THE CULT
	• Stalin's image is everywhere; his power cemented by his success as war leader. • His childhood home becomes a shrine. • Increasingly, portraits show him in god-like solitude, superior and apart. • The celebrations of his seventieth birthday are extremely elaborate, organised by 75 leading figures including the whole Politburo. There are galas and greetings almost every day from 21 December 1949 to August 1951.

SOCIALIST REALISM
The ideological philosophy that guided Soviet literature and the arts after 1934; all creative writing and art had to celebrate the achievements of the proletarian in his struggle to make a contribution to the Soviet achievement.

STORIES ABOUT THE CULT

In his book *Stalin: Breaker of Nations* (1991, page 213), Robert Conquest tells of some of the more absurd effects of the cult:

■ At a provincial meeting there was an ovation when Stalin's name was mentioned and no one dared to sit down first. When one old man could stand no longer and sat down, his name was taken and he was arrested the next day.

■ When a speech of Stalin's was published on a series of gramophone records, one side of one of the records consisted entirely of applause.

Khrushchev cited the example of Stalin marking a 1948 edition of the *Short Biography* about his own life: he marked the points where he thought the praise was insufficient. Stalin wanted the following sentence to be added: 'Although he performed his task as leader of the people with consummate skill and enjoyed the unreserved support of the entire Soviet people, Stalin never allowed his work to be marred by the slightest hint of vanity, conceit or self-adulation.' (Khrushchev in his secret speech at the Twentieth Party Congress in which he denounced Stalin. Taken from S. Talbolt (ed.), *Khrushchev Remembers*, vol. 1, 1977, page 629.)

B Rewriting history

Source 14.9a A famous photograph of Lenin addressing troops in 1920, with Trotsky and Kamenev on the steps to the right of the platform

Source 14.9b After Trotsky's downfall, the same photograph was published with Trotsky and Kamenev painted out

Source 14.9c In 1933, I. Brodsky painted the same scene on a giant canvas for the Central Lenin Museum in Moscow. Trotsky and Kamenev were replaced by two journalists. This photograph was taken for *Pravda* in 1940 and shows Red army and navy personnel staring at the work

FOCUS ROUTE

Why do you think Stalin found it necessary to rewrite the history of the revolution and the development of the Soviet state in the *Short Course*? Make a note of your answer.

Another significant aspect of the cult of the personality was the reinterpretation of history in Stalin's favour. In 1938, the *History of the All-Union Communist Party*, or *Short Course* as it was usually called, was published in the Soviet Union. In it, Stalin was given a much more important role in the October Revolution as chief companion to Lenin, his closest friend and disciple. Trotsky, on the other hand, was demoted to the role of bourgeois opportunist and given little credit. The other old Bolsheviks, especially Bukharin and his supporters, were designated 'enemies of the people' or were relegated to minor roles. All were dwarfed by the invincible heroes – Lenin and Stalin.

SOURCE 14.10 A photograph taken in April 1925 (above) and published again in 1939 (below)

The *Short Course* was not just another history book. It was *the* main history text for educational institutions across the USSR. It was the definitive version, replacing all the books that had had pages cut out or pasted over as leading Bolsheviks fell victim to the show trials and purges. According to the *Short Biography*, Stalin himself was the author of the *Short Course*. By 1948, it had sold 34 million copies in the Soviet Union and two million elsewhere.

As part of the process of reinterpretation, photographs were amended to support the new history. Stalin was added to photographs of Lenin to show that he had been his closest friend and adviser. Old 'heroes of the revolution' were airbrushed out of Soviet history. It was as if Stalin wanted them wiped from the collective memory of the period.

FOCUS ROUTE

1 Account for the relative success of the cult – why do you think it worked with the Russian people?
2 What conclusions can you reach about whether the adulation Stalin received was genuine? Make notes of your answers.

C How did Russians react to the cult?

Stalin received adulation on a scale and intensity that few leaders have known and, according to Robert Service, he had a 'craving for adulation' (*A History of Twentieth-Century Russia*, 1997, pages 250–51). Although the cult was a carefully contrived propaganda campaign, it does not seem that the adulation was entirely manufactured. Service maintains that genuine enthusiasm for Stalin was limited until the end of the 1930s when the mass indoctrination campaign reached its peak. Such enthusiasm as had been aroused was then heightened by the grave threat to the Soviet Union presented by the war. Robert Thurston, the revisionist historian, is convinced that the people believed that the show trials were genuine and that Stalin was rooting out wreckers and saboteurs. They believed that Stalin was their true guide and the person who cared for them. Only this, he claims (in *Life and Terror in Stalin's Russia 1934–41*, 1996), can account for the huge affection that people had for Stalin. Testimony from people who lived through the Stalinist period after 1945 seems to support this view, but it is more difficult to assess before 1939.

Sarah Davies, in her book *Popular Opinion in Stalin's Russia: Terror, Propaganda and Dissent 1934–41* (1997), identifies three ways in which people reacted to the Stalin cult. They viewed Stalin as:

1 Benefactor. Many, including Stakhanovites, some soldiers and the young intelligentsia, had reason to be grateful to Stalin because they had acquired power and status despite often humble origins. Khrushchev, who followed Stalin as leader of Russia, was an example of such a person. Stalin was admired as the prime agent in achieving the astounding changes brought about by industrialisation and collectivisation. A letter from one woman said: 'I live very well and I think that I will live even better. Why? Because I live in the Stalin epoch. May Stalin live longer than me! . . . All my children had and are having education thanks to the state and, I would say, thanks to the party, and especially comrade Stalin, for he, along with Lenin, opened the way for us simple people . . . I myself, an old woman, am ready to die for Stalin and the Bolshevik cause.'

2 Traditional defender of the people. In this Stalin played a role very similar to that of the tsars. Millions of petitions and letters were sent to him and other Communist leaders asking for help against misfortunes or the actions of local officials or bureaucrats. As in tsarist times, criticism was directed against local officials while the leaders were praised. Letters often began with cult-style greetings: 'Dear comrade Stalin! Our beloved *vozhd*, teacher and friend of the whole happy Soviet country'. Stalin and other leaders were often referred to as 'uncle' or seen as 'like a father'. The petitioners affirmed their loyalty while criticising the actions of the regime's agents on the ground. This was in line with Stalin's own message that officialdom was riddled with corruption and that the great father, Stalin, was on the people's side. It seems that this populist aspect of the cult was in tune with people's traditional ideas.

3 Charismatic leader. According to Davies, Stalin was perceived as a demi-god possessing superhuman abilities and superhuman wisdom. This was reflected in the icons and symbols of the *vozhd* that appeared in houses and in processions, very similar to the honouring of saints in the Christian tradition. Statues and images of Stalin abounded (see Source 14.8 on page 232), as did references to him as the 'sun' or the 'man-god' (see Source 14.13 on page 238). How far ordinary Russians actually believed this is difficult to say, but it does seem that this charismatic aspect of the cult was a significant feature for a large number, especially after the Second World War.

There was, of course, a substantial section of the population – intellectuals, experienced party members and workers – who were aware of the absurdities of the cult. There was active criticism, particularly early on, about the way Stalin had been elevated to some sort of mystical status. Some workers in the mid-1930s objected to the incessant declarations of love for Stalin. Many in the party felt that this was not how Lenin would have acted and still favoured collective leadership of a more anonymous nature – the dictatorship of the party, not an individual. Such criticism was less likely to be expressed after the purges got underway. But there is evidence that by 1938 the excessive propaganda was becoming counterproductive and that people were becoming cynical. Sarah Davies gives the following examples from 1938:

- a leaflet ridiculing the Supreme Soviet, where the 'people's elect' were allowed to shout out 'Hurray' a thousand times in honour of the *vozhd* and his stooges
- an anonymous letter from a Communist supporter complaining about the use of Stalin's name: 'Everything is Stalin, Stalin, Stalin. You only have to listen to a radio programme about our achievements, and every fifth or tenth word will be the name of comrade Stalin. In the end this sacred and beloved name – Stalin – may make so much noise in people's heads that it is very possible that it will have the opposite effect.'

However, even amongst those who did not like him, and there were very many, there was often respect and even admiration. There was a feeling that Stalin was a great leader in the Russian tradition, like one of the great tsars such as Peter the Great. He was tough and he was hard but he had achieved a great deal, industrialised the USSR and made it into a great world power that other countries respected. And on his death in 1953, there were many who wept, even those whose relatives had suffered persecution or died under his rule. The cult of the personality may not always have had a lot of depth, but it had penetrated all areas of Soviet society and played an important role in popularising Stalin and bringing solidity, confidence and coherence to that society during a period of rapid change and instability.

SOURCE 14.11 J. Lewis and P. Whitehead, *Stalin: A Time for Judgement*, 1990, pp. 66, 121, quoting two Russians who grew up in the 1940s

Alexander Avdeyenko
Looking back on my life, I now see that period as one of sincere enthusiasm, as genuine human happiness ... It would have been impossible for a common mortal to withstand the onslaught of Stalin, of the apparatus which was Stalin's, or the pressure which was put on people's reason, heart and soul. Day and night radio told us that Stalin was the greatest man on earth – the greatest statesman, the father of the nation, the genius of all time ... Man wants to believe in something great.

Pavel Litvinov
Stalin was like a god for us. We just believed he was an absolutely perfect individual, and he lived somewhere in the Kremlin, a light always in his window, and he was thinking about us, about each of us. That was how we felt. For example, somebody told me he was the best surgeon. He could perform a brain operation better than anyone else, and I believed it. I knew that he was busy with other things, but if he wanted to do it he would be better.

Sources 14.12 and 14.13, one a poem from 1917 and the other from 1936, give us some insight into how attitudes changed from the time of the October Revolution to the era of the Stalinist state.

1 a) What is the message in the first poem?
   b) How does the poet put over his message?
   c) Why might this be a poem you could march to?
   d) What insight does it give us into how some people might have felt in 1917?

2 a) What is the message in the second poem?
   b) What images of Stalin does the poet create?
   c) How does this message compare with the one in the first poem?
   d) What does it suggest about the way in which people viewed how Communism moved forward?

3 Are these poems useful for historians of this period?

SOURCE 14.12   Extracts from a poem by V. Kirilov, a young proletarian in 1917. Young Communists chanted or marched to poems like these

We are the countless, awesome legions of Labour . . .
Our proud souls burn with the fire of revolt . . .
In the name of our Tomorrow we shall burn Raphael,
Destroy museums, trample the flowers of art.
We have thrown off the heavy crushing legacy . . .
Our muscles crave gigantic work,
Creative pangs seethe in our collective breast . . .
For our new planet we shall find a new dazzling path.
We love life, its intoxicating wild ecstasy,
Our spirit is tempered by fierce struggle and suffering.
We are everybody, we are everything, we are the flame and the victorious light,
We are our own Deity, and Judge and Law.

SOURCE 14.13   Extracts from 'Song About Stalin' by M. Izakvosky, 1936. This is a typical poem from the late 1930s

For the sake of our happiness
He marched through all storms.
He carried our holy banner
Over our enormous land.
And fields and factories rose,
And tribes and people responded
To the call of our leader.

He gave us for ever and ever
Youth, glory and power.
He has lit the clear dawn of spring
Over our homes.
Let us sing, comrades, a song
About the dearest person,
About our sun, about the truth of nations,
About our Stalin let's sing a song.

KEY POINTS FROM CHAPTER 14   **The cult of the personality**

1 In the cult of the personality, Stalin was presented as a god-like figure, omniscient and omnipresent.
2 The cult was at its height at the end of the 1930s. Images of Stalin on posters and paintings, in books and as statues were everywhere in the Soviet Union.
3 Stalin enjoyed this adulation and encouraged the view of himself as a great hero of the past. He had history rewritten to reflect this view.
4 The cult also served an important purpose: it gave the Russian people a sense of confidence in troubled times – Stalin would see them through to a better society.

section

6

Soviet security or spreading revolution? Soviet foreign policy 1921–39

According to the orthodox Marxist view, revolution in the advanced states of Europe was essential for the success of the revolution in the USSR and, in March 1919, the Bolsheviks formed the Communist International – the Comintern – to help to produce this. The hostility of Western capitalist countries to the new Bolshevik regime and its Communist ideology was confirmed by their intervention in the Civil War. The Bolsheviks won the Civil War but found themselves engaged in a war with the Poles. By July 1920, however, the Polish army was in full retreat and Lenin realised this was an opportunity to spread the revolution. Lenin ordered the Red Army to pursue the Poles and then advance into Germany to encourage workers to rise up as part of the European-wide socialist revolution. But the Red Army was defeated and all attempts at revolution in Germany and Hungary collapsed.

The USSR now had to face up to being the only Communist nation in the world. Moreover, the draining experience of war, revolution and civil war had left the Soviet Union very vulnerable and in desperate need of economic help and consolidation. This presented the Bolshevik government with a serious foreign policy dilemma. How could it:

a) work to undermine capitalist governments?
b) achieve stable working diplomatic relations with them?

In this section, Chapter 15 examines the developments in Soviet foreign policy between 1921 and 1933 and Chapter 16 looks at the Soviet reaction to the aggressive policies of Hitler, who had strong anti-Communist views. It asks why the Soviet Union came to terms with Hitler and signed a non-aggression pact with Germany at the end of the 1930s.

SOURCE I A Communist cartoon of 1920. The caption reads 'Comrade Lenin cleans the world of filth'

Тов. Ленин ОЧИЩАЕТ землю от нечисти.

SOURCE 2 Lenin, February 1921

We have always and repeatedly pointed out to the workers that the underlying chief task and basic condition of our victory is the propagation of revolution at least to several of the more advanced countries.

SOURCE 3 Lenin explaining why the Soviet Union was attending the international conference at Genoa in 1922

We go to it because trade with capitalist countries (so long as they have not altogether collapsed) is unconditionally necessary for us.

SOURCE 4 Trotsky, 1930

The way out lies only in the victory of the proletariat of the advanced countries. Viewed from this standpoint, a national revolution is not a self-contained whole; it is only a link in the internal chain. The international revolution constitutes a permanent process, despite declines and ebbs.

SOURCE 5 Litvinov (Commissar for Foreign Affairs), December 1933

The ensuring of peace cannot depend on our efforts alone, it requires the collaboration and co-operation of other states. While therefore trying to establish and maintain relations with all states, we are giving special attention to strengthening and making close our relations with those which, like us, give proof of their sincere desire to maintain peace and are ready to resist those who break the peace.

SOURCE 6 Stalin, speaking at the Seventeenth Party Congress, 1934

The USSR would never be swayed by alliances with this or that foreign power, be it France, Poland or Germany, but would always base her policy on self-interest.

SOURCE 7 Molotov (Commissar for Foreign Affairs), January 1936

We toilers of the Soviet Union must count on our own efforts in defending our affairs and, above all, on our Red Army in the defence of our country.

What were the aims of Soviet foreign policy?

1 Study Sources 1–10. On your own copy of the table below, indicate which sources provide evidence of:
   a) the desire to spread revolution
   b) attempts to establish working relationships with other countries
   c) the desire to protect the Soviet Union's interests and ensure it could defend itself.

Source	Date	Desire to spread revolution	Establishment of working relationships	Defence of Soviet interests

2 What do these sources suggest about changes in Soviet foreign policy between 1920 and 1939?
3 Which events in Chart A on page 241 provide evidence to support your conclusions about changes in Soviet foreign policy?

SOURCE 8 Litvinov, May 1938, to the Director General of the Czech Foreign Office, comparing the situation with 1914–17

This time we shall observe the contest between Germany and the Western powers and shall not intervene in the conflict until we ourselves feel it fit to do so in order to bring about the decision.

SOURCE 9 Stalin at the Eighteenth Party Congress, March 1939

England and France have rejected the policy of collective security ... and taken a position of non-intervention ... the policy of non-intervention reveals an eagerness not to hinder Germany ... from embroiling herself in a war with the Soviet Union ...

... Be cautious and [do] not allow Soviet Russia to be drawn into the conflicts by warmongers who are accustomed to have others pull the chestnuts out of the fire.

SOURCE 10 The front page of a German weekly magazine, published after the Nazi–Soviet non-aggression treaty of 23 August 1939. It shows Stalin shaking hands with Ribbentrop, the German foreign minister

PHASE ONE

Extricating Russia from the war: October 1917–March 1918

October 1917	Decree on Peace
February 1918	Bolshevik cancellation of foreign debts
March 1918	Treaty of Brest-Litovsk

PHASE TWO

The Civil War: 1918–20

April 1918–September 1919	Foreign intervention in the Civil War
March 1919	Comintern (Third Communist International) set up to guide, co-ordinate and promote the Communist parties of the world.
April–October 1920	Russo-Polish war. Attempt to spread world revolution by arms defeated outside Warsaw in August.
July 1920	Second Congress of Comintern – laid on other Communist parties the overriding duty to protect the USSR.

PHASE THREE

The need for recovery and peace: 1921–27

1921	Secret discussions with Germany on military and economic co-operation. Anglo-Soviet trade agreement.
1922	Rapallo agreement with Germany – the two countries recognise each other diplomatically. Secret military co-operation.
1923	Soviets agree to the Curzon ultimatum (Curzon was British Foreign Secretary).
1924	Official recognition of USSR by Britain, France and Italy. 'Zinoviev letter' published in *The Times* newspaper in Britain.
1926	Treaty of Berlin with Germany extends the Treaty of Rapallo.
1927	Diplomatic relations between Britain and the USSR suspended (restored by Ramsay MacDonald in 1929).

PHASE FOUR

The left turn of the Comintern: 1928–33

1928	New, more radical Comintern line. Social Democrats (SPD) in Germany attacked as 'social fascists'. Foreign Communist party leaders suspected of following a line of their own are expelled from the Comintern and discredited. They are replaced by leaders obedient to Moscow. War scares: propaganda stressed the imminent danger of invasion.
1928–32	Rise in economic and military collaboration between the USSR and Germany.

PHASE FIVE

Collective security against fascism: 1934–39

March 1934	Trade agreement with Germany.
September 1934	Soviet entry into the League of Nations. Litvinov promotes a 'collective security' policy.
May 1935	Pacts with France and Czechoslovakia.
August 1935	Reversal of policy by the Comintern: now supports popular fronts.
1936–39	Soviet Union intervenes in Spanish Civil War.
November 1936	Anti-Comintern Pact involving Germany and Japan and, a year later, Italy.
September 1938	Munich agreement, Soviet Union excluded.
1938–39	Japanese attacks on Soviet territory in the Far East.
April 1939	Litvinov proposes a triple military alliance between the Soviet Union, Britain and France.
May 1939	Molotov replaces Litvinov as Commissar for Foreign Affairs.

PHASE SIX

The Nazi–Soviet Pact 1939

August 1939	Soviet-Anglo-French talks in Moscow.
23 August	Ribbentrop and Molotov sign the Nazi–Soviet non-aggression pact and a secret protocol dividing Eastern Europe into spheres of influence. (See the separate timeline – Chart 16E on page 262 – for the events leading to the pact of 1939.)

THE THIRD COMMUNIST INTERNATIONAL

The Comintern is described as the 'Third Communist International' because two previous organisations had been set up to encourage the spread of socialist ideas. The first was set up by Karl Marx in London in 1864 but was so riven by disputes that it soon fell apart. The second was a much looser association set up in Paris in 1889. It held international conferences to discuss Marxist theory but ceased to meet after the outbreak of the First World War.

FOCUS ROUTE

Note the differences between the three commissars under the following headings:

• background and experience of foreign countries
• status in the party
• attitude to Germany
• other policy differences.

■ B Commissars for Foreign Affairs

Lenin kept foreign policy very much in his own hands. As in the 1930s under Stalin, the leader and the Politburo made the crucial decisions. However, the Commissar for Foreign Affairs worked out the style and delivery of policy.

G. V. CHICHERIN (1872–1936)
Foreign Commissar April 1918–July 1930

An ex-Menshevik and an aristocrat by birth, Chicherin was a highly educated but rather emotional, chaotic man. He had been employed by the tsarist foreign ministry and had extensive experience working abroad. He was in jail in Britain from August 1917 to January 1918. Lenin described him as 'an excellent worker, extremely conscientious, intelligent and learned'. He was not a member of the Politburo.

The policies he is identified with
• He always favoured close relations with Germany and helped to bring about the Treaty of Rapallo.
• He was anti-British.
• Like Lenin, he believed that the USSR was most secure when the capitalist powers were disunited, and that if the USSR were involved in, rather than isolated from, the system of capitalist international relations then this would be more likely to occur. So he pursued a policy of *peaceful coexistence*.

M. M. LITVINOV (1876–1951)
Foreign Commissar July 1930–May 1939 (Deputy Commissar 1921–30 and 1941–46)

Litvinov was an ex-Menshevik, with a Jewish background. He had spent a long time abroad, including ten years in Britain; his wife was British. He was an exceptionally talented negotiator and very good at establishing friendly relations with statesmen and opinion leaders in the democracies; a model of organisation. His influence was restricted to foreign affairs: he was not a member of the Politburo.

The policies he is identified with
• He believed that preventing all wars was in the USSR's interest. Unlike Chicherin, he favoured disarmament and signing the Kellogg Pact to outlaw war. He was a familiar figure at Geneva once the USSR had joined the League of Nations.
• He was pro-British and deeply suspicious of Germany, even in the 1920s, and he only grudgingly accepted the Treaty of Rapallo.
• He favoured collective security against fascism.

V. M. MOLOTOV (1890–1986)
Foreign Commissar May 1939–March 1949

Molotov means hammer, quite an apt name. A Bolshevik from his youth, he was never exiled abroad and had no direct experience of the world outside Russia. A member of the Politburo from 1925 (unlike Chicherin and Litvinov), he was made leader of the Comintern in 1929. He became Stalin's deputy and together they signed many death sentences during the purges. Trotsky called Molotov a 'blockhead' and other colleagues referred to him as 'stone arse' but he did exert some influence over Stalin in foreign policy and has been called 'one of the toughest negotiators of the twentieth century'. His appointment as Commissar (replacing the anti-German Litvinov) in May 1939 has been seen as sending out an encouraging signal to Germany.

The policies he is identified with
He favoured improved relations with Germany. The Nazi–Soviet pact of 1939 is often referred to as the Ribbentrop–Molotov Pact.

When politicians make foreign policy, they are influenced by a number of different factors. For any given country, some factors are relatively constant while others vary according to the individuals involved and the circumstances in which they were operating. Here are some of the factors influencing Soviet foreign policy in the 1920s and 1930s.

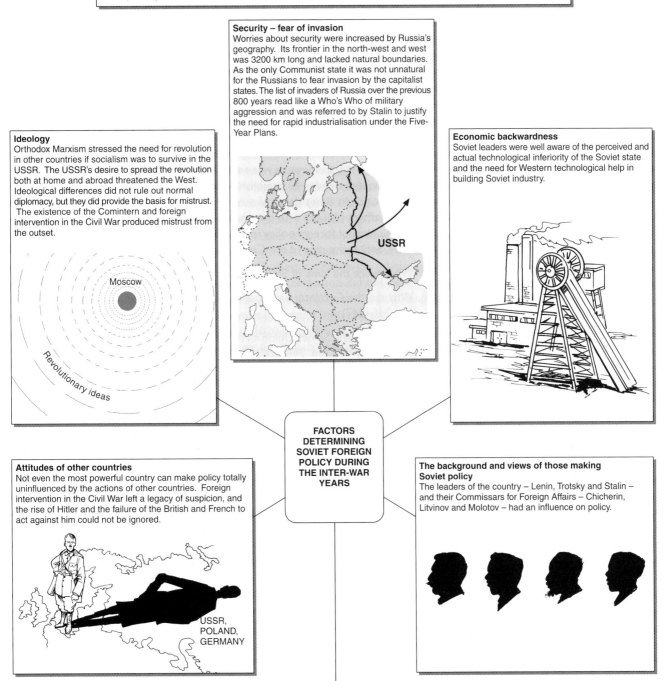

Security – fear of invasion
Worries about security were increased by Russia's geography. Its frontier in the north-west and west was 3200 km long and lacked natural boundaries. As the only Communist state it was not unnatural for the Russians to fear invasion by the capitalist states. The list of invaders of Russia over the previous 800 years read like a Who's Who of military aggression and was referred to by Stalin to justify the need for rapid industrialisation under the Five-Year Plans.

USSR

Ideology
Orthodox Marxism stressed the need for revolution in other countries if socialism was to survive in the USSR. The USSR's desire to spread the revolution both at home and abroad threatened the West. Ideological differences did not rule out normal diplomacy, but they did provide the basis for mistrust. The existence of the Comintern and foreign intervention in the Civil War produced mistrust from the outset.

Moscow

Revolutionary ideas

Economic backwardness
Soviet leaders were well aware of the perceived and actual technological inferiority of the Soviet state and the need for Western technological help in building Soviet industry.

FACTORS DETERMINING SOVIET FOREIGN POLICY DURING THE INTER-WAR YEARS

Attitudes of other countries
Not even the most powerful country can make policy totally uninfluenced by the actions of other countries. Foreign intervention in the Civil War left a legacy of suspicion, and the rise of Hitler and the failure of the British and French to act against him could not be ignored.

USSR, POLAND, GERMANY

The background and views of those making Soviet policy
The leaders of the country – Lenin, Trotsky and Stalin – and their Commissars for Foreign Affairs – Chicherin, Litvinov and Molotov – had an influence on policy.

The internal situation
At any given time, the internal situation was bound to impact on foreign policy. Thus the state of the country at the end of the Civil War, the power struggle to succeed Lenin, the Five-Year Plans and collectivisation all had an influence on foreign policy.

NEP PEASANTS OPPOSITION

FOCUS ROUTE

Which of the factors in Chart C do you think was most important in influencing Soviet foreign policy between 1920 and 1939? Place the factors in order of importance.

We will revisit your decisions at the end of the section.

246

ALONE IN A HOSTILE WORLD: HOW DID SOVIET FOREIGN POLICY DEVELOP BETWEEN 1921 AND 1933?

SOURCE 15.1 'Workers of the world unite!': the title page of *The Communist International*, a pamphlet published in Moscow in May 1919 and printed in several languages

SOURCE 15.2 A propaganda poster produced in Germany in 1919 by the Association for the Fight Against Bolshevism. The association was formed with support from the government and businesses to counter the threat of revolutionary influences on Germany

 # Why did the Comintern exist and what problems did it present?

In January 1919, when the revolutionary wave in Europe was at its peak, Lenin had called for an international congress of revolutionary socialists. In March 1919, a motley collection from 35 groups did meet in Moscow and the Comintern – the Communist International – was formed. The Comintern appealed at its first meeting to the workers of all countries to support the Soviet regime by all available means, including, if necessary, 'revolutionary means'. Such an appeal was likely to fuel fears in Western Europe, as the German propaganda poster (Source 15.2) shows. Winston Churchill, the British Chancellor of the Exchequer in 1924 and fiercely anti-Communist, voiced these fears: 'From the earliest moment of its birth the Russian Bolshevik Government has declared its intention of using all the power of the Russian Empire to promote world revolution. Their agents have penetrated into every country. Everywhere they have endeavoured to bring into being the "germ cells" from which the cause of Communism should grow.' His fears were shared by many others but, as Chart 15A on page 247 shows, attempts to stir up revolution in Europe were singularly unsuccessful.

The failure of revolutionary attempts in Berlin and Munich and of Bela Kun's Soviet Republic in Hungary, which lasted less than four months, demonstrated to Lenin that success could only be achieved if foreign Communist parties adopted the Bolshevik model. The second international congress organised by the Comintern in 1920 was a much larger affair than the first. It was highly stage-managed and designed to impress the delegates, who came from 41 countries. It took place as the Red Army moved towards Warsaw. One of its main aims was to bring foreign Communist parties under Comintern control. Twenty-one conditions were drawn up for membership of the Comintern, including the following:

- Communist parties had to be organised on Leninist principles of centralisation and discipline. (The British and Spanish delegates had demanded freedom of action for their Communist parties but it was not granted.)
- Parties had to prepare for civil war by establishing an underground organisation, by spreading revolutionary propaganda among the proletariat, peasantry and armed forces, and by setting up cells in trade unions and other worker organisations.
- Party programmes had to be approved by the Comintern; disobedience could mean expulsion.

This policy was understandable but it had two very important and damaging results:

1 Moscow insisted upon centralised control and discipline and made the national security of the USSR the top priority for all Communist parties in other countries. But this reduced the appeal of the Communist Party to the rank and file of workers in other countries and so party membership and influence declined everywhere in Europe.
2 The stated intentions of the Comintern – its threatening language and its aggressive ideology – and the financial support (real and imagined) it gave to its members seriously weakened the Soviet Union's chances of achieving reliable and stable commercial and diplomatic relations with the European countries.

Throughout his time in office, Chicherin petitioned the Politburo to separate the personnel, policies and activities of the Comintern from those of the Soviet government. In practice this did not happen. Key players like Zinoviev, Trotsky and Bukharin were all involved in the Comintern at different times and they could not be ignored. Any embassy was likely to contain an official whose main duty was Comintern matters and liaison with local Communists.

Key

■ / ⬚ Attempts by non-Russian Communists to seize power (all put down by armed forces)

■ Centres believed by Western powers to be training non-Russian Communists to carry out revolutionary activity in their own countries (countries affected shown in brackets)

★ Propaganda centres funded by the USSR to encourage revolutionary activity

▨ Countries with strong anti-Communist policies after 1926, forming a barrier between Russia and Western Europe

ALONE IN A HOSTILE WORLD: HOW DID SOVIET FOREIGN POLICY DEVELOP BETWEEN 1921 AND 1933?

TALKING POINT

Was the Comintern more of a hindrance than a help to the USSR by 1925?

Here are two examples of how the activities of the Comintern damaged diplomatic relations with Britain.

- In 1923, the British Foreign Secretary, Curzon, infuriated by the activities of Soviet agents in Persia, Afghanistan and India, threatened to cancel the Anglo-Soviet trade agreement of 1921 unless the Soviets abandoned these activities. The Soviets agreed to the 'Curzon ultimatum'.

- In 1924, the 'Zinoviev letter' – a letter supposedly from the Comintern to the British Communist Party instructing the latter to conduct propaganda in the armed forces and elsewhere – was published just before the British general election. It was a forgery, but it indicated how British opinion perceived the threat presented by the Comintern. The new Conservative government virtually suspended all dealings with the Soviet government throughout 1925.

■ **Learning trouble spot**

Britain's importance in the post-war years

In the 1920s and 1930s, Britain still had a huge empire 'on which the sun never set'. Britain was very much the major player on the world stage because the USA was pursuing an isolationist policy. Germany and the USSR took time recovering from war and the political turmoil of revolutions in 1917 and 1918 respectively; France was traumatised by the war which had been fought on its soil. Significantly, the Soviets considered Britain with its empire to be the centre of the capitalist world order and their main enemy. They made Britain a target for diplomatic recognition because it was an important country. If the USSR could establish relations with Britain, other countries would follow.

 # What were the Soviet Union's relations with Britain and Germany between 1921 and 1933?

Soviet Russia could not afford to remain isolated. It needed to trade with other countries and to bring in capital goods to help to revive its industry. There were also all sorts of other matters, such as the movement of people in and out of Russia, which needed to be sorted out by the normal round of diplomatic relations. These matters were handled largely by men working in the Commissariat for Foreign Affairs who had some diplomatic experience, like Chicherin, or by the new intake who soon became specialists in the field. There was often tension between these men and the revolutionary agitators working for the Comintern. What progress was made by conventional diplomacy?

FOCUS ROUTE

Draw a table with four columns and these headings:

Moves that strengthened/ maintained relations with Britain 1921–33	Moves that weakened relations with Britain	Moves that strengthened/ maintained relations with Germany 1921–33	Moves that weakened relations with Germany

As you work through this section, enter three events/actions in each column.

BRITISH GOVERNMENTS 1918–40

1918–22	Coalition government led by Lloyd George (Liberal) but dominated by the Conservatives
1922–23	Conservative government
1924	First Labour government, a minority government led by MacDonald
1924–29	Conservative government led by Baldwin
1929–31	Second Labour minority government led by MacDonald
1931–40	National governments, all dominated by the Conservatives and led successively by MacDonald, Baldwin and Chamberlain

Note: All Conservative-dominated governments had large majorities in parliament.

Relations with Britain

The Anglo-Soviet trade agreement of 1921 marked the first positive contact with the Soviet Union (trade was mutually profitable) although relations between the two countries were never easy. The Conservatives dominated British governments for most of the 1920s and 1930s and were particularly suspicious of Soviet activity in Britain and the empire. This was illustrated by Curzon's ultimatum in 1923 (see page 247).

Diplomatic relations were strained in 1926 by what the British government saw as subversive Soviet behaviour during the General Strike. The Soviet leadership saw the strike as a political act and the beginning of a proletarian revolution (they now thought Britain the most likely candidate for revolution). In reality, it was a dispute about wages. The Russian Central Council of Trade Unions sent a cheque for £26,000 (a considerable sum) to the Trades Union Congress (TUC), the national leadership of the trade unions. The TUC leadership sent it back to prevent the British government from claiming that they were in the pay of the Bolsheviks. All that Soviet policy had achieved was to encourage anti-Soviet die-hards in Britain. In 1927, the police mounted a full-scale raid on the premises of the Russian trade mission in London, which was suspected of being the centre of a Soviet spy ring. Known as the Arcos raid, it led to the breaking off of diplomatic relations.

Although it was Ramsay MacDonald's Labour governments which first recognised the USSR in 1924 and restored relations in 1929, historians have seen the very moderate Labour Party leadership as a major barrier to the spread of Communism in Britain.

Another Peace Pilgrimage.

THE DOVE: *" Are you sure we are in the right procession, Stanley?"*

SOURCE 15.3 A Low cartoon on the General Strike, published in the *Star*, 24 June 1926. The strike, which lasted for nine days in May 1926, was the culmination of bitter industrial disputes in the coal industry. Stanley Baldwin, the Prime Minister (riding the horse), was more conciliatory towards the strikers than other Conservatives, such as Winston Churchill (blowing the tuba)

Relations with Germany

It has been said that Germany and the USSR were natural allies in the 1920s. Both were outcast nations: Germany because it had been defeated in and blamed for the First World War, the USSR because of its Communist ideology and its refusal to support the Western powers in the First World War. The Rapallo Treaty of 1922 between the two countries was central to the Soviet Union's security. Although on paper it amounted to no more than the re-establishment of diplomatic relations, a renunciation of financial claims on each side and a promise of economic co-operation, it ended the isolation that both countries were experiencing. In the years that followed, it was underpinned by significant economic and military collaboration. In spite of the tensions caused by the activities of the Comintern, especially its involvement in Communist risings in Germany in 1921 and 1923 (in 1921, the Comintern spent 62 million marks and, in 1922, 47 million marks preparing for revolution in Germany, at a time of great hunger in Russia), co-operation was mutually beneficial (see Chart 15B on page 250).

After 1923 the chances of a Communist rising in Germany faded, removing the cause of tension between the two countries. However, in 1925 the Locarno treaties (a set of treaties between Western powers, which guaranteed the existing frontiers of Western Europe) indicated better relations between Germany, Britain and France. This worried Russia: would Locarno reintegrate Germany into the Western world and isolate the USSR? As a result, a whole clutch of trade treaties were signed between Germany and Russia on the eve of Locarno to reassure the Soviets. The Treaty of Berlin, signed in 1926, the same year that Germany joined the League of Nations, had the same purpose. It reaffirmed the terms of the Treaty of Rapallo and was to remain in force for five years. The USSR and Germany pledged neutrality if either were attacked by another power and Germany agreed to abstain from any League of Nation's trade or financial boycott of the USSR. Militarily and economically, though not politically, ties between the two countries grew stronger.

249

ALONE IN A HOSTILE WORLD: HOW DID SOVIET FOREIGN POLICY DEVELOP BETWEEN 1921 AND 1933?

250

ALONE IN A HOSTILE WORLD: HOW DID SOVIET FOREIGN POLICY DEVELOP BETWEEN 1921 AND 1933?

SOURCE 15.4 A locomotive produced in Germany is unloaded in Petrograd harbour in 1922

SOURCE 15.5 The German President, Hindenburg, welcomes Marshal Tukhachevsky (right) and a Soviet delegation in 1932. The Soviet army officers had come to observe German army manoeuvres

■ 15B Advantages of mutual co-operation between the USSR and Germany, 1922–32

Diplomatic advantages
Both ceased to be isolated outcasts. The USSR avoided the nightmare prospect of capitalist countries combining against it and Germany strengthened its bargaining position with Britain and France.

USSR   GERMANY

Military co-operation
German officers trained the Red Army in tank warfare and military aviation. The German army was able to train and experiment with weapons forbidden by the Treaty of Versailles – especially tanks, aircraft and gas. Co-operation reached its high point at the beginning of the 1930s.

Economic co-operation
Germany was the only major country to make significant long-term loans to the USSR. German financial and technical help was important during the NEP and the First Five-Year Plan. The USSR supplied markets for German heavy industry. By 1932, 47 per cent of total Russian imports came from Germany. German firms in the USSR manufactured guns, shells, aircraft and tanks.

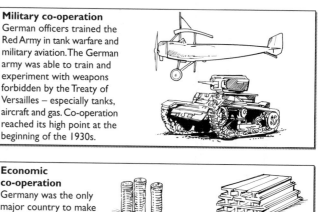

Loans, heavy industrial goods

USSR   GERMANY

Payment for imports, military manufacturing facilities

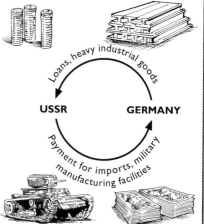

D How did Stalin change Soviet foreign policy between 1924 and 1932?

FOCUS ROUTE

Make notes to prepare for a discussion on the following issues:

1 How did Stalin and Trotsky differ on foreign policy?
2 How does Stalin's policy towards the Chinese Communist Party illustrate his attitude towards foreign Communists?
3 How did internal concerns shape Stalin's attitude towards the Comintern?

Stalin was not internationally minded like Lenin and he was not particularly interested in the activities of the Comintern. After Lenin's death, there were only three more Comintern congresses and Stalin never addressed them. The reason for this was that Stalin did not believe that the Comintern would bring about a revolution, even in 90 years. Stalin was committed to 'Socialism In One Country' – the idea that socialism could be built successfully in the Soviet Union without the necessity for revolution elsewhere. He thought it would be utter folly to risk the socialist transformation of Soviet Russia for the sake of possible revolution abroad. He dismissed the potential of foreign Communists to achieve revolutionary change. In his view, 'One Soviet tractor is worth ten good foreign Communists.'

This policy line brought splits in the party over foreign affairs for the first time since the Treaty of Brest-Litovsk. Many sided with Trotsky and his idea of 'Permanent Revolution'. Trotsky believed that revolution could not survive long in one country. Only when revolution had spread to Western Europe could socialism be established. If it did not spread it would, in time, succumb to a conservative Europe or be undermined by Russian backwardness. Trotsky and his supporters were alarmed by the way Stalin was sidelining the Comintern. Trotsky argued that under Stalin foreign Communist parties changed from being 'vanguards of world revolution' to the more or less pacifist 'frontier guards' of Soviet Russia.

Stalin, it seemed, was changing the focus of the Comintern from promoting world revolution to protecting the interests of the Soviet state. Nowhere is this clearer than in his policy towards the Communist Party in China, a policy bitterly attacked by Trotsky.

Why didn't Stalin support the Communists in China?

In 1911, there had been a revolution in China which resulted in the overthrow of the Manchu dynasty. A lengthy period of confusion followed with individual warlords controlling much of China. During this time, the Chinese Communist Party (CPC) was founded in 1921 with Soviet assistance. The policy of supporting a united anti-warlord front in China had been put forward by Lenin and backed by the Comintern. The CPC was to join the Guomindang (GMD), the Chinese Nationalists, as a 'bloc within'. The Nationalists represented the Chinese bourgeoisie. In 1925, Chiang Kai-shek, who had received military training in Moscow, became the leader of the GMD. Chiang sharply reduced the influence of the CPC within the GMD and showed strong anti-Communist tendencies. But Stalin continued to give Chiang Kai-shek military support. He thought that the Chinese Communists were too few to achieve anything on their own and needed to work with the Nationalists to bring about revolutionary change – the proletarian revolution would have to wait. He hoped that a Nationalist government would be a friend to Soviet Russia.

Then, in April 1927, Chiang struck. He massacred between thirty and forty thousand Communists and workers in Shanghai. Only a week before, Stalin had boasted at a party meeting that 'We [will] use the Chinese bourgeoisie and throw it away like a squeezed lemon.' Chiang had beaten Stalin at his own game. The policy had failed and the CPC under Mao Zedong adopted an independent policy. Trotsky, who had earlier criticised Stalin's China policy, felt that the massacres justified his attack on Stalin as the 'grave digger of the revolution'.

How did the Comintern change?

The leadership of the Comintern reflected the situation in the Soviet Union. Zinoviev was president from 1919 to 1926. When the United Opposition – Trotsky, Zinoviev and Kamenev – was defeated, Bukharin, Stalin's ally, succeeded Zinoviev. When Bukharin in turn was forced out, the loyal Stalinist Molotov succeeded him.

Similarly, the leadership of foreign Communist parties reflected Moscow's preoccupations. Working-class leaders were seen as less trouble than intellectuals, and so Thaelmann (Germany), Thorez (France) and Pollitt (Britain) became leaders of their national parties. In 1928, following a financial scandal, the German party decided to remove Thaelmann but the Comintern insisted he remained. The situation weakened the leaders' standing in their own countries but this did not worry Stalin. Foreign Communist leaders in the 1930s learned that the alternative to obedience to Moscow's orders was to be charged with being the agent of the capitalist police.

In the late 1920s, Stalin's attention was fixed very much on the internal politics of the Soviet Union as the struggle for the leadership of the Communist Party reached its final stage. In 1928, he made his 'left turn' (opting for extreme left-wing policies of rapid industrialisation) and moved against Bukharin and the right wing of the party. As Stalin moved to the left, so did the policy of the Comintern. Foreign Communist parties were instructed to denounce social democratic parties as 'social FASCISTS' because they co-operated with bourgeois parties and governments (mirroring the attack on Bukharin for his co-operation with the bourgeois elements of the peasantry and the NEP).

Probably the most damaging consequences of this new policy direction were felt in Germany where the KPD (the Communist Party) was instructed to attack the SPD (the Social Democrats) as 'social fascists'. This divided the left just at the time when the Nazis and fascism were beginning to grow stronger. Stalin rejected pleas for joint action by the left in Germany against the Nazis and thereby contributed to Hitler's rise to power. A theoretical justification was given for the policy: Hitler was the last stage of monopoly capitalism; a Nazi government would inflame social tensions and hasten a socialist revolution. This is why the KPD might say *'Nach Hitler Uns!'* which means 'After Hitler Us!' Unfortunately for the German Communists, this became true in a very different sense – they were Hitler's first victims!

FASCISM
Extreme nationalist political movement, originating in Italy in the 1920s and taken up by Nazi Germany in the 1930s.

253

ALONE IN A HOSTILE WORLD: HOW DID SOVIET FOREIGN POLICY DEVELOP BETWEEN 1921 AND 1933?

E Review: What was achieved in Soviet foreign policy between 1921 and 1933?

Between 1921 and 1933 conventional diplomacy had been much more successful than had the Comintern:

- the USSR was regarded as a European power once more
- there was no united capitalist front against the USSR
- foreign governments had begun to think they might be able to do business with the USSR
- valuable military and industrial gains had come from co-operation with Germany
- in 1933 the USA gave the USSR official recognition.

These were real gains, but in 1933 the world situation was deteriorating. Hitler had come to power in Germany and his anti-Communist intentions were well known. In September 1933, all Germany's military undertakings in the USSR were brought to an end. In January 1934, Hitler made a non-aggression pact with Poland, effectively ending the Treaty of Rapallo. In inter-war Europe, it was very difficult to be on good terms with both Poland and the Soviet Union. Indeed, the hope of regaining territory lost to Poland had been one of the chief factors that led Germany and the USSR to sign the Rapallo agreement. In his book *Germany and Europe, 1919–39* (1993), John Hiden comments that the non-aggression pact with Poland was 'a dramatic and decisive break ... and marked the virtual close of normal political exchange between Berlin and Moscow' (page 99). Furthermore, an expansionist Japan had, by its take-over of Manchuria between 1931 and 1933, shown itself to be a threat to the Far East. The makers of Soviet foreign policy were going to have to adjust to these changes.

TALKING POINT

How much change was there between 1921 and 1933? Do you agree with Adam Ulam's view: 'From the position of 1917–18, that Soviet Russia exists to promote the world revolution, the Communist view by 1928 had shifted to the position that the world revolutionary movement exists to defend and promote the interests of the USSR' (*Expansion and Coexistence*, 2nd edn, 1974, page 181)?

KEY POINTS FROM CHAPTER 15

Alone in a hostile world: how did Soviet foreign policy develop between 1921 and 1933?

1 Soviet foreign policy had two tracks: strengthening the security of the USSR and promoting world socialist revolution.
2 The existence of the Comintern complicated the USSR's relations with other countries.
3 The failure to spread revolution was a disappointment to Lenin and meant that Soviet security became the top priority in Soviet foreign policy.
4 Alone in a hostile world, the USSR felt very vulnerable after the Civil War and needed economic help and foreign trade.
5 The Treaty of Rapallo (1922) and good relations with Germany ended the USSR's isolation and were central to foreign policy in the 1920s.
6 Britain was seen as the main enemy and in spite of the trade agreement (1921) relations were strained throughout the 1920s.
7 Stalin adopted a policy of 'Socialism In One Country' which advanced the USSR's interests above those of world revolution.
8 Foreign Communist parties were totally subservient to the USSR. This reduced their appeal and proved disastrous for the Chinese Communist Party.
9 Switches in Soviet foreign policy were often determined by Stalin's domestic priorities such as the leftward turn in 1929.
10 By the end of 1932, the USSR was recognised as a European power again and there was no united front against her.

16

Why did the Soviet Union come to terms with Hitler?

CHAPTER OVERVIEW

It was Hitler rather than the Soviets who departed from the friendly relations that had existed since 1922. The Soviets renewed their commercial treaty with Germany in May 1933, but within Germany Hitler was attacking Communists. In January 1934, Hitler signed a non-aggression pact with Poland and refused to sign a mutual guarantee of frontiers with the USSR. Stalin realised that Hitler's aggressive nationalism necessitated a change of policy. In this chapter we examine the problems facing the Soviets in deciding what policy to adopt. Their first reaction was to seek collective security against fascism. While this policy was being pursued the Spanish Civil War erupted, posing a number of problems for Stalin. Then in 1938–39, Stalin decided to sign the Nazi–Soviet Pact. We look at why he did this and how historians have interpreted Soviet foreign policy after the rise of Hitler.

A What was collective security against fascism? (p. 255)

B How did the Spanish Civil War complicate the situation? (pp. 256–258)

C Why did the USSR make an agreement with Germany rather than with Britain and France in 1939? (pp. 259–264)

D How have historians disagreed over Stalin's foreign policy in the 1930s? (pp. 264–269)

ACTIVITY

Stalin wants your advice. He has asked you to write a report on whether the USSR should make an agreement with Germany or with Britain and France. Your report will have two parts:

1 Factual information for the main body of the report. You will find help for this in the Focus Route tasks in sections A–C.
2 Your recommendations. This will involve you drawing conclusions and giving your opinion, making the points that you think will weigh most heavily with Stalin.

You will find guidance on how to set out your report on page 261.

A What was collective security against fascism?

FOCUS ROUTE

To help to write your report (see the Activity on page 254) you will need to know what collective security against fascism meant. Make notes on it.

Collective security meant working with other states to stop fascist expansion. In the USSR the shift towards this can be seen in Litvinov's speech in December 1933 (Source 5 on page 240) and he is identified with this policy. The historian D. C. Watt argues in *How War Came* (1989, page 112) that up to the Munich Conference in September 1938, Litvinov was virtually in sole charge of Soviet foreign policy while Stalin said and did little. However, relations with Germany were never broken off and behind the scenes between 1935 and 1937 there were negotiations on improving economic and political relations. Molotov, in particular, wanted improved relations with Germany and was openly critical of the policy of collective security.

The Politburo had proposed that the USSR join the League of Nations, once referred to by Lenin as 'the robbers' den', and the Soviet Union became a member in September 1934. Litvinov was active in the League and had hopes that it could be an effective body. He denounced appeasement towards Germany as suicidal and urged the League to act decisively and resolutely to stop German aggression.

In May 1935, the Soviet Union signed mutual assistance pacts with France and Czechoslovakia. The Soviet Union was obliged to help the Czechs only if France came in, too. Although these pacts were good for the USSR's reputation as a supporter of collective security, neither was backed by military talks. Litvinov had no illusions: 'One should not place any serious hopes on the pact in the sense of real military aid in the event of war. Our security will still remain exclusively in the hands of the Red Army. For us the pact has predominantly a political significance, reducing the chance of war on the part of Germany and also of Poland and Japan.' The French saw the pact as a political measure to scare Hitler and not an agreement which would require any military action on their part.

In August 1935, the Comintern line of attacking Western social democratic and labour parties as 'social fascists' was completely overturned. The help of such parties was now sought in the creation of 'popular fronts' that aimed to contain the spread of fascism. Soviet policy was to support governments that pursued an anti-German, pro-Soviet foreign line. In France, for instance, this meant that the Communist leader, Thorez, went from stating that the Communists would not fight even if France were invaded to supporting rearmament and national defence.

Two popular front governments were formed in France and in Spain, but they were not successful. In Spain it proved an excuse for the right-wing rebellion which began the Spanish Civil War; in France Leon Blum's government did not last long, nor was it able to turn the pact with the USSR into military co-operation.

SOURCE 16.1 The International Brigades were supporters of the Republicans drawn from several countries and organised by the Comintern

FOCUS ROUTE

To write your report (see page 261) you need to study the evidence on the Spanish Civil War to see what lessons could be learned from it. These questions will help:

1 Did the Soviet Union make any gains by intervening in the Spanish Civil War?

2 What emerged about Britain and France's attitude to resisting fascism – was the collective security policy working?

TALKING POINT

Are there any grounds for a country to involve itself in another country's civil war?

ACTIVITY

1 Could Stalin have stayed out of the Spanish Civil War?

2 What factors do you think carried most weight in his decision to intervene?

3 Did the USSR benefit from having taken part?

4 How does Stalin's policy regarding Spain between 1936 and 1939 help historians to identify Stalin's foreign policy priorities, particularly his attitude to spreading revolution?

5 Find out more about the International Brigades. Has the fact that Spain was a cause championed by writers and poets, and that they have written some of the history, led to an exaggeration of the International Brigades' importance?

 # How did the Spanish Civil War complicate the situation?

Spain was a bitterly divided country, especially after the establishment of the Second Republic in 1931. On one side was the Republican left and on the other was the fascist right, the Nationalists. Civil war erupted in 1936. Army leaders, who could not accept the elected left-wing popular front government, launched an armed rebellion in July.

The Spanish Civil War was really all about Spanish issues but foreigners saw it as a battle between left and right. This made it difficult for Stalin to ignore, especially when Litvinov was enthusiastically pursuing collective security against fascism. What should the USSR, the champion of proletarian revolution, do in this war which captured the imagination of the left?

Germany and Italy were already involved in helping the Nationalists. Britain was the leading advocate of non-intervention and persuaded France not to help the Republicans. Many of the left in Europe saw it as a chance to fight back against fascism. 'We do not write History now, we make it,' wrote an enthusiastic volunteer for the Republican cause. The Soviet Union had to weigh up the advantages and disadvantages of intervening, as shown in Chart 16A. In the end the Soviets decided that there were more reasons to intervene than not, but Stalin's intervention was cautious and the gains that the USSR made from involvement were limited.

■ 16A How Spain and the European powers divided

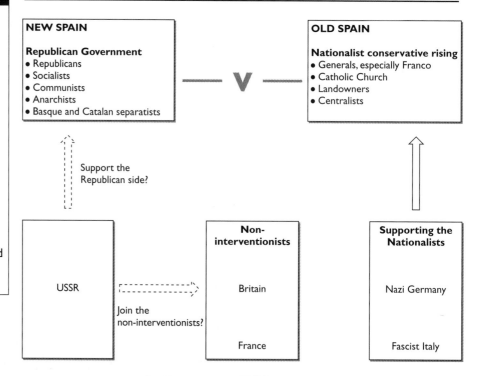

SOURCE 16.2 A Soviet fighter plane, one of around 1000 aircraft supplied by the USSR to the Republican side in the Spanish Civil War

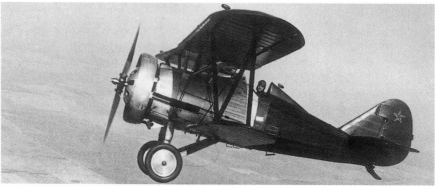

Ideology
The Spanish Civil War was seen as a battle between left and right. Could the USSR, the leader of the international proletariat, stand aside? Germany and Italy were intervening on the other side. Inaction would bring Trotskyite accusations of betraying the revolution.

Support for popular fronts
The Spanish government was just the sort of bourgeois democracy the Comintern's popular front tactics were designed to support.

Soviet security
France was the USSR's potential ally. Defeat of the Spanish Republic would leave France surrounded by fascist countries. This could affect Soviet security.

Diversionary effect
The war in Spain kept other European powers divided and allowed Stalin to carry out the purges without anxiety about external threats. Therefore it was worth prolonging.

Elimination of Trotsky's supporters
Trotskyites from all over the world were going to Spain to fight for the Spanish revolution. If Stalin intervened, the NKVD would have the opportunity to eliminate them.

Propaganda gains
Intervention would allow the USSR to present itself as the only world power ready to defend democracy against fascism.

Military experience
The war offered an opportunity to try out weapons and give officers and pilots experience of combat conditions.

Strategic issues
Spain was too far away to matter much to the USSR's vital interests.

Domestic considerations
The USSR was preoccupied with and weakened by the purges, especially the purges of the armed forces.

Reaction of Britain and France
Strong, successful intervention might lead to Spain becoming a Soviet satellite. Britain and France would be alarmed by this prospect and they might form an anti-Communist alliance with Germany and Italy.

STALIN'S DECISION
Stalin took the view that Spain was not suitable for Communism, nor could it survive there surrounded by bourgeois regimes. But the USSR needed to become involved to try to prevent any weakening of France's power or military situation.

The Nazi–Soviet Pact, August 1939

This pact referred directly to the Treaty of Berlin of 1926, which committed both countries to refrain from aggression and to observe neutrality in conflicts involving third parties. A secret protocol (whose existence was denied until 1991 by the USSR) defined future spheres of influence, with part of east Poland, plus Estonia, Latvia and Bessarabia (part of Romania) passing to the USSR.

Germany invaded Poland on 1 September 1939 and advanced very rapidly. The Soviet Union joined in on 17 September, attacking from the east. Poland was soon overrun. A new Nazi–Soviet treaty was agreed on 28 September: in return for giving Germany slightly more of Poland than was originally agreed, Lithuania was transferred to the Soviet sphere of influence. Important economic concessions were made by the Soviets to Germany, and the economic agreements made in October were crucial to Hitler's plans. The amount of grain and raw materials he gained from the USSR, together with the rubber from the Far East which came through the USSR, enabled Hitler to get round any Allied blockade. Without these supplies of natural rubber, neither the western campaigns of 1940 nor the later campaigns in the USSR could have been fought.

D   How have historians disagreed over Stalin's foreign policy in the 1930s?

FOCUS ROUTE

At the centre of the debate is the question of whether Soviet commitment to collective security was genuine or a poor second to an agreement with Germany.

1   Study Chart 16F on page 265. What is the position of the three interpretations on this issue?
2   Look at the different interpretations of the Nazi–Soviet Pact (Sources 16.10–16.14 on pages 264–267) which illustrate the different views and the argument that Stalin had no favoured option and just sought to do whatever suited the USSR best. What is your own interpretation?

SOURCE 16.7   The Russian view of the Munich Conference: Chamberlain and Daladier direct German expansion east

SOURCE 16.8 J. Haslam, *The Soviet Union and the Threat from the East, 1933–1941*, 1992, pp. 15–16. This quotation from one of the leading experts on Soviet foreign policy points to one reason why interpretation is difficult

265

Stalin's precise position on any given issue remained unclear and disputes over policy could and did arise within the upper reaches of the state and party apparatus; a process Stalin deliberately encouraged as a means of retaining ultimate control. In terms of diplomacy it meant that although Litvinov had considerable leeway in the conduct of day-to-day issues and essentially had Stalin's commitment (until 1939), he nonetheless faced intermittent opposition from other quarters that Stalin never entirely inhibited.

Three different interpretations of Soviet foreign policy in the 1930s

The official Soviet interpretation

The USSR pursued a clear and unambiguous policy of building a European-wide shield of collective security against Nazi aggression. Since the USSR represented the forces of historical progress it was bound to take the lead in opposing the barbarous schemes of Nazi Germany. Collective security failed because of the failure of the Western democracies to oppose Hitler's murderous plans. British ruling circles had been dreaming for a long time of a war between Germany and the Soviet Union. The Nazi-Soviet pact or, as Soviets refer to it, Russo–Germany non-aggression treaty, was necessitated by the grave threat of German and Japanese attacks on the USSR and what they saw as the West's betrayal of collective security.

Two contrasting Western views
1 The 'German' school

Stalin always preferred co-operation with Germany, whether Weimar or Nazi, to a defensive alliance with Western powers. He was only interested in the notion of collective security for as long as an agreement with Hitler remained out of reach. The Germans repeatedly rejected Soviet moves for closer co-operation. Gerhard Weinberg and, in extreme form, Robert Tucker take this view. In *World in Balance* (1981, page 7), Weinberg stresses the contacts between the head of the Soviet trade mission in Berlin and key figures making German economic policy.

Tucker argues that Stalin was following an ambitious and aggressive policy whereby he manoeuvred the capitalist states into a mutually destructive war from which the USSR would emerge unscathed and in a strong position to expand territorially all along its borders (see 'The Emergence of Stalin's Foreign Policy' in *Slavic Review*, 1977, pages 563–589 and pages 604–607). According to Tucker, collective security was a mask for Stalin's designs and a bait to attract Hitler. The purges were necessary to remove opposition to a deal with Hitler. The USSR struggled not for an alliance against Hitler but for the reconstruction of the Rapallo relationship between Germany and Russia.

2 The 'collective security' school

The USSR's campaign for collective security arose from a perceived need for the USSR to make common cause with the other states in opposition to Hitler's expansionist foreign policy. Jonathan Haslam wrote in *The Soviet Union and the Struggle for Collective Security in Europe* (1984, page 230): 'What is so striking from 1933–1939 is less the tentative soundings in Berlin – the echoes of Rapallo – than the merciless persistence with which the Russians so doggedly clung to the policy of collective security, a policy which so rarely showed any promise of success.' Geoffrey Roberts and Teddy Uldricks are other historians supporting this school of thought.

FOCUS ROUTE

Some would argue that Stalin always sought what was best for the USSR, and how this was achieved did not matter. Look for evidence which supports the different views and at the end of the topic come up with your own interpretation.

Why do historians disagree on Soviet foreign policy?

Until the 1990s, the study of Soviet foreign policy was problematic because it was difficult for Western historians to obtain access to records. Now that Communism has collapsed and records are more accessible, revelations may follow which could alter interpretations (see Source 16.14).

Just as the influence of the Cold War can be seen in the Soviet interpretation, it is not surprising that a Western interpretation of Soviet foreign policy as unscrupulous and double-dealing held sway at the same time. The Nazi–Soviet pact was seen as a typically treacherous Communist action. Also, since the pact encouraged Hitler to go ahead with his attack on Poland, the USSR could be said to bear a major responsibility for the outbreak of the Second World War. Soviet domination of Eastern Europe after the Second World War was further proof of the aggressive nature of its policy. This interpretation is likely to be held by historians who are very critical of Stalin and Communism.

A. J. P. Taylor's *Origins of the Second World War*, first published in 1961, is an excellent example of a book that challenged the existing orthodoxy that the war was Hitler's peculiar and special responsibility, and it forced historians to re-examine their views. Taylor believed that Soviet policy was one of improvisation, which was in line with his view that politicians do not carry out master plans but take advantage of opportunities as they arise. Taylor's view on Hitler and the war has not carried the field, but he was one of the pioneers of the collective security school of thought on the Soviet role. He argued that the Russians had always advocated collective security but did not want to be manoeuvred into resisting Germany alone, and that by signing the pact Stalin thought that he had 'escaped an unequal war in the present, and perhaps even avoided it altogether' (2nd edn, 1963, page 319).

■ 16F Why do historians disagree on Soviet foreign policy?

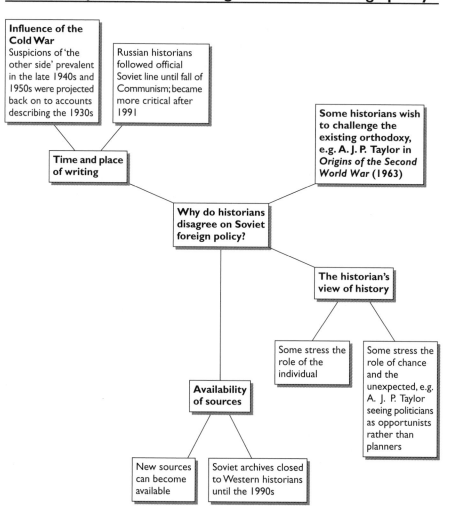

Influence of the Cold War
Suspicions of 'the other side' prevalent in the late 1940s and 1950s were projected back on to accounts describing the 1930s

Russian historians followed official Soviet line until fall of Communism; became more critical after 1991

Some historians wish to challenge the existing orthodoxy, e.g. A. J. P. Taylor in *Origins of the Second World War* (1963)

Time and place of writing

Why do historians disagree on Soviet foreign policy?

The historian's view of history

Some stress the role of the individual

Some stress the role of chance and the unexpected, e.g. A. J. P. Taylor seeing politicians as opportunists rather than planners

Availability of sources

New sources can become available

Soviet archives closed to Western historians until the 1990s

In the 1960s and 1970s, during the Vietnam war and the sharp criticism of American foreign policy, Soviet foreign policy was not seen as uniquely evil. Consequently, many historians felt that in coming to an accommodation with Hitler, Stalin was not acting very differently from the appeasers. A pact with Hitler did appear the safest option in August 1939.

Historians on the Nazi–Soviet Pact

SOURCE 16.9 R. C. Tucker, *Stalin in Power: The Revolution from Above, 1928–1941*, 1992, p. 592

Stalin in his party congress speech set in motion talks leading to an alignment with Berlin. He did so by professing a desire for peace and business relations with 'all' interested states and disclaiming any intention of 'pulling chestnuts out of the fire' for others. That raised the possibility of a negotiated neutrality which would insure Hitler against what he had to fear most: a two-front war. This, Stalin could calculate, would enable Hitler to unleash aggression and him, while remaining neutral, to take over territories in Eastern Europe on an agreed-upon basis. And given his expressed belief that the democracies were stronger than the fascist states, he could and evidently did calculate that the oncoming war between them would be a protracted one that would result in their mutual weakening or exhaustion while Soviet Russia was at peace and rebuilding its own strength.

SOURCE 16.10 G. Roberts, *The Soviet Union and the Origins of the Second World War*, 1995, p. 89

Hitherto the operational objectives of Soviet foreign policy had revolved around the project of a triple alliance with Britain and France. By 15th August that project was in the latter stages of its disintegration. The only clear goal of Soviet foreign policy from mid-August to mid-September 1939 was that of avoiding a war with Nazi Germany in Eastern Europe while Britain and France stood on the sidelines. A new policy of security through strategic political expansion and co-operation with Hitler was foreshadowed in the Nazi–Soviet pact, but this actualisation was slow and hesitant, an effect of a series of ad hoc responses and reactions to the dynamic events rather than the result of prior decision or planned policy.

SOURCE 16.11 M. Pankrashova, V. Sipols, *Why War was not Prevented*, 1970, pp. 154–55

In the face of the threat from Germany, the Soviet Union did everything possible to conclude a comprehensive and effective military-political anti-aggression pact with Britain and France. Such a pact under those conditions could have forced the aggressors to come to reason and could have preserved the peace and prevented war both in Europe and elsewhere. However, the negotiations showed that Britain and France had no desire to conclude a pact, that they were playing a game of pact negotiations; they proposed that the Soviet Union take on far-reaching commitments but did not, in turn, want to help the Soviet Union, if it was attacked, i.e., they did not want an equitable and mutually beneficial agreement. The ruling circles of Britain and France during that period wanted only one thing: to prod German aggression against the USSR. This was the whole idea behind the big political game they were playing.

Under the circumstances, the only way to preserve the security of the USSR – at least for a time – was for the Soviet government to accept the proposal made at that particular time by the German government to sign a non-aggression pact on its own.

SOURCE 16.12 P. M. H. Bell, *The Origins of the Second World War in Europe*, 1987, pp. 261–62

The Soviets held a central position, and could judge which set of talks would better serve their interests. It is reasonable to assume that these were twofold: to keep out of a European war, especially when they were actually engaged in serious fighting with the Japanese in the Far East – they did not seek a war on two fronts; and to secure territory – a sphere of influence which would add to Soviet security, internal as well as external. It would be advantageous to bring the Ukrainians in Poland under Stalin's control. The British and French offered nothing substantial under either heading.

The Germans on the other hand were able to meet both Soviet interests. Instead of a risk of war, they could offer certain neutrality. In terms of territory and spheres of influence, they came bearing gifts, ready to carve up Poland and to yield at once when Stalin asked for the whole of Latvia to be in his sphere instead of only a part, as Ribbentrop at first proposed. Moreover the Germans could deliver the goods forthwith, whereas the British and French could deliver nothing.

Between the two sides, the Soviet choice could hardly be in doubt. It is only surprising that so much obloquy [criticism] has been heaped upon Stalin's head for making the best deal he could get, and that so much criticism has been levelled at the British for their dilatoriness [lack of urgency] when nothing could have enabled them to match the German offers. The competition was decided on substance, not on method.

ACTIVITY

1 Read Sources 16.9–16.11 and assign each to one of the interpretations of Soviet foreign policy described on page 265.
2 Explain how Source 16.12 differs in its interpretation from Sources 16.9, 16.10 and 16.11.
3 Read Source 16.10 again. Explain why Roberts is likely to argue that the decision was made at a much later date than that suggested by Tucker in Source 16.9.

Section 6 Review: Soviet security or spreading revolution? Soviet foreign policy 1921–39

At the beginning of the 19 years we have been studying, no country wanted diplomatic relations with the Bolsheviks. By the end of the period the other major European powers, while still wary, were in Moscow negotiating with the USSR and the country was a member of the League of Nations. The country's diplomatic position had been restored, but for all the high hopes of the Comintern in 1919 there had been no successful Communist revolution outside the Soviet Union.

We began our study of foreign policy with an agreement with Germany, the Treaty of Brest-Litovsk, and we end with the Nazi–Soviet Pact. Through the former treaty, the USSR lost half of the grain, coal, iron and human population of the former Russian empire. Lenin had a fierce struggle to convince his colleagues of its necessity; he believed that the Bolshevik regime would have fallen in three weeks without it. It was a treaty no leading member of the government was prepared to sign, but Lenin did not expect it to last as he believed other revolutions would soon take place. Stalin did not sign the Nazi–Soviet Pact, but he chaired the discussions and was happy to propose a toast to Hitler after it had been signed. He did not expect this pact to last either, but he thought it would last longer than 22 months. In direct contrast to the Treaty of Brest-Litovsk, the USSR this time gained territory under the terms of the secret protocol. Neither treaty had anything to do with spreading revolution and everything to do with Soviet security.

ACTIVITY

1 Place the factors affecting Soviet foreign policy in order of importance. Justify your decisions.
2 What do you think was the priority of Soviet foreign policy – Soviet security or spreading revolution?

Soviet society in the 1920s and 1930s

17

Were Soviet culture and society transformed by the October Revolution?

CHAPTER OVERVIEW The Bolsheviks wanted to change society. Wherever revolutionaries seek to remake society, they challenge deep-rooted social institutions: the family, education and religion. In this chapter we focus on the experience of women after the revolution and also ask how much change there was in the family, religion, education and the arts. The first decade of Communism (1917–27) saw more equality for women, the most liberal divorce and abortion laws in Europe, an explosion of the arts, a fierce attack on religion and changes in education. But things did not always turn out as the revolutionary leaders intended.

A How much did life change for women and the family? (pp. 272–277)

B How did the Bolsheviks use artists and film-makers between 1918 and 1928? (pp. 278–283)

C How much change occurred in education? (pp. 284–285)

D What impact did the Bolsheviks have on religion? (pp. 286–287)

A # How much did life change for women and the family?

SOURCE 17.1 *Industrial Worker and Collective Farm Girl*, a statue by Vera Mukhina, 1935

SOURCE 17.3 Georgie Ryazhsky's portrait, *The Chairwoman*, 1928

SOURCE 17.2 *Kalyazin Lacemakers*, a painting by Evgeni Katsman, 1928

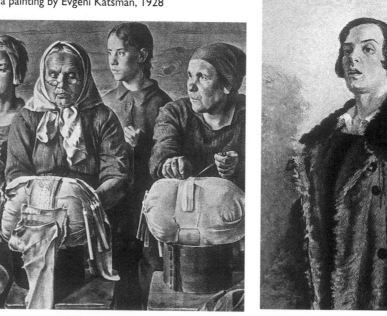

SOURCE 17.4 *Higher and Higher*, a painting by Serafima Ryangina, 1934

SOURCE 17.5 *New Moscow*, a 1937 painting by Yuri Pimenov

SOURCE 17.6 *A Mother* by Aleksandr Deineka, 1932

SOURCE 17.7 *Woman Metro-Builder with a Pneumatic Drill* by Aleksandr Samokhvalov, 1937

SOURCE 17.8 Gaponenko's *To Dine With the Mothers*, 1935

274

WERE SOVIET CULTURE AND SOCIETY TRANSFORMED BY THE OCTOBER REVOLUTION?

■ 17A Legislation on marriage and childcare

1917

- New divorce law – either partner could terminate a marriage on grounds of incompatibility. If one partner was not present at the divorce hearing, he or she was notified of the divorce by postcard.
- People's Commissar for Social Welfare passed laws which:
  - guaranteed paid maternity leave for two months before and after the birth
  - allowed nursing mothers to work shorter hours and take time to breastfeed their babies at work
  - excused women from heavy work or night work
  - set up a commission for the protection of mothers and infants, which made plans for maternity clinics, milk points and nurseries.

1920

Law passed allowing abortion to be performed under medical supervision. The Soviet state became the first country to legalise abortion on demand.

Women and the family

The new Communist state intended to bring about fundamental changes in the position of women in society. The key to this was economic independence: women should be able to have a job outside of the crushing drudgery of looking after a home and family (see the views of Alexandra Kollontai in Chart 17B, page 276). Lenin regarded the traditional bourgeois marriage as akin to slavery, with the woman the property of her husband and subjugated to his will. It was economic and sexual exploitation. Freeing women from their domestic role required the large-scale provision of facilities such as canteens, laundries, kindergartens and crèches; in other words, the socialisation of domestic services. This was a requirement which Lenin understood and supported.

Changes to women's role in the home also implied a fundamental change in the relationship between men and women. Once freed from the constraints of bourgeois marriage, there would be more equality between the sexes and sexual liberation because people would be freer to choose their partners. Therefore laws were passed immediately to make divorce easier and later, in 1920, to allow abortion on demand. The Bolsheviks had set the socialist dream for women in motion, but this soon collided with the economic realities of life in the Soviet state in the 1920s.

In 1919, the USSR had the highest marriage rate and, by the mid-1920s, the highest divorce rate in Europe, twenty-five times higher than in Britain. This situation did not work in women's favour. With easy divorce available, women were abandoned when they became pregnant. There were reports of young men registering more than fifteen short-lived 'marriages'. One survey of broken marriages from the end of the 1920s indicated that in 70 per cent of cases divorces were initiated by the men and in only seven per cent by mutual consent. By 1927, two-thirds of marriages in Moscow ended in divorce; across the country the figure was one-half. Due to the housing shortage, divorced couples often still lived together and domestic violence and rape were common.

The government was neither willing nor able to fund enough crèches or public canteens to free women from childcare and housework. When, in 1922, the idea of state provision for crèches, kitchens and laundries was costed, it added up to more than the entire national budget. The reality for many Russian children was not a network of socialist kindergartens but life in gangs that survived by begging, scrounging, stealing and prostitution. Hundreds of thousands had been made orphans by war and civil war. Malcolm Muggeridge, the English journalist and writer, reported seeing orphans 'going around in packs, barely articulate and recognisably human, with pinched faces, tangled hair and empty eyes. I saw them in Moscow and Leningrad, clustered under bridges, lurking in railway stations, suddenly emerging like a pack of wild monkeys, and scattering and disappearing' (quoted in R. Pipes, *A Concise History of the Russian Revolution*, 1995, page 326). Contemporaries estimated that in the 1920s there were between seven and nine million orphans, most of whom were under the age of thirteen.

SOURCE 17.9 O. Figes, *A People's Tragedy: The Russian Revolution, 1891–1924*, 1997, p. 197, writing of Russia before the revolution

For centuries peasants had claimed the right to beat their wives. Russian peasant proverbs were full of advice on the wisdom of such beatings: 'The more you beat the old women, the tastier the soup will be.'

A rival proverb [was] 'Women can do everything; men can do the rest.'

SOURCE 17.10 B. Williams, unpublished correspondence describing Soviet Russia in the inter-war years

It was a macho world for all the talk of equality. The nineteenth-century scientific ideas of in-built gender differences were still influential. Women cared and supported. Men built socialism. The iconography of the new state showed women with children or represented as peasants. The high-status proletarian was male, a metal worker or a blacksmith.

SOURCE 17.11 B. Williams, 'Kollontai and After: Women in the Russian Revolution' (unpublished lecture), quoting a Communist observer

In principle we separated marriage from economics, in principle we destroyed the family hearth, but we carried out the resolution on marriage in such a manner that only the man benefited from it ... The woman remains tied with chains to the destroyed family hearth. The man, happily whistling, can leave it, abandoning the women and children.

275

WERE SOVIET CULTURE AND SOCIETY TRANSFORMED BY THE OCTOBER REVOLUTION?

TALKING POINT

How important do you think employment is in changing the status of women in society today? Have increased economic independence, and higher positions in companies and public bodies, affected the lives of women and their relationships with men?

FOCUS ROUTE

Make notes on the following to prepare for a discussion:

- changes in the social and legal position of women after October 1917, including changes to the laws on divorce and abortion
- the difference between the socialist dream and the reality of childcare
- women's employment 1917–29
- the extent of women's political activity
- Alexandra Kollontai's ideas on women's emancipation, sex and marriage, and childcare.

Employment

During the First World War, the percentage of women in the urban workforce doubled; by 1917 it was about 47 per cent. After the Civil War, when five million men were discharged from military service, women suffered as men were given preference in jobs. Although women were paid less than men, employers regarded women as more expensive due to the time they took off work because of their home responsibilities. With the growth of urban unemployment during the NEP, women were forced from skilled to unskilled work – still predominantly in textiles and domestic service, and then from work to unemployment and into prostitution and crime. There were all-women gangs of thieves and 39 per cent of proletarian men used prostitutes in the 1920s. The result of all this was that the percentage of women in industrial labour by 1929 was practically the same as it had been in 1913. According to a survey in the 1920s, women in proletarian families worked an eight-hour day outside the home plus an extra five hours in domestic tasks; men did not help with the domestic work.

Participation in politics

You would imagine that a party that stressed the equality of women would promote this within their own party. But women's participation in the Communist Party did not make great strides in the 1920s. In 1917, women formed ten per cent of the party membership; in 1928, 12.8 per cent (156,000 women). At the party congress in 1918, only five per cent of the voting delegates were women and this percentage went down rather than up in succeeding years. Young, unmarried women had more time to be activists and female membership of the Komsomol (the Young Communist League) was much higher than party membership.

Women were up against two problems: Russian male chauvinism and the Marxist dislike of any separatist activity that could be interpreted as weakening the class struggle and proletarian unity. Traditional attitudes to women excluded them from party activities, as Sources 17.12 and 17.13 show. There were even reports of women being attacked or beaten by their husbands for being involved in party work.

In 1919, the party set up a women's department, Zhenotdel, to make women active defenders of the revolution through propaganda and agitation. However, in practice it focused on practical help such as social services, education and training, and making sure that new laws protecting women in factories were enforced, rather than on Alexandra Kollontai's more radical ideas about transforming women's role in society (see Chart 17B on page 276). Zhenotdel was abolished suddenly in 1930 on the grounds that it was no longer necessary.

SOURCE 17.12 J. McDermid and A. Hillyer, *Women and Work in Russia, 1880–1930*, 1998, p. 132

Before the revolution Kollontai tried to organise a meeting of women workers. Despite the promise of the St Petersburg committee of the party to provide a venue, when Kollontai and the women arrived, they found a sign on the door which read: 'The meeting for women only has been cancelled; tomorrow there will be a meeting for men only.'

SOURCE 17.13 B. Williams, 'Kollontai and After: Women in the Russian Revolution' (unpublished lecture), quoting a woman delegate who complained at a party congress that her activist husband forbade her to take part in public life

And in those very meetings which he forbids me to attend because he is afraid I will become a real person – what he needs is a cook and mistress wife – in those very meetings where I have to slip in secretly, he makes thunderous speeches about the role of women in the revolution, calls women to a more active role.

Paid work
Paid work outside the home should be the centre of women's lives. It would make them independent and personally fulfilled. As a good Marxist, she believed that a woman's rights and position in society 'always follow from her role in the economy and in production'. Capitalism oppressed women with the double burden of waged work and housework.

Marriage
The new marriage would be based on love, not on economic considerations or purely on sex, and would be unhindered by inequality, dependence or family ties. It need be neither monogamous nor long-lasting but it would be a true love relationship – the 'winged Eros' she writes about in her much misunderstood *Letter to Soviet Youth*. Like Lenin, she disapproved of the casual attitudes towards sex displayed by some Soviet youth in the 1920s.

Family life
The family could be transformed into something new: a network of collectives made up of a group of people working and living co-operatively together. Kitchens, dining rooms, laundries and childcare would be provided by the state.

Children
Motherhood was a duty but it ought not to be a burden. Once weaned, children would be the joint possession of the collective and possessiveness towards children would end. In the nurseries and kindergartens the new generation would learn to value the beauties of sociability, sharing and togetherness, and become accustomed to looking at the world from the perspective of the group and not through selfish eyes.

Workers' participation
Her belief in participation was not confined to women. The new society must be created from below. Trade unions must be preferred to the party bureaucracy. The party should return to the ideas of 1917. Trade unions, soviets and other elected workers' organisations should be trusted to run industry and create socialism themselves. Every party member should spend three months of every year working in factories or villages.

Alexandra Kollontai (1872–1952)

Alexandra Kollontai dominated Bolshevik theory and practice about 'the woman question' in 1906–22. The daughter of a wealthy general, her life was changed in 1896 after she visited a large factory. Shocked by the plight of the workers, which she saw as enslavement, she committed herself wholeheartedly to improving their living and working conditions. She plunged into revolutionary Marxism, leaving her husband and son. She was drawn into the Social Democratic Party, leaning towards the Mensheviks, but after the beginning of the First World War she committed herself to Lenin and the Bolsheviks. In 1917, she was on both the Central Committee of the Bolshevik Party and the Central Executive Committee of the Petrograd Soviet. She was appointed Commissar for Social Welfare after the revolution and drafted much of the 1917 legislation in this area. She resigned in protest over the Treaty of Brest-Litovsk.

After the Civil War, Kollontai was one of the leaders of the Workers' Opposition (see page 105) and clashed with Lenin. He stooped to a personal attack on her lifestyle. She had a succession of husbands and lovers: Shlyapnikov, the other leader of the Workers' Opposition, was her lover and she was married to Dybenko, a huge, black-bearded Bolshevik sailor and revolutionary hero seventeen years her junior.

The defeat of the Workers' Opposition effectively ended her political career. After this she was exiled to become a diplomat and in 1930–45 she was Soviet ambassador to Sweden; the King of Sweden was reported to be her lover. She wrote semi-autobiographical novels such as *Red Love* and *Love of Worker Bees*, putting forward her views on sex and the new woman. She retired to Moscow, the only surviving leading member of the opposition, and died in 1952 aged 80.

277

WERE SOVIET CULTURE AND SOCIETY TRANSFORMED BY THE OCTOBER REVOLUTION?

Enthusiasts to the left of Kollontai talked of free love, the abolition of marriage and forcibly removing children from the harmful influence of their parents to be brought up by the state. Kollontai did not, or at least did so with caution. Nevertheless, the pressure of the 'new morality' on girls led to 'liberty, equality and maternity!' Kollontai was increasingly associated with the corruption of Soviet youth rather than the liberation of Soviet women. There were some experimental communes but only one survived until the end of the 1920s. It had 168 members, only sixteen of whom were men. Student communes pooled all grants, books, even underclothes. One in Moscow forbade individual friendships. The fear of the 'new woman', prepared to sacrifice family, home and sometimes children for the cause, was widespread.

It is easy to overestimate the impact of these new ideas on Russian society in the 1920s. Although the family had been challenged by 'free' (unregistered) marriages, postcard divorces and abortion, the social radicalism of the decade can be exaggerated. Soviet law strongly emphasised the mutual responsibility of family members for each other's financial welfare and, as the state lacked the resources to provide social welfare, the family remained a key institution. There was an increase in promiscuity, but surveys in the 1920s suggest the increase was not as great as young men claimed. The majority held to traditional attitudes towards relationships and a large number dreamt of long-lasting partnerships based on love and marriage. Also, such change as did occur tended to be in the cities and not in the countryside, where the vast majority of the population remained unaffected by the concept of the new woman and freer sexual relations, as Source 17.14 indicates.

SOURCE 17.14 M. Hindus, *Black Earth*, 1926, pp. 165–67. In 1926 Maurice Hindus, an American academic, went back to the village in Russia where he had been born and talked to young people in the village

And what I asked, of the morality of young people? Had there been any changes since the Revolution? None, they replied. Girls were as strict as ever their mothers and grandmothers had been. Of course, a fellow could flirt with a girl, put his arm around her, hold her hand, kiss her, but only on the cheek, not on the lips – unless she was his fiancée. Otherwise – well – our girls were quite strong, a blow of their fists might even draw blood. Lapses in conduct were as rare as in the old times . . . it was the worst thing for a girl to submit to a man. Her betrayer is likely to abandon her, and no other man would have her as his wife. The girls knew that and took care of themselves.

And what, I further enquired, of the Young Communists? They laughed uproariously. Ekh, the Young Communists . . . some of them were against kissing and dancing, said it was all the invention of the capitalists to corrupt the peasant and the proletarian . . . and besides it was too much responsibility to be a Young Communist.

TALKING POINT

How far had women's lives and their position in society improved between 1917 and 1929?

LENIN'S VIEWS ON KOLLONTAI'S IDEAS

For Lenin, participation in the labour force plus socialisation of domestic duties equalled female emancipation. However, he thought that Kollontai's views on sex were completely unMarxist and anti-social. 'Of course . . . thirst must be quenched. But will the normal man, in normal circumstances, lie down in the gutter and drink out of a puddle, or out of a glass with a rim greasy from many lips?' was his attitude to casual sexual relationships – he deplored promiscuity. As far as he was concerned, young people required healthy sports and exercise rather than 'endless lectures and discussions on sex problems'. Lenin also condemned the Workers' Opposition as a deviation and radically wrong in theory.

FOCUS ROUTE

Make notes on:
- Proletkult
- the Bolshevik use of arts as propaganda
- cinema.

Anatoly Lunacharsky (1875–1933)
Lunacharsky was an intellectual, playwright and literary critic who was Commissar for Popular Enlightenment between 1917 and 1929. In the revolution he was a prominent and popular leader, second only to Trotsky as a crowd orator. He was creative and open-minded and encouraged artists, poets and musicians to work with the Bolsheviks. Although promoting proletarian culture, he also respected the cultural achievements of the past and was able to ensure that many historical buildings survived. At different times he was criticised by Lenin for his support of the avant-garde and Proletkult, and for trying to protect the Bolshoi theatre rather than using the money to set up reading rooms as part of the literacy campaign. Lunacharsky believed in allowing some artistic freedom and different schools of painting, literature and the performing arts did exist in the 1920s. He was replaced as Commissar in 1929.

LENIN'S VIEWS ON ART AND PROLETKULT

Lenin attacked all modern art as Futurism and was not keen on it. He believed that freedom in art was the freedom to 'elevate the masses, teach them and strengthen them'. He had no time for individual self-expression which he called 'bourgeois-anarchist individualism'. Lenin attacked the Futurist Mayakovsky's poem '150 Millions' as 'Rubbish, double-dyed stupidity and pretentiousness', declaiming 'And flog Lunacharsky for futurism'. Nor was he keen on Proletkult. He did not believe that you could invent a new proletarian culture; rather you should develop the best models and traditions from the existing culture from a Marxist world outlook.

B How did the Bolsheviks use artists and film-makers between 1918 and 1928?

Proletkult

Following the October Revolution, the Bolshevik government set up the Commissariat of Popular Enlightenment (Ministry of Education and Culture) headed by Anatoly Lunacharsky. The focus moved away from 'high art' – ballet, opera, fine art and museums – which was regarded as bourgeois and élitist, to 'popular culture' – art directed at the mass audience. Workers and peasants were encouraged to produce their own culture – Proletkult (proletarian cultural movement). This was to be a collective culture in which the 'I' of bourgeois culture would give way to 'we'. Some of the more extreme members of the Proletkult movement wanted to do away with existing libraries and art galleries, jettisoning the bourgeois culture of the past.

Proletkult was the idea of Alexander Bogdanov, Lunacharsky's brother-in-law. Bogdanov wanted to make art responsive to the needs of the working class and encouraged the masses to participate actively in making art. He set up studios, poetry circles, folk theatres and exhibitions. By 1920, there were around 400,000 Proletkult members, including 80,000 active in art studios and clubs. Bogdanov believed that proletarian art would move people towards Communism.

Lunacharsky was sympathetic to these ideas and believed that Proletkult should be independent of political control. Initially it was exempt from supervision. But it seemed to be developing as an independent working-class organisation, something the Bolsheviks would not tolerate, and so Lenin, antagonistic to the philosophy of Proletkult, had its regional and central offices shut down during 1921 and 1922.

How did the Bolsheviks use art in propaganda?

The Bolsheviks were anxious to harness art to the service of the new state. There had been a flowering of creativity in the arts in Russia in the years just before the revolution and this lasted into the 1920s. Innovators in the arts, the 'avant-garde', rejected the art of the past as linked with the bourgeois way of life which was to be destroyed. In the years immediately after the revolution, many of Russia's finest artists took part in the Soviet cultural experiment. The Bolsheviks wanted to keep well-known artists on their side if possible, and many artists, for their part, were encouraged by the ending of tsarist censorship. Indeed, artistic freedom was one area which the Bolsheviks encouraged in the first years after the revolution.

Artists of the avant-garde were excited by the revolution and embraced it. They wanted to communicate directly with the masses. Futurists like Mayakovsky and Malevich revolted against the boring old world. Like many fellow artists elsewhere in Europe, they were fascinated by machines and modern technology and wanted to reflect this in their art. Constructivists like Rodchenko, Tatlin and Lissitsky wanted to create a new proletarian culture based on the worker and on industrial technology. They concentrated on designing clothes, furniture, offices and everyday objects in an 'industrial style', using straight lines and geometrical shapes which they thought would liberate people. These two avant-garde schools influenced each other and sometimes it was difficult to tell a Futurist from a Constructivist.

279

WERE SOVIET CULTURE AND SOCIETY TRANSFORMED BY THE OCTOBER REVOLUTION?

Kasimir Malevich (1878–1935)

Malevich believed in the supremacy of geometric forms over realism and created his own system of art, Suprematism. Malevich is seen now as an important figure in the development of modern art though his work would have made a limited impact on workers, peasants and most Bolsheviks. He was regarded with suspicion and arrested in 1930. On his release he returned to more figurative painting but he did not toe the line completely. When he was buried in 1935, it was in a coffin decorated with Suprematist designs he had painted himself.

SOURCE 17.15 *Three Female Figures* K. S. Malevich, 1928–32

Vladimir Mayakovsky (1893–1930)

Mayakovsky was a young poet, playwright and artist of great energy who had joined the Social Democrats at the age of fifteen and was repeatedly jailed as a teenager for subversive activity. He was a Futurist and naturally welcomed the revolution wholeheartedly. He worked with the Bolsheviks producing posters and 3000 captions or slogans on a wide range of topics, from encouraging resistance during the Civil War to getting people to drink boiled water during an epidemic.

His play *The Mystery Bouffe* was a parody of the Biblical flood in which the unclean (proletariat) triumph over the clean (bourgeoisie). This was produced by Meyerhold (see page 299) as were the satires *The Bedbug* and *The Bath House*, fierce attacks on the smugness of petty leaders which exposed Communist bureaucracy. Both plays were soon withdrawn.

Mayakovsky was very egotistical: his first play was *Vladimir Mayakovsky* and his first book of poems *'I'*. His autobiography *I Myself* hardly showed him as the collective man. By 1930, he had grown disillusioned with the Communists. Always emotionally volatile, unhappy in love and denied a visa to go abroad, he committed suicide in April 1930. In 1935, when Mayakovsky was safely dead, Stalin proclaimed him 'the best and most gifted poet of our Soviet epoch'. Study of his work became compulsory in schools but his satires were not mentioned and neither was his interest in Futurism nor his suicide.

SOURCE 17.16 A ROSTA window poster produced by Mayakovsky to mark 'Remember Red Army Barracks Day' in 1920. The slogans read as follows: 1) We've finished off Russia's White Guards. That's not enough. 2) The ogre of world capitalism is still alive. 3) That means we still need the Red Army. 4) And that means we've got to help it out – the task is clear

SOURCE 17.17 Mayakovsky in front of propaganda posters in the window of ROSTA, the Petrograd telegraph office

Vladimir Tatlin (1885–1953)

Tatlin's 'Monument to the Third International' (the Comintern) was to be a tower twice the height of the Empire State Building. It was to be made of glass and iron and contain revolving glass shapes – cylinder, hemisphere, pyramid and cube – which would revolve at different rates: once a year, once a month or once a day. It was also to contain a propaganda centre equipped with telegraphy, telephone and radio, and a vast open-air screen. It was completely impractical and never got beyond the model stage.

SOURCE 17.18
Tatlin's Monument to the Third International 1919–20

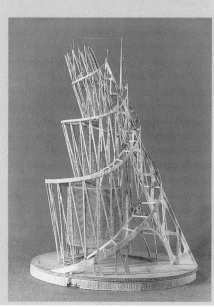

SOURCE 17.19   A classic image of Soviet industrial art from the mid-1920s. The caption reads 'Lenin is Steel and Granite'

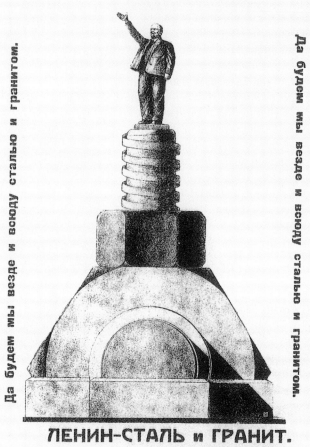

SOURCE 17.20   An illustration by Rodchenko for one of Mayakovsky's poems. This is an example of Constructivist art, showing new technology

SOURCE 17.21 Lissitsky's poster, *Beat the Whites with the Red Wedge*. Lissitsky was influenced by Malevich and the belief that the pure geometric form was superior to representational art. In this poster he expressed a political idea clearly and simply through an arrangement of geometric shapes

SOURCE 17.22 This monument, based on Lissitsky's famous *Beat the Whites with the Red Wedge* poster, was erected in Revolution Square as part of the celebrations for the first anniversary of the revolution in October 1918. As *Pravda* explained it, 'The white block representing the White Guards is pierced and cracked by the Red Wedge representing the great Red Army'

SOURCE 17.23 Lenin makes a speech at the unveiling of the memorial to Marx and Engels in Moscow, on the first anniversary of the October Revolution, in 1918

Agitational art

The avant-garde artists were drawn into producing propaganda for the Bolsheviks. Malevich and Lissitsky produced 'agitprop art' and their designs were reproduced on agitprop trains (mobile propaganda centres; see Source 6.10, page 92), ships and banners, and above all, on posters displayed in the Petrograd ROSTA (Russian Telegraph Agency) windows. More than 1000 ROSTA posters were created over a two-year period. Agitprop theatre broke down barriers between actors and audience, encouraging the audience to respond vocally to the actions of the play. Meyerhold and other directors produced street plays designed to stir up hatred of the old bourgeoisie and encourage people to support the new regime.

Lenin wanted to take art into the streets and had a plan for monumental propaganda. He proposed that the streets of the major cities should display posters and slogans to educate the citizens 'in the most basic Marxist principles and slogans'. So Moscow City Soviet was draped with the huge banner 'The proletariat has nothing to lose but its chains'. Even more important than these slogans, in Lenin's view, were statues 'of great figures of social and revolutionary activity'. He provided a list of 66 names and personally unveiled the joint statue of Marx and Engels on the first anniversary of the revolution.

Another element of mass agitational art was street processions. These built on a rich tradition of public festivals and, in the Orthodox tradition, icons were carried across the village or town, though now they were Communist rather than religious icons. May Day and the anniversary of the October Revolution became the great ritual festivals of the new atheist Marxist-Leninist state. Lenin encouraged popular revolutionary celebrations but he wanted them to be carefully organised and controlled rather than spontaneous.

Probably the best example of mass street theatre was the great re-enactment of the storming of the Winter Palace in November 1920. It involved 10,000 people and included the Winter Palace itself as, in the words of the director, 'a gigantic actor and a vast character in the play ... each one of the 50 windows of the first floor will in turn show a moment of the development of the battle inside.' There were fireworks and music – indeed it was far more dramatic and more damaging to the building than the original event. It was a stage-managed October as it should have happened, with Lenin directing.

Cinema

The shortage of supplies of film equipment made film production very difficult during the Civil War, but by the summer of 1918 the agitproptrains were in action and equipped to spread political propaganda through films, plays and other media far and wide. In the early 1920s a special unit, Proletkino, was formed specifically for the production of political films in line with party ideology.

In 1925, however, the Politburo's decision not to intervene in matters of form and style in the arts allowed the Soviet cinema a brief period of great creativity. The most outstanding film-maker of this period was Eisenstein, who was anxious to show the power of the people acting together, as in his famous film of the Bolshevik revolution, *October*. However, Soviet audiences tended to prefer Hollywood comedies to his sophisticated work. Although the number of cinemas grew fast, and 300 million tickets were sold in 1928, the cinemas were almost entirely restricted to the towns. In 1928, the first All-Union Party Congress on Film Questions met and tighter control was imposed. It ruled that films should be accessible to the mass audience, and emphasised socialist ideas along strict party lines.

SOURCE 17.24 A detail from a ROSTA window poster. The early posters were done as single copies but later ones were stencilled and reproduced hundreds of times. The posters were not always easy to interpret but the message of this one is very clear

SOURCE 17.25 B. Williams, *Lenin*, 2000, p. 162

Cinema was, in theory, the ideal medium of propaganda, visual, technological, controllable. Lenin was especially keen for it to be used in areas where cinemas 'are novelties, and where therefore our propaganda will be particularly successful'. He recommended concentration on documentary film and newsreels, the making of short agitki *on scientific topics, and encouraged the use of cinemas on agit-trains. He agreed that capital should be sought from private sources at home and abroad, 'on the condition that there should be complete guarantee of ideological direction and control by the government and the party', a statement which summed up his whole approach to the cultural revolution he so much desired. For Lenin propaganda, education and cultural development were not peripheral aims but absolutely central to the building of socialism.*

Sergei Eisenstein (1898–1948)

SOURCE 17.26 Still from Eisenstein's film *Battleship Potemkin*

Eisenstein was the best-known Soviet film director of the twentieth century. He worked with the Bolsheviks and for the Moscow Workers' Theatre before moving into the film industry. His first film was *Strike* (1924), with a clear message about how the workers were oppressed and how they could resist. Two of his best-known films were commissioned by the Central Committee: *Battleship Potemkin* (1925) and *October* (1928). His radical new filming techniques, editing together different images to build tension and produce a dramatic climax, are seen most famously in the 'Odessa Steps' scene in *Battleship Potemkin* and contributed to its huge international success.

October provided the classic heroic images of the revolution, but was far more dramatic than the reality; more people were killed and more damage was done to the Winter Palace than in the real event. However, the film was strongly criticised by the party leadership. The first All-Union Party Congress on Film Questions ruled that Socialist Realism was the only acceptable artistic style. In 1926, Stalin proposed that Eisenstein should make a film on the need for collectivisation. Eisenstein relied on his experimental style and focused on tractors and a cream separator to symbolise the transition from primitive farming to the mechanised modern agriculture. The film was excessively re-edited on Stalin's orders and re-titled *The Old and the New*. It was released in 1929.

Eisenstein was attacked during the Cultural Revolution of 1928 to 1931 (see page 291) and fell out of favour. He did not come back into favour until he made *Alexander Nevsky* in 1938. This film was commissioned by Stalin. It featured the Russian prince Alexander Nevsky who defeated invading German knights in a battle in 1242. The film was intended to strengthen Russian nationalism in the face of the growing threat from Nazi Germany. It ended with Nevsky saying 'Go tell everyone in foreign parts, anyone who comes to us with a sword will perish by the sword.' It was withdrawn after the Nazi–Soviet Pact in 1939. Eisenstein was later to make a two-part film on Ivan the Terrible, one of Stalin's heroes.

TALKING POINT

What does the rise, fall and rise again of Eisenstein tell us about the relationship between the government and the cinema?

How much change occurred in education?

For Lenin, education was an essential building block in creating a socialist society. Each child was to receive nine years of free, universal education. The aim was to combine education and political propaganda; Lenin did not believe that education could be 'politically neutral'. The 1919 Party Programme defined schools as 'an instrument for the Communist transformation of society'. Even learning the alphabet could carry a political message: A = All power to the soviets, B = Bolsheviks, C = Communist; and simple rhymes spelt out the achievements of Soviet power. Pupils were to be cleansed of 'bourgeois' ideas. Religious teaching was to be replaced by an emphasis on Communist values and atheism.

Schools were placed under the Commissariat for Enlightenment. The head of the Commissariat, Lunacharsky, was interested in progressive Western teaching ideas, such as those of John Dewey which stressed 'learning by doing' and the importance of work and play. So between 1919 and 1920, schools were encouraged to follow a more liberal line focusing on the development of the child's personality. The authority of teachers was reduced and they were designated as 'school workers' who shared administrative control with committees drawn from older pupils and factory workers. Teachers were forbidden to discipline pupils or set homework and examinations. Some radicals wanted to do away with schools altogether.

On the whole, schooling was a disaster area. The new school system failed, although in many areas it was never put into use. The vast majority of teachers were not Communists (3.1 per cent in primary schools and 5.5 per cent in secondary schools), had a poor understanding of progressive methods and did not know what was expected of them. Teaching went on much as it had done before the revolution, only worse because teachers had lost their authority. As a result, this more liberal approach was abandoned and more traditional methods restored with the introduction of the NEP in 1921.

Matters did not, however, improve much. Under the NEP, financial pressures meant that the idea of universal schooling had to be abandoned. Many children left school: by 1923, the numbers of schools and pupils were barely half the totals of two years earlier. Schools did not have the proper resources and the teachers were very badly paid (in 1925, a teacher received a fraction of an industrial worker's pay). There was also a lasting legacy of falling standards and failure of authority in many schools (see Source 17.27).

SOURCE 17.27 R. Pipes, *A Concise History of the Russian Revolution*, 1995, p. 315. Pipes believes that the following extract, written in the style of a fifteen-year-old boy's diary, reflects the atmosphere of the early Soviet classroom

October 5

Our whole school group was outraged today. This is what happened. A new school worker came to teach natural science, Elena Nikitishna Kaurova, whom we named Elnikitka. She handed out our assignments and told the group: 'Children!'

Then I got up and said: 'We are not children.'

To which she: 'Of course you are children, and I won't call you any other way.'

I replied: 'Please be more polite or we may send you to the devil.'

Elnikitka turned red and said: 'In that case be so good as to leave the classroom.'

I replied: 'In the first place, this is not a classroom but a laboratory and we are not expelled from it . . . you are more like a teacher of the old school. Only they had such rights.'

That was all. The whole group stood up for me. Elnikitka ran off like she was scalded.

285

WERE SOVIET CULTURE AND SOCIETY TRANSFORMED BY THE OCTOBER REVOLUTION?

In the 1920s there were two main strands in the school curriculum:

- general education, which included learning about Communism and the history of the revolution
- practical education, focusing on technical subjects and industrial training, with visits to factories, state farms and power stations.

The Bolsheviks wanted to increase the number of party members, especially those from working class or peasant backgrounds, who had engineering and technical skills. However, the new Soviet citizen was also to have a knowledge of culture as well as industrial skills. The emphasis on indoctrination remained throughout the 1920s, but a survey in 1927 of schoolchildren aged eleven to fifteen showed that they had become increasingly negative towards Communist values as they got older, and nearly 50 per cent still believed in God.

Literacy

Before the revolution, the illiteracy rate was about 65 per cent. This explains some of the Bolshevik emphasis on visual propaganda, and sending agitprop trains all over the country. The Bolsheviks attached great importance to universal literacy so that all citizens could be both exposed to their propaganda and taught modern industrial skills. In December 1919, the 'liquidation of illiteracy' was decreed for all citizens aged between eight and 50. Illiterates who refused to learn faced criminal prosecution. Tens of thousands of 'liquidation points' were set up in cities and villages and between 1920 and 1926 some five million people in European Russia went through literacy courses.

Youth organisations

The Bolsheviks did not leave indoctrination to non-Communist teachers. They had a mission to capture the hearts and minds of the young. Two youth organisations were set up: the Pioneers for children under fifteen and the Komsomol for those from the age of fourteen or fifteen into their twenties. The duty of these organisations was to inculcate Communist values and to promote loyalty to the working class. In later years, they were used as instruments as social control and to promote discipline in schools. The Pioneers were much like the Boy Scouts, with activities, trips and camping. The Komsomol was much more serious and was used by the Communist Party to take propaganda into the towns and villages and to attack religious beliefs and bourgeois values. Komsomol membership was seen as a preparation for entry into the Communist Party. The Komsomol played a very important role in the Cultural Revolution of 1928–31 (see page 289).

SOURCE 17.28 *He Who is Illiterate is Like a Blind Man. Failure and Misfortune Lie in Wait for Him on All Sides.* A poster promoting literacy from 1920

НЕГРАМОТНЫЙ тот-же СЛЕПОЙ
ВСЮДУ ЕГО ЖДУТ НЕУДАЧИ И НЕСЧАСТЬЯ.

КНИГИ

SOURCE 17.29 A member of the Komsomol

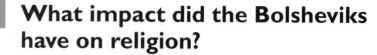

D What impact did the Bolsheviks have on religion?

The Bolsheviks were aggressively atheistic. They saw religion as a sign of backwardness. Lenin declared that the party's aim was to 'destroy the ties between the exploiting classes and the organisation of religious propaganda', and replace it with scientific education. Lenin forecast that 'Electricity will take the place of God. Let the peasant pray to electricity; he is going to feel the power of the central authorities more than that of heaven.' This attitude brought the Bolsheviks into direct conflict with the Orthodox Church, which was central to the lives of millions of peasants and an integral part of the village community.

In January 1918, the Bolsheviks issued the Decree on the Separation of Church and State which declared that the Church could not own property, church buildings had to be rented and religious instruction in schools was outlawed. Priests and clerics were declared 'servants of the bourgeoisie'. This meant that they were not allowed to vote and did not receive ration cards, or got those of the lowest category. Patriarch Tikhon, the head of the Orthodox Church, denounced the Bolsheviks and called upon the faithful to resist them by all possible spiritual means. The battle was on for the people's soul.

The Bolsheviks mounted an enormous propaganda onslaught. In 1921, the Union of the Militant Godless was established, with branches across the country. It held events such as debates to prove that God did not exist. It had its own newspaper which attacked the clergy as fat parasites living off the peasantry. Relics and icons were ridiculed – for example, weeping icons were shown to be operated by rubber squeezers. Peasants were taken for rides in planes to show there was no God in the sky. Atheist art showed a pregnant Virgin Mary longing for a Soviet abortion. At the same time, Communism was promoted as the new 'religion'. Public and private religious rituals were Bolshevised: Christmas and Easter became Komsomol Christmas and Easter; instead of baptisms, children were 'Octobered', with new names such as Revolyutsiya and Ninel (Lenin spelt backwards); Red weddings were conducted in front of a portrait of Lenin rather than an altar, with the couple making their vows both to each other and to the principles of Communism.

SOURCE 17.30 Red Army soldiers looting a church

This anti-clerical propaganda was accompanied by more direct action, particularly after 1921. Lenin used the famine of 1921–22 to demand that the Church surrender its valuables, including consecrated vessels used in rituals, for famine relief. Instructions were sent to local soviets to seize the valuables. But there was bitter resistance. Unarmed civilians, often old men and women, fought soldiers equipped with machine guns. More than 8000 people were executed or killed in 1922 in the anti-Church campaign, including the Metropolitan of Petrograd (a leading churchman only just below the Patriarch in rank), 28 bishops and 1215 priests.

The Politburo was alarmed by this level of resistance and decided to suspend the action. But Lenin, who saw this as the opportunity to smash the Church, overruled them. The Russian historian Volkogonov, who has enjoyed unrestricted access to Russia's archives, has seen in Lenin's papers an order from him demanding to be informed, on a daily basis, about how many priests had been shot.

SOURCE 17.31 Lenin, quoted in R. Pipes, *A Concise History of the Russian Revolution*, 1995, p. 338

It is now and only now, when in regions afflicted by the famine there is cannibalism and the roads are littered with hundreds if not thousands of corpses, that we can (and therefore must) pursue the acquisition of [church] valuables with the most ferocious and merciless energy, stopping at nothing in suppressing all resistance ... The greater the number of representatives of the reactionary bourgeoisie and reactionary clergy we will manage to execute in this affair, the better ...

There was also a campaign to split the Church from within. The 'Living Church' movement, backed by the OGPU (which had replaced the Cheka), hailed the revolution of October 1917 as a 'Christian deed' and denied that the Communists persecuted the Church. The Soviet government, it declared, alone in the world was striving to realise 'the ideal of the Kingdom of God'. Tikhon gave in, frightened that the Church would be split permanently. The Orthodox Church leadership gave no more trouble to the Communists.

Nevertheless, the Orthodox religion was not destroyed. Surveys of the peasantry in the mid-1920s revealed that 55 per cent were still active Christians. They continued to support priests with voluntary donations and carried out centuries-old religious practices. It is a mark of the durability of the Orthodox faith that the collapse of Communism in 1991 saw the immediate revival of the Church and large congregations for services.

KEY POINTS FROM CHAPTER 17

Were Soviet culture and society transformed by the October Revolution?

1 Soviet Russia had the most liberal divorce and abortion laws in Europe, but generally they worked against women. Childcare was supposed to become the collective responsibility of the state; in reality seven to nine million children lived on the streets in gangs of orphans.

2 Alexandra Kollontai was the only woman among the leading Bolsheviks, but the impact of her radical feminist ideas was limited.

3 The Bolsheviks believed in mass art that had to serve the new state. Some avant-garde artists were initially attracted to the regime but the relationship soured as political control increased.

4 Lenin was especially keen on the cinema and Eisenstein was an outstanding film-maker, but political control curbed his freedom later on.

5 Education was an essential element in building socialism but schools in the 1920s were not one of the Bolsheviks' successes.

6 The campaign to liquidate adult illiteracy had a higher success rate.

7 The Bolsheviks were aggressively atheistic and over 8000 believers were killed in the anti-Church campaign of 1922. However, religious belief persisted, especially amongst the peasants.

18

Culture and society in a decade of turmoil

CHAPTER OVERVIEW
The second decade of Communist rule began with the Cultural Revolution of 1928–31. It involved a return to the class struggle of the Civil War, with attacks on bourgeois specialists in the industrial workplace and on kulaks in the countryside. Its radical programme had an impact on the arts, education and religion. It was followed by a 'Great Retreat': a return to traditional values in the family, an emphasis on academic standards and discipline at school, and a more conservative style in the arts.

A What was the impact of the Cultural Revolution? (pp. 288–291)

B Women and the family in the 1930s – was there a 'Great Retreat' back to family values? (pp. 291–295)

C What was the impact of Socialist Realism in the arts? (pp. 296–301)

D What happened in education after the Cultural Revolution? (pp. 301–302)

E Soviet society at the end of the 1930s: had 'a new type of man' been created? (pp. 303–306)

What was the impact of the Cultural Revolution?

FOCUS ROUTE

Make notes on the impact of the Cultural Revolution in different parts of Soviet life by examining:

• religion
• education
• the arts.

The Cultural Revolution was part of a great upheaval in the USSR associated with the 'socialist offensive' which began at the end of the 1920s with the First Five-Year Plan. There was a return to the class warfare of the Civil War and a repudiation of everything that had gone with the compromise of the NEP. This was seen in the attack on bourgeois specialists in industry, the Nepmen and the kulaks. It was accompanied by an attack on the old intelligentsia and bourgeois cultural values. Non-Marxists working in academic subjects such as history, philosophy and science, in the cinema, the arts and literature, in schools, in architecture and in town planning were denounced. There was an attempt to find truly 'proletarian' approaches in all these fields. So it was labelled the 'Cultural Revolution'.

The Cultural Revolution was more than an attack on bourgeois values. There was a vision of what the socialist future might be like, of a society transformed. People believed great changes were imminent. They had visions of new cities with large communal living spaces where money was no longer the main means of rewarding people and transacting exchanges. There would be a 'new Soviet Man'.

Young Communists, in particular, enthusiastically took up the challenge and took the lead in taking the attack forward on many fronts. They mounted a fierce attack on religion in the villages, broke up 'bourgeois' plays by booing and criticised painters and writers who did not follow the party line. The activists had been itching to move forward towards a more proletarian society with proletarian values. They pushed matters further than the leadership wanted. The Cultural Revolution was not simply a manipulation from above; it gained a momentum of its own.

SOURCE 18.1   A Komsomol activist interviewed in Munich after the war and quoted in S. Fitzpatrick, *Everyday Stalinism*, 1999, p. 37

I saw that the older generation, worn out after years of the war and the postwar chaos, were no longer in a position to withstand the difficulties involved in the construction of socialism. I thus came to the conclusion that the success in transforming the country depended entirely on the physical exertions and the will of people like myself.

The role of the Komsomols in the Cultural Revolution

The Komsomol (Young Communist League) had been set up in 1918 to help the party. Its members were aged fourteen to twenty-eight and by 1927 it had two million members. It was an exclusive club: many applicants were rejected on grounds of immaturity or insufficiently proletarian social origins. The membership was enthusiastic and leapt at the opportunity to drive the Cultural Revolution. They were to fulfil a number of roles between 1929 and 1933:

- being 'soldiers of production' in the industrial drive; one of the first directors of the Magnitogorsk site described the local Komsomol as 'the most reliable and powerful organising force of the construction'
- imposing labour discipline; leading and joining shock brigades
- enforcing collectivisation and collecting state procurements of grain, etc.
- leading the campaign against religion
- keeping an eye on bureaucracy, exposing official abuses, unmasking hidden enemies
- weeding out students whose families had been members of the 'former people', attacking non-party professors and teachers, with the aim of making the intelligentsia proletarian
- reporting on the popular mood.

SOURCE 18.2   R. Service, *A History of Twentieth-Century Russia*, 1997, p. 199

There is no doubt that many young members of the party and the Komsomol responded positively to the propaganda. The construction of towns, mines and dams was an enormously attractive project for them. Several such enthusiasts altruistically devoted their lives to the communist cause. They idolised Stalin, and all of them – whether they were building the city of Magnitogorsk or tunnelling under Moscow to lay the lines for the metro or were simply teaching kolkhozniki *(collectivised peasants) how to read and write – thought themselves to be agents of progress for Soviet society and for humanity as a whole. Stalin had his active supporters in their hundreds of thousands, perhaps even their millions ... Stalin's rule in the early 1930s depended crucially upon the presence of enthusiastic supporters in society.*

ACTIVITY

Study Sources 18.1–18.3. What was the role of the Komsomols in the Cultural Revolution?

SOURCE 18.3   A Soviet slogan

The future belongs to the Komsomols.

TALKING POINT

Does any Cultural Revolution require a body of people like the Komsomols in order to carry it through?

CASE STUDY: KOMSOMOL ACTIVITIES IN SMOLENSK

The worker and student Komsomols in Smolensk were given a major role in leading the collectivisation drive and overseeing all aspects of the harvest. The Smolensk archive contains the following resolutions passed at a Komsomol committee meeting for the whole area in April 1931:

1 Participation in the collectivisation drive, universal Komsomol enrolment in kolkhozes, and active leadership in preparation for the spring sowing
2 A major role in fulfilling the figures for industrial production during the year
3 An intensified campaign to enlist industrial and farm workers in the Komsomol and to establish a Komsomol cell in every kolkhoz and sovkhoz (state farm)
4 Prepare for military service, help to liquidate illiteracy among draftees, and provide political instructors for them.

The Komsomol members were also called upon to serve as pace-setters in industry and transport. They were required to enrol in technical courses to improve their qualifications, to organise shock brigades, and to encourage competition between different groups of workers. They were also expected to conduct campaigns to shame the laggards and discourage loitering on the job.

This change in attitude has been called the 'Great Retreat': marriage was to be taken seriously, and children urged to love and respect their parents, 'even if they are old-fashioned and do not like the Komsomol' (*Pravda*, 1935). The change in emphasis can be seen in the new Family Code of May 1936 in which:

- abortion was outlawed except where there was a threat to the woman's life and health, and for women with hereditary diseases
- divorce was made harder: both parties were required to attend divorce proceedings and the fee for registering a divorce was raised to 50 roubles for the first divorce, 150 for the second and 300 for any subsequent divorce
- child support payments were fixed at a quarter of wages or salary for one child, a third for two, and 50–60 per cent for three or more children
- mothers with six children were to receive cash payments of 2000 roubles a year – a really substantial amount – for five years, with additional payments for each child up to the eleventh.

Around the same time, laws were passed against prostitution and homosexuality, and having illegitimate children was stigmatised.

The birth rate did rise from under 25 per 1000 in 1935 to almost 31 per 1000 in 1940. Newspapers reported prosecutions of doctors for performing abortions and some women were imprisoned for having abortions, although the punishment for women in these circumstances was supposed to be public contempt, rather than prosecution.

SOURCE 18.6 A poster with the slogan 'The wide development of a network of crèches, kindergartens, canteens and laundries will ensure the participation of women in socialist reconstruction'

SOURCE 18.5 Women expressing milk at a factory. Their babies were given the milk while the mothers worked in the factory

By the early 1930s, Soviet doctors were performing 1.5 million abortions a year. Abortion rates were highest in the cities. Statistics, especially for illegal abortions, are notoriously unreliable, but in *Popular Opinion in Stalin's Russia: Terror, Propaganda and Dissent 1939–41*, (1997, p. 65) S. Davies provides some figures for Leningrad

Year	Births (per thousand of population)	Abortions (per thousand of population)
1930	21.3	33.9
1931	21.3	36.3
1932	20.7	34.0
1933	17.0	36.7
1934	15.9	42.0

Divorce declined in Leningrad, but so too did marriage and by 1939 the marriage/divorce ratio was not much better than in 1934 – about 3.5 marriages for every divorce. Because of the high rate of desertion by husbands, many women ended up as the sole breadwinner for families which often consisted of a mother, one or two children, and the irreplaceable *babushka* (grandmother) who ran the household. At all levels of society, though most notably at its lower levels, it was women who bore the brunt of the many problems of everyday life in the USSR. However research, including interviews with refugees carried out by Harvard University's Russian Research Center, shows that the family was resilient and the state's change of attitude to the family in the middle of the 1930s was positively received.

TALKING POINT

A draft of the Family Code was published for public discussion. In the debate on abortion in the USSR there was nothing about the foetus's 'right to life' and little on women's right to control their own bodies (unlike the debate in the USA in the late twentieth century). The big issue was whether women whose material circumstances were very poor should be allowed to have abortions. The shortage of urban housing, which forced families into miserably confined spaces, and the high rate of desertion by husbands were major factors in this. While almost all participants in the discussion agreed that access to abortion should be restricted, total prohibition was deeply unpopular with urban women. How important do you think abortion on demand is to women's rights?

Juvenile crime was perceived as an increasing problem in the first half of the 1930s. For juvenile offenders, the law was relatively mild and rehabilitation was preferred. In 1935, Voroshilov, a member of the Politburo, signalled a change when he urged that the NKVD should be instructed to clear Moscow immediately not only of homeless adolescents but also of delinquents out of parental control. 'I don't understand why we don't shoot these scoundrels,' he concluded. A Politburo decree in April 1935 allowed just that. It made violent crimes committed by juveniles from twelve years of age punishable in the same way as those committed by adults, though the archives show no examples of actual executions of adolescent hooligans. This was followed by a law 'on the liquidation of child homelessness and lack of supervision', which increased NKVD involvement in attempting to get children off the streets and into appropriate institutions. Parents could be fined for the hooliganism of their children and risked having them taken away and placed in orphanages where parents would have to pay for their maintenance.

SOURCE 18.7   S. Fitzpatrick, *The Russian Revolution 1917–1932*, 1994, p. 151

The old-style liberated woman, assertively independent and ideologically committed on issues like abortion, was no longer in favour. The new message was that the family came first, despite the growing numbers of women who were receiving education and entering professional careers. No achievement could be greater than that of the successful wife and mother. In a campaign inconceivable in the 1920s, wives of members of the new Soviet élite were directed into voluntary community activities that bore a strong resemblance to the upper-class charitable work that Russian socialist and even liberal feminists had always despised. At a 'national meeting for wives' in 1936, the wives of industrial managers and engineers described their successes in cleaning up factory kitchens, hanging curtains in the workers' hostels, advising the working girls on personal hygiene and how to keep out of trouble, and so on.

SOURCE 18.8   S. Kotkin, *Magnetic Mountain: Stalinism as a Civilisation*, 1995, p. 179

In the Magnitogorsk newspaper in May 1936 abortion was pronounced 'an evil holdover from the order whereby an individual lived according to narrow, personal interests and not in the interests of the collective. In our life there is no such gap between personal and collective life. For us it seems that even such ultimate questions as the family and the birth of children are transformed from personal to social issues.' This was a long way from the 'abolition of the family as the basic cell of society' announced in the Magnitogorsk newspaper back in 1930.

SOURCE 18.9   A statement in the Soviet press in 1934, quoted in N. Timasheff, *The Great Retreat: The Growth and Decline of Communism in Russia*, 1946

There are people who dare to assert that the Revolution destroys the family; this is entirely wrong: the family is an especially important phase of social relations in socialist society . . . One of the basic rules of Communist morals is that of strengthening the family . . . The right to divorce is not a right to sexual laxity. A poor husband and father cannot be a good citizen. People who abuse the freedom of divorce should be punished.

SOURCE 18.10   *Pravda*, 28 May 1936

When we talk of strengthening the Soviet family we mean the fight against the wrong attitudes towards marriage, women and children. Free love and a disorderly sex life have nothing in common with Socialist principles or the normal behaviour of a Soviet citizen . . . The outstanding citizens of our country, the best of Soviet youth, are almost always devoted to their families.

SOURCE 18.11   Extracts from letters sent to *Rabonitsa*, a women's magazine, in 1936. These letters would have been carefully selected for publication

From Tatanya Koval of the Lubchenko collective farm, Kiev district
I can't find the words to express my gratitude to the Party and the Government, to dear comrade Stalin for his care of us women . . . My children are my joy. I've never had an abortion, and I'm not going to have any. I've borne children and I shall go on bearing them.

From Nina Ershova, Moscow
If a mother has seven children one has to be sent to school, another to the kindergarten, the third to a crèche; and then in the evening Mother has to collect them all, give them supper, look after their clothes, put them to bed . . . Well, then that mother . . . won't have a single minute left to herself. This surely means that women will be unable to take part in public life, unable to work.

This new law undoubtedly has much in its favour, but it is still too early to talk of prohibiting abortion. We must first develop our communal restaurants so that a woman does not have to bother about dinners, suppers and breakfast . . . We must have more and better crèches and kindergartens, more laundries.

ACTIVITY

Study Sources 18.7–18.11.

1 What change do these sources suggest is taking place in attitudes to the family?
2 How do Sources 18.8–18.11 show how the Soviet regime was managing this change in attitudes?
3 Which letter writer in Source 18.11 is closest to the original revolutionary view about abortion and the role of women in society?

FAMILY LOYALTY OR CONSCIENCE OF THE NATION?
THE CASE OF PAVLIK MOROZOV

The real Pavlik

In a trial in 1932, thirteen-year-old Pavlik testified that his father, a poor peasant who had become chairman of the village soviet, had taken property confiscated from the kulaks. Pavlik's furious grandfather and cousin later stabbed him and his younger brother to death in the woods.

The legend of Pavlik

Pavlik's father secretly helped local kulaks by selling them false documents. In court Pavlik denounced him as a traitor. When Pavlik later denounced kulaks in the village for hiding and spoiling their grain, some of them ambushed him and killed him in the woods. They received the death sentence.

His symbolic importance

The legendary Pavlik was celebrated in song, statue and story. Those who were young in the 1930s recall being told at Pioneer and Komsomol meetings that it was their duty to report all suspicious events, following Pavlik's example.

Pavlik embodied the 'good' Soviet citizen who was 'above all, a member of the Soviet community, and only incidentally of the family group with which he could only identify himself if the group was in tune with the whole Soviet group. In rejecting his family and in denouncing his father, Pavlik Morozov was simply turning towards the group of which he was fundamentally a member. With the years, his story assumed a more definite content. More than towards the group, it was towards the Father of the group that he turned, towards Stalin ... Is it surprising that in the years of the purges his example was followed by countless children? ... the constantly presented influence of this example must not be underestimated for it had gradually placed the whole of society under Stalin's parental authority.' (Helene Carrère D'Encause, *Stalin: Order Through Terror*, 1981, pages 76–77)

TALKING POINT

1 How do you explain the differences between the real and the legendary Pavlik?
2 It has been argued that in the 1930s, in some respects, families drew closer for self-protection. 'We talked freely only in our own family. In difficult times we came together' (Harvard Project quoted in S. Fitzpatrick, *Everyday Stalinism*, 1999, page 140). Do you think this was more likely to happen than children following Pavlik's example?

C What was the impact of Socialist Realism in the arts?

FOCUS ROUTE

Make notes on what happened in the 1930s in the following areas:

• painting
• music
• literature
• cinema.

■ 18C Key events in the arts, 1931–38

1931	Stalin makes a speech emphasising the value of the tsarist-educated intelligentsia.
1932	A party resolution is passed abolishing aggressive and competing proletarian organisations. RAPP is abolished and the Union of Composers and the Union of Architects are formed.
1933	Union of Writers formed. Zhdanov outlines the doctrine of 'Socialist Realism'.
1934	Architectural competition to design the 'Palace of Soviets' is won by a plan to build a 300-metre tower (taller than the Empire State Building) topped by a 100-metre statue of Lenin (taller than the Statue of Liberty). (It is never built.)
1936	Stalin criticises Shostakovich's opera *Lady Macbeth of Mtsensk*. The party issues decrees against 'formalism' in architecture and painting. (Formalism is defined as 'non-accessible, non-realistic, non-socialist'.)
1937–39	Purges hit the arts: around 1500 writers are killed, including the poet Mandelstam, the theatre director Meyerhold and the short story writer Babel.
1938	Eisenstein makes the film *Alexander Nevsky* which is in tune with growing nationalism and concern about impending war.

In the middle of 1931, Stalin proclaimed the Cultural Revolution at an end. A decree of April 1932 abolished all proletarian artistic and literary organisations and ordered all artists to come together in a single union. There was a dramatic reversal of the official attitude to the intelligentsia. Avant-garde artists were excluded from the mainstream of artistic life. The leading realist artists and sculptors became very successful, guided down the path of Socialist Realism.

SOURCE 18.12 *Industrial Worker and Collective Farm Girl*, a sculpture by Vera Mukhina exhibited at the Paris Fair in 1937

What was Socialist Realism?

Although the origins of 'Socialist Realism' lay with Lenin's view that art and literature must educate the workers in the spirit of Communism, the term appears for the first time in 1932. In 1934, the newly founded Union of Writers proclaimed Socialist Realism to be the 'definitive Soviet artistic method'. Stalin liked realism – art which could be easily understood by the masses and which told a story. It would be a good vehicle for propaganda. Zhdanov said that 'Soviet literature must be able to show our heroes, must be able to glimpse our tomorrow.' Socialist Realism meant seeing life as it was becoming and ought to be, rather than as it was. Its subjects were men and women, inspired by the ideals of socialism, building the glowing future.

Art

From the beginning of the 1930s, Soviet paintings swarmed with tractors, threshing machines and combine harvesters or else peasants beaming out of scenes with tables groaning with food. It was at the height of the purges that Vera Mukhina's famous *Industrial Worker and Collective Farm Girl* (Source 18.12) was sculpted – a massive image of the Soviet people striding into a joyful future.

SOURCE 18.13 *A Collective Farm Feast*, a painting by Alesandr Gerasimov, 1937. Paintings like these were intended to reflect 'the "typical" or exceptional characteristics of the new life: i.e. the Party's concern for the labourers, which transformed inordinately heavy work into a joyful festival. Reality was very different. But such paintings were given the name in the USSR not of surrealism but of socialist realism' (I. Golomstock, *Totalitarian Art*, 1990)

■ 18D Some other titles of Socialist Realist art

Expulsion of the Kulaks (1931)
Construction of a Railway Bridge in Armenia (1933)
In the Struggle for Fuel and Metal (1933), a poster
Stakhanovites in a Box at the Bolshoi Theatre (1937)
The Factory Party Committee (1937)
Collective Farmers Greeting a Tank (1937)
Stalin and Voroshilov in the Kremlin (1938)

Anna Akhmatova (1888–1966)
Akhmatova is considered to be one of the greatest poets in Russian history. Much of her work was banned in the 1920s for being bourgeois and individualistic and she stopped writing for publication in the 1930s. It was not until after Stalin's death in 1953 that her work was published again in the Soviet Union.

The content of pictures was more tightly controlled. Artists were now given quite detailed guidelines when they were commissioned to produce specific works on a given subject. There were almost no pictures of domestic and family scenes. 'To judge from art alone Soviet man passed his entire existence in the factories, on the fields of collective farms, at party meetings and demonstrations, or surrounded by the marble of the Moscow metro!' (I. Golomstock, *Totalitarian Art*, 1990, page 193). Museum directors and their staffs received bonuses if they exceeded their targets for visitors – a big incentive to organise mass visits to their exhibitions. This ensured that more people were exposed to the message of Socialist Realism.

Music

Socialist Realism extended to music, too. Music was to be joyous and positive. Symphonies should be in a major key. Folk songs and dances and 'songs in praise of the happy life of onward-marching Soviet Man' were the acceptable sounds of music. Shostakovich's new opera *Lady Macbeth of Mtsensk* was attended by Stalin. He did not like it. It was criticised in *Pravda* in an article entitled 'Muddle instead of Music' and banned. Shostakovich never composed another opera.

Literature

By mid-1932, Stalin decided that the RAPP (Russian Association of Proletarian Writers) had served its purpose: it was criticised as being too narrow and was abolished. It was replaced by the Union of Soviet Writers which included non-proletarian and non-party writers and had Maxim Gorky (see page 301), himself a non-party member, as its first head. The degree of state control, however, was just as strong and Socialist Realism was proclaimed to be the basic principle of literary creation. In this climate, some great writers like Isaac Babel, Boris Pasternak and the poet Anna Akhmatova practised 'the genre of silence' and gave up serious writing altogether. According to Robert Service, 'No great work of literature was published in the 1930s and all artistic figures went in fear of their lives' (*A History of Twentieth-Century Russia*, 1997, page 248).

What were Socialist Realist novels like?

For Stalin, writers were the 'engineers of human souls', and Socialist Realism was 'the guiding principle': 'Literature should not be a single step away from the practical affairs of socialist construction.' From late 1929, many literary organisations began to organise writers into brigades and sent them to construction sites, kolkhozes and factories. Simple, direct language and cheap mass editions were demanded to make books accessible to a newly literate readership. There was nothing subtle about the titles: *Cement*, *The Driving Axle*, *How the Steel was Tempered*, and *The Great Conveyor Belt*.

Case study: Isaak Brodsky (1884–1939)

Brodsky first came to notice when his picture of Lenin won the painting section of a competition held in Petrograd. Lenin was to remain Brodsky's main subject and his style that of the documentary photograph. His pictures, such as *Lenin's Speech at a Workers' Meeting*, portray both Lenin and the masses – two idealised elements of the USSR. The famous *Lenin at Smolny* shows Lenin absorbed in his work and his simple lifestyle despite the Civil War raging outside.

Brodsky's reputation grew in the 1920s but his style – 'too photographic' – fell out of favour during the Cultural Revolution. He was expelled from the Association of Proletarian Artists. By 1932, the Cultural Revolution was over and Brodsky was one of Stalin's favourite artists. His picture of Lenin in front of the Kremlin was the basis for the massive May Day decorations in 1932, in which Lenin and Stalin were paired as they were to be so often in the 1930s. Brodsky slavishly declared, 'A painting must be living and comprehensible. I have remembered these words of Comrade Stalin for ever.' In 1934, Brodsky was made director of the All Russian Academy of Arts and became the first artist to be awarded the Order of Lenin. He died in 1939.

SOURCE 18.16 *Lenin's Speech at a Workers' Meeting at the Putilov Factory in May 1917* by Isaak Brodsky, 1929

SOURCE 18.17 *Lenin in Smolny* by Isaak Brodsky

ACTIVITY

1 Why was Meyerhold so criticised?
2 How well do Brodsky's paintings and methods illustrate Socialist Realism?
3 What do the experiences of Brodsky, Gorky and Meyerhold tell us about the relationship between artists and the Bolsheviks?

Case study: Maxim Gorky (pen name of A. M. Peshkov; 1868–1936)

Gorky's novels and plays gave him an international reputation and earnings which were large enough to be one of the Bolsheviks' main sources of income before 1917, although he was never actually a member of the party. The pseudonym he adopted means 'bitter' and, sent out to work at the age of eight, he knew more about the seamy side of life than almost any other Russian author. He was a humane and democratic socialist. He was critical of Lenin's seizure of power in 1917 and deeply distressed by the terror during the Civil War. The destruction appalled him and he helped to preserve both works of art and artists and intellectuals in the aftermath of the revolution. He became increasingly disillusioned with the Bolsheviks: even as early as the beginning of 1918 he wrote, 'It is clear Russia is heading for a new and even more savage autocracy.' Gorky left the country in 1921.

Stalin was desperately anxious for Gorky to return so that he could demonstrate that the most celebrated living Russian author was an admirer of the system. Gorky returned for a visit in 1928 when his sixtieth birthday was celebrated and he became a permanent resident in 1931. In 1934, he was made the first president of the Soviet Writers' Union. Former colleagues who had criticised the Bolsheviks felt he had sold out. He was flattered on a grand scale – the main street of Moscow was renamed after him, as was his birthplace Nizhny Novgorod – but he was never to be allowed to leave the Soviet Union again. By the end of his life, he regarded himself as under house arrest.

Although Gorky's health had been deteriorating, the circumstances and timing of his death have been regarded with suspicion. He died in June 1936 while receiving medical treatment. This was very convenient for Stalin, coming two months before the first show trial which Gorky was bound to have criticised openly. At his show trial in 1938 Yagoda, who was head of the NKVD in 1936, confessed to having ordered Gorky's death.

SOURCE 18.18   Gorky (left) with Stalin

In his notebooks, found after his death, Gorky compared Stalin to 'a monstrous flea which propaganda and the hypnosis of fear had enlarged to incredible proportions'. Stalin, though, led the mourners at his funeral and Gorky's ashes were placed in a niche in the Kremlin wall.

D What happened in education after the Cultural Revolution?

In the middle of 1931, the Cultural Revolution came to an end. A Central Committee resolution criticised the project method and the 'withering away of the school'. Compare the extract in Source 18.19 with Shulgin's ideas (page 290).

Stalin was outraged by the state of schools in 1931. The Komsomol's 'Cultural Army' had done enormous damage to local education authorities and wreaked havoc in the schools. Stalin needed educated workers to work in skilled jobs and be able to take advantage of the higher education and training schemes that were now on offer. The Central Committee ordered a fundamental shift in educational policy. The core recommendation was that the teaching of physics, chemistry and mathematics in particular 'must be based on strictly delineated and carefully worked out programmes and study plans', and that classes should be organised on a firm timetable. Examinations, homework, textbooks and rote learning reappeared. Discipline was emphasised and the authority of parents and teachers over pupils was supported; in the late 1930s school uniforms reappeared.

SOURCE 18.19   Central Committee resolution of 25 August 1931

[The school's basic failing is that it] does not give a sufficient amount of general knowledge, and does not adequately solve the problem of training fully literate persons with a good grasp of the bases of sciences (physics, chemistry, mathematics, native language, geography and so on) for entrance to the technicums and higher schools.

FOCUS ROUTE

Make notes answering the following questions:

1 Did the Cultural Revolution have any lasting impact?
2 How far was radical change replaced by conservatism?
3 What was the impact of the changes on one subject: history?

In universities, there was also a return to something much more like the situation before the revolution. Entrance to university was based more on academic success than on class or political criteria. Examinations, degrees and academic titles were restored.

History, nationalism and education

'I like your book immensely,' wrote Lenin in the preface to M. N. Pokrovsky's *Brief History of Russia*. Published in 1920, it became *the* Soviet school text book. Pokrovsky was a historian who had been a Bolshevik since 1915 and became Deputy Commissar for Education. It was a straightforward Marxist work, which saw the whole of Russian history in terms of class struggle and included long descriptions of the brutal beatings of serfs by their owners and the dreadful working and living conditions of industrial workers. Economic forces drove history onwards, leading inevitably to socialism. Tsars and generals were barely mentioned, as Pokrovsky believed personality mattered very little in history.

The two most famous first-hand Bolshevik accounts of the revolution, John Reed's *Ten Days that Shook the World* (1919) and Trotsky's *History of the Russian Revolution*, presented the revolution as a popular rising and emphasised the role of the proletariat rather than the party in making the revolution. Lenin wrote in the foreword to Reed's book that he wanted to see millions of copies published in all languages – Stalin was much less keen, perhaps because he was not mentioned, and no Russian editions were published between 1930 and 1956.

Soon after the revolution, history was banished as a school subject because it was seen as irrelevant to contemporary life and had been used under the tsars to develop patriotism and reinforce the values of the ruling class. In the Cultural Revolution one notable historian, Professor Tarle, a non-Marxist historian and Russian patriot, who had written about Peter the Great and Ivan the Terrible, was attacked for glorifying the idea of monarchy and imprisoned. Professors could be identified as bourgeois specialists, too.

For Stalin, the Cultural Revolution was part of the great transformation of the USSR, but it did not reflect his ideas on history. By 1934, Pokrovsky had come under attack for reducing history to an abstract record of class conflict without names, dates, heroes or stirring emotions. Historians were now required to write about the imperial past in positive terms and Ivan the Terrible and Peter the Great, who expanded that empire, were looked on particularly favourably by Stalin. The term *rodina* (motherland), despised by the old Bolshevik internationalists, came back into common use. In May 1934, a decree on history teaching was issued declaring that the old ways must be replaced with 'mandatory consolidation in pupils' memories of important historical events, historical personages and chronological dates'. History faculties were restored in the universities of Moscow and Leningrad. Professor Tarle was released from prison to reoccupy his university chair in Moscow. In the new school history texts, which appeared in 1937, the years 1917–37 are 'presented as the finale of embattled Russia's long march through history from humble beginnings in the tenth century to world leadership and greatness under Lenin–Stalin' (R. C. Tucker, *Stalin in Power: The Revolution from Above, 1928–1941*, 1992, page 53). The past and its interpretation was important to Stalin. In Soviet history books, he emerged as one of the main architects of the revolution, the close companion and adviser to Lenin, and a hero of the Civil War.

TALKING POINT

What are the advantages and disadvantages of schools following a national curriculum in history and other subjects?

ACTIVITY

1 How did interpretations of history change between the 1920s and the mid-1930s?
2 How did individual historians fare?
3 Did this add up to a 'Great Retreat' in history?

E Soviet society at the end of the 1930s: had 'a new type of man' been created?

Socialist construction involved not only building the structures of the socialist state but also creating the right sort of citizens to live in it. New Soviet Man would embody the morality, values and characteristics that a good Soviet citizen should possess. He would be a willing servant of the state with the right attitudes, far removed from the illiterate, uneducated peasant who exemplified the backwardness which had cursed the USSR in the past. New man was part of new modern industrial society, above all a proletarian with a sense of social responsibility and moral virtue. Creating citizens like this was the objective of the proletarianisation that was such an important part of the Cultural Revolution of 1929–31 (see page 288). The changes were aimed mainly at the young through the education system and the Komsomol youth organisation but all sorts of pressures were also brought to bear on adult workers in order to make them conform (see Chart 18E on page 304).

Pavel Korchagin, the hero of Nikolai Ostrovsky's novel *How the Steel was Tempered* (see page 298), is the archetypal new man who puts the interests of his comrades, the Bolsheviks and the revolution before himself – an example of self-sacrifice and moral virtue. Soviet writers from the mid-1920s onwards presented to the public new Soviet heroes who overcame hardship and obstacles in the cause of the construction of the new socialist society.

The idea that people could be programmed in this way drew support from the spurious theories of the Soviet scientist Trofim Lysenko, who believed that human beings could acquire characteristics that could be passed on from one generation to the next. Stalin was very much influenced by Lysenko's thinking and came to believe that socialist characteristics could be passed on if people were taught the right habits and attitudes. It was this notion of socialist programming that appalled writers such as George Orwell and Aldous Huxley, who in their books *1984* and *Brave New World* put the case against totalitarianism and its apparent need to crush individuality and the human spirit.

THE FORERUNNER OF ORWELL AND HUXLEY

Yergeny Zamyatin is not as well known in the West as Orwell and Huxley but his novel *We*, written in 1924, was the forerunner of their books. In this Dystopia (a nightmare Utopia) the people are robot-like, known by numbers and have lives programmed in every detail. The story of D503's 'pitiful struggle against the ruler – the bald Benefactor – is a plea for the right of the individual to live his life without oppressive interference from the state'. The book was banned in the USSR for sixty years. Robert Service in *A History of Twentieth Century Russia*, page 139.

Was a new type of man produced in Magnitogorsk?

If the new man were to be created, surely it would be at a place like Magnitogorsk where a great steel plant and a town of 150,000 people were created from nothing between 1929 and 1939? Stephen Kotkin, in his book *Magnetic Mountain: Stalinism as a Civilisation* (1995), has produced a remarkable study of the town, and what follows is based on his research. The aim at Magnitogorsk was to build not only an industrial giant but also a socialist paradise (see Chart 18E).

FOCUS ROUTE

Make notes on the forces trying to create the new man in Magnitogorsk and the evidence that the creation of a new man still had some way to go. What conclusion would you reach – had a new type of man been created?

Housing
In Magnitogorsk housing was not just for shelter; it was also designed to mould people. It was largely communal, and in every barracks there was a 'Red corner' with the barracks wall newspaper, shock-worker banners and pictures of Lenin and Stalin. It was intended to be a cultural training ground in which the dwellers could read, listen to lectures, watch films and discuss political issues.

Education
Virtually everyone in Magnitogorsk, even those who worked full time, attended some form of schooling, which reinforced the socialisation and politicisation being experienced at work. The school curriculum combined basic education with technical subjects and 'the spirit of socialism'. Compulsory courses in Marxism-Leninism began at an early age.

Public holidays
These took place on the anniversary of the October Revolution and on 1 May. The May Day parade was a highly organised procession, based on people's different places of work, with numerous floats, portraits of the leaders and Communist slogans.

Speaking Bolshevik
In Magnitogorsk you identified yourself as a 'Soviet worker' and learned to say the right things in the right way. The 'Dear Marfa!' letter (Source 12.23 on page 189) is a classic example. Kotkin found that workers in Magnitogorsk still spoke in the same way as they had in the 1930s, fifty years later.

Shock workers and socialist competition
An individual's work history recorded his or her profession, party status, record on absenteeism, study or course attendance, production achievements and how often their equipment broke down. The work histories of the shock worker, the award winner, and those who succeeded in socialist competition were made public and used to decide the distribution of material rewards.

Entertainment
More than 600,000 seats a year were sold at the cinema in Magnitogorsk: it was easily the most popular form of entertainment and a key mechanism for spreading socialist values. All Soviet films shown there carried forceful political messages. Foreign films were for pure entertainment, but no recognisably anti-socialist or overtly pro-capitalist popular culture was permitted. Newsreels were shown before and after every film. The inhabitants of Magnitogorsk read avidly: 40,000 books were sold in January 1936 and 10,000 people held library cards. Nikolai Ostrovsky's novel How the Steel was Tempered was the most frequently borrowed book from the Magnitogorsk libraries.

Censorship
'Censors were quintessential "social engineers", with the media serving as their instruments – or weapons, as Lenin wrote – in the battle to construct a Communist society. The instructional messages emanating from reading matter, radio, and, especially, films were paralleled by training received in schools' (S. Kotkin, Magnetic Mountain: Stalinism as a Civilisation, 1995)

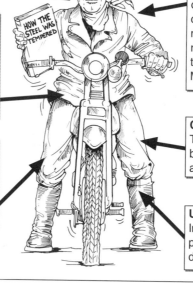

Campaigns to improve behaviour
There were campaigns to improve men's behaviour towards women and to discourage alcohol consumption.

Use of agitators
In 1936, 214 agitators were employed to discuss political issues and present interpretations of domestic and international events.

EVIDENCE THAT THE CREATION OF NEW SOVIET MAN STILL HAD SOME WAY TO GO

Housing
Private housing was never entirely eliminated, even in 1938. Privately owned mud huts (which had no 'Red corners') made up 17.5 per cent of the living space in Magnitogorsk. In the latter half of the 1930s, there was a shift away from barracks to providing apartments for families, as part of the pro-family policies then being adopted.

Preferences in entertainment
Next to the cinema, the most popular entertainment was performances of French wrestling (scripted wrestling). Attempts were made to use the circus at Magnitogorsk as a vehicle for propaganda about the Five-Year Plans and socialist construction but such attempts failed miserably – in Beyond the Urals (1942) John Scott describes such attempts as 'ludicrous'.

Limited success in campaigns to improve behaviour
The campaigns to improve men's behaviour towards women and to discourage alcohol consumption had very limited success.

Opposition to Stakhanovites
The case of the Magnitogorsk Stakhanovite (see page 192) shows the resentment that could be aroused. One worker remarked that Stakhanovism was an attempt to enslave the working class – he was arrested and sentenced to forced labour. Anti-Stakhanovite jokes show this resentment was felt all over the country.

The leverage that workers had
There was a perpetual labour shortage. Managers, desperate to meet their targets, could not afford to sack workers for breaking the rules on absenteeism and so on, and were prepared to take on workers sacked elsewhere. As we have seen, Magnitogorsk was a revolving door.

What was the national picture?

Magnitogorsk is just one example of the massive change that took place in the USSR in the 1930s. The regime was committed to economic, social and cultural transformation. In the First Five-Year Plan, there was massive social dislocation as ten million peasants changed occupations and moved into the towns.

By 1939, the combination of the technical education opportunities granted by the Cultural Revolution and the opportunities for upward mobility created as a result of rapid industrialisation and the purges meant that a working class/peasant governing élite had been virtually achieved. Khrushchev, Brezhnev and Kosygin, who became key Soviet leaders in the 1950s, 1960s and 1970s, were among the 150,000 workers and Communists entering higher education during the First Five-Year Plan.

But was the mass of the people transformed? The attitude of the people to the regime is one way of assessing this. The historian John Barber estimated that one-fifth of all workers enthusiastically supported the regime and its politics, while another minority opposed, although not overtly. This left the great mass of workers, who were neither supporters nor opponents but nonetheless more or less 'accepted' the regime for its social welfare policies. NKVD soundings of popular opinion in the 1930s indicate that the regime was relatively, though not desperately, unpopular in Russian towns but much more unpopular in the villages, especially in the first half of the 1930s. The post-NEP situation was compared unfavourably with the NEP and Stalin was compared unfavourably with Lenin, mainly because living standards had fallen. The arbitrary nature of terror and rewards encouraged fatalism and passivity in the population. The historian Sheila Fitzpatrick in her book *Everyday Stalinism* (1999) has found that 'a degree of scepticism, even a refusal to take the regime's most serious pronouncements fully seriously, was the norm'. *Homo Sovieticus*, who emerges in the 1930s, may or may not be a new man, but he had to be a survivor and one 'whose most developed skill involved the hunting and gathering of scarce goods in an urban environment'.

ACTIVITY

Make a presentation to the rest of the class. Your presentation will cover changes in Soviet culture and society in the 1920s and 1930s. This can be done in groups or individually. If done in groups, it is important that each individual has a chance to participate so that the teacher can assess his or her performance.

1 In a group, divide up the topics. Some topics are bigger than others, so two students might cover women and the family, one education, and so on.
2 Subdivide topics for individual presentations, e.g. the arts could be divided into painting, street theatre and agit-prop, literature, film and music. Students could research and report on individuals such as Malevich, Shostakovich and Mayakovsky.

WAS THERE A 'GREAT RETREAT'?

Trotsky denounced Stalin as the leader of a new privileged class and saw this as part of Stalin's betrayal of the revolution. The 1930s were a time of great shortage so access to special food rations and other scarce goods at low prices in special élite stores, together with access to better services and housing, was at the heart of privilege.

Does this inequality, combined with the change by the middle of the 1930s to more conservative policies on family values, divorce, abortion, education and the arts which we have already noticed, signify a retreat? Historians have debated this issue. Some, like Sheila Fitzpatrick, argue that there was a retreat, contrasting the revolutionary spirit of the Civil War and Cultural Revolution with the mid-1930s. They point to:

- the acceptance of hierarchy and social privilege
- respect for authority and tradition
- the return to traditional values in education, the family and the arts.

Historians who challenge this interpretation, like Stephen Kotkin and Ewan Mawdsley, argue that the creation of the new working class and the new intelligentsia meant that:

- there was no retreat on private ownership of land and the means of production, or on hiring labour
- the rest of the world saw Communist Russia as still distinctly anti-capitalist
- Stalinist culture may have embraced many of the traditions of nineteenth-century Russian realism but the content was 'modern': it was promoted to achieve objectives which the regime chose to stress – economic activity, the socialist utopia, national defence and adulation of the leader. It reflected a changing and advancing rather than a retreating society.

KEY POINTS FROM CHAPTER 18 Culture and society in a decade of turmoil

1 The Cultural Revolution of 1928–31 coincided with industrialisation and collectivisation. It saw a return to the class struggle of the Civil War.
2 The Komsomols were particularly active in enforcing the Cultural Revolution in education and art and intensifying the attack on religion.
3 After the Cultural Revolution there was a return to traditional values in many areas of Soviet society. This has been called the Great Retreat.
4 Abortion was outlawed and divorce was made harder after the introduction of the 1936 Family Code, which emphasised the value of family life.
5 In education, discipline, exams and traditional procedures were brought back.
6 Socialist Realism was the guiding principle for all artists from 1932 onwards.
7 Art was even more tightly controlled than it had been in the 1920s. Artists rose, like Brodsky, or fell, like Meyerhold, depending on how closely they followed the dictates of Socialist Realism.
8 Great writers like Pasternak were silent; lesser ones produced novels about the Five-Year Plans.
9 The Soviets were trying to produce a new type of man.
10 Their success was very limited. In spite of Stalin's terror, the Soviet people were survivors and remained sceptical.
11 There has been a debate among historians about whether there was a Great Retreat or not.

8

Conclusion

19

Was Stalinism Lenin's baby?

CHAPTER OVERVIEW

GLASNOST
Russian word for openness associated with Mikhail Gorbachev's liberalising policies in the late 1980s characterised by a relaxation of censorship, opening of Soviet archives, and willingness to examine critically and in public what took place during the Stalin years of power.

The period from the end of the 1930s through to Stalin's death in 1953 is called 'high Stalinism'. It has certain defining features and historians have suggested various explanations for why it developed. One of the main areas of debate is the extent to which the Stalinist state was the creation of Lenin – Lenin's baby. Some historians see Stalin as the natural heir of Lenin, others see a break between the two regimes, believing that Stalin changed the course of Communist history for the worse. This has been a significant historical debate because it has influenced events and policy in Russia in the *GLASNOST* and post-Soviet eras.

A How can we explain Stalinism? (pp. 307–309)

B Did Lenin beget Stalinism? (pp. 310–313)

C Why is this historiographical debate relevant today? (pp. 314–315)

D A Red tsar? (pp. 316–317)

FOCUS ROUTE

Make notes on the main features of Stalinism.

A How can we explain Stalinism?

'High Stalinism' is the name given to the period from the late 1930s through to Stalin's death in 1953. In this period, Stalinism was at its height, with the cult of the personality in full flow, Stalin's dominance assured by the purges and the command economy in full operation. It can be defined by listing its main characteristics or features.

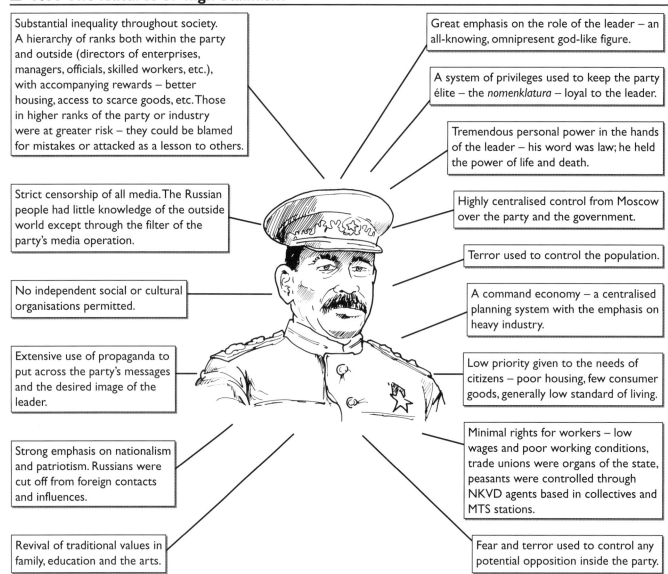

Substantial inequality throughout society. A hierarchy of ranks both within the party and outside (directors of enterprises, managers, officials, skilled workers, etc.), with accompanying rewards – better housing, access to scarce goods, etc. Those in higher ranks of the party or industry were at greater risk – they could be blamed for mistakes or attacked as a lesson to others.

Strict censorship of all media. The Russian people had little knowledge of the outside world except through the filter of the party's media operation.

No independent social or cultural organisations permitted.

Extensive use of propaganda to put across the party's messages and the desired image of the leader.

Strong emphasis on nationalism and patriotism. Russians were cut off from foreign contacts and influences.

Revival of traditional values in family, education and the arts.

Great emphasis on the role of the leader – an all-knowing, omnipresent god-like figure.

A system of privileges used to keep the party élite – the *nomenklatura* – loyal to the leader.

Tremendous personal power in the hands of the leader – his word was law; he held the power of life and death.

Highly centralised control from Moscow over the party and the government.

Terror used to control the population.

A command economy – a centralised planning system with the emphasis on heavy industry.

Low priority given to the needs of citizens – poor housing, few consumer goods, generally low standard of living.

Minimal rights for workers – low wages and poor working conditions, trade unions were organs of the state, peasants were controlled through NKVD agents based in collectives and MTS stations.

Fear and terror used to control any potential opposition inside the party.

What explanations have been put forward for the Stalinist dictatorship?

Stalinism in the 1930s seems to have little to do with the original aims and ideals of the 1917 revolution – freedom, equality between men and women, democracy and a good lifestyle for all based on sharing and co-operation. Commentators condemn the terror and atrocities committed during the Stalinist dictatorship and claim that Stalin betrayed the revolution and its ideals. So, how can we explain the Stalin dictatorship and the form it took? Some of the main explanations are given below.

1 Stalin's personality

Stalin's desire to dominate and be the hero of the revolution, his love of adulation, his conviction that he knew the right policies to follow and must not be thwarted, his paranoid behaviour and desire to get rid of individuals and groups who stood in his way, his tendency to use violence and terror to crush opposition and pursue his policies – all these traits influenced the system that emerged, particularly the nature of the purges and the use of terror. Stalin's personality is more fully considered on pages 230–238.

2 The circumstances surrounding the revolution and the Civil War

Lenin and a small minority had seized power in October 1917. They had refused to work with other socialist parties and had become isolated. Also, the country was in ruins after the war and there was a chaotic situation rapidly running out of control. To stay in power, to keep a lid on the explosive situation and suppress disorder, the Bolsheviks were ruthless – they launched the Red Terror, set up the Cheka and created an increasingly authoritarian state.

The Civil War also had a profound effect on the Bolshevik Party. It enforced on them military discipline, which demanded party unity above all else and strict obedience. It led to the development of a combative and a siege mentality that made them see enemies and conspiracies everywhere. It was a life-and-death struggle which saw them become hardened, pitiless and intolerant in their dealings with opposition. This mentality continued into the 1930s. The regime was not confident it could hold on to power and still saw enemies all around. Faced with this fear and insecurity, it resorted to terror and violence to resolve its problems. All this fed into Stalinism.

3 Economic reasons – was Stalin necessary?

Alec Nove argues (see page 197) that Soviet Russia was in an economic impasse at the end of the 1920s. It was still a backward country dependent on a peasantry unwilling to support the state's industrialisation and modernisation plans. Also, the anticipated world revolution had failed to materialise, leaving it isolated in the world and without the support of other countries to develop its industry and build socialism. For the majority of Bolsheviks, the only way out of this impasse was the 'socialist offensive' of 1928 and the launching of the rapid industrialisation and collectivisation programme.

Nove believes that once the decision had been taken to industrialise rapidly, it was bound to bring the party into conflict with the people because it would inevitably mean that their living standards would be hit and the party would be unpopular. The party would therefore have to use coercive methods 'on a grand scale' with a strong police state and 'party members fully employed in enforcing these drastic policies' (*Was Stalin Really Necessary?*, 1964, pages 25–26). The socialist offensive would also involve the mass mobilisation of society – the use of wartime allusions and appeals to patriotism, warnings about the dangers of enemies and wreckers within and without, the encouragement of criticism of officials – which was a key feature of Stalinism. In these sorts of circumstance, Nove contends, a leader like Stalin was the one the party wanted because he had the qualities to carry them through this tough period.

4 The nature of the central planning system

The command economy requires the hierarchical organisation of society into ranks and levels with a 'supremo' at the top. With such a complex process to co-ordinate, involving thousands of products and hundreds of economic enterprises, there has to be an authority that issues instructions from the top. These are passed down to people at different levels who have to take decisions about the allocation of scarce supplies and materials. Then instructions are passed down from above to lower levels. Stalin used a system of rewards and wage differentials to encourage people at different levels to do their jobs, develop their skills and keep the workers' production rate up.

5 Russian history

Russia had a history of autocracy, with officials whose duty it was to serve the state and the tsar. State control over the people was normal and the state had played a commanding role in the growth of capitalism and industry in tsarist Russia. There were no habits or traditions of democratic political institutions. People were used to the idea of a strong leader who prevented anarchy and disorder. So Stalin tapped into a strong tradition in the role he adopted as a godlike figure who would provide strong leadership and see the Russian people through a difficult time. He seemed to see himself as a modernising leader in the style of Peter the Great (see page 317).

6 Stalinism was inherent in Leninism

All the apparatus of the Stalinist state – rule by one party, centralised control, central planning, secret police and the use of terror – was in place before Stalin became leader. Stalin used and extended these to their logical conclusion (see pages 310–313 for a fuller discussion).

B Did Lenin beget Stalinism?

There is an important debate about the extent to which Stalinism was a natural continuation of the ideas, policies and institutions of Lenin's regime. We can identify two clear schools of thought amongst historians, as outlined in Chart 19B.

■ 19B Contrasting views of historians

Stalin was the natural heir of Lenin – there is a clear line of continuity from one to the other. Stalin's dictatorship was a logical extension of Lenin's authoritarian and centralised regime. You can find all the key features of Stalinism in the Leninist state.

No! The Stalinist state was very different from the one that would have developed under Lenin if he had lived. Things went wrong for the Soviet Union when Stalin became leader. When he made the Great Turn in 1928 he fundamentally altered the institutions – party, government, economy, education – of Soviet society. He exercised personal control and used terror to a degree that would have been unimaginable under Lenin. No doubt about it – there is a clear break between Lenin and Stalin. Stalin perverted the course of the Communist Revolution.

ACTIVITY

1 Read the short extracts from different historians writing about the continuity between Lenin and Stalin (Sources 19.1–19.6).
2 The line below represents the two extremes in the debate. Decide where on the line the views of each historian should be placed. Some will be at the ends of the line, others will go part-way along the line, closer to one end than the other. Mark the source numbers in the relevant position on your own copy of the line.

Clear break between Leninism and Stalinism |————————| **Continuity between Leninism and Stalinism**

SOURCE 19.1 R. Medvedev, 'The Political Biography of Stalin' in R. C. Tucker (ed.), *Stalinism, Essays in Historical Interpretation* 1977

One could list the various measures carried out by Stalin that were actually a continuation of anti-democratic trends and measures implemented under Lenin, although it could be said that here we presume that Lenin never could have gone so far in this direction. In most respects, however, there is no continuity between Stalinism and Leninism. In pursuing a course aimed at abolishing NEP, in putting through a hasty policy of forced collectivisation, carrying out mass terror against the well-to-do peasants in the countryside and against the so-called bourgeois specialists in the cities, employing mainly administrative rather than economic methods to carry out industrialisation, categorically forbidding any opposition inside or outside of the party, and thus reviving, under other circumstances, the methods of War Communism, in all this, as in so many other ways, Stalin acted, not in line with Lenin's clear instructions, but in defiance of them, especially of Lenin's last writings of 1921–2, where he laid out the path of the construction of the socialist society.

SOURCE 19.2   R. Pipes, *Three Whys of the Russian Revolution*, 1998, pp. 83–84

I believe that Stalin sincerely regarded himself as a disciple of Lenin, a man destined to carry out his agenda to a successful conclusion. With one exception, the killing of fellow Communists – a crime Lenin did not commit – he faithfully implemented Lenin's domestic and foreign programmes. He prevented the party from being riven by factionalism; he liquidated the 'noxious' intelligentsia; he collectivised agriculture, as Lenin had desired; he subjected the Russian economy to a single plan; he industrialised Russia; he built a powerful Red Army . . . and he helped unleash the Second World War, which had been one of Lenin's objectives as well.

SOURCE 19.3   O. Figes, *A People's Tragedy: The Russian Revolution 1891–1924*, 1997, p. 807

On the one hand, it seems clear that the basic elements of the Stalinist regime – the one-party state, the system of terror and the cult of the personality – were all in place by 1924. The party apparatus was for the most part an obedient tool in Stalin's hands. The majority of its provincial bosses had been appointed by Stalin himself . . . On the other hand, there were fundamental differences between Lenin's regime and that of Stalin. Fewer people were murdered from the start. And, despite the ban on factions, the party still made room for comradely debate.

SOURCE 19.4   G. Gill, *Stalinism*, 1990, pp. 62–63

What is important is that these events were not a natural flow-on of earlier developments; they were sharp breaks resulting from conscious decisions by leading political actors. This means that those arguments that see Stalinism as the inevitable product of the 1917 revolution or of Leninism/Bolshevism are mistaken. Both the revolution and the corpus of theory which the Bolsheviks carried with them had elements which were consistent with the Soviet phenomenon (just as they had elements which were totally inconsistent with it). However, it needed the direct intervention on the part of the political actors in introducing the revolution from above and the terror to realise the Stalinist phenomenon in Soviet society.

SOURCE 19.5   I. Deutscher, *The Prophet Unarmed: Trotsky 1921–29*, 1959, pp. 464–65

Trotsky did not perceive the ascendancy of Stalinism as an inevitable result of the Bolshevik monopoly of power. On the contrary, he saw it as the virtual end of the Bolshevik government. We have traced the transitions through which the rule of the single party had become the rule of the single faction and through which Leninism had given way to Stalinism. We have seen that the things that had been implicit in the opening phase of this evolution had become explicit and found an extreme exaggerated expression in the closing phase . . . Only the blind and the deaf could be unaware of the contrast between Stalinism and Leninism. The contrast shows in the field of ideas and in the intellectual climate of Bolshevism even more strongly than in the matters of organisation and discipline.

SOURCE 19.6   R. Service, 'Lenin: Individual and Politics in the October Revolution', *Modern History Review*, September 1990

Lenin was not the Devil incarnate. He genuinely adhered to at least some ideals which even non-socialists can see as having been designed to benefit the mass of humanity. Lenin wanted to bring about not a permanent dictatorship, but a dictatorship of the proletariat which would eventually eradicate all distinctions of social and material conditions and would rely decreasingly upon authoritarian methods. Ultimately Lenin wanted to abolish not only the secret police and the army but the whole state as such. If Lenin was therefore to be miraculously brought back to life from under the glass case in his mausoleum, he would be appalled at the use made of his doctrines by Stalin. Lenin was no political saint. Without him Stalin could not have imposed Stalinism. Institutionally and ideologically, Lenin laid the foundations for a Stalin. But the passage from Leninism to the worse horrors of Stalinism was not smooth and inevitable.

CONTINUITY BETWEEN LENIN AND STALIN

• One-party state
Lenin created the one-party state. He dealt ruthlessly with other socialist parties – Mensheviks and Socialist Revolutionaries – and was intolerant of opposing views. Stalin's control of the one-party state allowed him to crush all those who opposed or criticised him.

• Use of terror
Lenin was ruthless and used terror to achieve his ends. He was a 'class warrior' and waged 'class warfare'. He mercilessly attacked the bourgeoisie, the 'former people'. One of his first actions was to create the Cheka. Stalin likewise pursued 'class warfare' against the kulaks to force through collectivisation. Stalin used the methods he had learnt from Lenin. Lenin had set up labour camps for oppositionists in the early 1920s.

• Centralised and bureaucratic state
Lenin created a highly centralised and authoritarian state. This may in part be due to the circumstances after the revolution, particularly during the Civil War, but he had not dismantled the apparatus of the state in any way before he died. Stalinism is rooted in centralism: he extended the power of the centre to an enormous degree.

Lenin created a bureaucratic state that needed a bureaucrat and administrator to run it. Stalin was just the sort of wily operator required to prevent it collapsing. He revelled in bureaucracy and in running the party and government machine.

• Party and the people
Under Lenin the party became detached from the people. Lenin considered that the workers in the early 1920s were 'uncultured' and ill-educated (the older members of the working class had died in the Civil War or were in the party already). Lenin and the party leadership decided that the party alone knew the right path to follow and that they would have to lead and cajole the people along this path. Once this decision had been taken, dictatorship was ensured. Stalin simply continued this process and took it to its logical conclusion.

• Party democracy and control
Lenin destroyed democracy in the party with the 'ban on factions' in 1921. He used this to end the problem of splits during the crisis of 1921, but it created a situation whereby the party leadership could do what it wanted and dismiss any opposition within the party. Also, most of the new generation of party members in the 'Lenin Enrolment' of 1924–25 were a 'green and callow mass' (Trotsky) who knew little about Marxism and were more inclined to follow orders than take an active part in democratic debate. The Civil War had also encouraged centralisation and military-style discipline within the party. So under Lenin, power was concentrated at the top and this facilitated Stalin's policies in the 1930s.

• Purges
Lenin instigated purges in the party to weed out elements he did not approve of.

• The economy
The economy under Lenin was largely in the hands of the state. Central planning had always been a feature of Bolshevik economic policy. During the NEP, the state controlled key industries and banking. It also regulated agriculture, e.g. by fixing prices. Lenin wanted to increase the power of the state to direct the economy. Stalin did just this.

• Mass mobilisation
Both Lenin and Stalin mobilised the workers to carry out their policies. Lenin did this for the October Revolution and during the Civil War. Stalin mobilised the workers to carry through rapid industrialisation and collectivisation in the early 1930s and again in the Stakhanovite campaign in the mid-1930s.

A CLEAR BREAK BETWEEN LENIN AND STALIN

• Centralised state
Authoritarian, centralised control was forced on Lenin by circumstances after the Revolution; it was not his choice. It is unlikely that he would have extended it to the degree that Stalin did.

• Cult of the personality
Stalin developed the cult of the personality and the idea of the supreme leader, the fount of wisdom in the party. Lenin would have deeply objected to this. This aspect of the Stalinist state was not built on Leninism.

• Purges
The party purges instigated by Lenin were non-violent, involving the withdrawal of party cards. Stalin used terror inside the party, which Lenin was always against. Lenin would never have countenanced the killing of leading Bolsheviks and other party members. This was the result of Stalin's personality and motives – he wanted to crush his enemies, remove all opposition and impose his vision of the future on the Soviet Union.

• Use of terror
Stalin employed terror as part of the fabric of his personality. He had a brutal streak and resorted to terror when threatened or thwarted. Lenin would never have set in motion the mass terror of the 1930s, particularly the mass enforced collectivisation of the peasants.

• Leninism
Lenin always objected to the term Leninism. He regarded himself as a Marxist. He saw Marxist theory as progressive, leading the way to socialism. Stalin developed the cult of Leninism and used it as an ideological orthodoxy to justify his actions.

• National minorities
Lenin wanted the national minorities to stay in the Soviet Union by choice. Stalin wanted to bend them to the will of Moscow, mould them to Russian control and make them adopt a style of Communist life as laid down from the centre. Lenin would not have crushed the national minorities in the way Stalin did.

• Party, government and bureaucracy
Lenin was very worried by the power of the party and the bureaucracy. He originally conceived of the government, the Sovnakom, running the country with the Politburo as a court of appeal for decisions. In practice, the party filled key posts in government and soviets. Lenin wanted to dismantle the stranglehold of the party machine and increase internal democracy but died before this could take place. Stalin reinforced bureaucracy in party and government.

• Peasantry
Lenin had stated clearly that the peasantry should not be coerced into collective farms.

Developing the argument

To a large extent, the debate hinges on the view you take of Lenin. If you see Lenin as a ruthless tyrant who seized power for his own political purposes, who used terror as a matter of course, and imposed his will on the people through an authoritarian one-party state, then you are likely to take the view that Stalinism was the logical extension of Leninism. This is the view taken by anti-Communist historians during the Cold War.

If, however, you take the view that Lenin was forced by circumstances – the Civil War, terrible economic conditions and the failure of world revolution to materialise – to develop a highly centralised state after the revolution then you are likely to see a break between Lenin and Stalin. The Bolsheviks could not have anticipated the problems they would face, they were changed by the Civil War and they became more authoritarian to cope with the situation as it developed. In this view, Lenin, if he had lived, would have allowed a more enlightened state to develop, would have encouraged more democracy in the party and would not have supported forced collectivisation or the purges of the 1930s. This has been described as the 'cuddly' view of Lenin and is more likely to be taken by left-wing historians and by revisionist historians.

In 'The Passage from Leninism to Stalinism' (unpublished lecture, January 1999), Robert Service draws on research from newly opened archives to suggest that Lenin was more ruthless than has sometimes been supposed. He actively encouraged terror to smash his enemies and was a fierce class warrior. We can see this in his attitudes towards the peasants and the Church (see pages 286–287). This is a long way from the cuddly view of Lenin. He moulded the state out of chaos after the First World War and it was a one-party authoritarian state. It is this that pushes Robert Service to the continuity side of the argument. However, Service is keen to point out that Lenin did have a vision of a utopian state where there would be no violence and terror and where the Russian people would enjoy the fruits of socialism. For Lenin, violence was a means to an end.

Of course, the problem with these arguments is that we cannot know what Lenin would have done. It may well be that, faced with the same situation as Stalin at the end of the 1920s, he would have become impatient and forced the pace. He was no great lover of the peasants and might have been prepared to use more forceful tactics. However, before he died he emphasised that coercion should not be used against the peasants. It is also clear that he was worried by the extent of bureaucracy and the lack of democracy in the party and intended to do something (though we don't know what) about this. And it is unthinkable that he would have killed his Bolshevik comrades and adopted the leadership style, entailed in the cult of the personality, that Stalin adopted.

Where does this leave us? We can definitely identify features of Stalinism in Leninism. Stalin fell back on tried and trusted methods used by Lenin – class warfare against peasants and terror against political opponents. Also, the way in which Lenin had organised the party and the state facilitated Stalinism and made it likely that control would fall into the hands of the best manipulator of the apparatus. The ban on factions provided Stalin with a mechanism to deal with opposition inside the party.

On the other hand, it is also clear that the 'Great Turn' initiated and implemented by Stalin, wrought great changes on the party and the people of the USSR – political, economic and cultural changes. The Soviet state of the 1930s was very much his construction. Also, Stalin extended and intensified Leninist methods, like class warfare and terror, to a degree unimaginable under Lenin. He was the executioner of Lenin's comrades and was responsible for the deaths of millions.

It is probably fair to say that Stalinism was built on the foundations of the Leninist state, even though it took a shape of which Lenin probably would not have approved.

FOCUS ROUTE

Make notes on the historiographical debate about the continuity between the Leninist and Stalinist states.

C Why is this historiographical debate relevant today?

The debate about the continuity between the regimes of Lenin and Stalin is more than just of academic interest to historians; it has influenced the recent history of Russia. But first we need to look at the story of the way historians have viewed this topic.

Post-war consensus – the traditional view

The post-1945 interpretation amongst historians in the West, found in the works of Leonard Schapiro and Adam Ulam and developed more recently by Richard Pipes, reflects the 'traditional' view of totalitarianism. For these writers, Lenin and a small group of Bolsheviks seized power and imposed their will on an unwilling populace. To stay in power, they applied a regime of terror within the framework of a highly centralised state. The October Revolution was a malignant process which would always end in political dictatorship. For them, Lenin and Stalin are virtually the same: Stalin carries on what Lenin started and Stalinism is simply the fully developed version of Lenin's repressive creed of revolution. However, most of these historians, such as Schapiro, hold Stalin personally responsible for the excesses of the 1930s and the level of human suffering endured by the Russian people.

This view was held not only in the West. The prominent Soviet dissident Alexander Solzhenitsyn held that there was a direct link between Stalinism and the institutions set up by Lenin. He says that the apparatus of Stalinism – the one-party state, the secret police, the ban on factionalism – were all in place before Stalin assumed the leadership.

Clear break between Lenin and Stalin

The idea that Stalin was the natural heir of Lenin was challenged right from the beginning. As far as Trotsky was concerned, Stalinism was a perverted form of Leninism which arose as a result of Stalin's personality. For Trotsky, the purges marked the clear division between Bolshevik philosophy and Stalinism: 'The present purge draws between Bolshevism and Stalinism a whole river of blood' (Trotsky, 1937). Isaac Deutscher, the biographer of Stalin and Trotsky, takes a similar line, believing that Stalin perverted the basically democratic nature of Leninism into a personal dictatorship. He sees the terror, party dictatorship and ideological intolerance as products of the Civil War.

The main challenge to the post-1945 traditional view arrived in the 1970s. The Russian dissident historian and Leninist, Roy Medvedev, argued (*Let History Judge*, 1972) that Stalin distorted Lenin's noble vision and is alone responsible for the mass murder and terror of the 1930s. He claims that things went badly awry when Stalin took over and launched the rapid industrialisation drive and forced collectivisation. He believes that if Lenin had lived a little longer, the NEP would have survived and the USSR would have taken a slower, more humane route to socialism. Medvedev attaches a great deal of importance to Stalin's personality because he believes that the Soviet system of the 1930s would have been quite different under a different leader.

Revisionist historians in the West in the 1970s and 1980s have taken a similar line. Probably the best exponent of the revisionist position in this debate is Stephen Cohen. In *Rethinking the Soviet Experience* (1985, pages 38–70) he acknowledges that the Bolshevism of 1921–28 contained the 'seeds' of Stalinism, but he suggests that the seeds of Stalinism can also be found in other areas of the Russian historical and cultural tradition, and in events like the Civil War and the international situation the USSR found itself in at the end of the 1920s. Cohen stresses the differences between Stalinism and Leninism. He says that the authoritarianism before 1929 was very different from that of the 1930s, when it went to extremes. He sees, for example, the policies towards the peasants as a virtual civil war, the terror as a holocaust that victimised tens of millions of people, and the leader cult as the 'deification of a despot'. For him, the difference in degree divides Stalinism from Leninism.

How did these views affect events in Soviet Russia?

In the 1980s, Mikhail Gorbachev and leading members of the Communist Party were influenced by the writings of Medvedev and Cohen. They came to believe that things had gone wrong in the USSR at the point where Lenin died and Stalin took over. They thought that if they could return to the NEP-style economy of 1924–25 and inject a little market capitalism back into the USSR, then they could set the Soviet Union on the way to a more humane and socially just form of Communism. This was contained in their ideas of *PERESTROIKA*. The economy that emerged in the 1980s did indeed have similarities with the NEP period – the emergence of private traders who became increasingly rich while others remained poor, property speculation, low wages for workers, the growth of crime and prostitution, and so on. But it did not deliver the economic growth they needed and the failure of these policies led to the total collapse of Communism in 1991.

Reviewing Lenin

Towards the end of the Communist period, Gorbachev had initiated what he called *glasnost* or openness. Novels that had been banned were made available to the public; for example, Alexander Solzhenitsyn's *Gulag Archipelago* (a study of the Soviet labour camp system) was published in 1989. Part of this *glasnost* process was a re-evaluation of the Soviet past. Russian archives began to open up in a way they had not before. There was a comprehensive attack on Stalin, and many of his victims, such as Bukharin, were rehabilitated.

But it was not long before Lenin himself came under scrutiny. As more documents about Lenin were uncovered so his ruthlessness and cruelty became more apparent. He was attacked, in particular, for his use of terror, for his callousness in the Civil War and as the originator of the labour camps and forced labour. In the West, Richard Pipes in his book *The Unknown Lenin* (1996) revealed more details about Lenin's repressive policies in the Civil War period. The Russian historian Dimitri Volkogonov (a former general in the Red Army) changed his position. In his earlier biography of Stalin in 1988, Volkogonov argued that Lenin was trying to build democracy back into the state and break down bureaucracy, and that the failure to remove Stalin in 1924 condemned the Soviet Union to dictatorship and totalitarianism. However, by the time he came to write his biography of Lenin in 1994, having gained access to new archival evidence, he identified Lenin as the chief architect of the Communist state based on terror and coercion.

> *PERESTROIKA*
> **Russian word for rebuilding or reconstruction, used by Mikhail Gorbachev to describe the reform policies introduced by him in the mid- to late 1980s.**

TALKING POINT

How is a knowledge of history important to today's politicians? Can a little knowledge do more harm than good?

Can you think of any examples where past events have influenced British politicians or been used by them to justify their policies?

ACTIVITY

Write an essay answering the following question: Was Stalinism Lenin's baby?

In your essay, refer to the historiographical debate surrounding this issue and mention the views of historians.

When you are writing essays, you have to develop a line of argument. This means arguing a particular case and supporting it with evidence. Often you can take one of the three approaches below:

1 'Yes' – you agree with the essay title and supply the points and supporting argument (with evidence) to show why you agree.
2 'No' – you take the opposite view, arguing against the essay title. In this case you would argue that Stalin changed the course of Soviet Russia, creating a system that was more to do with his priorities and personality than with Lenin's.
3 'Yes ... but' – where you can argue the case for the proposition in the essay title (supplying supporting evidence) but also put the case against the proposition. At the end, you weigh up the argument and come down on one side or the other.

D A Red tsar?

There is a strong case for arguing that the traditions of Russian history preceding the revolution played an important role in determining the shape and character of Stalinism. The Stalinist state that emerged in the 1930s had many similarities with the tsarist state of the nineteenth century. In both systems, state control over people was regarded as normal and in both you find the idea of a strong authority figure, one who knows the right course to follow and can lead the Russian people, like children, out of the darkness into the light. The icons of tsarism and Stalinism – the pictures, statues and imagery – are very similar in portraying them as godlike leaders.

This is not to say that Stalinism was somehow inevitable. What is suggested is that, given the chaotic and difficult circumstances in which the Russians found themselves, they retreated to or slipped into traditional solutions which they understood well and with which they were familiar. In Chart 19D, the similarities of the two systems – tsarism and Stalinism – are compared. Tsarism was based on three guiding principles: autocracy, orthodoxy and nationalism. These are used as the basis for comparison.

ACTIVITY

Write a short essay under the title: Stalin the Red Tsar. Decide how far you think this statement is fair and what the main similarities between the tsarist state and the Stalinist state were. Draw on material from the beginning and end of this book and your own knowledge.

■ 19D Similarities between tsarism and Stalinism

Tsarism	Stalinism
Autocracy	
Rule by a supreme leader, the tsar, who makes major decisions and has power of life and death over his subjects. He was given divine status.	Stalin was supreme leader of the Soviet Union, with power to sign death warrants. He was portrayed as a god-like figure in the cult of the personality.
The tsar was supported by an élite – the nobility whose prime role was to serve the tsar. Their positions of influence in the government, armed forces and civil service were held through the patronage of the tsar.	Stalin was supported by the *nomenklatura* – an élite who held the top positions in the party, government, armed forces, etc., through the patronage of Stalin. He kept their support by the threat of removing privileges – access to scarce goods, best apartments, etc.
There was a huge government bureaucracy, slow, unwieldy and impenetrable, with corruption at lower levels.	There was a huge, faceless bureaucracy in government and party which led to 'death by paper'. In local areas 'inner circles' of government and party officials and industrial managers cooked up deals to suit themselves, often ignoring instructions from the centre.
There was a well-developed system of ranks and privileges.	A system of ranks developed in the 1930s from the *nomenklatura* downwards. Being a party official or member brought power and privileges commensurate with the level. The command economy demanded there be officials and managers at different levels and wage differentials between workers.
The secret police – the Okhrana – were used to support the state and deal with critics and opposition.	There was extensive use of the secret police (OGPU, then NKVD) in all aspects of Soviet life – government, party, economic spheres and prison system (the Gulag) – and at all levels. They performed a monitoring role, with power to root out opposition to party leadership.
Internal passports, residence permits and visas were used to control the movement of the population.	Internal passports, residence permits and visas were used to control the movement of the population.
There was lack of free speech – censorship of the press and banning of political parties (except between 1906 and 1914).	There was lack of free speech – censorship of the press and banning of rival political parties.
There was no tradition of democratic political institutions.	There were no genuinely democratic institutions although soviets were designed to be a purer form of democratic participation.

Tsarism	Stalinism
Orthodoxy	
The tsar's power was underpinned by the Russian Orthodox Church, a branch of Christianity. Russians saw their Orthodox beliefs as special and believed they had a mission to spread their beliefs to other parts of the world. They believed they were the upholders of the 'true' Christian faith.	Stalinism was underpinned by Marxism–Leninism which became an orthodoxy trotted out by Stalin to justify his actions. It was treated as a quasi-religion. Russians believed they had a mission to spread Communist beliefs throughout the world by encouraging world revolution.
Nationalism	
There was a strong emphasis on Russian nationalism and patriotism. There were attempts to export the Russian way of life to other parts of the empire through the policy of Russification. Tsars throughout the nineteenth century were looking to expand their empire and to become a major dominant power in European affairs.	Stalin emphasised nationalism in 'Socialism in One Country' – the idea that Russians could build socialism on their own without outside help. There were appeals to nationalism and patriotism in the Five-Year Plans. People who did not co-operate were denounced as traitors and 'enemies within'. Stalin was keen on Russian domination of both government and party in the other Soviet republics, although some concessions were made to regions developing their own national traditions. In foreign policy, Stalin pursued a very nationalistic line, putting Soviet security above everything else, even to the point of doing a deal with Hitler. Any tsar would have been proud of Stalin's foreign policy, particularly the successful expansion after the Second World War, with the USSR's becoming a superpower.
Economic change was led from above. The middle classes were weak in tsarist Russia and the state had been the main agent in promoting industrial growth and the development of the railways. The state had borrowed money from abroad and squeezed resources from the peasantry to do this.	In 1928, Stalin mounted the 'revolution from above'. He decided to enforce change on the peasantry and go for rapid industrialisation through the command economy. He could get very little money from abroad and so extracted resources from the peasantry and industrial proletariat (resulting in a low standard of living for most workers) to achieve his industrial transformation.
Tsars like Peter the Great and Ivan the Terrible saw themselves as leaders who were enforcing change on the nobility and others to create a strong Russian state. Peter also saw himself as a moderniser bringing Russia out of the dark ages. Ivan broke the nobility, torturing them and executing them on suspicion of treason, ensuring their loyalty to the state. His agents, the Oprichniks, wore black uniforms; their insignia was a dog's head on a broom, signifying their dog-like devotion to the tsar and their duty to sweep away treason.	Stalin saw himself as being in the same tradition as Peter the Great and Ivan the Terrible, taking the Soviet Union towards socialism and making it into a great industrial power, respected in the world. He praised Peter in 1928, on the eve of the Great Turn, for building mills and factories to strengthen the defences of the country. When watching Eisenstein's film about Ivan he remarked that Ivan's fault lay in not annihilating enough of his enemies. Like Ivan, Stalin was prepared to deal harshly with any opposition. He believed he was acting in the interests of his country and its people.

KEY POINTS FROM CHAPTER 19   Was Stalinism Lenin's baby?

1 Stalinism, which was at its height after the mid-1930s, has certain defining features.

2 Historians have put forward a number of reasons to explain why it took the form it did.

3 There is a debate amongst historians about how far the system that developed under Stalin was his own creation and how far it was a continuation of the ideas and policies of Lenin before 1924.

4 Some historians believe that the Stalinist regime was the logical extension of the centralised state that developed under Lenin and that there is a clear line of continuity between the two.

5 Others believe that there is a clear distinction between Lenin and Stalin and believe that Stalin corrupted the 1917 Revolution and took Soviet Russia along the path to a new class system, tyranny and mass murder.

6 A reasonable conclusion to reach is that Stalinism was built on the foundations of the Leninist state but developed in ways of which Lenin would probably not have approved.

7 This debate was of great relevance to events in the USSR in the lead-up to the fall of Communism in 1991. Soviet Communist leaders, notably Mikhail Gorbachev, believed they could return to the conditions of the NEP period just before 1924 and develop a more humane and economically dynamic form of Communism.

8 Stalin has been called the 'Red Tsar' because his regime had many features in common with the tsarist regime before 1917, and seemed to fall back on traditional styles and solutions with which the people were familiar.

20

Stalinism: a final assessment

At the start of the book we looked at the tsarist regime in pre-revolutionary Russia. By the end of the 1930s, after two decades of Communism, there had been enormous changes. A backward rural state had been turned into a great industrial power, one that was soon to become a world superpower. Yet the Stalinist state had many features in common with its tsarist predecessor. The system of personalised control that developed with the growth of the Stalinist dictatorship was certainly not new. Traditional patterns of control – involving a god-like leader, the chief benefactor and protector of the people, and the culture of blaming officials rather than the leader – found their way into the Stalinist repertoire and seemed to sit comfortably with the Russian people. Moreover, the use of new techniques of propaganda served to make the control even more effective and gave rise to the notion of a 'totalitarian' state.

However, the image of the totalitarian state is that of a well-oiled, efficient machine, carrying out instructions from above. The Stalinist state was far from this: it was full of contradictions and inefficiencies. This was in part due to the breakneck speed of industrialisation whereby Stalin hoped to compress into a few years a process that had taken centuries in the West. Policies were often ill conceived and introduced so rapidly that they had unintended consequences that proved counterproductive. Collectivisation met the immediate needs of the Soviet state but saddled the Soviet Union with an inefficient, unproductive agricultural system. The command economy was a rough and ready tool that was well suited to achieving rapid growth in the 1930s but led to the creation of a vast, unresponsive bureaucracy unable to deliver the goods after the Second World War. Terror and propaganda served to mobilise the population in the 1930s but were, by their very nature, incapable of producing a critical élite capable of reforming the system.

In the same way that the tsarist system became unstable when reform was attempted, so the Soviet Union collapsed in 1991 when Mikhail Gorbachev tried to reform the Soviet economy. As under tsarism, the system had failed to engage the people in legitimate political processes and institutions. They had become cynical towards the party's claims of superiority and so, when the economy collapsed, the people rejected those who had set themselves up as the unaccountable leaders of political and economic life. It was a system that was unable to reform itself.

We should be wary of judging Stalinism in the light of the collapse of Communism, although it is clear that some of the fundamental structures created then contributed hugely to the problems faced by the Soviet Union in the 1970s and 1980s. Historical hindsight is a wonderful thing. None of these problems was apparent to Stalin or the people involved in the great experiment of socialist construction in the 1930s. The Stalin revolution did produce 'heroic' successes; many people were better off materially and had opportunities that they would not have had under a tsarist regime. But it also produced a fearful society in which arrests and trials had a terrible impact on human relationships. Life for many was hard and millions died or were repressed by an authoritarian regime that denied its people their fundamental human rights.

THE SAFETY-NET SOCIETY

Although the Soviet regime, largely because of its lack of market mechanisms to reduce costs and manage the distribution system, did not deliver the economic prosperity that developed in Western Europe, it did for some years after the war provide food, shelter, clothing, health care and employment at a safety-net level. People had a peaceful, predictable framework in which they could live their lives. At the beginning of the twenty-first century, many Russian people bemoan the loss of such security, since free-market economics have left them uncertain, exposed, jobless and poor. Some look back with nostalgia to the Stalinist era, which they see as one of achievement, stability and strength.

The final remarks come from Stalin and his mother, at their last meeting in 1935, as recalled by the doctor of Stalin's mother.

Stalin: Why did you beat me so hard?

Mother: That's why you turned out so well . . . Joseph – who exactly are you now?

Stalin: Remember the tsar? Well, I'm like a tsar.

Mother: You'd have done better to have become a priest.

SOURCE 20.1   A French poster from the 1930s, depicting Stalin dominating the masses

SOURCE 20.2   *The Morning of our Fatherland*, a painting by F. Shurpin, 1948

Dates in brackets are dates of first publication.

Abraham, R., *Alexander Kerensky, The First Love of the Revolution*, Columbia University Press, 1987

Acton, E., *Rethinking the Russian Revolution*, Edward Arnold, 1990

Alliluyeva, S., *Twenty Letters to a Friend*, Penguin, 1968

Avrich, P., *Kronstadt 1921*, Princeton University Press, 1970

Babel, I., *Collected Stories*, trans. D. McDuff, Penguin, 1994

Bell, P. M. H., *The Origins of the Second World War in Europe*, Longman, 1987

Blinkhorn, M., *Democracy and Civil War in Spain, 1931–1939*, Routledge, 1988

Bullock, A., *Hitler and Stalin: Parallel Lives*, Harper Collins, 1991

Carmichael, J., *A Short History of the Revolution*, Sphere Books, 1967

Carr, E. H., *The Russian Revolution from Lenin to Stalin*, Macmillan, 1979

Carr, E. H., *Socialism in One Country*, Macmillan, 1958

Carrère D'Encause, H., *Stalin: Order Through Terror*, Longman, 1981

Chamberlain, W. H., *The Russian Revolution 1917–21*, Macmillan, 1935

Cohen, S., *Bukharin and the Bolshevik Revolution*, OUP, 1974

Cohen, S., *Rethinking the Soviet Experience*, OUP, 1985

Conquest, R., *The Great Terror: A Reassessment*, Pimlico, 1990

Conquest, R., *The Harvest of Sorrow*, Hutchinson, 1986

Conquest, R., *Lenin*, Fontana, 1972

Conquest, R., *Stalin and the Kirov Murder*, Hutchinson, 1989

Conquest, R., *Stalin: Breaker of Nations*, Weidenfeld & Nicolson, 1991

Cullerne Brown, M., *Art under Stalin*, Phaidon Press, 1991

Dallin, D. J. and Nikolaevsky, B. I., *Forced Labour in Soviet Russia*, Hollis & Carter, 1948

Daniels, R. V. (ed.), *The Stalin Revolution*, Heath, 1990

Davies, R. W., *Soviet Economic Development from Lenin to Khrushchev*, CUP, 1998

Davies, R. W., 'Stalin and Soviet Industrialization', *History Sixth*, March 1991

Davies, R. W., Harrison, M. and Wheatcroft, S. G. (eds), *The Economic Transformation of the Soviet Union, 1913–1945*, CUP, 1994

Davies, S., *Popular Opinion in Stalin's Russia: Terror, Propaganda and Dissent 1934–41*, CUP, 1997

De Robien, L., *The Diary of a Diplomat in Russia, 1917–18*, Praeger Pubishers, 1969

Deutscher, I., *Stalin*, rev. edn, Pelican, 1966

Deutscher, I., *The Prophet Unarmed: Trotsky 1921–29*, OUP, 1959

Deutscher, I., *The Prophet Outcast: Trotsky 1929–40*, OUP, 1963

Duranty, W., *I Write as I Please*, Simon & Schuster Inc., 1935

Fainsod, M., *Smolensk Under Soviet Rule*, Harvard University Press, 1958

Farmborough, F., *Nurse at the Russian Front*, Futura, 1977

Figes, O., *A People's Tragedy: The Russian Revolution 1891–1924*, Pimlico, 1997 (1996)

Fitzpatrick, S., *Everday Stalinism*, OUP, 1999

Fitzpatrick, S., 'Revolution and Counter-Revolution in the Schools' in Daniels, R. V. (ed.), *The Stalin Revolution*, Heath, 1990

Fitzpatrick, S. (ed.), *Stalinism: New Directions*, Routledge, 2000

Fitzpatrick, S., *The Russian Revolution 1917–1932*, OUP, 1994 (1982)

Fitzpatrick, S., *Stalin's Peasants*, OUP, 1994

Getty, J. A., *The Origins of the Great Purges*, CUP, 1985

Getty, J. A., 'The Politics of Stalinism' in Nove, A. (ed.), *The Stalin Phenomenon*, Weidenfeld and Nicolson, 1993

Getty, J. A. and Manning, R. (eds), *Stalinist Terror – New Perspectives*, CUP, 1993

Getty, J. A. and Naumov, O. V., *The Road to Terror: Stalin and the Self-Destruction of the Bolsheviks, 1932–39*, Yale University Press, 1999

Getzler, I., *Kronstadt 1917–1921: The Fate of Soviet Democracy*, CUP, 1983

Gill, G., *Stalinism*, Macmillan, 1990

Goldman, E., *My Disillusionment in Russia*, Garden City, 1923

Goldman, E., *My Further Disillusionment in Russia*, Garden City, 1924

Golomstock, I., *Totalitarian Art*, Harper Collins, 1990

Harris, J., 'The purging of local cliques in the Urals region 1936–7' in Fitzpatrick, S. (ed.), *Stalinism: New Directions*, Routledge, 2000

Haslam, J., *The Soviet Union and the Struggle for Collective Security in Europe*, Macmillan, 1984

Haslam, J., *The Soviet Union and the Threat from the East, 1933–41*, Macmillan, 1992

Hiden, J., *Germany and Europe, 1919–39*, Longman, 1993 (1977)

Hindus, M., *Black Earth*, T. Fisher Unwin, 1926

Hosking, G., *A History of the Soviet Union*, Fontana, 1985

Howson, G., *Arms for Spain*, John Murray, 1998

Kenez, P., *A History of the Soviet Union from the Beginning to the End*, CUP, 1999

Kennedy, P., *The Realities Behind Diplomacy*, Fontana, 1981

Khrushchev, N., *Khrushchev Remembers*, Vol. 1, ed. S. Talbot, Penguin, 1971

Khrushchev, N., *Khrushchev Remembers: The Glasnost Tapes*, 1990

Kotkin, S., *Magnetic Mountain: Stalinism as a Civilisation*, University of California Press, 1995

Kravchenko, V., *I Chose Freedom: The Personal and Political Life of a Soviet Official*, Robert Hale, 1947

Krivitsky, W. G., *I Was Stalin's Agent*, Hamish Hamilton, 1939

Lewin, M., 'Society, State and Ideology during the First Five-Year Plan', 1976, in Ward, C. (ed.), *The Stalinist Dictatorship*, Edward Arnold, 1998

Lewis, J. and Whitehead, P., *Stalin: A Time for Judgement*, Methuen, 1990

Lincoln, B., *Red Victory: A History of the Russian Civil War*, Simon & Schuster, 1989

McCauley, M., *Russia 1917–41*, Sempringham, 1997

McDermid, J. and Hillyer, A., *Women and Work in Russia, 1880–1930*, Longman, 1998

Mandelstam, N., *Hope Against Hope*, Collins/Harvill, 1971

Manning, R., 'The Soviet Economic Crisis of 1936–40 and the Great Purges' in Arch Getty, J. and Manning, R. (eds), *Stalinist Terror – New Perspectives*, CUP, 1993

Mawdsley, E., *The Russian Civil War*, Birlinn, 2000 (1987)

Mawdsley, E., *The Stalin Years*, University of Manchester Press, 1998

Medvedev, R., *Let History Judge*, Macmillan, 1972 (1971)

Medvedev, R., 'The Political Biography of Stalin' in Tucker, R. C. (ed.), *Stalinism: Essays in Historical Interpretation*, Norton, 1977

Moynahan, B., *The Russian Century*, Random House, 1994

Nove, A., *An Economic History of the USSR, 1917–91*, Penguin, 1992 (1969)

Nove, A., *Was Stalin Really Necessary?*, Allen & Unwin, 1964

Nove, A. (ed.), *The Stalin Phenomenon*, Weidenfeld and Nicolson, 1993

Orlov, A., *The Secret History of Stalin's Crimes*, Jarrold, 1954

Ostrovsky, N., *How the Steel Was Tempered*, Moscow, 1952

Pankrashova, M. and Sipols, V., *Why War was not Prevented*, Novosti Press, Moscow, 1970

Pasternak, B., *Doctor Zhivago*, Collins Fontana, 1975 (first published in English 1958)

Pipes, R., *A Concise History of the Russian Revolution*, Harvill Press, 1995

Pipes, R., *Russia Under the Bolshevik Regime, 1919–24*, Harvill Press, 1994

Pipes, R., *Three Whys of the Russian Revolution*, Pimlico, 1998

Pipes, R., 'The Great October Revolution as a clandestine coup d'état', *Times Literary Supplement*, November 1992

Pipes, R. (ed.), *The Unknown Lenin*, Yale University Press, 1996

Pomonarev, B. N., *History of the Communist Party of the Soviet Union*, Moscow, 1960

Radzinsky, E., *Stalin*, Sceptre, 1997 (1996)

Ransome, A., *Six Weeks in Russia in 1919*, George Allen and Unwin, 1919

Rappaport, H., *Joseph Stalin: A Biographical Companion*, 1999

Read, C., *From Tsar to Soviets: The Russian People and their Revolution 1917–21*, UCL Press, 1996

Reed, J., *Ten Days that Shook the World*, Penguin, 1977 (1919)

Roberts, G., *The Soviet Union and the Origins of the Second World War*, Macmillan, 1995

Sakwa, R., *The Rise and Fall of the Soviet Union 1917–1991*, Routledge, 1999

Schapiro, L., *1917*, Temple Smith, 1984

Scott, J., *Behind the Urals*, Secker and Warburg, 1942

Serge, V., trans. and ed. P. Sedwick, *Memoirs of a Revolutionary 1901–1941*, OUP, 1967 (1963)

Service, R., *A History of Twentieth-Century Russia*, Penguin, 1997

Service, R., *Lenin, A Biography*, Macmillan, 2000

Service, R., 'Lenin: Individual and Politics in the October Revolution', *Modern History Review*, September 1990

Service, R., *The Russian Revolution 1900–1927*, 2nd edn, Macmillan 1991 (1986)

Sholokhov, M., *Virgin Soil Upturned*, Penguin (1935)

Smith, S., *Red Petrograd: Revolution in the Factories 1917–1918*, CUP, 1983

Solzhenitsyn, A., *The Gulag Archipelago*, Vols 1–2, Collins/Harvill, 1974, 1975

Sukhanov, N. N., *Notes on the Revolution*, 1922; trans. and ed. J. Carmichael, *The Russian Revolution 1917: A Personal Record*, OUP, 1955

Talbott, S. (ed.), *Khrushchev Remembers*, Vol. 1, Penguin, 1977

Taylor, A. J. P., *Origins of the Second World War*, 2nd edn, Penguin, 1963 (1961)

Taylor, R. (trans. and ed.), *The Film Factory: Soviet Cinema in Documents, 1936–1939*, Routledge and Kegan Paul, 1988

Thomas, H., *The Spanish Civil War*, 3rd edn, Penguin, 1977

Thurston, R., *Life and Terror in Stalin's Russia 1934–41*, Yale University Press, 1996

Timasheff, N., *The Great Retreat: The Growth and Decline of Communism in Russia*, Dutton, New York, 1946

Tucker, R. C., 'The Emergence of Stalin's Foreign Policy' in *Slavic Review*, 1977

Tucker, R. C., *Stalin in Power: The Revolution from Above, 1928–1941*, Norton, 1992

Tucker, R. C. (ed.), *Stalinism: Essays in Historical Interpretation*, Norton, 1977

Ulam, A., *Expansionism and Coexistence*, 2nd edn, Praeger, 1974

Vasilievski, L. A. and L. M., *Kniga o golode*, 1922

Vernadsky, G., *A Source Book of Russian History*, Vol. 3, Yale University Press, 1972

Volkogonov, D., *Lenin: Life and Legacy*, Harper Collins, 1994

Volkogonov, D., *Stalin*, Weidenfeld and Nicolson, 1988

Volkogonov, D., *The Rise and Fall of the Soviet Empire*, Harper Collins, 1998

Ward, C., *Stalin's Russia*, Edward Arnold, 1993

Ward, C. (ed.), *The Stalinist Dictatorship*, Edward Arnold, 1998

Watt, D. C., *How War Came*, Heinemann, 1989

Weinberg, G., *World in the Balance*, Hammer, 1981

Weissberg, A., *Conspiracy of Silence*, Hamish Hamilton, 1952

Westwood, J., *Endurance and Endeavour*, OUP, 1973

Williams, B., *Lenin*, Longman, 2000

Williams, B., *The Russian Revolution 1917–21*, Historical Association Studies, 1987

p.26 source 2.1 *A People's Tragedy, the Russian Revolution* by O. Figes, published by Pimlico. Used by permission of The Random House Group Limited; **p.27** source 2.2 *A People's Tragedy, the Russian Revolution* by O. Figes, published by Pimlico. Used by permission of The Random House Group Limited; source 2.3 *The Russian Revolution 1917–1921* by B. Williams, from 'Historical Association Studies', Blackwell Publishers, 1987, pp.8–9; **p.37** source 3.2 *A Short History of the Revolution* by J. Carmichael, Sphere Books, 1967, pp.80–81; **p.40** source 3.3 *A People's Tragedy, the Russian Revolution* by O. Figes, published by Pimlico. Used by permission of The Random House Group Limited; **p.43** sources 3.5, 3.6, 3.7 figures from *Ten Days that Shook the World* (illustrated edition), by J. Reed, Penguin Books, 1977; **p.46** source 3.10 *A People's Tragedy, the Russian Revolution* by O. Figes, published by Pimlico. Used by permission of The Random House Group Limited; source 3.12 *Alexander Kerensky, The First Love of the Revolution*, by R. Abraham, © Columbia University Press, 1987, p.207. Reprinted with the permission of the publisher; **p.51** source 4.2 *A Short History of the Revolution* by J. Carmichael, Sphere Books, 1967, p.116; **p.60** source 4.6 'The Great October Revolution as a Clandestine *Coup d'Etat*' by R. Pipes, *Times Literary Supplement*, November 1992; source 4.7 *A People's Tragedy, the Russian Revolution* by O. Figes, published by Pimlico. Used by permission of The Random House Group Limited; source 4.8 *Rethinking the Russian Revolution*, by E. Acton, 1990, p.177. Reproduced by permission of Edward Arnold Limited; **p.61** source 4.9 *The Russian Revolution, 1917–21* by B. Williams, from 'Historical Association Studies', Blackwell Publishers, 1987, pp.46–7; source 4.10 *Rethinking the Russian Revolution*, by E. Acton, 1990, pp.203–4. Reproduced by permission of Edward Arnold Limited; **p.62** source 4.15 *A Short History of the Revolution*, by J. Carmichael, Sphere Books, 1967, p.193; **p.63** source 4.16 *A People's Tragedy, the Russian Revolution* by O. Figes, published by Pimlico. Used by permission of The Random House Group Limited; **p.67** source 1 *A People's Tragedy, the Russian Revolution* by O. Figes, published by Pimlico. Used by permission of The Random House Group Limited; **p.68** source 4 *From Tsar to Soviets: The Russian People and their Revolution 1917–1921*, by C. Read, UCL Press, Taylor and Francis, 1996, p.178; source 7 *A People's Tragedy, the Russian Revolution* by O. Figes, published by Pimlico. Used by permission of The Random House Group Limited; **p.86** source 6.4 *A History of Twentieth Century Russia*, by R. Service, Allen Lane, 1997, pp.105–6. Copyright © Robert Service, 1997; **p.87** source 6.5 *Memoirs of a Revolutionary 1901–1941*, by V. Serge, translated and edited by P. Sedwick, Oxford University Press, 1963, p.92, by permission; source 6.6 *The Russian Civil War*, by E. Mawdsley, Birlinn, 1987, pp.277–78; **p.94** source 6.14 *Doctor Zhivago* by Boris Pasternak © Giangiacomo Feltrinelli Editore, 1958. English translation © Harvill, 1958. Reproduced by permission of the Harvill Press; **p.95** source 6.15 *Collected Stories* by Isaac Babel, translated by David McDuff, Penguin Books, 1994. Copyright © David McDuff, 1994; **p.96** source 6.16 *The Russian Revolution 1917–1921* by B. Williams, from 'Historical Association Studies', Blackwell Publishers, 1987, pp.62–3; **p.99** source 6.18 *A People's Tragedy, the Russian Revolution* by O. Figes, published by Pimlico. Used by permission of The Random House Group Limited; **p.101** source 6.20 *My Disillusionment in Russia*, by E. Goldman, Garden City, 1923, pp.8–9; source 6.22 *The Diary of a Diplomat in Russia 1917–1918*, by L. de Robien. Copyright © 1969 by Praeger Publishers. Reproduced with permission of Greenwood Publishing Group Inc., Westport, CT; **p.104** source 7.3 *From Tsar to Soviets: The Russian People and their Revolution 1917–21*, by C. Read, UCL Press, Taylor and Francis, 1996, p.192; source 7.4 *The Russian Revolution 1917–1932*, by S. Fitzpatrick, Oxford University Press, 1994, p.86, by permission; source 7.5 *From Tsar to Soviets: The Russian People and their Revolution 1917–1921*, by C. Read, UCL Press, Taylor and Francis, 1996, p.266; source 7.6 *A People's Tragedy, the Russian Revolution* by O. Figes, published by Pimlico. Used by permission of The Random House Group Limited; **p.107** source 7.10 *Red Victory: A History of the Russian Civil War*, by W. Bruce Lincoln. Copyright © 1989 by W. Bruce Lincoln (New York: Simon and Schuster); sources 7.13, 7.14 *From Tsar to Soviets: The Russian People and their Revolution 1917–1921*, by C. Read, UCL Press, Taylor and Francis, 1996, p.277; **p.112** source 7.18 figures from *An Economic History of the USSR, 1917–1991*, by Alex Nove, Penguin Books, 1969, p.89. Third revised edition 1992, copyright © Alex Nove, 1969, 1972, 1982, 1979, 1992; **p.133** source 8.10 *From Tsar to Soviets: The Russian People and their Revolution 1917–1921*, by C. Read, UCL Press, Taylor and Francis, 1996, p.164; source 8.12 *A Short History of the Revolution*, by J. Carmichael, Sphere Books, 1967, p.83; source 8.13 'Lenin: Individual and Politics in the October Revolution', by R. Service, from *Modern History Review*, Philip Allan Updates, September 1990; source 8.14 *A History of the Soviet Union from the Beginning to the End*, by Peter Kenez, Cambridge University Press, 1999, pp.27–8; **p.146** source 9.3 *A History of the Soviet Union*, by G. Hosking, HarperCollins Publishers Ltd., 1985, p.140; source 9.4 *The Prophet Unarmed: Trotsky 1921–1929*, by I. Deutscher, Verso Publishers, 1959, p.93; source 9.5 *Socialism in One Country*, by E. H. Carr, Macmillan, 1958, p.151; **p.147** source 9.8 *Stalin's Russia*, by C. Ward, 1993, pp.35–6. Reproduced by permission of Edward Arnold Limited; source 9.9 *Stalin: Breaker of Nations*, by R. Conquest, Weidenfeld and Nicolson, 1991, pp.129–30; **p.150** source 1 *The Russian Revolution 1917–1932*, by S. Fitzpatrick, Oxford University Press, 1994, pp.9–10, by permission; **p.166** source 11.6 *I Chose Freedom: The Personal and Political Life of a Soviet Official*, by V. Kravchenko, Robert Hale Limited, 1947, p.104; source 11.8 *Memoirs of a Revolutionary 1901–1941* by V. Serge, translated and edited by P. Sedwick, Oxford University Press, 1963, p.247, by permission; **p.168** source 11.13 *I Chose Freedom: The Personal and Political Life of a Soviet Official*, by V. Kravchenko, Robert Hale Limited, 1947, p.130; source 11.14 *The Harvest of Sorrow*, by R. Conquest, 1986, p.233. Reproduced with permission of Curtis Brown Ltd., London, on behalf of Robert Conquest. Copyright Robert Conquest, 1968; **p.171** source 11.16 *An Economic History of the USSR, 1917–1991*, by Alex Nove, Penguin Books, 1969, pp.180, 186. Third revised edition 1992, copyright © Alex Nove, 1969, 1972, 1982, 1979, 1992; **p.172** source 11.17 *Stalin's Russia* by C. Ward, 1993, p.47. Reproduced by permission of Edward Arnold Limited; source 11.18 *A History of Twentieth Century Russia*, by R. Service, Allen Lane, 1997, pp.181–82. Copyright © Robert Service, 1997; **p.175** source 12.1 *Magnetic Mountain: Stalinism as a Civilisation*, by S. Kotkin, © 1997 The Regents of the University of California, 1995, p.35; source 12.2 *Hitler and Stalin: Parallel Lives*, by A. Bullock, HarperCollins Publishers Ltd., 1991, p.298; source 12.3 *An Economic History of the USSR, 1917–1991*, by Alex Nove,

Photo credits

The Publishers would like to thank the following for permission to reproduce copyright material:

Cover: David King Collection; **pp.vii–viii** David King Collection; **pp.1–15** David King Collection; **p.19** Hulton Getty; **pp.22–25** David King Collection; **p.28** Popperfoto; **p.29–41** David King Collection; **p.45** *t* David King Collection, *b* Hulton Getty; **p.46** Mary Evans Picture Library; **p.47, p.53** Art Collection Harry Ransom Humanities Research Center, University of Texas, Austin; **p.51** David King Collection; **p.54** Hulton Getty; **p.55, p.57** David King Collection; **p.63** Ronald Grant Archive; **pp.85–92** David King Collection; **p.93** *t* David King Collection, *c* British Library 85/1856.g.8 12 (01A12973P), *b* British Library 85/1856.g.8 28 (01A12973P); **p.98** *t* Popperfoto, *b* David King Collection; **pp.100–103** David King Collection; **p.106** *t* David King Collection, *b* Hulton Getty; **p.107** David King Collection; **p.109** Hulton Getty; **p.112** David King Collection; **p.24** *tl, tr, bl* David King Collection, *br* State Russian Museum, St Petersburg; **p.125** *all* David King Collection; **p.128** Hulton Getty; **pp.129–139** David King Collection; **p.151** *tr, bl, cr* David King Collection, *tl* and *br* Corbis UK Ltd; **p.158** Topham Picturepoint/Novosti; **p.159** *t* and *bl* David King Collection, *cr* Roger Viollet, Paris; **p.166, p.167** *b* David King Collection; **p.167** *t* Topham Picturepoint/Novosti; **pp.174–206** David King Collection; **p.208** Roger Viollet, Paris; **pp.209–215** David King Collection; **p.218** *both* © Colonel Danzig Baldayer/Zweitausendeins (www.Zweitausendeins.de, e-mail: info@Zweitausendeins.de); **pp.219–242** David King Collection; **p.246** *t* David King Collection, *b* German-Russian Museum, Berlin-Karlhorst; **p.249** by David Low from *The Star* 24 June 1926; reproduced courtesy Evening Standard/Atlantic Syndication/British Library of Political and Economic Science, London School of Economics; **p.250** *t* Bundesarchiv, Koblenz, *c* Ullstein Bilderdienst; **p.255** David King Collection; **p.256** Popperfoto; **p.259** *l: A piece missing, Tovarish* from *Evening Standard* 3 April 1939, *r: What, no chair for me?* from *Evening Standard* 30 September 1938; both by David Low courtesy Evening Standard/ Atlantic Syndication/Centre for the Study of Cartoons and Caricature, University of Kent, Canterbury, CT2 7NU, Kent; p.264, p.272 *all*, p.273 *tl, tr* and *br* David King Collection, *cr* AKG London, *bl* State Russian Museum/Petrushka (e-mail: petrushkanet@hotmail.com); **p.276, p.279** *cr* and *bl* David King Collection, *t* Bridgeman Art Library; **p.280** *tl* Society for Cooperation in Russian and Soviet Studies, London, *b* Bridgeman Art Library; **pp.281–282** David King Collection; **p.283** Ronald Grant Archive; **pp.285–286** David King Collection; **p.292** *l* David King Collection, *r* International Instituut voor Sociale Geschiederies, Cruquiusweg 32, 1019 AT Amsterdam, Netherlands; **p.295** TASS; **p.296** Society for Cooperation in Russian and Soviet Studies, London; **pp.297–319** David King Collection.

t = top, *b* = bottom, *l* = left, *r* = right, *c* = centre

*Every effort has been made to contact copyright holders, and the publishers apologise for any omissions which they will be pleased to rectify at the earliest opportunity.